COMPUTE!'s

128 Programmer's Guide

The Editors of COMPUTE!

COMPUTE!™ Publications, Inc. abc
One of the ABC Publishing Companies
Greensboro, North Carolina

Printed in the United States of America

10 9 8 7 6 5 4 3 2 1

ISBN 0-87455-031-9

COMPUTE! Publications, Inc., Post Office Box 5406, Greensboro, NC 27403, (919) 275-9809, is one of the ABC Publishing Companies, and is not associated with any manufacturer of personal computers. Commodore 64 and Commodore 128 are trademarks of Commodore Electronics Limited.

Contents

Foreword

COMPUTE!'s 128 Programmer's Guide is a book you'll want at your side whenever you're programming or using the Commodore 128. It's not intended to replace the *128 System Guide*. Instead, it's a source of additional ideas, programming advice, and technical information. It covers the 128 in all of its several modes, and every explanation is written in the clear, easy-to-read style that's the hallmark of COMPUTE! publications.

BASIC programmers, for instance, will make frequent reference to the detailed explanation of every 128 BASIC command. Machine language devotees will be particularly interested in the ROM maps and listings of Kernal routines. And if you've bought the 128 for its CP/M capabilities, you'll find the discussion of CP/M commands and Z80 machine language invaluable.

This book begins with a brief survey of the 128's many capabilities, and instructions on how to enter programs in BASIC and machine language. Chapter 1 contains valuable programming advice as well as a discussion of each BASIC command. Graphics, music and sound, and machine language are all examined in detail. Chapters are also devoted to the disk drive and other peripherals, CP/M operations, machine language programming, and system architecture.

The authors—the technical staff of COMPUTE! Publications—have distilled years of computer experience and many hours of research into the pages of *COMPUTE!'s 128 Programmer's Guide*. For almost every level of programming, from rank beginner to veteran programmer, this book can be your guide to greater understanding of your machine and more effective programming methods. It not only teaches, but is also a thorough reference for the experienced programmer.

Acknowledgments

Every book is the work of many hands. The authors would particularly like to thank their families and friends, who supported them throughout this endeavor, as well as everyone at COMPUTE! who provided advice and assistance in this exciting, satisfying project.

Ottis R. Cowper
David Florance
Todd D. Heimarck
John Krause
George W. Miller
Kevin Mykytyn
Philip I. Nelson
Tim Victor

October 1985

Introduction

The Commodore 128 offers a lot to programmers; it's three computers in one. It can operate as a Commodore 64 with 64K of memory, BASIC 2.0, and 6502/8502 machine language. It's also a Commodore 128 with 128K of memory (expandable to 512K), BASIC 7.0, and 8502 machine language. Finally, it's a CP/M computer with a transient program area (TPA) of 59K, a variety of languages available, and Z80 machine language. Plus, you can purchase versions of Logo, Pilot, C, Comal, Pascal, COBOL, and many more languages. In one computer, you can choose to work with two BASICs, two versions of machine language, and three different operating systems. Where do you begin?

If you're a VIC or 64 owner who is already familiar with programming, you may want to start with Chapter 1, which explains BASIC in detail. The 128 has many new commands to make programming easier. You could then move on to the sections on graphics, music, machine language, or peripherals. Readers who have come to the 128 with a CP/M background may want to start with the CP/M chapter. And if the 128 is your first computer, you should probably start with the *System Guide,* the 400-page book that came with your 128 and which provides a good introduction to programming. *COMPUTE!'s 128 Programmer's Guide* was not written to replace the *System Guide* as an introduction to BASIC. Rather, it is a guide for programmers, a reference book, and a source of ideas.

Even if you're comparatively new to programming, you should not have difficulty understanding most parts of this book. We've tried to avoid jargon whenever possible, and explain each subject in clear, everyday language.

However, certain technical terms are unavoidable: For instance, the most descriptive name for the BASIC computer language is simply "BASIC." The term *microprocessor* is universally understood to mean the computer's main chip—the "electronic brain" that controls everything else—and so on. When a technical term is first introduced, it's italicized and described.

The Commodore 128 has 128K of memory. You can think of this as the equivalent of 131,070 characters, but what does that really mean? A single memory location can hold a *byte* or number in the range 0–255. The term K stands for *kilobyte* and refers to a 1,024-byte package of memory (128 * 1,024 = 131,070). Less often, you'll see the term *page*, which refers to a 256-byte memory zone. In most cases, the words *location* and *address* are interchangeable, both referring to a particular one-byte-long space in the computer's memory.

Just as memory is divided into single byte-size locations, a byte can be divided into individual *bits*, or binary digits. A byte contains eight bits, each of which represents a binary (base 2) number of 1 or 0.

We all understand decimal numbers. When referring to the 1,024th memory location in the computer, we'll ordinarily call it location 1024 (since the computer doesn't accept commas in numbers, we use 1024 instead of 1,024). In many cases, it's helpful to programmers to know the *hexadecimal* (base 16) form of an address as well. One reason for this is that all of the major subdivisions in computer memory occur at spots that divide evenly in hexadecimal, not decimal. BASIC program space, for instance, starts at decimal location 7168—which looks very odd unless you realize that the hexadecimal equivalent of 7168 is $1C00. This location falls at an even page boundary in memory (7168/256=28). A dollar sign ($) in front of a number tells you that it's hexadecimal. Thus, we'll usually refer to the 1,024th byte in memory as location 1024 ($0400).

If hexadecimal numbers sound confusing or difficult to you, don't worry about it. You won't need to deal with them very often in ordinary programming. And BASIC provides two functions (DEC and HEX$) that make it easy to translate from one number base to another (see Chapter 1). Or you can use the machine language monitor (see explanation below) to convert into four different number bases—decimal, hexadecimal, binary, and even octal.

How to Type In BASIC Programs

Many of the programs in this book contain special control characters (cursor controls, color keys, reverse video, etc.). To make it easy to know exactly what to type when entering one of these programs into your computer, we have established the following listing conventions.

Generally, program listings will contain words within braces which spell out any special characters: {DOWN} would mean to press the cursor-down key. {5 SPACES} would mean to press the space bar five times.

To indicate that a key should be *shifted* (hold down the SHIFT key while pressing the other key), the key would be underlined in our listings. For example, S would mean to type the S key while holding the SHIFT key. This would appear on your screen as a heart symbol. If you find an underlined key enclosed in braces (for example, {10 N}), you should type the key as many times as indicated. In that case, you would enter ten SHIFTed N's.

If a key is enclosed in special brackets, [<>], you should hold down the *Commodore key* while pressing the key inside the special brackets. (The Commodore key is the key in the lower-left corner of the keyboard.) Again, if the key is preceded by a number, you should press the key as many times as necessary.

Rarely, in programs for the 128, you'll see a solitary letter of the alphabet enclosed in braces. These characters can be entered by holding down the CTRL key while typing the letter in the braces. For example, {A} would indicate that you should press CTRL-A.

Quote Mode

The cursor is moved around the screen with the CRSR keys. Sometimes a programmer will want to move the cursor under program control. That's why you see all the {LEFT}'s, {HOME}'s, and {BLU}'s in our programs. The only way the computer can tell the difference between direct and programmed cursor control is the quote mode.

Once you press the quote (the double quote, SHIFT-2), you are in the quote mode. If you type something and then try to change it by moving the cursor left, you'll only get a bunch of reverse-video lines. These are the symbols for cursor left. The only editing key that isn't programmable is the DEL key; you can still use DEL to back up and edit the line. Once you type another quote, you are out of quote mode.

You also go into quote mode when you insert spaces into a line. In any case, the easiest way to get out of quote mode is to just press RETURN. You'll then be out of quote mode, and you can cursor up to the mistyped line and fix it.

Refer to the following table when entering cursor and color control keys:

When You Read:	Press:	See:	When You Read:	Press:	See:
{CLR}	SHIFT CLR/HOME		‹1›	COMMODORE 1	
{HOME}	CLR/HOME		‹2›	COMMODORE 2	
{UP}	SHIFT ↑ CRSR ↓		‹3›	COMMODORE 3	
{DOWN}	↑ CRSR ↓		‹4›	COMMODORE 4	
{LEFT}	SHIFT ← CRSR →		‹5›	COMMODORE 5	
{RIGHT}	← CRSR →		‹6›	COMMODORE 6	
{RVS}	CTRL 9		‹7›	COMMODORE 7	
{OFF}	CTRL 0		‹8›	COMMODORE 8	
{BLK}	CTRL 1		{ F1 }	f1	
{WHT}	CTRL 2		{ F2 }	SHIFT f1	
{RED}	CTRL 3		{ F3 }	f3	
{CYN}	CTRL 4		{ F4 }	SHIFT f3	
{PUR}	CTRL 5		{ F5 }	f5	
{GRN}	CTRL 6		{ F6 }	SHIFT f5	
{BLU}	CTRL 7		{ F7 }	f7	
{YEL}	CTRL 8		{ F8 }	SHIFT f7	
			←	←	
			↑	SHIFT ↑	

How to Type In Machine Language Programs

One of the Commodore 128's powerful built-in features is its machine language (ML) monitor. Since the machine language programs in this book must be typed in with the monitor, you'll need to know how it works. A *monitor* is simply a program, just as BASIC itself is a program. Its chief purpose is to simplify the process of writing an ML program. But it has other uses, even if you're not interested in machine language.

Getting In and Out of the Monitor

To activate the monitor from BASIC, type MONITOR and press RETURN (you may abbreviate the keyword MONITOR as MO followed by SHIFT-N). If you press the function key F8

(SHIFT-F7), the computer automatically enters the MONITOR command for you. Try entering the monitor and notice that the 128 prints two lines of characters over the blinking cursor, but don't worry about them now. We'll return to them later on.

Once you are in the monitor, the rules of BASIC no longer apply. For instance, try entering the BASIC command LIST. Since the monitor doesn't recognize BASIC commands, it prints a question mark after LIST and moves the cursor to the next line. The question mark is the monitor's all-purpose error message. Since it is a much simpler program than BASIC, the monitor doesn't print English error messages as BASIC does. Instead, it prints a question mark on the line that has a mistake, leaving it up to you to recognize the error.

Getting back to BASIC from the monitor is easy. Simply type X and press RETURN. The computer prints READY to signal that BASIC is working again. X stands for *exit*. You can always use this command to escape from the monitor and return to BASIC.

There may be times when you enter the monitor unintentionally. For instance, exit to BASIC and enter the following line:

POKE 8192,0:SYS 8192

The 128 makes a beep sound and activates the monitor just as if you had executed a MONITOR command. The value 0 which we put in location 8192 stands for BRK (break) in machine language. Like the BASIC STOP command, the BRK instruction causes the computer to stop executing an ML program. But instead of returning to BASIC, the computer returns to the monitor. When this happens unexpectedly during a BASIC program, it is usually the result of performing a SYS command that sends the computer to the wrong address: The 128's memory ordinarily contains a huge number of zero bytes. As soon as the computer hits one, it performs BRK and puts you in the monitor.

Typing In an ML Program

Most of the machine language programs in this book must be entered (typed in) and saved with the 128's built-in machine language monitor. This is done for two reasons. First, entering a program with the monitor is no more difficult than entering a BASIC program. And it's far easier for you to understand a program in this form than if it were listed in the usual way—as a group of raw numbers in BASIC DATA statements.

Let's begin with a simple example. The monitor's A command lets you *assemble* (write) a machine language program. Activate the monitor as described above, then type in the following lines. Just as in BASIC, you should press RETURN after typing each line.

```
A 2000 LDA  #$41
A 2002 JSR  $FFD2
A 2005 RTS
```

The A at the beginning of the line means "assemble the following machine language instruction." The number (2000, etc.) is the hexadecimal address where you want to put the instruction. The actual instruction (LDA #$41, etc.) is in *mnemonic* form. As you probably know, machine language—the computer's native tongue—consists of pure numbers. While it's possible to write an ML program as a string of raw numbers, it's hard for most of us to remember which number belongs to each machine language instruction. To simplify the process, descriptive three-letter labels (called *mnemonics*) have been invented for each machine language instruction. For instance, the mnemonic JSR stands for "Jump to SubRoutine." When you type JSR in a line, the monitor converts the mnemonic into the correct machine language instruction.

Note that although you had to enter A 2000 for the first line, the monitor automatically prints A followed by the correct number (with a leading 0) for later lines. This is a convenience feature, similar to automatic line numbering utilities in BASIC. After the monitor prints A 02006, press RETURN without typing anything. When you are done entering the program, your screen should look like this:

```
A 02000 A9 41    LDA #$41
A 02002 20 D2 FF JSR  $FFD2
A 02005 60       RTS
A 02006
```

This version of the program looks different from the first version. What do these extra characters mean? The leading 0 in front of each address signifies *bank 0*. This is part of the 128's internal memory management, a topic we'll return to in Chapter 7. At this stage, you can ignore the bank number in front of the address (except when using the G command; see explanation below).

In addition to the leading zeros, the monitor prints extra numbers on each line between the address and the mnemonic. In the first line, for instance, it adds A9 41. These are hexadecimal numbers representing the actual byte values which the monitor placed in memory to form this program. This portion of the display is called the *byte field*. When typing in ML programs, you can also ignore the byte field: It's just something the monitor creates to give you extra information.

To simplify the task of entering ML programs, we will list only the characters that you actually need to type in. For example, the example program would appear in this form:

```
2000 LDA #$41
2002 JSR  $FFD2
2005 RTS
```

Remember, you must start an assembly by typing A followed by the address where the program begins. For succeeding lines, all you need to enter are the mnemonics themselves. Since you're probably anxious to see what this program does, let's exit the monitor and try it out. Press X to return to BASIC, then enter the command BANK 15:SYS 8192. The computer prints the letter A. Not too impressive, but at least we know that it works. The BASIC equivalent of this program is PRINT CHR$(65). The hexadecimal number $41 translates to decimal 65, the character code value for the character A. The instruction JSR $FFD2 goes to the computer's built-in character printing routine, which takes care of putting the character on the screen.

Disassembling and Editing

Another important monitor function is *disassembly*. This is similar to LISTing a BASIC program. Reenter the monitor, then enter D 2000 2005. The computer prints your program on the screen, much as it appeared when you finished assembling it. On the left of each line is the address (with a leading 0), in the middle are the bytes composing each instruction, and on the right is the mnemonic field which contains the mnemonic for each instruction. This time, however, the A's in front of each line have been replaced with periods. The period character (.) is another monitor command that works much like the A command. The monitor prints a period in front of each disassembled line so that you can reassemble the line if needed.

To illustrate, let's change the program to make it print the letter B. Move the cursor to the instruction LDA #$41 in the first line, then change the 41 to 42. If you exit the monitor and perform SYS 8192 from BASIC, you'll see that the change was successful. Use this technique whenever you wish to correct or modify an ML program you've typed in. Note that you must make the change in the mnemonic field of the line, not in the byte field.

Saving and Loading

The 128's monitor can save any memory area to disk or tape. In most cases, you'll be using this command to save machine language programs. But you can also use it (like the BSAVE command in BASIC) to save other data such as custom character definitions, sprite shapes, and so on.

The monitor's Save and Load commands are very similar to their BASIC equivalents. To save the example program to disk, enter S "*filename*" 8 2000 2006 (inserting the filename of your choice). The first number after the filename is the device number—in this case it's 8, the device number of the disk drive. If you replace the 8 with a 1, the 128 assumes you want to save the file to tape. The second and third numbers in the command are the starting and ending addresses of the memory area you want to save. Notice that we must give an ending address which is *one higher in memory than the true ending address*. This is due to a peculiarity of the monitor and is not necessary when saving from BASIC via BSAVE.

The command L "NAME" 8 loads the program NAME from disk into memory. Again, if you replace the 8 with 1 (or omit it altogether), the 128 assumes you are using tape. Note that starting and ending addresses are not required to load a file: The file itself contains a load address which is used to put the program back into the same memory area it was saved from.

Number Conversions

In the previous examples, we used only hexadecimal numbers for monitor input. Most monitor output (disassembly, etc.) is in hexadecimal form, and the monitor expects hex input unless you specify otherwise. But there will be many times when you need to convert hexadecimal numbers to some other form. For instance, before using the example program from BASIC, we needed to know the decimal address for the SYS. The monitor has a built-in number converter that makes such conversions easy.

To demonstrate, move the cursor to a blank line and enter the hex number $2000 (note the leading $ symbol). The computer prints the following conversions:

$2000
+8192
&20000
%10000000000000

This display shows the number in four different forms: hexadecimal (base 16), decimal (base 10), octal (base 8) and binary (base 2). As you can see, a different leading symbol ($, +, &, or %) is used to identify each number base. If you type a number preceded by any of these symbols, the monitor automatically displays the number in all four bases. For instance, enter +7168 to find the hexadecimal, octal and binary equivalents of decimal 7168.

In addition to converting numbers, the monitor will accept input in number bases other than hexadecimal. All that's required is that you precede the number with the appropriate symbol. For instance, the command S "NAME" 8 +1024 +2023 is the same as S "NAME" 8 0400 07E7. In both cases, the monitor saves the contents of locations 1024–2023 to disk. In this example, the + symbol before the numbers 1024 and 2023 tells the monitor they are decimal numbers.

Monitor Commands

Here is a list of all the monitor commands, with a short explanation of the commands not already discussed.

A (Assemble). See explanation above.

C (Compare Memory). The Compare command compares two areas of memory and indicates which bytes (if any) are not the same. You must provide the starting and ending address of the first block of memory, followed by the starting address of the block you want to compare. For example, the command C 2000 20F0 3000 compares the areas from $2000–$20F0 and $3000–$30F0. The computer compares the two blocks byte by byte and prints the address of any byte in the second area that does not match. If nothing is printed, the contents of both memory areas are identical.

D (Disassemble Memory). See explanation above.

F (Fill Memory). This command fills a memory area with the value you designate. For instance, the command F 2000 2FFF 41 puts the value $41 (decimal 65, the letter A) in every location from $2000–$2FFF. The first and second values are the starting and ending addresses of the area you want to fill, and the third number is the value you want to put there.

G (Go). Go to the specified address and execute the ML program found there. For example, G 2000 causes the computer to execute the program at $2000. If the program calls any of the computer's internal ROM routines, you *must preface the address with a bank number in hexadecimal*. For example, G F2000 correctly executes an ML program which uses ROM calls. Chapter 7 explains how the 128 manages different banks of memory. If you intend to execute an ML program from within the monitor, end the program with a BRK instruction rather than RTS. BRK always returns you to the monitor rather than to BASIC.

H (Hunt). The Hunt command looks for a specified combination of bytes within the area you specify. The first two values after the command are the starting and ending addresses of the area you wish to search. The next value is the number (or string of characters) you are seeking. For example, the command H 2000 3000 D2 FF searches the area from $2000–3000 for the address $FFD2. Note that the search bytes must be typed in exactly the way they would appear in memory. You can also search for a character string; simply precede the string with an apostrophe (SHIFT-7). The command H 2000 3000 'DOG searches the same memory area for the characters DOG. When the target bytes are found, the monitor prints the address where the designated sequence begins.

L (Load). See explanation above.

M (Memory). This important command permits you to display any memory area or modify individual bytes. Let's try a quick example. Exit to BASIC and enter the following program:

```
10 REM THIS IS WHAT A BASIC PROGRAM
20 REM LOOKS LIKE WHEN STORED IN MEMORY
```

Now reenter the monitor and enter

M 1C00

Location $1C00 (7168) is where BASIC programs normally begin on the 128. You should see the following display:

Memory Dump from Monitor

```
>01C00 00 24 1C 0A 00 8F 20 54:
>01C08 48 49 53 20 49 53 20 57:
>01C10 48 41 54 20 41 20 42 41:
>01C18 53 49 43 20 50 52 4F 47:
>01C20 52 41 4D 00 4B 1C 14 00:
>01C28 8F 20 4C 4F 4F 4B 53 20:
>01C30 4C 49 4B 45 20 57 48 45:
>01C38 4E 20 53 54 4F 52 45 44:
>01C40 20 49 4E 20 4D 45 4D 4F:
>01C48 52 59 00 00 00 32 33 2C:
>01C50 31 36 2C 31 2C 32 3A FE:
>01C58 1C 20 32 3A E2 20 32 2C:
```

Several features of the display are notable. As you've probably gathered, the numbers at the left represent addresses. Each screen line shows the contents of several bytes (8 on a 40-column screen, 16 on an 80-column screen) in hexadecimal form. The rightmost portion of the line displays the same bytes in character form, highlighted in reverse video. Values that can't be printed as characters are printed as periods. In this case, we're looking into the memory area where BASIC programs are stored. Note that all the characters from the BASIC REM statements are visible in the character portion of the display.

Each line of the display begins with a > symbol. Just as the period is a substitute for the A command, the > symbol works much like the M command. In addition to displaying the contents of memory, M lets you change whatever you like. For instance, move the cursor to the second line of the display (it begins with >01C08), change the third value in the line from 53 to 59 and press RETURN. In the character display to the right, you see THIX instead of THIS. Now exit the monitor and LIST the program from BASIC to confirm that the program was actually changed. In this manner, you can change the contents of any memory location in the computer. Note that an error (?) results if you try to modify a ROM address with M.

When only one address is specified after M, the computer displays 12 rows of bytes (a total of 96 bytes in 40 columns or 192 in 80 columns). By specifying a starting and ending address, you can display a smaller or larger range of bytes. For instance, M 1C00 2000 displays all the locations from $1C00–2000. M always displays an entire line of bytes. Once you have a memory display on the screen, you can display succeeding areas by typing M followed by RETURN.

R (Register Display). This command displays the contents of several important registers (locations) in the microprocessor chip itself. When you enter the monitor, it automatically executes an R command before doing anything else. The display looks like this:

```
   PC  SR AC XR YR SP
;01C00 00 00 00 00 00
```

The Program Counter (PC) indicates the address of the last ML instruction executed before entering the monitor. This provides another way to execute ML programs from within the monitor: Simply change the address under PC to the starting address of your program, then execute a G command without specifying an address. The other registers are explained in Chapter 6. Note that the semicolon character (;) is a synonym for the R command.

S (Save Memory). See explanation above.

T (Transfer). The Transfer command moves an entire block of memory to some other location in the computer. Like the Compare command, it requires three addresses. First come the beginning and ending addresses of the block of memory you want to move, then the starting address of the area where you want to put the block. For instance, enter these commands:

```
M 1C00 1D00
T 1C00 1D00 2000
M 2000 2100
```

As you can see, the contents of locations $1C00–1D00 have been copied exactly into locations $2000–2100. You might think of this as a "copy" command, since it does not disturb the original memory area.

V (Verify). This works much like the BASIC VERIFY command, comparing the contents of memory (usually an ML program) to the contents of a disk file. For example, the command

V "NAME" 8 2000 compares the contents of the disk file NAME to the ML program beginning at location $2000 (note that no ending address is required; the command V compares bytes until it reaches the end of the disk file). The 8 indicates the device number: Change it to 1 for tape. If you omit the starting address, Verify begins verifying at $1C00, the place where BASIC programs usually start. If an error is found, the monitor prints ERROR; otherwise, the cursor simply reappears when the operation is done.

X (Exit). Exit the monitor and return to BASIC.

@ (Disk Command). The @ symbol permits you to read the status of the disk drive or send a command to the drive. It works much like the @ command in Commodore's familiar "DOS Wedge" program. If you enter @ by itself, the monitor reads and displays the drive status (0, OK, 0, 0 indicates all is well). If you wish to send a disk command, you must include the device number (usually 8) before the command. For instance, the command @8 V0 validates the disk, as if you had used the BASIC command OPEN 15,8,15:PRINT"V0." Chapter 4 explains the various disk commands in detail.

Quick Reference Table

Command	What It Does
A (Assemble)	Assemble a machine language instruction
C (Compare)	Compare two areas of memory
D (Disassemble)	Disassemble a machine language instruction
F (Fill)	Fill a memory area with the specified value
G (Go)	Execute a machine language program at the specified address
H (Hunt)	Hunt for certain bytes in the specified memory area
L (Load)	Load from disk or tape into memory
M (Memory)	Display or change the specified memory area
R (Register)	Display or change the microprocessor's registers
S (Save)	Save the specified memory area to disk or tape
T (Transfer)	Transfer the contents of one memory area to another
V (Verify)	Compare the specified memory area with a file on disk or tape
X (Exit)	Exit the monitor
. (Assemble)	Similar to A
> (Memory)	Similar to M
; (Register)	Similar to R
@ (Disk)	Read disk status or send disk command

Chapter 1

BASIC Programming

BASIC Programming

Almost every microcomputer programmer knows one or more dialects of BASIC. After all, BASIC comes standard with most personal computers, making it perhaps the most widely known language for micros.

If your first computer was a VIC or 64, expect to be surprised by BASIC 7.0, the version in the 128. You can do almost anything, even complex high-resolution graphics or multivoice musical compositions, without a single PEEK or POKE. Readers with a CP/M background may have worked with Microsoft BASIC or another version of BASIC. You'll recognize some of the commands like PRINT USING, but we think you too will be surprised by the power of BASIC on the 128.

For 64 Programmers: The Transition to 128 BASIC

A word of caution to aficionados of the 64: Whether you're a tyro or an expert, you'll find you have some BASIC 2.0 habits to unlearn. Many of the techniques you may have memorized are no longer necessary.

Of course, since BASIC 7.0 includes everything from BASIC 2.0 (as well as adding much more), you don't have to change if you don't want to. But why use a line like 10 GET A$:IF A$=""THEN10 when you could say 10 GETKEY A$? Why POKE 53281 to change the background color when the COLOR statement is available? A favorite programming utility that renumbers a program, deletes lines, or lists the directory is unnecessary when you have BASIC commands to do all of those things. You probably know how to read the disk error channel with OPEN 15,8,15: INPUT#15,E,E$: PRINT E,E$: CLOSE15. That method still works if you like a lot of typing, but you might as well just PRINT DS$. It even works in direct mode, so you can say goodbye to the DOS Wedge.

Those two workhorses, IF-THEN and FOR-NEXT, aren't obsolete, but they've been improved in many ways. You now have an ELSE that executes when the IF condition is false. BEGIN-BEND lets you extend a THEN or an ELSE to cover several lines. FOR-NEXT loops are still valuable for repetitions of calculations and actions. But a DO-LOOP is open-ended; it is flexible enough to continue WHILE a condition is true or UNTIL a condition is false. You can also leave a DO-LOOP with an EXIT. If you jump out of an ordinary FOR-NEXT loop enough times, you'll eventually fill up the stack and get an OUT OF MEMORY error. And the RESTORE command can now include a line number, to set the READ-DATA pointer to a specific line.

The famous SID sound chip is directly accessible through BASIC commands. You no longer need to consult a list of SID registers to figure out how to play a note or two of music. Creating hi-res graphics in 64 mode still requires a knowledge of bit-masking with ANDs and ORs. And it helps to have a few machine language routines to set up or clear the hi-res screen. But programming hi-res graphics in 128 mode can be done completely in BASIC. Throw away the graph paper (or the long program) you once used for drawing sprites: BASIC 7.0 includes a built-in sprite editor named SPRDEF. Once you've built a sprite, you can move it, check for collisions, and more with a few simple statements.

BASIC 7.0 also provides several new ways to print to the screen. The PRINT statement has been extended to include PRINT USING, which lets you format variables before they're printed to the screen. PUDEF assigns definitions to the characters that appear in PRINT USING statements. And the CHAR statement allows you to print to both text and hi-res screens. Since you specify the X and Y positions, CHAR is like the PRINT AT command so popular in other BASICs.

Variables, too, are easier to manage. MID$ can still find one string in the middle of another, but it can also reassign part of an existing string. For instance, T$="A STRING": MID$(T$,2,4)= "NYTH" makes A$ into "ANYTHING." INSTR is like a random access MID$—it tells you the position of one string inside another. It could tell you that "JONES" is inside the name "SAM JONES", starting at the fifth character.

PRINT FRE(0) tells you how much memory is left for BASIC programs, while FRE(1) returns the free memory left for variables. Programs are kept in memory bank 0, separate from bank 1 where variables are stored. So adding or changing a program line doesn't destroy variable definitions.

If you've ever alphabetized a large array or written a program that performs hundreds or thousands of calculations, you know that such tasks can take many minutes—sometimes even hours—for BASIC to complete. The FAST command doubles the speed of the processor, and thus halves the time spent on calculations, sorts, and other time-consuming jobs. If you're working in 40 columns, the display will blank until you order a SLOW.

Machine language programmers can call up the built-in machine language monitor. It's similar to other popular monitors and includes commands for assembling, disassembling, memory dumps, and more. Then you can start up the program with the new version of the SYS command, which allows you to send values to the A, X, Y, and P registers. DEC and HEX help you easily translate between decimal and hexadecimal numbers. When the program finishes, you can look at the last values in these registers with RREG (Read REGister). There's also an XOR (eXclusive OR) function in BASIC.

A Brief Introduction to BASIC

If you've never programmed in BASIC, the *System Guide* that came with your 128 is the best place to start learning. It contains many good programming examples and thorough explanations. Here is a brief outline of how BASIC programs are handled in the 128.

Starting Programs

The RUN command starts up a BASIC program. But if you turn on your 128 and enter RUN, all you'll see on the screen is another READY prompt and a blinking cursor. When you first turn on the computer, there's no BASIC program in memory. You must either type in a program or load one from tape or disk. Once you've put a program in memory, you can type LIST to look at it. Or just press the F7 key, which is predefined as LIST followed by a RETURN.

While a program is running, the computer is said to be in *program mode*. There are some commands, like GET and INPUT that work only inside a program. If the program stops or ends, the computer prints READY and the cursor starts blinking. When the computer is waiting for instructions, it is in *immediate mode* (also called *direct mode*). A few commands, like CONT, work only in direct mode. Others, like LIST, NEW, and RUN, are most often used in direct mode, though you may find occasion to use them in a program.

Program Flow

Every line in a BASIC program starts with a number between 0 and 63999 (note the absence of commas—you'd never enter 63,999 as a line number). It's common to number lines by tens, which lets you go back later and add a line or two if necessary. The 128 automatically sorts the lines from low to high: If you type line 500 and then line 10, LIST will show you that line 10 has been inserted in its proper place, ahead of 500. Each line number should be followed by at least one BASIC command. You can put more than one command on a line if you separate them with colons.

When you type RUN, the computer switches into program mode and starts executing (performing) the program, starting at the lowest line number. In a simple program, the computer works methodically, line by line. When it reaches the highest line, the program stops, and you're back in immediate mode. But there are several things that can disrupt or divert the program's journey from the lowest to the highest line number:

- An error can stop the program in its tracks.
- STOP and END tell the computer to stop running the program. The RUN/STOP key also works like a STOP command. STOP and END are designed to get you out of program mode back to direct mode. You can send the 128 back to the program with RUN, or use CONT (CONTinue) to restart the program at the point where it stopped.
- GOTO works like a permanent detour. The computer jumps to the line number you've specified. GOSUB (GO to SUBroutine) is a temporary rerouting of program flow. The program goes to the line number after the GOSUB and continues execution until it comes across the RETURN statement. RETURN ends the subroutine, and the program goes back to the command just after the GOSUB that called the subroutine.
- There are also several loop commands and decision-making commands (see below) that can change the program flow.

Variables

A variable has a name and a value. Entering the line 10 LET A=10 assigns the value 10 to the variable called A. Since the equal sign (=) is all you need to assign the value, LET is superfluous (thus, it's almost never used). You'll often see lines like 10 B=A+2, which assigns the current value of A (plus 2) to the variable B.

The names of *numeric* variables always start with a letter A–Z followed by either a letter or a number. Legal numeric variables include A, B, X, HI, ZZ, G5, G4. You can use more than two characters in a variable name, but only the first two are significant: For instance, the computer considers USA to be the same variable name as USNAVY. Numeric variables can include fractions and can have a maximum value, positive or negative, of about 10^{38} (10 to the thirty-eighth power, a 1 followed by 38 zeros). Very large and very small numbers are converted to exponential form. Enter A = 8000000000000000: PRINT A and the result should be 8E15, which means 8 * 10^{15} (8 times 10 to the fifteenth power).

String variables are always followed by a dollar sign. Again, only the first two characters in the variable name are significant: A$, Z$, GH$, IJ$, U9$ are examples of string variables. The equal sign is used to assign values to string variables, and you must enclose the string (but not the variable name) in quotation marks: Z$ = "HELLO": G$ = Z$: PRINT G$. This type of variable can hold up to 255 characters.

The final variable type, *integer,* is less frequently used. An integer variable is labeled with one or two characters followed by a percent sign, such as A%, B%, YS%, P2%. Integer variables always round down to the nearest whole number, so a line like Q% = 5.9 would put the value 5 into Q%. Integer variables are limited to a range of −32768 to 32767.

You can also create *arrays* of variables by putting a number or numeric variable in parentheses after one of the three variable types. Arrays are like numbered lists. A$(5) would represent the sixth string variable on the list called A$—sixth, because arrays start counting at zero.

Statements

Statements are orders to the computer. The statement (command) RUN tells the 128 to leave direct mode and run the program currently in memory. The statement LET A=15 assigns the value 15 to variable A. The statement PRINT "THE VALUE OF A IS"; A puts a string and a value on the screen.

Functions

Functions don't operate alone, as many statements do. Functions take one value as input and return another as output: In short, they're information-providers. Functions are often found in assignment statements, such as T1 = SQR(9) which finds the square root of 9 and stashes it in the variable T1. You can also nest one function inside another: B$ = STR$(INT(LOG(C*8)/LOG(BA))) is perfectly valid.

Input/Output

Some commands get information from the keyboard, from data files, or from other peripherals. Others send information out to a device hooked up to the computer (PRINT is a good example). Type NEW to clear the current program from memory and enter this program:

```
10 PRINT "PRESS A KEY"
20 GETKEY A$
30 PRINT "YOU CHOSE" A$: GOTO 10
```

Line 10 sends output to the screen, line 20 gets a keypress from the keyboard and puts the value into variable A$, and line 30 prints to the screen again and sends the program back to 10 (note that you can put more than one command on a line if they're separated by a colon).

Making Decisions

One of the two most powerful things a computer can do is make decisions. IF TM = 10 OR H < K THEN GOTO 500 is an example. The IF is followed by the expression TM = 10 OR H < K. The equal sign here is not assigning a value, but comparing the value in TM with the number 10. The two are either equal or not equal. The expression H < K also compares two values. If the number in H is really less than K, the expression is true. But the two are linked by a logical operator OR. If one *or* the other is true (or both are true), THEN takes over and sends the program to line 500. If both expressions are false, THEN never does anything. The computer ignores everything after THEN on that line, and proceeds to the next line of the program.

It's a fork in the road where two things could happen. If one expression is true, the whole OR operation is true and the computer moves on to 500. If not, it continues on.

Decision makers include commands like IF-THEN-ELSE, ON-GOTO, ON-GOSUB, WHILE, UNTIL, BEGIN-BEND. Though each set of decision-making commands serves a similar purpose, they have different advantages, too. The time spent learning the ins and outs of decision makers will return valuable dividends.

Loops

The other power commands are the loopers. They make the computer repeat a series of actions over and over. Sometimes the loop repeats a certain number of times and then ends (see FOR-NEXT in the list of commands). In other cases, the loop is open-ended, meaning that it runs WHILE an expression is true or UNTIL something becomes false (see DO-LOOP). DO-LOOPs are useful hybrid forms of decision-maker and loop.

Algorithms

The best way to learn programming is to experiment. You can't break a computer by making programming mistakes. You'll find yourself inventing *algorithms,* a fancy word for programming techniques. Say that you want to write a program that alphabetized a list of ten names.

You might start by asking the user (the person using the program) for input. The names typed in would be stored in a string array, to be sorted later (or maybe you'd prefer to sort the names as they're typed in—it's up to you). Once the list has been established, you can alphabetize the names. Finally, you'll want to print them on the screen.

There's no ALPHABETIZE command built into BASIC, so you'll have to invent one. One of the simplest techniques is a *bubble sort* (unfortunately, it grows slower and slower as the list becomes longer, but that's no problem when we're sorting only ten items). Here's the basic idea: Set up a loop inside a loop. The first starts at the end and works toward the beginning while the inner loop starts at the beginning and loops forward to the counter in the first loop. Within that loop, you compare one item on the list with its neighbor. If they're out of order, switch them. The result is an alphabetized list.

The program looks like this (type it in to test it out):

```
10 T = 10: REM TOTAL NUMBER OF ITEMS ON THE LIST
20 DIM N$(10): REM SET UP SIZE OF STRING ARRAY
30 PRINT "PLEASE ENTER";T;"NAMES TO BE
   ALPHABETIZED."
40 FOR J = 1 TO T: INPUT N$(T): NEXT: REM USER INPUT
50 FOR J = T-1 TO 1 STEP -1: PRINT J;
60 FOR K = 1 TO J
```

```
70 IF N$(K) > N$(K+1) THEN TEMP$ = N$(K): N$(K)
   = N$(K+1): N$(K+1) = TEMP$
80 NEXT K: REM END INNER LOOP
90 NEXT J: REM WHEN IT FINISHES, THE LIST IS SORTED
100 PRINT: PRINT"THE RESULTS:"
110 FOR J = 1 TO T: PRINT T, N$(T): NEXT
```

BASIC Keywords

Before beginning the keyword section of this chapter, please note the typing conventions used to denote format: The keyword is always capitalized and printed in boldface. A mandatory parameter—something which must always be included with the keyword—is shown in ***boldface italics*** (**POKE *address, value***). An optional parameter—one which is not needed in every case—is shown in *italics* (**MID$(*string$***, *position, number of characters***)**).

ABS

Numeric function
Returns the absolute value of a number or numeric variable.

Format: ABS(*number*)
Modes: Immediate and program
Token: 182 ($B6)
Abbreviation: A SHIFT-B
Same as BASIC 2.0

This function converts the argument (in parentheses) to a positive number. Positive numbers remain unchanged. For negative arguments, the value returned is positive, the equivalent of the argument multiplied by −1. In short, ABS strips off minus signs.

ABS is used when only the magnitude of a number—and not its sign—is significant:

```
10 INPUT A,B
20 PRINT"THE DIFFERENCE BETWEEN"A"AND"B"IS"
   ABS(A-B)
```

It's also useful when you simply want to get rid of a negative sign:

```
ON ABS(F>3)+1 GOTO 100,200
```

AND

Logical operator
Performs a logical AND on two expressions or numbers.

Format: ***expression1* AND *expression2***
Modes: Immediate and program
Token: 175 ($AF)
Abbreviation: A SHIFT-N
Same as BASIC 2.0

If both expressions are true, the result of the AND operation is true. If either is false, the entire ANDed expression is false. This operator allows you to test for several conditions:

```
100 A1 = 100: A2 = 100: B$ = "GRAPEFRUIT": M$ =
    "ORANGE"
110 IF A1 = A2 AND B$ = M$ THEN PRINT "BOTH ARE THE
    SAME":ELSE PRINT "NOT THE SAME"
```

In this example, both expressions must be true for the message to be printed. While it's true that A1=A2, it's not true that B$=M$, so the test fails and the IF statement is false.

This operator can also be used for bit-masking (testing numbers to see whether individual bits are on or off). For example, PRINT 71 AND 143 gives an answer of 7, which results from the bit patterns of each number:

```
    01000111 (71)
AND 10001111 (143)
=   00000111 (7)
```

Note that 1's appear in the answer only where the first two numbers both contained a 1. This way of using AND is often found in PEEKs and POKEs when a certain bit or series of bits need to be tested.

APPEND

Disk command
Opens an existing disk file, so information can be added.

Format: APPEND#*file number,"filename"*,*Ddrive number,Udevice number*
Modes: Immediate and program
Tokens: 254 14 ($FE $0E)
Abbreviation: A SHIFT-P
Not available in BASIC 2.0

APPEND works like OPEN or DOPEN, but it is used to append or write new data to the end of the sequential file specified. The logical file number can range from 1–255. APPEND opens the file and positions the pointer to the end of the file, causing subsequent PRINT# statements to add data to the file. The default drive number is 0, the device number 8, so if you're using a single 1541 or 1571, you don't need to include drive or device numbers.

One acceptable version of this command is

APPEND#1,"DATAFILE"

Note that the disk should already contain a file called DATAFILE. You may use a string variable as the filename if you enclose the variable in parentheses:

APPEND#1,(N$),D0,U8

APPEND may be used in immediate or program mode, but is most often used under program control. Here is how to perform an append operation in BASIC 2.0 (64 mode):

OPEN *file number,device number,channel,"drive number:filename,S,A"*

The following statement opens DATAFILE for an append in BASIC 2.0:

OPEN1,8,2,"0:DATAFILE,S,A"

ASC

String conversion function

Converts a character from a string or string variable to a Commodore character code number.

Format: ASC(*character$*)
Modes: Immediate and program
Token: 198 ($C6)
Abbreviation: A SHIFT-S
Same as BASIC 2.0

All printable characters and most of the keyboard functions (CLR/HOME, cursor keys, CTRL codes, and so on), have a corresponding character code value. For a complete list of Commodore character codes, see Appendix A.

The ASC function takes any string expression and returns the code for the first character in that string. (An easy way to remember how it works is that ASC "asks" for an

ASCII value.) The following program line waits for the RETURN key to be pressed by looking for a character code of 13.

```
100 DO: GET A$: LOOP UNTIL ASC(A$)=13
```

ATN(X)

Numeric function
Returns the arctangent (in radians) of the argument.

Format: **ATN(*slope*)**
Modes: Immediate and program
Token: 193 ($C1)
Abbreviation: A SHIFT-T
Same as BASIC 2.0

In trigonometry, ATN (arctangent) is the complement of the TAN (tangent) function. ATN converts the slope of a line (the Y-position divided by the X-position) into an angle measured in radians. Say you wanted to aim a telescope at the tip of a building. You could use the height of a building (Y-position) and its distance from you (X-position) to figure out what the telescope's angle would be:

```
10 PRINT"WHAT IS THE HEIGHT OF THE BUILDING AND
   HOW FAR AWAY IS IT?"
20 INPUT H,D: A1 = ATN(H/D): A2 = A1*180/π
30 PRINT"SET THE TELESCOPE FOR";A1;"RADIANS
   OR";A2;"DEGREES."
```

AUTO

Programming utility
Turns automatic line numbering on and off.

Formats: **AUTO *increment*** (turns AUTO on)
AUTO (turns it off)
Mode: Immediate only
Token: 220 ($DC)
Abbreviation: A SHIFT-U
Not available in BASIC 2.0

AUTO followed by a number tells the 128 to start automatically numbering lines. When you press RETURN to enter a line, the next line number is printed just below it. This can save typing when you're entering a long program. The number after AUTO determines the increment—the difference between successive line numbers. If you press RETURN on a blank line, AUTO is still turned on, but it won't list another line number until you enter a line. This feature lets you skip over a range of lines.

To completely turn off automatic line numbering, type AUTO by itself, without a number. RUN also disables autonumbering.

AUTO 10	—start numbering by tens
100 PRINT "TEST THE AUTO FEATURE"	—enter line 100
110	—next line number, ten higher than the previous, appears automatically

BACKUP

Disk command
Copies an entire disk to another on a dual drive.

Format: BACKUP D*source drive* TO D*destination drive*,U*device number*
Modes: Immediate and program
Token: 246 ($F6)
Abbreviation: BA SHIFT-C
Not available in BASIC 2.0

BACKUP makes a backup disk, copying all files and information on the source disk to the destination disk. The backup disk need not be formatted. Everything on the source disk is copied, so any information previously stored on the destination disk will be destroyed. BACKUP defaults to device 8. A dual disk drive (such as the 1572) is required; you can't use BACKUP with two single drives. There is no similiar command in DOS for BASIC 2.0 (64 mode), although Commodore PET computers have a version of BACKUP.

For example, BACKUP D0 TO D1 copies all files from the disk in drive 0 to the disk in drive 1.

BANK

Memory control
Selects one of the 16 memory banks, numbered 0–15.

Format: BANK *banknumber*
Modes: Immediate and program
Tokens: 254 2 ($FE $02)

Abbreviation: B SHIFT-A
Not available in BASIC 2.0

The 128 has 128K of RAM and 52K of ROM, yet it can "see" only 64K (65536 bytes of memory) at one time. To compensate, it can choose from 16 possible arrangements (banks) of 64K. In some arrangements, the 128 sees only RAM; in others, it sees a combination of RAM, ROM, and I/O chips. Bank 0 contains the RAM which holds BASIC programs, and bank 1 is the RAM where BASIC variable definitions are stored. The ROM and I/O chips have addresses in bank 15. Character ROM is found in bank 14.

The BANK command sets up a pointer to which bank will be active for PEEK, POKE, SYS, and other memory-related commands. For more about banks, see Chapter 7.

Commodore 64 programmers should recognize what this line does:

```
BANK 15: POKE 53280,1
```

BEGIN

Program control (decisions)
Marks the beginning of a block of statements executed after a THEN or an ELSE.

Formats: IF (*statement*) THEN BEGIN: (*several lines or statements*): BEND
or
IF (*statement*) THEN (*action1*): ELSE BEGIN (*several lines or statements*): BEND

Modes: Immediate and program
Tokens: 254 24 ($FE $18)
Abbreviation: B SHIFT-E
Not available in BASIC 2.0

Most commands are limited in length to a single line. But there are times when you may want to execute several commands as part of a THEN or an ELSE. BEGIN and BEND allow you to define a block of statements that will be active only within the context of a THEN or an ELSE.

```
710 PRINT "PLAY AGAIN? (Y/N)
720 GETKEY P$: IF P$= "N" THEN BEGIN:
730 PRINT "YOUR HIGH SCORE WAS"; HS
740 IF HS > TH THEN PRINT "...A NEW RECORD": GOSUB
    500: REM SAVE HS TO DISK
```

750 PRINT"THANKS FOR PLAYING.": END
760 BEND: ELSE GOTO 400: REM START ANOTHER GAME

A couple of noteworthy items in the example above: A response of N in line 720 triggers the BEGIN block. It covers all the lines up to 760, where BEND turns off the block and checks the ELSE (which refers back to the IF in 720, not the IF in 740). Line 740 does two things after the IF: It prints something and calls a subroutine. So, if you can fit the actions following a THEN onto one line, you don't need BEGIN/BEND. If you type Y after the prompt, the program would skip the whole block, from BEGIN to BEND, and start execution after the ELSE in line 760.

BEND

Program control (decisions)
Signals the end of a BEGIN/BEND block that would be set in motion by THEN or ELSE.

Format: see BEGIN
Modes: Immediate and program
Tokens: 254 25 ($FE $19)
Abbreviation: BE SHIFT-N
Not available in BASIC 2.0

See BEGIN/BEND above for details on the use of BEND.

BLOAD

Disk command
Loads a binary file from disk.

Format: BLOAD *"filename",Ddrive number,Udevice number,Bbank number,Paddress*
Modes: Immediate and program
Token: 254 17 ($FE $11)
Abbreviation: B SHIFT-L
Not available in BASIC 2.0

The LOAD and DLOAD commands load standard BASIC programs into the beginning of BASIC memory. BLOAD loads a binary file, which could be a machine language program, sprite definitions, function key definitions, character ROM, or any section of memory you may have elected to save with the BSAVE command.

It's similar to BASIC 2.0's LOAD "filename",8,1 but more flexible. Any file may be forced to load at any specified memory location.

The only necessary parameter is the *filename*. *Drive number* is the number of the disk drive containing the disk with the program file, either 0 (the default value) or 1. *Device number* is usually either 8 or 9, with 8 the default value. *Bank number* is one of the 16 memory banks available on the 128 (you're generally limited to banks 0 and 1). *Address* is the memory location within the memory bank where the file is to be loaded. If the address is omitted, the binary file loads back to the area from which it was saved.

This command loads a file called SPRITES into bank 0, starting at position 3584, from drive 0, device 8:

BLOAD "SPRITES",D0,U8,B0,P3584

With a single disk drive (a 1541 or 1571), you don't need to indicate the drive or device:

BLOAD "SPRITES",B0,P3584

BOOT

Disk command

Used by itself, loads and runs CP/M or any other autoboot disk. When a filename is included, BOOT performs an absolute load of a machine language program and executes the program beginning at the starting address.

Formats: BOOT *"filename"*,*Ddrive number,Udevice number*
or
BOOT

Modes: Immediate and program
Tokens: 254 27 ($FE $1B)
Abbreviation: B SHIFT-O
Not available in BASIC 2.0

BOOT loads an executable binary file from disk, beginning at the predefined starting address, and starts it up. The default drive is 0, and the default device is 8.

BOOT "MLGAME" loads and runs the program file MLGAME using the default parameters of device 0, and drive 8.

BOOT by itself with no program name checks track 1, sector 0 on the disk for autoboot instructions. If a CP/M disk is there, for example, CP/M loads and runs. Chapter 4 explains the autoboot process and shows how to create your own autobooting disks.

BOX

Graphics command

Draws a square or rectangle on the hi-res screen.

Format: BOX *color source, Xcoord1, Ycoord1*, *Xcoord2, Ycoord2, angle, paint flag*
Modes: Immediate and program
Token: $E1
Abbreviation: None
Not available in BASIC 2.0

BOX draws a rectangle with one corner at the point defined by (Xcoord1, Ycoord1) and the opposite corner at the point defined by (Xcoord2, Ycoord2). If the second set of coordinates is omitted, the corner is defined as the current position of the pixel cursor. The rectangle may be rotated at any angle from 0 to 360 degrees (the default value is 0, no rotation). Setting *paint flag* to 1 causes the rectangle to be filled as it is drawn. If this value is omitted or set to 0, the rectangle is not filled.

The following program draws a filled rectangle rotated 45 degrees at the center of the screen.

```
10 GRAPHIC 4,1
20 BOX 1,100,100,50,50,45,1
```

For more about this and other graphics commands, see Chapter 2.

BSAVE

Disk command

Saves a binary file from specified memory locations in RAM or ROM.

Format: BSAVE *"filename"*, *Ddrive number, Udevice number, Bbank number*, ***Pstart address* TO *Pend address***
Modes: Immediate and program
Tokens: 254 16 ($FE $10)
Abbreviation: B SHIFT-S
Not available in BASIC 2.0

SAVE and DSAVE are designed for saving BASIC programs. When you want to save a hi-res screen, sprites you've created, or other sections of memory outside the realm of BASIC, use BSAVE.

The *filename* can be up to 16 characters, as long as no file by that name already exists on the disk. *Drive number* is either 0 or 1 (0 is the normal value for a single-drive system). *Device number* defaults to 8, the standard value for a single-drive system. *Bank number* is a number between 0 and 15 specifying which bank of memory holds the data you're saving. *Start address* is the first memory location you wish to save. *End address* is the address of the last memory location to be saved. (Note that the end address for BSAVE is the actual last byte to be saved, whereas for files saved from the monitor the end address is the last location plus one.)

BSAVE is useful for saving machine language programs and sprite data. The following statement saves the binary data in memory locations 3584 through 4096 (from bank 0) to a file called "SPRITES":

BSAVE "SPRITES", B0, P3584 TO P4096

This statement saves the current contents of the hi-res screen:

BSAVE "PICTURE", B0, P7168 TO P16383

And the following saves the uppercase/graphics character set patterns:

BSAVE "CHARSET", B14, P53248 TO P55296

BUMP

Graphics function
Detects collisions between sprites or between sprites and background.

Format: BUMP(*collision type*)
Modes: Immediate and program
Tokens: 206 3 ($CE $03)
Abbreviation: B SHIFT-U
Not available in BASIC 2.0

If the number in parentheses is 1, BUMP returns a binary pattern indicating which sprites have collided. Setting *collision type* to 2 returns a value indicating which sprites have collided with the background.

After a collision has occurred (see COLLISION for an easy way to check for this), the following routine tells you which sprites have been bumped:

```
500 B = BUMP(1): SN = 0: E = 1
510 DO WHILE SN < 8: IF B AND E THEN PRINT "SPRITE"; SN
520 SN = SN + 1: E = E*2: LOOP
```

For more detailed examples and further explanation, see Chapter 2.

CATALOG

Disk command

Lists the programs on the current disk, without disturbing the program in memory.

Format: CATALOG *Ddrive number, Udevice number, wildcard string*

Modes: Immediate and program

Tokens: 254 6 ($FE $06)

Abbreviation: C SHIFT-A

Not available in BASIC 2.0

The CATALOG command displays the directory of the disk (or of the disk in the specified drive of a dual drive system). The default value for the drive is 0, and the default value for the device is 8. Displaying a disk directory by using the CATALOG command does not affect the program currently in memory. (See DIRECTORY for more details about wildcards.)

CATALOG (without any parameters) displays the directory of the disk on drive 0, device 8, using the default values. CATALOG,D1,U9,"A*" displays the directory of all files starting with the letter A on the disk on drive 1, device 9.

CHAR

Graphics command

Prints a string, in the color specified, on any of the hi-res or text screens.

Format: CHAR *color source,**column,row**,string$,reverse flag*

Modes: Immediate and program

Token: 224 ($E0)

Abbreviation: CH SHIFT-A

Not available in BASIC 2.0

CHAR positions the printing of a string in any graphics mode. It is especially useful for printing text on hi-res drawings. In text mode, it is similar to the PRINT AT (PRINT@) command found in some BASICs, and can replace the dozens of cursor commands often used to move around the screen in 64 mode.

The *color source* can be 0 (background color) or 1 (foreground color). *Column* is the X coordinate from 0 to 79 and *row* is the Y coordinate (0–24). On a 40-column screen, any column higher than 39 makes CHAR wrap around to the next line. You can print strings or string variables, but not numbers. If you wish to print a numeric value, use the STR$ function to convert it to a string. To print the characters in reverse, set the reverse flag to 1.

The following program prints the title COMMODORE 128 PROGRAMMER'S GUIDE in the center of the screen, then frames it with a BOX command.

```
10 GRAPHIC 2,1
20 CHAR 1,4,12,"COMMODORE 128 PROGRAMMER'S
   GUIDE",1
30 BOX 1,29,94,291,105
```

CHR$

Number to string conversion function
Converts a number into the character or function represented by the corresponding Commodore character code—the converse of ASC.

Format: CHR$(*char number*)
Modes: Immediate and program
Token: 199 ($C7)
Abbreviation: C SHIFT-H (includes the $)
Same as BASIC 2.0

The following program waits for the user to press the RETURN key (RETURN is the same as CHR$(13)) and then prints several CHR$ functions. CHR$(147) clears the screen, CHR$(5) turns the cursor to white, and CHR$(7) rings the bell (turn up the volume to hear the bell). For a complete list of Commodore character codes, see Appendix A.

```
100 DO:GET A$:LOOP UNTIL A$=CHR$(13)
110 PRINT CHR$(147);CHR$(5);CHR$(7);"YOU PRESSED
    RETURN."
```

CIRCLE

Graphics command
Draws all or part of a circle, ellipse, or polygon on the hi-res screen.

Format: CIRCLE *color source, **Xcenter, Ycenter, Xradius, Yradius**, start angle, end angle, rotation, segment*
Modes: Immediate and program
Token: 226 ($E2)
Abbreviation: C SHIFT-I
Not available in BASIC 2.0

Before a circle can be drawn, a graphics area in memory must be available. Otherwise, a NO GRAPHICS AREA error will occur. Use the GRAPHIC command to allocate 9K for the hi-res work area.

The *color source* is a number from 0–3 (see COLOR for a list of colors and color sources). When figuring out the center coordinates, remember that the multicolor screen has half as much horizontal (X) resolution as an ordinary hi-res screen. Adding a plus (+) or minus (−) to X and Y locates the circle center at a position relative to the current pixel cursor. If you have previously used the SCALE command, the circle is drawn within the scaled screen. WIDTH commands also affect the size of the lines in the circle.

The X *radius* controls how wide the circle is, and the *Y radius* defines the height. To draw a circle that looks perfectly round, you may have to experiment with smaller Y radiuses.

The starting and ending angles are necessary only for drawing arcs (circle segments). Likewise for the rotation. The segment defaults to 2 degrees. Larger segments make the sides flatter. A segment angle of 72, for example, draws a pentagon. For a square, insert a segment angle of 90 degrees.

The following program draws an ellipse and a half of an ellipse to form a bowl shape.

```
10 GRAPHIC 2,1
20 CIRCLE 1,160,80,50,20
30 CIRCLE 1,160,80,50,40,90,270
```

CLOSE

General input/output
Closes an open file on disk, tape, printer, modem, or other peripheral.

Format: CLOSE ***file number***
Modes: Immediate and program
Token: 160 ($A0)
Abbreviation: CL SHIFT-O

Same as BASIC 2.0

CLOSE closes a logical file which was previously established by OPEN or DOPEN. Follow CLOSE with the same logical file number used in the corresponding OPEN statement. For example, after opening a file to the printer with OPEN 3,4 you should close it with CLOSE 3. (In this case, the logical file number is 3 and the device number for the printer is 4; you're not closing the printer, you're closing the communication channel associated with file 3 which you used to send information to the printer.)

It is prudent to CLOSE a file as soon as you are done with it. In some cases, a naked PRINT# statement (see line 40) is required to assure that all data is output before you close the file. This clears any buffer that might contain characters. In the following example, note that nothing happens at the printer until you press RETURN. The printer saves up the characters sent in an internal buffer.

```
10 OPEN 3,4 : REM OPEN FILE TO PRINTER
20 GETKEY A$ : REM GET CHARACTER FROM KEYBOARD
30 IF A$ <> CHR$(13) THEN PRINT#3,A$;: PRINT A$: GOTO 20
40 PRINT#3: CLOSE 3
```

Attempting to CLOSE a file that is not currently open is acceptable, but if you try to OPEN an already open file, a FILE OPEN error is generated. To avoid the possibility of an error message, some programmers issue a CLOSE right before each OPEN.

CLR

Control over variables
Clears all variables and resets variable pointers.

Format: CLR
Modes: Immediate and program
Token: 156 ($9C)
Abbreviation: C SHIFT-L
Same as BASIC 2.0

This command makes the computer "forget" the values of all variables, including FOR-NEXT loop counters and arrays. It also unDIMensions arrays, clears the return addresses for subroutines and resets the pointer to DATA statements. It does not affect the current program in memory, but does get rid of all variables.

CLR also erases all file numbers, which makes the computer think all files have been closed. However, the CLR statement does not affect the actual state of the files on disk, tape, or modem. To avoid problems like unclosed files on the disk or tape (which can result in loss of programs), you should always be sure that all files are closed before executing a CLR.

There aren't many instances where CLR is necessary except in 64 mode. Whenever you move the top of BASIC down to protect a section of memory from variables, issue a CLR to reset the pointers.

In BASIC 7.0, CLR is also used as part of the GRAPHIC CLR statement which deallocates the hi-res screen. See GRAPHIC for more details.

CMD

Type: General input/output
Redirects system output to a previously opened file.

Format: CMD *file number*
Modes: Immediate and program
Token: 157 ($9D)
Abbreviation: C SHIFT-M
Same as BASIC 2.0

CMD is most often used along with PRINT or LIST. PRINT is the 128's all-purpose output command, which lets you display strings, numbers, or variables on the screen. LIST is a variation on PRINT which also defaults to the screen.

CMD reroutes output that would normally go to the screen to another device such as the disk drive or the printer. It must be preceded by an OPEN statement to establish a logical file (communication channel) for the desired device. For example, these statements redirect the normal output of LIST to a printer file designated as logical file 3:

```
OPEN 3,4 : REM OPEN FILE TO PRINTER
CMD 3 : REM REDIRECT OUTPUT TO FILE 3
LIST : REM PROGRAM IS LISTED ON PRINTER RATHER
   THAN SCREEN
PRINT#3 : REM MAKE SURE ALL DATA IS SENT
CLOSE 3 : REM ALWAYS CLOSE A FILE WHEN YOU'RE DONE
   USING IT
```

You may add a filename after a CMD statement if you separate it with a comma. This has the effect of PRINTing the name before any other output takes place. For instance, in the preceding example CMD 3,"PROGRAM NAME" causes the printer to print PROGRAM NAME at the top of the program listing. Of course, you may substitute a string variable for the filename (A$="PROGRAM NAME":CMD 3,A$).

COLLECT

Disk command
Cleans up the Block Allocation Map of a disk.

Format: COLLECT *Ddrive number,Udevice number*
Modes: Immediate and program
Token: 243 ($F3)
Abbreviation: COLL SHIFT-E
Not available in BASIC 2.0

COLLECT frees otherwise inaccessible disk space by making available any sectors allocated to improperly closed files. Improperly closed files (informally known as *poison* or *splat* files) are marked in the disk directory with an asterisk (*). Typing COLLECT by itself performs a disk validation on drive 0 of device 8, the standard values for a single-drive system.

During the COLLECT procedure, the disk drive looks at all disk files and determines which disk sectors the files occupy. It marks the sectors in use as allocated in the Block Allocation Map (BAM). Any sectors not active are deallocated and freed up for future use by programs or files.

COLLECT is the same as the disk validate command in BASIC 2.0 (OPEN 15,8,15,"V0":CLOSE 15). This can also be used in BASIC 7.0 in lieu of COLLECT.

COLLISION

Graphics command
Sets up a GOSUB which will be triggered by a sprite collision.

Formats: COLLISION ***type, line number*** (turns on collision-checking)
COLLISION ***type*** (turns it off)
Modes: Immediate and program
Token: 254 23 ($FE $17)
Abbreviation: CO SHIFT-L
Not available in BASIC 2.0

COLLISION tells the 128 to start watching for sprite collisions.

There are three types of collisions:

- sprite-to-sprite collision
- sprite-to-character collision
- light pen

The collision type follows the COLLISION command. Usually, nothing happens immediately after execution of COLLISION, unless a sprite is turned on and is touching another sprite or a character.

While COLLISION is in effect, the 128 continues running the current program in memory. But as soon as a collision occurs, the program finishes whatever command is being processed and then does a GOSUB to the line number specified. RETURN marks the end of the collision routine and sends the program back to the program line that was interrupted. Within the subroutine, you can check what happened and which sprites are involved with the BUMP function.

COLOR

Graphics command
Stores a color into a color source register.

Format: COLOR ***color source, color number***
Modes: Immediate and program
Token: 231 ($E7)
Abbreviation: COL SHIFT-O
Not available in BASIC 2.0

Color sets the background, border, and foreground screen colors. The color sources are numbered as follows:

0 40-column (composite) background
1 40-column foreground
2 Multicolor 1
3 Multicolor 2
4 40-column border
5 Character color (40- or 80-column)
6 80-column (RGB) background

The color numbers range from 1 to 16 (80-column RGB colors appear in parentheses if different from 40-column composite colors):

1	Black	4	Cyan (Light Cyan)
2	White	5	Purple (Light Purple)
3	Red	6	Green

7	Blue	12	Dark Gray (Dark Cyan)
8	Yellow (Light Yellow)	13	Medium Gray
9	Orange (Dark Purple)	14	Light Green
10	Brown (Dark Yellow)	15	Light Blue
11	Light Red	16	Light Gray

An easy way to remember color numbers is to look at the color keys at the top of the keyboard. The numbers 1–8 are exactly as printed on tops of the keys 1–8. For the secondary colors underneath, add eight to the key on which it is printed.

Each color on the 40-column screen contains a chroma (color) value and a luma (brightness) value. If you're working with a monochrome monitor or a black-and-white TV, you can display four different levels of brightness (shades of gray), corresponding to white and the three shades of gray (plus black, which has no brightness). With a monochrome monitor and 80-column mode, you can also set brightness (intensity). Note that SPRCOLOR, and not COLOR, assigns colors to sprites. The colors for sprites can be different from the colors on the foreground and background. The following program may bring back some old memories for Commodore 64 owners.

```
10 COLOR 0,7
20 COLOR 5,15
30 COLOR 4,15
```

CONCAT

Disk command

Appends one file to the end of a second.

Format: CONCAT ***"second file"****, Ddrive number* **TO** ***"main file"****, Ddrive number, Udevice number*

Modes: Immediate and program

Token: 254 19 ($FE $13)

Abbreviation: C SHIFT-O

Not available in BASIC 2.0

CONCAT attaches a second file to a main file. The second file (listed first after CONCAT) remains unchanged on the disk. The main file contains both the original data and the data from the second file, in that order. The optional device defaults to 8, and the drive defaults to 0. If you own a dual drive, you can concatenate files from drive 0 to drive 1 and vice versa.

The statement CONCAT "BUGGY" TO "HORSE" adds the contents of "BUGGY" to "HORSE." The file called BUGGY stays on the disk as it was before the concatenation. The original portion of HORSE remains unchanged, but a copy of the data in BUGGY is tacked onto the end.

CONT

Program control
Resumes execution of a program following a STOP, an END, or the pressing of the RUN/STOP key.

Format: CONT
Mode: Immediate only
Token: 154 ($9A)
Abbreviation: None in BASIC 7.0 (C SHIFT-O in BASIC 2.0)
Same as BASIC 2.0

CONT continues program execution after it has been stopped with STOP or END. Since the program's variables remain intact, CONT lets you restart the program where it left off. This is very useful for debugging programs; you may insert a STOP or END statement in the program (or press RUN/STOP), PRINT the value of any variable or LIST a section of the program, and then resume execution with CONT.

This command cannot be used if the program stops because of an error or if you cause an error after the program stops. Likewise, CONT cannot be used (and generates a CAN'T CONTINUE error) if you add or change program lines during the interim, or simply press RETURN over an existing line. However, you are allowed to change variable values. Enter this short example:

```
10 A$="FIRST"
20 PRINT A$;:GOTO 20
```

Run the program, then halt it by pressing the RUN/STOP key. Now enter A$="SECOND":CONT in direct mode. The program now prints the new string.

CONT cannot be used in program mode. See RESUME for details of the program mode equivalent.

COPY

Disk command
Makes an exact copy of a disk file.

Format: COPY ***"source file"***, *Ddrive number* **TO** ***"copy file"***, *Ddrive number, Udevice number*
Modes: Immediate and program
Token: 244 ($F4)
Abbreviation: CO SHIFT-P
Not available in BASIC 2.0

As its name implies, this command copies files from one disk to another on a dual drive system. You must include the drive numbers (0 and 1) on a dual drive. If you omit the drive numbers, COPY defaults to drive 0, so it creates a second copy with a different name on the same disk (on single or dual drive systems). When copying between drives, you may use the same name for both files. The default parameters are device 8, and drive 0.

COPY "SPROUT",D0 TO "SPROUT",D1 copies the file SPROUT from the disk in drive 0 onto the disk in drive 1. Both files are named SPROUT.

COPY "HUBCAP" TO "NEWHUBCAP" copies HUBCAP into a new file called NEWHUBCAP on the same disk.

COS

Numeric function
Returns the cosine of an angle measured in radians.

Format: COS (*angle*)
Modes: Immediate and program
Token: 190 ($BE)
Abbreviation: None
Same as BASIC 2.0

This trigonometric function finds the cosine of an angle. The angle must be given in radians, not degrees. To convert from degrees to radians, divide by 180 and multiply times π (the π symbol, which is a constant with the value of pi, is obtained by typing SHIFT-↑, next to the RETURN key). Given an angle that's part of a right triangle, the cosine is the same as the length of the adjacent side divided by the hypotenuse. If the hypotenuse is equal to one, the cosine is the X coordinate.

DATA

Variable control
Holds information for the READ statement.

Format: DATA ***item1****, item2, item3, item4, ...*
Modes: Program only
Token: 131 ($83)
Abbreviation: D SHIFT-A
Same as BASIC 2.0

DATA statements work like high-speed memory-based sequential files. For short to medium lists of information, DATA statements may be preferable to tape or disk files. With DATA lines, the program does not have to go through the process of opening, reading, and closing disk or tape files, because the data is right there in the program.

DATA statements are always used in conjunction with READ commands. READ searches for the next item in a DATA statement and puts it into a variable. READ and DATA are often used to POKE short machine language programs into memory or to keep track of lists of information (prices, state capitals, etc.).

You must follow the DATA statement with at least one piece of information (a string or number). And the variable type used in READ (string or numeric) should match the type of information held in the DATA statement. You can place several items in a DATA statement by separating them with commas. A string that contains a comma should be enclosed in quotation marks; otherwise, the computer interprets the comma as a separator. Quotation marks have a higher level of authority than commas, so strings inside quotes are read from beginning to end. Quotation marks also allow you to include shifted characters and special control characters like the clear-screen reversed heart or CTRL-G (the bell sound).

READ starts at the first DATA statement and continues until there are no more. Each item is read only once. To reuse selected DATA statements, you can include a RESTORE command, with or without a line number. See READ and RESTORE for more information about DATA statements.

DCLEAR

Disk command
Closes all open files and clears disk channels.

Format: DCLEAR *Ddrive number,Udevice number*
Modes: Immediate and program
Token: 254 21 ($FE $15)

Abbreviation: DCL SHIFT-E
Not available in BASIC 2.0

This command is the same as OPEN 15,8,15,"I0": CLOSE15 in BASIC 2.0. DCLEAR closes all files and clears all open channels on the specified device number. In doing so, it performs a disk initialize—the Block Allocation Map (BAM) is copied from the disk into disk drive memory. The default value for the drive is 0, and the default value for the device is 8, so these parameters are unnecessary if you have a single 1541 or 1571 drive.

DCLOSE

Disk command
Closes open disk files

Format: DCLOSE#*logical file ON Udevice number*
Modes: Immediate and program
Token: 254 15 ($FE $0F)
Abbreviation: D SHIFT-C
Not available in BASIC 2.0

By itself, DCLOSE closes all files currently open. The default value for the device is 8.

DCLOSE closes all open files on the default device 8 (single or dual drive). DCLOSE #1 closes logical file 1. DCLOSE ON U9 closes all files currently open on device 9, a second (single or dual) disk drive.

DEC

Numeric function
Converts a hexadecimal string to a decimal number.

Format: DEC(*hexadecimal$*)
Modes: Immediate and program
Token: 209 ($D1)
Abbreviation: None
Not available in BASIC 2.0

The DEC function converts hexadecimal numbers (often used in machine language programming) into decimal numbers, the form ordinarily used in BASIC. The hexadecimal string must be in the range 0–FFFF. For example, PRINT DEC("D000") translates the hex number $D000 into decimal 53248. Hexadecimal numbers are often written with a preceding $ (as the

$D000 in the previous sentence); this should be omitted when using DEC. Note that the machine language monitor (see the Introduction) also performs decimal, hexadecimal, octal, and binary number conversions.

DEF FN

Numeric function
Defines a function for use later in the program.
Format: DEF FN ***function name(variable)*** **=** ***expression***
Modes: Program only
Tokens: DEF 150 ($96); FN: 165 ($A5)
Abbreviations: DEF: D SHIFT-E; FN: None
Same as BASIC 2.0

DEF allows you to define numeric functions. The rules for naming functions are the same as for numeric variables: The name must begin with a letter, other characters can be either letters or numbers, and only the first two characters of the name are significant. A function can have the same name as an existing variable, but that practice may lead to confusion.

The definition on the left of the equal sign (=) must include a variable name in parentheses. Any numeric variable can be used, since its value is not actually used when the function is called. The variable serves only as a marker. When you later use the defined function, the actual value in parentheses is substituted for the marker variable wherever that variable appears in the expression on the right side of the equal sign.

The expression on the right can be any valid numeric formula, and can include other BASIC functions (such as SQR, PEEK, RGR, and so on) or even other defined functions. It is not necessary to use the argument variable in the expression, in which case the number or variable in parentheses is simply a dummy value.

If the expression on the right contains a variable not mentioned in the left-side definition, the actual value of the variable counts when the function is called. That is, DEF FNAA(X) = X * HR defines a function called AA that multiplies a number by a variable HR. If you later ask the computer to PRINT FNAA(5), the current value of the variable X doesn't matter because it was only used as a marker in the definition. But the value held by HR does matter and the computer calculates 5 * HR.

DEF FN allows you to create custom functions that are more flexible and powerful than BASIC's predefined functions. For example, the following defined function calculates cosines in degrees instead of the usual radians:

```
10 DEF FNCS(Z)=COS(Z*π/180)
20 INPUT"ANGLE";A
30 PRINT"COSINE";FNCS(A):PRINT:GOTO 20
```

DELETE

Programming utility
Removes a range of lines from a BASIC program.

Format: DELETE *first line-last line*
Mode: Immediate only
Token: 247 ($F7)
Abbreviation: DE SHIFT-L
Not available in BASIC 2.0

The DELETE command removes one or many lines from a BASIC program. It can be followed by one line number, to remove just one line, or by a range of line numbers. If the first line number in the range is omitted, all lines up to the line number that follows the dash will be deleted. Omitting the second line number from the range will delete every line which comes after the starting line number. If no lines exist within the range of the DELETE statement, no error will occur and no lines will be deleted. Use this command with care, since its effects can't be undone.

DIM

Variable control
Establishes a size for an array of variables.

Format: DIM *array(size1,size2,size3,...), array(size), array(size)...*
Modes: Immediate and program
Token: 134 ($86)
Abbreviation: D SHIFT-I
Same as BASIC 2.0

A variable array is a series of variables identified by their subscripts in parentheses: A$(5), YT%(2,3), and G2$(9) are typical. The values are collected under a single variable name, but have different subscripts. Quite simply, an array is a list of variables.

Arrays default to a size of 11 elements, numbered 0–10. DIM allows you to predefine the DIMensions of an array. Once an array has been dimensioned, you cannot change the size of the array unless you perform a CLR (which erases all variable data).

Arrays are valuable for alphabetizing and sorting lists of information:

```
10 INPUT "HOW MANY STUDENTS";G
20 DIM N$(G), GR(G)
30 FOR J=1 TO G
40 INPUT "STUDENT NAME"; N$(J): INPUT "GRADE"; GR(J)
50 NEXT: H=0: L= 1E10
60 FOR J=1 TO G: IF GR(J) > H THEN X1 = J: H=GR(J)
70 IF GR(J) < L THEN X2 = J: L=GR(J)
80 NEXT
90 PRINT "THE BEST MARK IS" N$(X1);GR(X1)
100 PRINT "THE LOWEST IS" N$(X2); GR(X2)
```

DIRECTORY

Disk command

Displays the directory of a disk.

Format: DIRECTORY *Ddrive number,Udevice number,wildcard$*

Modes: Immediate and program

Token: 238 ($EE)

Abbreviation: DI SHIFT-R

Not available in BASIC 2.0

DIRECTORY prints to the screen the contents of a disk, without affecting the program currently in memory. The default value for the drive is 0, and the default device is 8. The top line lists the disk name and ID given when the HEADER command was used to format the disk. To the left of each filename is the number of disk sectors used by the file; to the right of each name is the file's type. A PRG file is most often a program, and SEQ marks a sequential data file.

When you first turn on the 128, the F3 key is defined as DIRECTORY plus RETURN, so you can simply press F3 to see what's on a disk. Press CTRL-S or the NO SCROLL key to pause the display, or the Commodore key to slow down the scrolling. The DIRECTORY command cannot print a directory on a printer. Here is how to print out a paper copy of the directory:

LOAD "$0",8
OPEN4,4:CMD4:LIST
PRINT#4:CLOSE4

The * and ? characters can be used as *wildcards* to generate directories that show only particular files. Wildcards are easy to use: DIRECTORY "A*" lists directory information only for those files whose names start with the letter A. DIRECTORY D0,"ML?.OBJ" lists only the directory information for files containing the characters "ML" for the first two characters and ".OBJ" as the last four characters. In the second example (using a question mark), MLD.OBJ, ML .OBJ, and ML3.OBJ would all appear in the directory listing, whereas files that did not start and end with exactly those characters would not.

DLOAD

Disk command
Loads a BASIC program from disk.

Format: DLOAD*"program name"*,*Ddrive,Udevice*
Modes: Immediate and program
Token: 240 ($F0)
Abbreviation: D SHIFT-L
Not available in BASIC 2.0

DLOAD loads a BASIC program into memory in bank 0. The program name may be up to 16 characters long. DLOAD defaults to drive 0 and device 8. An asterisk (*) or question mark (?) may be used as wildcards in the name. You may also use a string variable to specify the name (in which case the string variable must be enclosed in parentheses).

DLOAD "MYPROG" loads the file named "MYPROG" from the disk in drive 0, device 8. DLOAD "MYPROG",D1,U9 loads the file named "MYPROG" from the disk in drive 1 of device 9 in a second dual-drive system.

DLOAD "W*" loads the first file in the directory beginning with the character W. DLOAD (N$) loads the file named by the variable N$. Loading a BASIC program file under program control causes the loaded program to begin executing at its first line as soon as the load is complete.

DO

Program flow (loops)
Sets the beginning of a DO-LOOP structure.

Formats: DO *WHILE/UNTIL condition* **... LOOP**
DO ... LOOP *WHILE/UNTIL condition*
Modes: Immediate and program
Token: 235 ($EB)
Abbreviation: None
Not available in BASIC 2.0

A DO-LOOP is similar to a FOR-NEXT loop: each repeats a series of actions. But a FOR-NEXT loop repeats a given number of times. FOR J=1 TO 12, for example, would loop exactly 12 times. DO-LOOPs are flexible: You can make the actions keep repeating WHILE a condition remains true or UNTIL a condition becomes true (the same as repeating WHILE the condition is false). You can also insert an EXIT to break out of the loop somewhere in the middle. If no WHILE, UNTIL, or EXIT appears in the loop, it continues forever—or until you press the STOP key.

The WHILE and UNTIL conditions can be attached to the DO or to the LOOP. Logical operators are allowed: DO WHILE (*condition1*) AND (*condition2*) makes the loop continue as long as both conditions are true.

It is legal to nest DO-LOOPs, up to several levels deep. However, keep in mind that the first DO must match up with the last LOOP, the second DO must be paired with the second-to-last LOOP, and so on. EXIT sends the program out of the current loop: If you EXIT an inner loop, the outer loop is still active.

Normally, the conditions tested will be comparisons like P=16 or A$<>"" which return a value of −1 if they're true or a 0 if they're false. But variables are also allowed. DO WHILE G means, in effect, continue the loop while G is not equal to zero. And DO UNTIL G continues as long as G is equal to zero—until it holds a nonzero value. Here are some typical uses of DO.

```
10 REM FIBONACCI SEQUENCE - LOOP UNTIL A KEY IS
   PRESSED.
20 B=1
30 DO: C=A+B: A=B: B=C: PRINTC,: GETK$: LOOP WHILE
   K$=""
```

```
10 REM GUESSING GAME - EXIT IF GUESS IS RIGHT
20 PRINT "PLEASE THINK OF A NUMBER FROM 1 TO 100"
30 PRINT "AND I WILL TRY TO GUESS IT."
40 H=100:L=1
50 DO: G=INT((H-L)/2)+L:T=T+1
60 PRINT "IS IT";G;"?"
70 PRINT "(H)IGH, (L)OW, OR (J)UST RIGHT"
80 GETKEY K$: IF K$="H"THEN H=G:ELSE IF K$="L" THEN
   L=G: ELSE IF A$<> "J" THEN 80: ELSE EXIT
90 LOOP
100 PRINT "I GUESSED THE NUMBER IN ONLY";T;"TRIES."
```

DOPEN

Disk command

Opens a disk file for input or output.

Formats: DOPEN#*logical file, "filename,* *type",Ddrive,Udevice,W*
DOPEN#*logical file, "relative file"*,*Lrecord size*

Modes: Immediate and program

Token: 254 13 ($FE $0D)

Abbreviation: D SHIFT-O

Not available in BASIC 2.0

DOPEN is always followed by a logical file number and a filename. The file number is important: Whichever number you choose must be used when the file is read from (with GET# or INPUT#) or written to (with PRINT#). The file number can be any number in the range 1–255, but file numbers greater than 127 have a special meaning. For file numbers 128 and above, PRINT# automatically adds a linefeed character (CHR$(10)) after each RETURN character (CHR$(13)) it sends. The filename can be any combination of up to 16 characters. A string variable can be used as filenames if you enclose it in parentheses.

The two most common types of files are marked in the directory as PRG, for PRoGram, and SEQ, for SEQuential. Program files usually hold programs, while sequential files hold information used by programs. If no file type is specified, DOPEN attempts to open the named file for reading regardless of its type. To restrict DOPEN to a particular file type, add ,P after the filename (but before the closing quotes) to open the named file if it's a program file, or add ,S to open the file if it's sequential.

The device number defaults to 0, the drive number to 8.

To open a new sequential or program file for writing, add a ,W at the end of the statement. If no file type is specified (by ,P or ,S following the filename), the computer creates a sequential file.

The third file type is relative, labeled REL in the directory. To create a new relative file, you must follow the file name with ,L (for length) and a record size. (Unlike the ,S and ,P type designations, the ,L must be *outside* of the quotes that surround the filename.) The ,L is not required when reopening an existing relative file for reading, and neither ,L nor ,W is required to open an existing relative file for writing. Chapter 4 explains relative files in detail. Two other file types that you'll rarely see are: USR, used infrequently for DOS routines, and DEL (for DELeted, but not scratched files).

DOPEN#3,"FILE1" opens an existing program or sequential file named FILE1 for reading, or an existing relative file named FILE1 for both reading and writing. DOPEN#3,"FILE1,P" opens an existing file named FILE1 for reading only if it's a program file. DOPEN#3,"FILE1",W creates a new sequential file and prepares it for writing. DOPEN#3,"FILE1,P",W does the same for a program file. DOPEN#3,"FILE1",L20 creates a relative file with a record length of 20 characters. The following lines show how to specify a filename with a variable:

```
10 INPUT"NAME FOR DATA FILE";F$:IF F$="" THEN 10
20 DOPEN#6,(F$),W
30 PRINT "FILE ";F$;" OPENED FOR WRITING"
40 CLOSE 6
```

DRAW

Graphics command
Puts a line on the hi-res screen.

Formats: DRAW *color source,Xcoord1,Ycoord1* TO *Xcoord2,Ycoord2*
DRAW TO *Xcoord,Ycoord*
Modes: Immediate and program
Token: 229 ($E5)
Abbreviation: D SHIFT-R
Not available in BASIC 2.0

DRAW is used to draw points and lines on the hi-res and multicolor screens. The first example statement shown above draws a line from position (Xcoord1, Ycoord1) to position (Xcoord2, Ycoord2). If the second set of coordinates is omitted from this statement, a point is turned on. The second example draws a line from the current pixel cursor to the point (Xcoord, Ycoord). This program draws a series of rays originating from one point.

```
10 GRAPHIC 2,1
20 FOR A=1 TO 150 STEP 4
30 DRAW 1,0,75 TO 319,A
40 NEXT A
```

Chapter 2 contains additional information about DRAW.

DS

Programming utility (reserved variable)
Returns a number corresponding to a disk error code.

Format: DS
Modes: Immediate and program
Token: None
Abbreviation: None
Not available in BASIC 2.0

DS is a reserved variable which reports a status code for the most recent disk operation. It is closely related to another reserved variable, DS$ (see below). While DS can be assigned to another (numeric) variable or printed to the screen, its value can only be changed indirectly, by a disk operation. Generally, if the value of DS is 0, then the last disk operation was successful. One of two exceptions to this rule occurs when the disk drive hasn't been used since it was turned on. A freshly powered-up drive returns a status code of 73. Also, after creating a new relative file (with RECORD) or expanding an existing relative file, DS will hold a 50 (representing RECORD NOT PRESENT).

```
100 BLOAD "A FILE"
110 IF DS <> 0 THEN PRINT "I COULDN'T LOAD THE FILE"
```

Appendix B contains a complete list of disk status codes and their meanings.

DSAVE

Disk command
Saves the program currently in memory to disk.

Format: DSAVE *"program name"*, *Ddrive, Udevice*
Modes: Immediate and program
Token: 239 ($EF)
Abbreviation: D SHIFT-S
Not available in BASIC 2.0

DSAVE stores a BASIC program on disk. A filename of up to 16 characters must be included. The default drive is 0, the default device is 8.

DSAVE "STAR GATE" stores the program to the disk in drive 0 of device 8 with the name STAR GATE. DSAVE (A$) saves a program with the name specified in the variable A$. (A$ cannot be a null string; if it is, you'll get a MISSING FILENAME error message.) And DSAVE "NEXTTRY",D1,U9 stores a program named NEXTTRY on a disk in drive 1 of device 9.

If something goes wrong during the save, the light on the disk drive will start blinking. You can find out what went wrong by entering PRINT DS$ (see below).

DS$

Programming utility (reserved variable)
Returns the current status of the disk drive.

Format: DS$
Modes: Immediate and program
Token: None
Abbreviation: None
Not available in BASIC 2.0

Like DS, DS$ is a reserved variable which reports the drive status following the most recent disk drive operation. But DS$ gives a string as its result. If the disk command worked correctly, DS will hold a value of zero, and PRINT DS$ will display "00, OK, 00, 00".

The first two characters in DS$ are the same error number that DS gives, but DS$ adds an error message to go with the number. Also included are the numbers of the disk track and sector that were being accessed when the error occurred. For many disk errors, like FILE NOT FOUND, these values are meaningless and zeros are displayed. Here's what the screen shows when you try to load a nonexistent file named NO FILE:

```
DLOAD "NO FILE"
SEARCHING FOR 0:NO FILE
?FILE NOT FOUND ERROR
READY.
PRINT DS$
62, FILE NOT FOUND,00,00
READY.
```

Here's what it takes to do the equivalent of PRINT DS$ in BASIC 2.0 (note that since it uses an INPUT# statement, this routine works only in program mode):

```
100 OPEN 15,8,15
110 INPUT#15,A,B$,C,D
120 CLOSE 15
130 PRINT A;B$;C;D
```

Appendix B contains a complete list of disk error messages.

DVERIFY

Disk command
Compares, byte by byte, the program in memory with a program on disk.

Format: DVERIFY *"program name",Ddrive number,Udevice number*
Modes: Immediate and program
Token: 254 20 ($FE $14)
Abbreviation: D SHIFT-V
Not available in BASIC 2.0

DVERIFY is a way of double-checking the success of a SAVE or DSAVE. It makes the 128 read each byte of a BASIC program on disk and compare it with the values in program memory. The default value for the drive is 0, and the default value for the device is 8.

If a graphic area is allocated or deallocated after a SAVE, an error will occur, even though the program may be valid, because BASIC text is moved from its original location whenever you allocate or deallocate a hi-res graphics area.

DVERIFY "FORECAST" compares the BASIC program currently in memory to the program file named "FORECAST" on drive 0, device 8.

DVERIFY "FORECAST",D1,U9 verifies the program file "FORECAST" found on the disk on drive 1 of device 9.

EL

Programming utility (reserved variable)
Holds the line number of the most recent error.

Format: **EL**
Modes: Immediate and program
Token: None
Abbreviation: None
Not available in BASIC 2.0

The reserved variable EL (Error Line) holds a number that tells you where a BASIC error occurred. It's most useful for handling errors that have been caught by the TRAP statement. EL lets you handle an expected error, like a user input that's out of bounds, while stopping the program for any unexpected problems.

```
100 TRAP 1000
110 INPUT "SCREEN COLOR";C
120 BANK 15: POKE 53280,C-1: REM THE POKE IS ONE LESS
    THAN THE COLOR #
130 END
1000 IF EL=120 THEN RESUME 110 ELSE PRINT ERR$(ER);
    " ERROR IN LINE";EL
```

ELSE

Program control (decisions)
Allows an IF statement to pick one action or another.

Format: IF ***condition*** **THEN** *BEGIN* ***action****...BEND: ELSE BEGIN action...BEND*
Modes: Immediate and program.
Token: 213 ($D5)
Abbreviation: E SHIFT-L
Not available in BASIC 2.0

ELSE is always found as part of an IF-THEN statement. It is found most often in the same program line as the IF and THEN, but can also follow a BEND that ends a BEGIN-BEND block. ELSEs can be chained, as in this example:

```
50 IF A=5 THEN 500: ELSE IF A>B THEN PRINT "OUT OF
   BOUNDS": ELSE GOTO 40
```

The first ELSE occurs only if it's *not* true that A=5. It leads into another IF, to test whether A is greater than B. If that is true, OUT OF BOUNDS is printed and the program continues at the next line (skipping over the ELSE). But if A is less than or equal to B, then it is not true that A>B and the second ELSE takes effect, sending the program to line 40.

END

Program control
Causes a program to stop running and return to immediate mode.

Format: END
Modes: Immediate and program
Token: 128 ($80)
Abbreviation: None
Same as BASIC 2.0

END stops the execution of a BASIC program and returns you to immediate mode. If a program contains no END statement, execution ends after the computer performs the last program line. If the program contains additional statements after END, you may use CONT to restart it. END is most often used to separate a series of subroutines at the end of the program from the main program. For example, if the first subroutine starts at line 500, adding 499 END would prevent the program from "falling through" to the lines containing the subroutines.

ENVELOPE

Sound and music
Defines the shape of a sound to emulate a real instrument.

Format: ENVELOPE *number*, *attack, decay, sustain, release, waveform, pulse width*
Modes: Immediate and program
Tokens: 254 10 ($FE $0A)
Abbreviation: E SHIFT-N
Not available in BASIC 2.0

ENVELOPE is used with the PLAY statement to allow the 128 to simulate musical instruments. *Number* selects which of the ten available envelopes (numbered 0–9) is being specified or redefined. It is the only mandatory parameter. If only the number is specified, the predefined settings for that ENVELOPE are used. *Attack* defines the attack rate, *decay* sets the decay rate, *sustain* sets the sustain rate (the volume of the sound after the attack and decay have finished), and *release* sets the release rate. All four aspects of the ADSR are numbers in the range 0–15. Note that attack, decay, and release are time periods, but sustain is a volume. The sustain volume stays constant for as long as the voice is turned on.

Waveform (0 = triangle, 1 = sawtooth, 2 = pulse, 3 = noise, 4 = ring modulation) allows the user to select one of five waveforms, and *pulse width* (0–4095) sets the width of the pulse waveform (relevant only if you select that waveform). If one of the optional parameters is not defined, it retains the previous value for that envelope.

```
10 ENVELOPE 7,15,9,9,0,2,2048 :REM LONG ATTACK
15 TEMPO 32
20 PLAY "T7 O4 C D E F G A B O5 C"
```

ER

Programming utility (reserved variable)
Returns the most recent error code.

Format: ER
Modes: Immediate and program
Token: None
Abbreviation: None
Not available in BASIC 2.0

The reserved variable ER gives the code number for the most recent BASIC error. If no error has occurred, its value is −1. You can use ER to handle different errors in different ways. If an error results from user input, you could print an error message and make some attempt to correct it, but in most cases you'll want the program to end if a syntax error occurs. ER can also be used as input to the ERR$ function (see below) to print BASIC's error message.

This program traps errors caused by trying to divide a number by zero. Try running it and entering a variety of numbers, including zero.

```
10 TRAP 800
20 DO PRINT "ENTER A NUMBER"
30 INPUT A: B = 10/A: PRINT "THAT GOES INTO
   TEN";B;"TIMES"
40 LOOP
800 IF ER = 20 THEN PRINT: PRINT"I'M SORRY, ZERO IS
   NOT ALLOWED. PLEASE TRY AGAIN": RESUME 30
810 PRINT ERR$(ER): END
```

For a complete list of BASIC error codes and messages, see Appendix B.

ERR$

Programming utility (reserved variable)
Returns a string describing the most recent error.

Format: ERR$(ER)
Modes: Immediate and program
Token: 211 ($D3)
Abbreviation: E SHIFT-R
Not available in BASIC 2.0

Error handling routines can access BASIC's own error messages with the ERR$ function. The ERR$ function returns a string containing the error message that BASIC would have printed if the error hadn't been trapped. Most often, the ER function is used as its parameter:

PRINT ERR$(ER)

BASIC has 41 error messages, numbered 1–41. Using a number outside this range causes an ILLEGAL QUANTITY error. When no BASIC error has occurred since a RUN, RESUME, CLR, or NEW statement, the ER variable holds a value of −1. When the error code has been cleared, ERR$(ER) generates an ILLEGAL QUANTITY error.

EXIT

Program flow (loops)
Makes the program jump to the statement following the LOOP which marks the end of a DO-LOOP.

Format: EXIT
Modes: Immediate and program
Token: 237 ($ED)
Abbreviation: EX SHIFT-I
Not available in BASIC 2.0

A DO-LOOP structure can be defined to repeat UNTIL or WHILE an expression is true. But the UNTIL and WHILE conditions must be stated at the beginning or end of the loop. EXIT allows you to stop execution in the middle of a loop. When an EXIT occurs, the program proceeds to the first statement following LOOP. For more details, see DO.

EXP

Numeric function
Raises the number e (2.71828183) to the power specified—the inverse of the LOG function.

Format: EXP(*n*)
Modes: Immediate and program
Token: 189 ($BD)
Abbreviation: E SHIFT-X
Same as BASIC 2.0

The mathematical constant e (2.71828183) is a special quantity, the base of the natural system of logarithms. Complex math operations can be expressed in terms of simpler operations using logarithms, exponents of powers of the numbers. For example, two numbers can be multiplied or divided simply by adding or subtracting their logarithms. This can be a useful tool in many mathematical operations. EXP performs the equivalent of e ↑ n, and tends to return values that are much greater than the argument n. The range of allowable values for the argument is approximately −88 to 88. EXP's converse function, LOG—the natural logarithm—can turn a very large number into a much smaller one that's easier to manipulate. Then EXP can turn the logarithm back into the original number. The following program shows some of the ways you can perform other math operations with EXP and LOG. Lines 30 and 40, for instance, illustrate how BASIC calculates powers and roots:

```
10 PRINT"16 * 2 =";EXP(LOG(16)+LOG(2))
20 PRINT"16 / 2 =";EXP(LOG(16)-LOG(2))
30 PRINT"16 ↑ 2 =";EXP(LOG(16)*2)
40 PRINT"SQR(16)=";EXP(LOG(16)/2)
```

FAST

Time control
Causes the processor clock to double in speed; also turns off the 40-column screen

Format: FAST
Modes: Immediate or program
Tokens: 254 37 ($FE $25)
Abbreviation: None
Not available in BASIC 2.0

The internal clock that drives the 8502 chip normally runs at 1 MHz (one million cycles per second). FAST makes the clock run twice as fast, so calculations take only half as much time. Disk access also speeds up (although only slightly). Because the 40-column VIC-II video chip can't keep up at this faster speed, the 40-column screen blanks to the same color as the border when fast mode is in effect (the 80-column screen is unaffected). Because FAST doubles the clock speed, it's very helpful in calculation-intensive programs. To remind the user that something is happening, you may want to change the border color occasionally, using the COLOR command.

Fast mode is controlled by bit 0 of location $D030 (location 53296, in bank 15 in 128 mode), so it can also be turned on by entering POKE 53296,1 and turned off with POKE 53296,0. This works in either 64 or 128 mode (but be warned that turning FAST off in this manner *does not* restore the screen); in 128 mode, you should precede the POKE with a BANK 15 statement.

```
10 SLOW:TI$="000000":FOR J=1 TO 30000: NEXT: PRINT
   TI/60"SECONDS NORMALLY"
20 FAST
30 TI$="000000":FOR J=1 TO 30000: NEXT: SLOW: PRINT
   TI/60"SECONDS IN FAST MODE"
```

FETCH

Memory control

Transfers values from memory expansion into main memory.

Format: **FETCH** ***bytes,address1,bank,address2***
Modes: Immediate and program
Tokens: 254 33 ($FE $21)
Abbreviation: F SHIFT-E
Not available in BASIC 2.0

FETCH is the opposite of STASH, and allows you to retrieve blocks of data from the special memory expansion modules available for the 128. Include the number of bytes to retrieve, the starting address (in the current 128 bank) where they should be stored, the expansion module bank you are copying from, and the address in that expansion module bank where the bytes are currently stored. Expansion module memory can thus be used for storing programs or data in a manner similar to disk or tape. Chapter 7 contains more information about the expansion module.

FILTER

Sound and music

Assigns values to the filter for creating special sound effects.

Format: FILTER ***frequency,*** *lowpass, bandpass, highpass, resonance*

Modes: Immediate and program

Token: 254 3 ($FE $03)

Abbreviation: F SHIFT-I

Not available in BASIC 2.0

FILTER allows you to define the characteristics of the SID chip filter, which lets certain audio frequencies through while suppressing others. It's similar to a phonograph's tone control which boosts the treble or bass depending on which way the knob is turned.

Defining the filter is not enough by itself, you must also turn it on. Put an X1 in the PLAY statement to enable the filter. X0 turns it off. Each of the three voices is independent of the others, so it is possible to filter one or more voices while leaving the others unfiltered.

When the filter is set up and turned on (with X1), the sound is shaped according to your specifications. Note that the *frequency* accepts numbers in the range 0–2047, while SOUND takes numbers from 0–65535. Thus, every increment of the filter frequency corresponds to 32 steps in the SOUND statement.

The cutoff frequency determines what happens to the sound. There are three basic ways to filter. A lowpass filter allows only sounds *below* the cutoff frequency (like turning up the bass on a stereo). Highpass filters allow only high frequencies through. And bandpass filters cut off the notes both above and below the given frequency. It's possible to combine these different filters: Turning on both highpass and lowpass gives you a bandstop, or "notch reject" filter which passes all but a narrow range of frequencies.

For each filter position in the FILTER statement, a 1 turns on the specified type of filtering and a 0 turns it off. The *resonance* (0–15) is optional: It controls the degree to which the filter affects frequencies near the cutoff points. Increasing the resonance value makes the effects of a filter more pronounced.

```
10 FILTER 1047,1,0,1,13
20 PLAY "X1 O4 C D E F G F E D C"
```

FN

Numeric function
Returns a value from a previously defined function.

Format: FN *function name(number)*
Modes: Immediate and program
Token: 165 ($A5)
Abbreviation: None
Same as BASIC 2.0

FN allows you to use the functions you previously defined with DEF FN (see DEF). If DEF included a marker variable on both sides of the equal sign (=), the argument in parentheses is substituted for the marker in the expression. If the variable did not appear in the expression, the value in parentheses has no effect on the value returned by the function.

The following example shows how a defined function might perform a metric conversion:

```
10 DEF FN DC(X)=INT(5*(X-32)/9)
20 INPUT "TEMPERATURE (FAHRENHEIT)";T
30 PRINT FN DC(T)"DEGREES CELSIUS":PRINT:GOTO 20
```

As an example of a function where the argument variable is not used in the expression, the following program prints asterisks at the rate of one per second. The number in parentheses in the FN statement is a dummy value and has no effect on the value returned:

```
10 DEF FN TM(Q)=VAL(RIGHT$(TI$,2))
20 T1 = FN TM(1)
30 IF FN TM(255) = T1 THEN PRINT"*";:GOTO 20
40 GOTO 30
```

FOR

Program flow (loops)
Marks the beginning of a FOR-NEXT loop.

Format: FOR *index* = *start* TO *finish* *STEP increment*
Modes: Immediate and program
Token: 129 ($81)
Abbreviation: F SHIFT-O
Same as BASIC 2.0

FOR-NEXT loops let you repeat a series of actions. The *index* is a numeric variable that begins with the *start* value and increases by the STEP value every time the loop cycles. The

STEP can be any number, including fractions and negative numbers. A negative STEP value makes the loop count backwards, which is helpful in some cases. If you omit the STEP statement, the FOR-NEXT loop defaults to an increment of one.

The index variable is available for calculations within the loop. For instance, you might PEEK a series of memory locations (FOR A = 0 TO 50: PRINT PEEK(1024 + A);: NEXT), fill up an array (FOR J = 0 TO 10: D(J) = J: NEXT), or do any other task that requires a changing variable.

NEXT can include the index variable, but it's not necessary in most cases. It marks the end of the loop. When NEXT executes, the index is increased by the STEP size and the computer does a comparison to the *finish* value. If the new index value is higher, the loop ends. Otherwise, the loop repeats again.

Because of inexactness with floating point fractions (a problem of all binary computers, not just the 128), you should avoid fractions in the step size unless they're divisible by powers of two (1/2, 1/4, 1/8, and so on). The following example illustrates why:

```
10 FOR X = 1 TO 5 STEP .1: PRINT X,: NEXT
15 PRINT: PRINT
20 FOR X = 1 TO 50: PRINT X/10,: NEXT
```

The 128 rounds the number .1 to a binary number that's very close, but not exactly equal, to a tenth. As the loop progresses, the rounding errors become more exaggerated. The second form of the loop, counting in whole numbers, is better.

FRE

Numeric function
Returns the number of free bytes of memory in a specified bank.

Format: FRE(*bank*)
Modes: Immediate and program
Token: 184 ($B8)
Abbreviation: F SHIFT-R
Enhanced BASIC 2.0 statement

FRE prints the amount of memory available for BASIC text and variables. In 64 mode (BASIC 2.0), the argument is a dummy value and the number returned is the amount of memory available for both programs and variables. If the number of bytes free exceeds 32767, a negative value is reported. The following expression gives the true value in all cases:

```
FR=FRE(0)−65535*(FRE(0)<0).
```

In BASIC 7.0 (128 mode), the number in parentheses makes a difference. FRE(0) reports the number of bytes free for BASIC program storage, while FRE(1) reports how much memory is available for variable storage.

This example (for BASIC 7.0) shows how FRE can be used to make sure there is sufficient room for a string array before it is dimensioned:

```
10 INPUT "DIMENSION";NN: MM=7+3*(NN+1)
20 IF FRE(1)-MM<0 THEN PRINT"INSUFFICIENT
   MEMORY":GOTO 10
30 DIM A$(NN):PRINT FRE(1)"BYTES REMAIN"
```

GET

Keyboard input
Reads one character, or a null string if no key has been pressed, from the keyboard.

Format: GET ***variable***
Mode: Program only
Token: 161 ($A1)
Abbreviation: G SHIFT-E
Same as BASIC 2.0

After a key is pressed, its character code value is put into the keyboard buffer. Technically, GET doesn't check the keyboard directly; it looks at the keyboard buffer to see if anything is there. If no key had been pressed, a null character is returned. The following line uses GET within a DO-LOOP to wait for the letter Q to be pressed.

```
10 DO: GET R$: LOOP WHILE R$<>"Q"
```

In many cases, GETKEY (see below) is preferable because it waits for a keypress. But sometimes GET is more flexible:

```
50 PRINT "PRESS E TO END"
60 DO: X=X+1: PRINTX, X*X:
70 GET A$: IF A$="E" THEN EXIT
80 LOOP
```

Because GET doesn't stop to wait for a key, the loop continues until the user presses E. If you substitute GETKEY in line 70, the program pauses after the PRINT statement in 60.

GETKEY

Keyboard input
Waits for a keypress and then takes the character from the keyboard buffer.

Format: GETKEY ***variable***
Mode: Program only
Tokens: 161 249 ($A1 $F9)
Abbreviation: GETK SHIFT-E
Not available in BASIC 2.0

When GETKEY executes, the 128 checks for a keypress. If none has occurred, the computer waits for the user to press a key. This differs from GET, which continues on whether or not a key has been pressed.

```
10 GETKEY R$: REM WAITS FOR USER TO PRESS ANY KEY
10 GETKEY A: REM WAITS FOR A NUMERIC KEY
```

GET#

File input
GET# takes one character from a specified file.

Format: GET# ***file number, variable***
Mode: Program only
Token: 132 ($84)
Abbreviation: None
Same as BASIC 2.0

GET# is similar to GET in that it reads one character. But GET# is used when you wish to read a character from a file that has been opened to a peripheral device such as a disk or tape drive or modem. GET# does not operate in direct mode. In the following example, note that the logical file number in the OPEN statement (the first number after OPEN, a 1) is the same number placed directly after the GET# command.

```
10 OPEN 1,8,15
20 GET#1,A: PRINT A
30 CLOSE 1
```

See Chapter 4 for more information on file handling.

GO 64

System command
Switches the computer from 128 mode to 64 mode.

Format: GO 64
Modes: Immediate and program
Token: 203 ($CB)
Abbreviation: None
Not available in BASIC 2.0

The command GO 64 is used to switch the computer from 128 mode to Commodore 64 mode. When it is issued in direct mode, the 128 asks for confirmation ("ARE YOU SURE?") before actually changing modes. Since it erases the program being edited, and since no command to return to 128 mode exists in 64 mode, this precaution is well-advised. But no double-checking occurs when GO 64 is executed in program mode.

GOSUB

Program control
Transfers execution temporarily to the subroutine beginning at the specified line number.

Format: GOSUB ***line number***
Modes: Immediate and program
Token: 141 ($8D)
Abbreviation: GO SHIFT-S
Same as BASIC 2.0

GOSUB temporarily sends the program to a subroutine at the designated line number. When that routine is finished, a RETURN statement causes the program to resume execution where it left off—with the next statement following the GOSUB that initiated the subroutine. GOSUB must be followed by a line number (GOSUB 1000); you may not use a variable in place of a line number. Here is a simple example of how GOSUB works.

```
10 PRINT"MAIN PROGRAM WORKING HERE"
20 GOSUB 50
30 PRINT"BACK TO MAIN PROGRAM AGAIN"
40 END
50 PRINT"SUBROUTINE ACTIVE NOW"
60 SLEEP 2
70 RETURN
```

BASIC is designed to run through a program from beginning to end. But two things in this example disrupt the normal program flow: Line 20 contains GOSUB 50, which diverts the program to line 50. The RETURN in line 70 sets things right, sending BASIC back to the statement immediately after the GOSUB (line 30). The second break occurs at line 40, which prematurely ends the program run. The END is necessary to prevent the program from falling through to the subroutine.

Every subroutine initiated with GOSUB must end with RETURN: If you exit the routine in some other fashion (with GOTO, for instance), the computer's stack area of memory may become clogged, causing an OUT OF MEMORY error.

GOSUB also works in immediate mode. For instance, after running the example program, you can execute the subroutine alone by typing GOSUB 50 and pressing RETURN. Using GOSUB from immediate mode can cause odd (but usually harmless) error messages if the routine you GOSUB to uses input statements like GET or INPUT. See also RETURN.

GOTO

Program control

Format: GOTO *line number*
Modes: Immediate and program
Token: 137 ($89)
Abbreviation: G SHIFT-O
Same as BASIC 2.0

GOTO causes the computer to jump to a line in the program and perform the statements it finds there. The program then continues in normal line-by-line order unless another GOTO or similar statement is encountered. GO TO, as two words, is also acceptable; the two words are tokenized as two bytes (GO, as in GO 64, and TO).

Like GOSUB, this command must be followed by a line number (a variable is not acceptable). For example, GOTO 1000 transfers control to line 1000. If the specified line does not exist, an UNDEF'D STATEMENT error results.

```
10 PRINT "START HERE,"
20 GOTO 40
30 PRINT "NEVER GET HERE"
40 PRINT " AND END THERE."
```

This command is often used to transfer control after a condition-testing statement such as IF. Since GOTO can jump backward as well as forward, it can also be used in loops.

```
10 J=100
20 PRINT "THE VALUE OF J IS";J:J=J+1
30 IF J<201 THEN GOTO 20
```

Another acceptable form of line 30 is IF J<201 GOTO 20. You may also use THEN by itself, as in IF J<201 THEN 20.

GRAPHIC

Graphics command

Sets the screen display to one of several graphics modes.

Formats: **GRAPHIC** *mode, clear, split*
GRAPHIC CLR

Modes: Immediate and program

Token: 222 ($DE)

Abbreviation: G SHIFT-R

Not available in BASIC 2.0

GRAPHIC, followed by a number from 0–5 sets the graphics mode of the computer:

0 40 columns (composite or monochrome monitor, or television)
1 Hi-res graphics
2 Hi-res graphics (split screen)
3 Multicolor graphics
4 Multicolor graphics (split screen)
5 80 columns (RGB or monochrome monitor)

The new screen is not cleared unless the optional *clear* parameter is equal to 1 (or you issue a SCNCLR command). If a split screen mode is chosen, the screen will be divided at the line chosen by the *split* parameter. If a split is not defined, the default for the start of text is line 20 (lines are numbered vertically from 0–24, where 0 is the top line). The hi-res and multicolor screens require 9K of memory ($1C00–$2000 for color and $2000–3FFF for the bit map), so the first time you establish a hi-res screen with GRAPHIC, the computer moves the start of BASIC up to $4000 (decimal 16384) in memory bank 0. The GRAPHIC CLR command reverses this process, reclaiming the 9K graphics work area for BASIC. This command should be necessary only if you run out of memory for BASIC programs and you're no longer using any kind of hi-res graphics.

The following program selects a multicolor split screen, clears the screen, and sets text to start on line 12.

```
10 GRAPHIC 4,1,12
20 PRINT SPC(14);"THIS IS TEXT"
```

GSHAPE

Graphics command
Places a shape previously stored in a string onto the hi-res screen.

Format: GSHAPE *string$,* *Xcoord, Ycoord, mode*
Modes: Immediate and program
Token: 227 ($E3)
Abbreviation: G SHIFT-S
Not available in BASIC 2.0

GSHAPE is like a rubber-stamp function for the hi-res screen. First, you must create a shape and save it into a string variable with SSHAPE (Save SHAPE). Then, use GSHAPE to recall the shape and place it anywhere on the screen.

The string variable is required. If you omit the optional X and Y coordinates, GSHAPE puts the shape at the current location of the pixel cursor. You can include plus (+) or minus (−) signs to position the shape at a location relative to the pixel cursor as well. The *mode* parameter affects the shape as follows:

Mode	Effect
0	No changes to shape (default)
1	Inverse shape
2	OR with foreground
3	AND with foreground
4	Exclusive-OR with foreground

If you don't supply a mode parameter, GSHAPE defaults to mode 0 (no change).

Mode setting 2 (OR) causes the shape to blend in with the other shapes on the screen. A mode value of 3 ANDs the shape with the foreground so that the only pixels that show up are the ones contained in *both* the shape and the picture on the screen. Mode 4 can be used to erase the shape from the screen and create simple animation without sprites.

The following program draws a house shape, then stores the shape in A$ with SSHAPE. A GSHAPE command randomly places the houses on the hi-res screen.

```
10 GRAPHIC 2,1
20 BOX 1,10,10,30,20
30 DRAW 1,30,10 TO 20,3:DRAW TO 10,10
40 SSHAPE A$,9,2,31,21
50 FOR A=1 TO 50
```

```
60 GSHAPE A$,15+RND(1)*280,15+RND(1)*120,2
70 NEXT A
```

HEADER

Disk command
Formats a blank disk.

Format: HEADER"*disk name*",I*disk identifier*,D*drive number*, U*device number*
Modes: Immediate and program
Token: 241 ($F1)
Abbreviation: HE SHIFT-A
Not available in BASIC 2.0

Before you can use a brand new disk, it must be formatted. The disk name can be up to 16 characters long. The disk ID is specified by an I followed by any two characters—letters, numbers, or even graphics symbols. There is one odd (and obviously unintentional) restriction: The first character of the ID cannot be an F or you will get a SYNTAX ERROR message. BASIC sees the required I followed by an F as the keyword IF. Using more than two characters for the ID also causes a SYNTAX ERROR.

It is very important to use a unique ID for every disk you format. The name you specify is for your benefit. The disk drive identifies a disk solely by its ID, so if you take a disk out of the drive and replace it with another which has the same ID, the drive may not recognize that disks have been changed. This could cause the drive to scramble the entire disk, rendering it unreadable. The ID number cannot be changed without reformatting the disk. However, the old ID can be "reused" if the disk is reformatted. To do this, omit the ID from the HEADER statement. When reusing the ID, the formatting is much faster than the standard HEADER.

The drive number defaults to 0 (if you have a dual drive, you can specify drives 0 or 1). The device number defaults to 8 for a single-drive system.

HEADER"WORK DISK",I01 formats a disk called WORK DISK with an ID of 01, on drive 0, device 8.

HEADER"REFORMAT 10/85" will work with a previously formatted disk.

HEADER"JOHN'S DISK",IAB,D1,U10 uses the optional parameters to format a disk called JOHN'S DISK with an ID of AB, on drive 1 of a dual drive that is device 10.

The equivalent for HEADER in 64 mode's BASIC 2.0 is OPEN 1,8,15,"N0:*filename,id*":CLOSE 1.

HELP

Programming utility
Highlights the line where an error has occurred.

Format: HELP
Modes: Immediate and program
Token: 234 ($EA)
Abbreviation: HE SHIFT-L
Not available in BASIC 2.0

The HELP command displays the statement that caused the most recent BASIC error. The statement responsible for the error is displayed in underlined text on the 80-column display, and in reversed text on 40-column screens. When the guilty statement is part of a multistatement line, the highlighted display identifies the exact source of the difficulty.

```
?SYNTAX ERROR IN 100
READY.
HELP
100 FOR X=1 TO 10:PRINT X:NXET
READY.
```

Although HELP can be used in a program, its usefulness there is limited to error-handling routines triggered by the TRAP command. You'll need HELP most often in direct mode just after an error. An easier way to call this command is to press the HELP key.

HEX$

Programmer's aid
Converts a decimal number to a hexadecimal string. The decimal number must be in the range 0–65535.

Format: HEX$ (*decimal number*)
Modes: Immediate and program
Token: 210 ($D2)
Abbreviation: H SHIFT-E
Not available in BASIC 2.0

The HEX$ function is handy for converting decimal (base ten) numbers to hexadecimal (base 16). In hex, the numbers above

9 are numbered A–F, where A is 10 and F is 15. BASIC accepts only decimal numbers, unless you convert them with the DEC function. But the built-in machine language monitor (see the Introduction) uses hexadecimal notation, unless you preface numbers with a + for decimal or % for binary.

IF

Program control (decisions)
Tests the truth or falsity of an expression before conditional execution of a THEN block.

Format: IF ***condition*** **THEN** *BEGIN* ***action****...BEND: ELSE BEGIN* ***action****...BEND*
Modes: Immediate and program
Token: 139 ($8B)
Abbreviation: None
Enhanced BASIC 2.0 structure

BASIC prefers to take straight pathways, beginning at the first line in the program and ending at the last. IF builds a fork in the road. If the condition is true, the computer takes the THEN branch. If not, it either moves to the ELSE block (if one exists) or goes on to the next line. The condition is usually a comparison (IF M<16 compares the value in variable M to see if it's less than 16) or a conjunction: IF (B$=Z$) OR (H=Y+6) is true if one or the other comparison is true.

Although people think of truth and falsity as abstract concepts, the computer has to translate everything to numbers. Comparing two numbers to see if they're equal is the same as subtracting one from the other to see if the result is zero (this is a common technique in machine language).

Once a comparison has been made, BASIC assigns a value to the expression as a whole. True statements are worth −1, false statements are 0. Since everything evaluates to a number, the condition after an IF can be a numeric expression, as in IF B THEN PRINT "B IS NOT EQUAL TO ZERO." A value of zero makes B false, but any nonzero value convinces the computer that it's true. One thing to watch out for is multiple statements after an IF:

```
50 IF N = 5 AND QT < X+1 THEN Z = 15: PRINT "STILL
   PART OF THEN"
60 GOTO 600
```

The THEN in line 50 encompasses everything from Z to the end of the line. The IF statement drops to the next line if the condition is false. You can put several statements after a THEN and they will be activated only if the IF condition is true. For this reason, you should avoid putting NEXTs anywhere after a THEN: If you do, the FOR-NEXT loop won't work properly.

You don't have to follow an IF with THEN; GOTO also works:

```
10 A = 5: IF A=5 GOTO 500
499 END
500 PRINT "IT WORKED"
```

See also BEGIN/BEND for examples of THEN and ELSE blocks.

INPUT

Keyboard input

INPUT takes data (up to 160 characters in 128 mode) from the keyboard and puts it into a variable.

Format: INPUT ***variable***
Mode: Program only
Token: 133 ($85)
Abbreviation: None
Enhanced BASIC 2.0 statement

INPUT makes the program halt temporarily, to allow the user to type in information. The computer prints a question mark and waits for the user to enter data. Pressing the RETURN key ends execution of INPUT. The computer stores the data, if it was acceptable, into the string or numeric variable following the INPUT statement. The length of the reply is limited by the input buffer—80 characters in 64 mode, 160 characters in 128 mode.

10 INPUT X expects a numeric value to be typed in.
**20 INPUT X$** gets a string and puts it in variable X$.

It is possible to use text as a part of the INPUT statement. Use this format to include a prompt to the user:

```
10 INPUT "YOUR NUMBER";X
15 PRINT "THE NUMBER YOU TYPED WAS";X
20 INPUT "YOUR NAME";X$
25 PRINT "HELLO THERE, ";X$
```

In these examples, the semicolon forces the question mark to print next to the prompt. INPUT can also handle more than one variable. If multiple INPUTs are desired, use this syntax:

```
10 INPUT X,Y,Z
20 INPUT "TYPE IN THREE NAMES";R$,S$,T$
```

Notice the commas. They tell the computer to expect more than one INPUT. INPUT does not work in direct mode, and the default value for variables is the value previously typed in.

INPUT#

File input

INPUT# takes in data (up to the length of the input buffer) from files that have been opened for reading.

Format: INPUT# ***file number, variable***
Mode: Program only
Token: 132 ($84)
Abbreviation: I SHIFT-N
Enhanced BASIC 2.0 statement

In 64 mode, the longest string you can INPUT# is 88 characters. In 128 mode, INPUT# can handle up to 160 characters. Like INPUT, it does not work in direct mode. Usually the files are disk or tape files, or a peripheral device such as a modem. The following program reads through and prints a sequential text file:

```
10 DOPEN#1,"FILENAME,S"
20 DO UNTIL 64 AND ST = 64
30 INPUT#1,A$: PRINTA$: LOOP
40 DCLOSE#1
```

For more about file-handling statements, see Chapter 4.

INSTR

String function

Finds the position of a substring within a larger string.

Format: INSTR(*main string,substring*,*start char*)
Modes: Immediate and program
Token: 212 ($D4)
Abbreviation: IN SHIFT-S
Not available in BASIC 2.0

Returns the starting position within the main string of a substring. If the starting position parameter is included, the search for the substring begins at the specified character position in the main string. Otherwise, the search begins with the first character. For example, A$="PATRICK HENRY": PRINT INSTR(A$,"HENRY") prints the number 9, because INSTR finds HENRY starting at the ninth character in A$.

If the substring is not found, the value returned is zero. Other than specifying a starting position outside the range 1–255, no parameter values for INSTR cause error messages. For example, INSTR returns a zero when either or both strings are null, the substring is longer than the main string, or you specify a starting position greater than the length of the main string. As the following example shows, one useful application of INSTR is to determine the position of a given character within a string:

```
10 INPUT M:M$=STR$(M)
20 DP=INSTR(M$,"."):IF DP=0 THEN M$=M$+".00":GOTO 40
30 IF DP<LEN(M$)-2 THEN M$=LEFT$(M$,DP+2)
40 PRINT M$:GOTO 10
```

INT

Numeric function
Converts a number to an integer by rounding down to the next whole number.

Format: **INT(*number*)**
Modes: Immediate and program
Token: 181 ($B5)
Abbreviation: None
Same as BASIC 2.0

INT returns the integer (whole number) portion of the argument—the portion to the left of the decimal point if the number has a fractional component. This is not the same as rounding. INT(4.99999) is truncated to 4 rather than rounded to 5. Be careful when using this function with negative numbers. Since INT rounds down, INT (−12.1) returns a value of −13.

INT is used to discard the fractional portion of a number when only a whole number value is needed, as the following example illustrates:

```
10 N=RND(1)*10: REM PICK A NUMBER FROM 0 TO 9.9999999
20 PRINT N,INT(N):GOTO 10
```

INT is not always necessary. Many BASIC statements—for example, CHR$, POKE, and PEEK—automatically truncate any fractional remainder. PRINT CHR$(65.889) is the same as CHR$(65), so there's no need to use INT before these statements unless you need the integer number for some other purpose.

JOY(x)

Special input function
Finds the current state of a joystick.

Format: JOY(*n*)
Modes: Immediate and program
Token: 207 ($CF)
Abbreviation: J SHIFT-O
Not available in BASIC 2.0

JOY returns a value which indicates the position of the joystick and/or whether the firebutton is being pressed. The number in parentheses should be either 1 or 2, depending on which joystick port you wish to read.

JOY(*n*)	Joystick direction
0	center
1	north
2	northeast
3	east
4	southeast
5	south
6	southwest
7	west
8	northwest

JOY adds 128 to the above values to indicate that the joystick button is pressed. For example, a value of 135 indicates that the button is being pressed while the stick is held to the left (west).

```
10 IF JOY(1)=3 THEN PRINT "YOU PUSHED THE JOYSTICK
   EAST"
20 IF JOY(1)=129 THEN PRINT " YOU FIRED TO THE NORTH"
30 GOTO 10
```

KEY

Programming utility
Controls the programmable function keys.

Formats: KEY ***key#,string***
or
KEY
Modes: Immediate and program
Token: $F9
Abbreviation: K SHIFT-E
Not available in BASIC 2.0

The KEY command lets you define the 128's programmable function keys. The KEY command alone prints out a list of the current definitions of all eight function keys. By including a key number and a string in the command, you can reprogram one function key. Enter the following line in immediate mode, and the F1 key will henceforth renumber the program in memory by tens, starting with line 100.

KEY 1,"RENUMBER 100,10" + CHR$(13)

CHR$(13) is the character code for the RETURN key and should be added to KEY definitions if you want them to execute immediately upon pressing the function key. The total number of characters used in all eight key definitions must be less than 241.

LEFT$

String function
Reads characters from the left side of a string.

Format: LEFT$(*string$,number*)
Modes: Immediate and program
Token: 200 ($C8)
Abbreviation: LE SHIFT-F (includes the $)
Same as BASIC 2.0

LEFT$ returns a substring consisting of the leftmost characters of the specified string. The value specified for the number of characters in the substring must be in the range 1–255; otherwise, an ILLEGAL QUANTITY ERROR will result. If the string has not been defined or if it has been defined as a null string (a string with no characters and a length of zero), then the substring returned is a null string. If the original string has fewer characters than the number specified for the substring, then the substring will be the same as the original. For example, LEFT$("ABC",6) returns ABC.

LEFT$ is used when you want only a portion of an existing string. For example, the following program segment uses LEFT$ to check the first character in an input string:

```
100 INPUT "PLAY AGAIN";AN$
110 IF LEFT$(AN$,1)<>"Y" THEN END
120 RUN
```

LEN

String function
Finds the length of a string or string variable.

Format: LEN(*string$*)
Modes: Immediate and program
Token: 195 ($C3)
Abbreviation: None
Same as BASIC 2.0

This function lets you measure the length of the specified string. If the string has not been previously defined or if it has been defined as a null string (""), then the value returned is zero. The maximum length of a string is 255 characters.

The following example illustrates how LEN can test the length of an input string and adjust the FOR-NEXT loop accordingly:

```
10 W$="":INPUT W$
20 IF LEN(W$)=0 THEN 10
30 IF LEN(W$)>16 THEN PRINT "TOO LONG":GOTO 10
40 FOR J=1 TO LEN(W$):PRINT TAB(J);MID$(W$,J,1):NEXT
```

LET

Control over variables
Assigns a value to a variable.

Format: LET *variable = expression*
Modes: Immediate and program
Token: 136 ($88)
Abbreviation: L SHIFT-E
Same as BASIC 2.0

LET is always optional. The line LET Q = 15: LET G$ = "GREETINGS" puts the value 15 into variable Q and the string GREETINGS into G$. But the equal sign (=) by itself works just as well: Q = 15: G$ = "GREETINGS".

LIST

Programming utility
Prints all or part of the program in memory.

Format: LIST *start line–end line*
Modes: Immediate and program
Token: 155 ($9B)
Abbreviation: L SHIFT-I
Enhanced BASIC 2.0 statement

LIST is followed by (optional) line numbers. The following examples illustrate the various formats:

```
LIST           : REM LISTS ALL OF THE PROGRAM
LIST 200       : REM LISTS ONLY LINE 200
LIST 100-199: REM LISTS 100-199 INCLUSIVE
LIST -50       : REM LISTS UP TO 50
LIST 500-      : REM LISTS 500 AND FOLLOWING LINES
```

The LIST command instructs BASIC to display all or part of the current BASIC program. If it is typed with no operands, the entire program is printed to the screen. In BASIC 2.0, LIST can be executed in program mode, but the program stops when the listing is done. The program below executes correctly in BASIC 7.0, listing itself 10 times. But in BASIC 2.0, it will only list itself once before jumping back to immediate mode.

```
100 FOR C=1 TO 10
110 LIST
120 NEXT C
```

To list a program to a printer, use these two lines:

```
OPEN 4,4: CMD4: LIST
PRINT#4: CLOSE4
```

To list a disk directory to the printer, LOAD "$0",8 before entering the two lines above. Also, remember that the F7 key is predefined as LIST plus a RETURN. To list a program, it's convenient to reach for the upper-righthand corner.

LOAD

Program file-handling
Loads a program from tape or disk.

Tape Format: LOAD *"program name",1,1*
Disk Format: LOAD *"drive number:**program name**",**device number**,relocating flag*

Modes: Immediate and program
Token: 147 ($93)
Abbreviation: L SHIFT-O
Same as BASIC 2.0

LOAD brings a program or other data from disk or tape into the computer's memory. The format of the command is very similar to that of SAVE. If no filename is used, the 128 assumes you want to load the next filename on tape and issues an appropriate prompt. When a filename is added, the 128 searches for a program of that name. Here are some typical LOAD statements:

LOAD : REM LOAD NEXT PROGRAM ON TAPE
LOAD "PROGRAM NAME" : REM LOAD "PROGRAM NAME" FROM TAPE
LOAD "PROGRAM NAME",1 : REM SAME AS PRECEDING EXAMPLE
LOAD "PROGRAM NAME",1,1 : REM NONRELOCATING TAPE LOAD (MACHINE LANGUAGE)
LOAD "0:PROGRAM NAME",8 : REM LOAD "PROGRAM NAME" FROM DISK
A$="0:PROGRAM NAME" : LOAD A$,8 : REM SAME AS PRECEDING EXAMPLE
LOAD "1:PROGRAM NAME",9,1 : REM NONRELOCATING DISK LOAD (MACHINE LANGUAGE) FROM DRIVE 1, DEVICE 9

The first number after the filename is the device number (1 for tape; usually 8 for disk, although other numbers may be used if multiple drives are connected). If this number is not followed by anything else (or if it is followed by ,0), the computer automatically puts the program in the usual memory location for a BASIC program. If you put ,1 after the device number, the computer loads the program into the same memory location it was saved from: This method is ordinarily used to load machine language programs.

LOCATE

Graphics command
Moves the pixel cursor on the hi-res screen to the coordinates specified.

Format: LOCATE ***Xcoord,Ycoord***
Modes: Immediate and program
Token: 230 ($E6)

Abbreviation: LO SHIFT-C
Not available in BASIC 2.0

The pixel cursor's location can determine what happens when certain graphics commands are executed. For example, given two corner coordinates, BOX draws a rectangle. But if you leave off the location of one corner, BOX defaults to the current pixel cursor location. To see if a certain pixel on the screen is turned on or off, first set the pixel cursor (PC) location, and then use the RDOT function.

The following program sets the pixel cursor to the center of the screen, then draws a line to the top lefthand corner.

```
10 GRAPHIC 1,1
20 LOCATE 160,100
30 DRAW TO 0,0
```

LOG

Numeric function
Returns the natural logarithm of the argument.

Format: LOG(*number*)
Modes: Immediate and program
Token: 188 ($BC)
Abbreviation: None
Same as BASIC 2.0

Natural logarithms are based on the constant e, approximately 2.71828183. The use of the name LOG is slightly different from normal mathematical convention. Generally, the natural log (log to the base e) is referred to as ln(x); the term log(x) usually refers to the common logarithm (log to the base 10). To find the common log of a number, PRINT LOG(X)/LOG(10), where X is any positive number.

For example, if you insert a 41, PRINT LOG(41)/LOG(10) gives you a value of 1.61278386. If you now enter PRINT 10 ↑ 1.61278386, the answer is 41.0000003 (a slight rounding error has affected the answer, which should be exactly 41).

The inverse of LOG is EXP. PRINT LOG(EXP(X)) should return X. See EXP for more on logarithms.

LOOP

Program flow (loops)
Marks the end of a DO-LOOP.

Format: DO ... LOOP
Modes: Immediate and program
Token: 220 ($EC)
Abbreviation: LO SHIFT-O
Not available in BASIC 2.0

LOOP marks the end of a DO-LOOP structure. The BASIC commands within the loop will repeat without end until one of three things happens: a WHILE condition becomes untrue, an UNTIL condition becomes true, or an EXIT is issued. When a DO-LOOP finishes, the program continues at the next statement following the LOOP. See DO for examples.

MID$

String function
Finds (or assigns) a substring from the middle of a string.

Format: MID$(*string$, position*, *number of characters*)
Modes: Immediate and program
Token: 202 ($CA)
Abbreviation: M SHIFT-I (includes the $)
Enhanced BASIC 2.0 statement

MID$ returns a substring beginning at the specified character position in the original string. If you specify a value for the number of characters in the substring, the number must be in the range 1–255. If you don't specify a length for the substring, MID$ returns a substring composed of all characters from the starting character position to the end of the original string. If the string has not been defined or if it has been defined as a null string, then the substring returned is the null string. If the original string has fewer characters than the number specified for the substring, then the substring will be shorter than the specified length. For example, MID$("ABC",2,4) returns a string of only two characters, BC, instead of the specified four.

MID$ can also assign a string to the middle of another string. For example, B$="MINNESOTA": MID$(B$,6,3) = "HAH" changes B$ into MINNEHAHA. This feature of MID$ is not available in BASIC 2.0 (64 mode). The following program illustrates some of the string manipulations possible with MID$:

```
10 INPUT T$:S$=""
20 FOR J=LEN(T$) TO 1 STEP -1
30 S$=S$+MID$(T$,J,1):PRINT MID$(T$,J),S$
40 NEXT J
```

MONITOR

Machine language utility
Enables the built-in machine language monitor.

Format: MONITOR
Modes: Immediate and program
Token: 250 ($FA)
Abbreviation: MO SHIFT-N
Not available in BASIC 2.0

MONITOR takes you out of the BASIC editor and into the machine language monitor. It can be entered by typing MONITOR, by holding down the RUN/STOP key when you turn on (or reset) the 128, or by SYSing to a machine language routine that ends with the BRK (BReaK to monitor) instruction. The monitor allows you to read, write, and edit machine language programs. Refer to the Introduction for a detailed explanation of all the commands available in the monitor.

MOVSPR

Graphics command (sprites)
Moves sprites around the screen.

Formats: MOVSPR *sprite number, Xcoord, Ycoord*
MOVSPR *sprite number, ±Xcoord, ±Ycoord*
MOVSPR *sprite number, distance; angle*
MOVSPR *sprite number, angle #speed*
Modes: Immediate and program
Token: 254 6 ($FE $06)
Abbreviation: M SHIFT-O
Not available in BASIC 2.0

MOVSPR positions sprites on the screen or starts them moving around the screen. You must define the sprite and turn it on before you'll see anything appear on the screen.

The first sample statement shown above places a sprite at a specific position on the screen. The second (with plus and minus signs) moves a sprite to a location relative to its current position. In the third example (note the semicolon), a sprite is relocated a given distance and angle—zero degrees is straight up, 90 is to the right, and so on. The final example (with the # character) starts movement at a given angle and speed. While the rest of the program runs, the sprite will continue to move at that angle.

NEW

Program control
Clears the current program and variables from memory.

Format: NEW
Modes: Immediate and program
Token: 162 ($A2)
Abbreviation: None
Same as BASIC 2.0

NEW resets all BASIC program and variable pointers to their initial values. Use this command to clear memory before you start typing a new program. Although NEW works within programs, too, you should be cautious about using it in this way since the program will erase itself the instant it encounters the NEW statement.

Although programs seem to disappear after NEW, they are not actually erased from memory. NEW simply resets the pointers that tell BASIC where the program text and variables are located. If you should accidentally type NEW, you can recover the pointers fairly easily. Try this:

1. Enter the machine language monitor with MONITOR.
2. Memory locations 45–46 (hex $2D–2E) point to the beginning of BASIC. To look at those two bytes, enter M +45 or M 2D (the plus sign in front of the 45 indicates you're using a decimal number).
3. Unless you've been moving memory locations around, the two numbers after 002D should be either 01 1C or 01 40, depending on whether or not you've allocated a hi-res graphics area. The numbers are listed in low-byte/high-byte format, so the addresses would really be $1C01 or $4001.
4. Cursor down to a blank line and type X, for eXit to BASIC.
5. Enter this line (if the start of BASIC was at $4001, substitute that number in the POKE DEC statement):

   BANK 0: POKE DEC("1C01"), 1: BANK 15: SYS DEC("5EE5")

   LIST to make sure your program is back in memory.

NEXT

Program flow (loops)
Marks the end of a FOR-NEXT loop.

Format: FOR *index* = *start* TO *finish* *STEP increment* **...**
NEXT *index*

Modes: Immediate and program
Token: 130 ($82)
Abbreviation: N SHIFT-E
Same as BASIC 2.0

A FOR-NEXT loop begins at the FOR statement and ends at NEXT. The index variable initially holds the value in *start* and increments by the STEP size (if STEP is left off, the index variable counts by ones). As soon as it exceeds the *finish* value, the loop ends. So NEXT is like a GOTO that repeatedly sends the program back to the statement just after the FOR, until the index variable reaches a predefined value.

```
10 FOR J = 1 TO 5: PRINT "OUTER LOOP PASS NUMBER"; J
20 FOR K = 4 TO 1 STEP −.5: PRINT K;
30 NEXT K
40 PRINT
50 NEXT
```

NEXT can be followed by the index variable name (line 30), or can appear by itself. The computer keeps track of which loop is currently active.

NOT

Logical operator
Performs a ones complement bitwise negation.

Format: NOT *expression*
Modes: Immediate and program
Token: 168 ($A8)
Abbreviation: N SHIFT-O
Same as BASIC 2.0

NOT is a logical operator like AND, OR, and XOR, but it operates on a single argument rather than two. Using it on a number is the equivalent of adding one and changing the sign. PRINT NOT 8 will print the number −9 on the screen. It's the same as PRINT −(8+1). You can also use NOT on expressions. For example, IF NOT (A$ = "GLORY") THEN PRINT "SHAME" means if the condition inside parentheses is *false,* print the message. If (A$ = "GLORY") is true, NOT negates it, making IF see it as false. If the expression is false, NOT (false) yields a true statement. IF A$ <> "GLORY" THEN PRINT "SHAME" does the same thing and is a bit easier to understand.

Since NOT also has the effect of reversing all bits in the value it operates on, it can be used to control the settings of particular bits in memory locations. For example, to turn on bit 6 of a location without changing the setting of any other bit, you OR the contents of the location with 64, since the binary bit pattern for 64 has only bit 6 set. To turn off that bit, you could calculate which number has a binary bit pattern with only bit 6 clear, but it's faster to use NOT(64) instead. The following example turns multicolor mode on and back off by switching bit 7 of location $D8.

```
10 POKE 216,PEEK(216) OR 128
20 SLEEP 5
30 POKE 216,PEEK(216) AND NOT(128)
```

ON

Program flow

Performs a GOTO or GOSUB based on the value of a numeric variable.

Formats: ON ***variable*** **GOTO** ***line****, line, line, line*
ON ***variable*** **GOSUB** ***line****, line, line, line*
Modes: Immediate and program
Token: 145 ($91)
Abbreviation: None
Same as BASIC 2.0

ON lets you branch to one of several possible destinations, depending on the value of the *variable* that follows ON. The variable must evaluate to a positive number or zero (if it's negative, an ILLEGAL QUANTITY error occurs). If the number is zero or larger than the number of lines included in the list following GOTO or GOSUB, the program continues to the next statement.

In the statement 50 ON J GOTO 100,200,5 the variable J controls where the program branches. The same thing could be done (though much less efficiently) with several IF-THENs: 50 IF J = 1 THEN GOTO 100: ELSE IF J = 2 THEN GOTO 200: ELSE IF J = 3 THEN GOTO 5.

ON-GOSUB works the same as ON-GOTO, but it branches temporarily to a subroutine which must end with a RETURN. After the RETURN, the programs resumes with the first statement following the ON-GOSUB. For more information, see the entries under GOTO and GOSUB.

OPEN

General input/output

Establishes a communications link with a peripheral such as a disk drive, tape drive, printer, or modem.

Formats: OPEN *file number, device,* *secondary address, "filename,type,mode"*

OPEN *file number, device, secondary address, "command string$"*

Modes: Immediate and program

Token: 159 ($9F)

Abbreviation: O SHIFT-P

Same as BASIC 2.0

OPEN establishes a channel for communication between the computer and a specified data file or peripheral device. Consider this example:

```
10 OPEN 3,4,7 : REM OPEN CHANNEL TO PRINTER
```

The first number, 3, designates the logical file number. Other input/output statements such as PRINT# and GET# use this number to identify the file. The second number (4) is the device number: In Commodore systems device 4 is ordinarily the printer. Here are the device numbers you'll see most often:

Device No.	Device
0	Keyboard
1	Datassette
2	RS-232 devices (usually a modem)
3	Screen
4–7	Printer(s)
8–15	Disk drive(s)

The third number after OPEN (7 in this example) sets the secondary address. The secondary address has different meanings depending on which device is addressed: In this case, a secondary address of 7 selects a printer mode (uppercase/lowercase). When opening a file to disk, you must also include a filename within quotation marks after the secondary address, as shown here.

```
OPEN 2,8,2,"ASCII LISTING,S,W" : REM OPEN SEQUENTIAL
  DISK FILE
CMD 2 : REM REDIRECT OUTPUT TO LOGICAL FILE 2
LIST : REM LIST PROGRAM IN MEMORY
PRINT#2 : REM MAKE SURE ALL DATA IS PRINTED
CLOSE 2 : REM ALWAYS BE SURE TO CLOSE DISK FILES
```

Similar statements can be used to create a text file on tape. In the case of tape, however, the filename is optional. A filename suffix such as the one used here (,S,W) is appropriate only for disk files. See also the entry for DOPEN.

OR

Logical operator
Performs a logical or bitwise OR on two expressions.

Format: ***expression1* OR *expression2***
Modes: Immediate and program
Token: 176 ($B0)
Abbreviation: None
Same as BASIC 2.0

OR, like the other logical operators AND, NOT, and XOR, can be used to test truth and falsity of expressions, and is also useful for bit-masking operations.

You'll find it often in IF-THENs or other conditional tests. IF (A=5) OR (B=16) THEN PRINT "GAME OVER": END is a good example. Here we're testing the truth of two expressions. The variable A might be equal to five, in which case (A=5) is true, but if A isn't five, the expression is false. The same goes for (B=16). So if either one (or both) of the expressions is true, the whole OR is true and the THEN is executed.

When OR is applied to true/false situations, the 128 considers true statements to be worth −1 and false statements to be 0. These two values have special properties. Any number ORed with zero returns the original number, and any number OR −1 gives you back −1.

When 0 and −1 are not part of the expression, OR works on individual bits. To see how this works, go into the monitor (enter MONITOR). Type + 129 followed by RETURN, then type + 7 and press RETURN. As you'll see, the first number is 10000001 in binary form, and the second is 00000111. Now exit to BASIC (enter X) and enter PRINT 129 OR 7. The answer is 135 because of the bit patterns:

```
     10000001  (129)
OR   00000111  (7)
 =   10000111  (135)
```

If either one of the numbers contains an "on" bit (1) in a certain position, the bit is on in the answer. The only place you'll find off bits is where both numbers contained a zero in the same position. This method of masking bits is most useful for turning on individual bits of memory addresses (see the example for NOT).

PAINT

Graphics command
Fills a specified section of the screen with one color.

Format: PAINT *color source, Xcoord, Ycoord, mode*
Modes: Immediate and program
Token: 223 ($DF)
Abbreviation: P SHIFT-A
Not available in BASIC 2.0

PAINT fills any shape on the hi-res screen with the color source indicated. If you perform PAINT with no parameters, it fills with the current foreground color, starting at the present pixel cursor location. Use color 0 to select the background color, 1 for the foreground, 2 for the first multicolor, or 3 for the second multicolor.

The X and Y coordinates can specify absolute screen locations or locations relative to the pixel cursor. If a plus sign (+) or minus sign (−) comes before the coordinate number, the coordinate number is added to or subtracted from the pixel cursor's current coordinate. So PAINT 1,160,100 tells the computer to start filling the area at 160,100 with color source 1 (foreground). But PAINT 1,+5,−12 begins painting at the cursor X position plus 5, and Y position minus 12.

PAINT fills shapes, continuing in each direction until an edge is found. If the shape has two edges that don't connect, the color spills through. It's possible for PAINT to fill the entire screen if you're not careful about defining the edges of shapes.

If the *mode* is undefined (or 0), the fill continues until it reaches the color source specified. If mode equals 1, PAINT fills until a nonbackground color is found (this is useful only in multicolor mode).

This program draws three boxes and fills them with blue, white, and red to create a flag. You could make a similar picture by setting the paint flag to one in the BOX command, but the outline effect would be missing.

```
10 GRAPHIC 4,1
20 COLOR 0,1: COLOR 1,7: COLOR 2,2: COLOR 3,3: COLOR 4,1
```

```
30 FOR A=0 TO 100 STEP 50
40 BOX 2,A,0,50+A,140
50 PAINT A/50+1,A+1,1,1
60 NEXT A
```

PEEK

Memory control
Returns the number held in a memory location.

Format: PEEK(*address*)
Modes: Immediate and program
Token: 194 ($C2)
Abbreviation: PE SHIFT-E
Enhanced BASIC 2.0 statement

PEEK examines the contents of a memory location and tells you what number is stored there. The address must be in the range 0–65535. PEEK works within the current memory bank, so it is sometimes necessary to use a BANK command to make sure you're looking at the correct section of memory. There's no need to specify a bank number in BASIC 2.0.

PEEK is the opposite of POKE, which stores a number into a byte. Refer to the memory map for a description of accessible memory locations.

```
10 BANK 0: PRINT PEEK(2598): REM SHOULD RETURN A
   ZERO FOR BLINKING CURSOR
20 POKE 2598,255: REM TURNS CURSOR TO BLANK SPACE
30 PRINT PEEK(2598): REM SHOULD PRINT A 255
40 POKE 2598,64: REM TURNS CURSOR TO SOLID BLOCK
50 PRINT PEEK(2598): REM NOW IT IS 64
```

Commodore 64 programmers who are familiar with the abbreviation P SHIFT-E (which the 128 recognizes as PEN) should note the new abbreviation PE SHIFT-E.

PEN

Special input function
Returns the current coordinates of the light pen.

Format: PEN(*n*)
Modes: Immediate and program
Token: 206 4 ($CE $04)
Abbreviation: P SHIFT-E
Not available in BASIC 2.0

PEN(*n*) returns coordinates for the light pen, where *n* is a number from 0–4. The X coordinate can take even values from 60 to 320, and the Y coordinate can range from 50 to 250 (notice that these numbers don't match up with the coordinate system used for hi-res graphics). Here are the values which PEN returns, depending on which value you supply within the parentheses.

n	**Value returned**
0	X coordinate for 40 columns
1	Y coordinate for 40 columns
2	X coordinate for 80 columns
3	Y coordinate for 80 columns
4	pen trigger

The values returned depend on what type of television or monitor you're using. The 40-column screen returns pixel coordinates and the 80-column screen returns character rows and columns.

PI (π)

Numeric constant
Always holds the value 3.14159265.

Format: π
Modes: Immediate or program
Token: 255 ($FF)
Abbreviation: None
Same as BASIC 2.0

Pi is a constant important in trigonometric functions. To type a pi character, hold down the SHIFT key and press the up-arrow (↑, to the left of the RESTORE key). An unusual property of pi is that if you GET or GETKEY a pi from the keyboard, its character code value is 222. But if you INPUT A$ and then PRINT A$, it has a value of 255. If you PEEK into a BASIC program or use the memory display command of the monitor, the pi character is always 255 (hex $FF).

PLAY

Sound and music
Plays a note—or a complete melody.

Format: PLAY ***string$***
Modes: Immediate and program
Token: 254 4 ($FE $04)

Abbreviation: P SHIFT-L
Not available in BASIC 2.0

PLAY allows you to play a melody. The music is defined by the string of characters following PLAY, which may either be placed inside quotation marks or stored in a string variable. The string can contain any combination of parameters from the following list:

Parameter	Range of values
Voice	V 1–3
Octave	O 0–6
Tuning Envelope	T 0 (piano)
	1 (accordion)
	2 (calliope)
	3 (drum)
	4 (flute)
	5 (guitar)
	6 (harpsichord)
	7 (organ)
	8 (trumpet)
	9 (xylophone)
Volume	U 0–15
Filter	X 0–1 (off or on)
Note Values	A, B, C, D, E, F, G
Accidentals	# (sharp)
	$ (flat)
Rhythmic Values	S (sixteenth)
	I (eighth)
	Q (quarter)
	H (half)
	W (whole)
	. (dotted)
	M (finish measure)
	R (rest)

```
10 REM LA DONNA IL MOBILE
20 PLAY "V1 O4 T0 U12 X0 QE QE QE .IG SF HD QD QD QD .IF
SE HC"
```

Chapter 3 provides additional details about how to use PLAY.

POINTER

Programming aid
Returns the memory address of a variable.

Format: POINTER(*variable name*)
Modes: Immediate and program
Token: 206 10 ($CE $0A)
Abbreviation: PO SHIFT-I
Not available in BASIC 2.0

On rare occasions, you may want to find the location in memory where a variable is stored. Since variables always use memory bank 1, be sure to issue a BANK 1 command before you start PEEKing into memory locations for variables. Floating point numbers, integers, and strings all have slightly different formats:

Floating point: Five bytes for floating point representation of number.
Integer: Two bytes, plus three empty bytes.
String: One byte for length, two for pointer to memory address holding the string, two empty bytes.

Array variables dispense with the extra unused bytes. Floating point arrays use five bytes per element, integer arrays two bytes, and string arrays use three (plus one byte for each character in the string). The following program finds the variable A, prints out the two bytes for the variable name, plus five for its value, and then changes the name of the variable to B.

```
10 BANK 1: A = 15: P = POINTER (A)
20 FORJ= P-2 TO P + 4: PRINT J, PEEK(J)
30 PRINT "THE VALUE OF A IS"; A
40 POKE P-2, 66: REM A LEGAL NAME CHANGE
50 PRINT "NOW A IS:";A
60 PRINT "BUT B IS:";B
```

POKE

Memory control
Stores a number into a memory address.

Format: POKE *address, value*
Modes: Immediate and program
Token: 151 ($97)
Abbreviation: PO SHIFT-K
Enhanced BASIC 2.0 statement

The POKE command stores a number in a memory location within the current bank (it's the opposite of PEEK, which lets you examine the contents of a particular location). The number to be stored must be in the range 0–255, and the memory location must be in the range 0–65535. Negative values aren't allowed in either position.

Because the 128 can address up to 16 memory banks, POKE behaves somewhat differently in 128 mode than in 64 mode. BANK 0: POKE 16000,1 puts a number into BASIC program space, while BANK 1: POKE 16000,1 affects a memory location in bank 1, where variables are stored. Note that most of bank 15 cannot be POKEd because ROM (Read Only Memory) cannot be written to. You *are* allowed to POKE to I/O registers such as the SID chip and the CIA chips. The memory map in Appendix D describes most important memory locations.

POKE is frequently used with READ and DATA to put machine language programs, sprite definitions, or custom character sets into memory. It can also pass parameters to machine language programs. 64 programmers who are familiar with the abbreviation P SHIFT-O (which the 128 recognizes as POT) should note the new abbreviation PO SHIFT-K.

POS

Cursor function
Returns the current location of the text cursor.

Format: POS(*number*)
Modes: Immediate and program
Token: 185 ($B9)
Abbreviation: None
Enhanced BASIC 2.0 statement

POS tells you the position of the cursor on the current screen line. The number in parentheses is a dummy argument, meaning that you must include some number in this position, but it doesn't matter what you choose. POS(15) works just the same as POS(1).

In BASIC 2.0, a *logical* screen line can consist of up to two physical 40-column screen lines. If more than 40 characters are printed before a carriage return, the logical line wraps around to the next physical line. Thus, POS can return values in the range 0–79. In BASIC 7.0, the value returned will always be in the range 0–39 for the 40-column screen or 0–79 for the 80-column screen. POS can determine only the position of the cursor on the screen; it cannot, for example, determine the position of a printer head during PRINT# operations.

Use POS when you need to know where the cursor is presently located. The following example uses POS to center a box of width N on the 40-column screen:

```
10 INPUT N:R=(40-N)/2-1
20 FOR J=0 TO 9:FOR K=0 TO 38:PRINT " ";
30 IF POS(0)>R THEN PRINT"{RVS}";
40 IF POS(0)>N+R THEN PRINT"{OFF}";
50 NEXT K:PRINT:NEXT J
```

POT

Special input function
Reads the paddles (or other potentiometers) plugged into the joystick port.

Format: POT(*n*)
Modes: Immediate and program
Token: 206 2 ($CE $02)
Abbreviation: P SHIFT-O
Not available in BASIC 2.0

POT(*n*) returns the position of a paddle, where the value *n* specifies which of the four possible paddle inputs (numbered 1–4) you want to read. The resulting value is in the range 0–255, unless the paddle button is also pressed, in which case 256 is added to the paddle reading. Thus, a reading of 393 indicates a paddle position of 137 with the button pressed (137 + 256 = 393).

```
10 X=POT(1):IF X> 256 THEN PRINT "FIREBUTTON IS
   PRESSED"
20 PRINT X:GOTO 10
```

Game paddles are analog, rather than digital, devices. Turning the knob varies the resistance of the potentiometer (variable resistor) in the paddle controller, which changes the voltage of the paddle input. Special circuitry in the SID chip translates this voltage into a number. The values returned by POT may vary slightly even if the paddle is not turned, resulting in "jumpy" numbers. You may find it helpful to read the paddles several times and average the results to smooth out the slight variations.

PRINT

General output
Displays information on the screen.

Format: PRINT *expression*
Modes: Immediate and program
Token: 153 ($99)
Abbreviation: ?
Same as BASIC 2.0

In most cases, PRINT simply displays characters on the screen. But PRINT can send output to any device; when used with CMD it can send print to a printer, disk or tape drive, modem, and so on.

PRINT is one of the most frequently used statements in BASIC. You are probably familiar with its most common use—putting messages on the screen, as in PRINT"PRESS ANY KEY TO CONTINUE." PRINT accepts virtually any kind of data:

PRINT"HELLO"	*literal string*
PRINT A$, B$(20)	*string variables*
PRINT 123	*literal number*
PRINT A, B(20)	*numeric variables*

Two or more data items can be combined in one PRINT statement. The result depends on how the items are separated. Consider this example:

```
10 A$="DOG":B$="CATCHER"
20 PRINT A$ B$
30 PRINT A$B$
40 PRINT A$;B$
50 PRINT A$,B$
```

```
DOGCATCHER
DOGCATCHER
DOGCATCHER
DOG       CATCHER
```

If you separate data items with a semicolon (or don't separate them at all), PRINT displays them without any intervening spaces. A comma causes them to be separated into 10-space columns across the screen. When a PRINT statement ends without a comma or semicolon, the computer performs a carriage return after the statement, moving down one line and returning to the left edge of the screen.

```
10 PRINT "DOG";:PRINT"CATCHER"
20 PRINT "DOG":PRINT"CATCHER",
30 PRINT "DOGCATCHER"
```

PRINT statements can also include control characters—special characters that perform a printing function rather than putting a character on the screen. For instance, PRINT CHR$(147);CHR$(5) clears the screen and changes the character color to white. Here are some typical combinations of PRINT and a function that returns a value:

```
10 PRINT ASC("H");ASC("I")
20 PRINT CHR$(72);CHR$(73)
```

```
72        73
HI
```

```
10 A$="DOGCATCHER"
20 PRINT LEFT$(A$,3)
30 PRINT MID$(A$,4,3)
40 PRINT RIGHT$(A$,7)
```

```
DOG
CAT
CATCHER
```

```
PRINT "END OF PROGRAM=";PEEK(4624)+256*PEEK(4625)
```

PRINT USING

General output

Prints items to the screen in predefined formats.

Format: PRINT USING *"format"; expression,* *expression, expression...*

Modes: Immediate and program

Token: $FB (USING)

Abbreviation: ? US SHIFT-I

Not available in BASIC 2.0

PRINT USING is a variation of PRINT that permits you to format output in a certain way. Consider this example:

```
X=1234.56:PRINT USING "#$#,###.##";X,543.21
```

```
$1,234.56    $543.21
```

The characters within quotation marks (the format field) define the format for printing the numeric values that come after the semicolon. The period and comma show where the decimal place and comma should be placed in the printed result. The #$ character sequence creates a floating dollar sign which will be placed immediately to the left of the first digit of the printed number. Though frequently used to format numeric data, PRINT USING can also be used with strings. The format field must contain at least as many # symbols as you expect the string to have (if the format field is shorter, the string will be truncated). Include an equal sign (=) to center the string in the field, or a greater than sign (>) to right-justify the string.

USING is also legal within a PRINT# command. With PRINT# USING, you can control the formatting of information sent to files or to the printer.

PRINT#

Input/output
Prints characters to a previously opened file.

Format: PRINT# ***file number,expression***
Modes: Immediate and program
Token: 152 ($98)
Abbreviation: P SHIFT-R
Same as BASIC 2.0

PRINT# sends output to a specified file after you have used OPEN (or DOPEN) to open a channel to the device or create a logical file. It must be followed by a file number which matches the number in the preceding OPEN statement:

```
10 OPEN 2,8,3,"TEST,S,W": REM OPEN SEQUENTIAL DISK FILE
   NAMED TEST
20 PRINT#2,CHR$(65);"BC": REM OUTPUT "ABC" TO THE
   DISK FILE
30 CLOSE2
```

Note that the file number (2 in this case) must be followed by a comma. As with PRINT, you can control spacing by putting semicolons or commas between different data items.

PUDEF

General output
Defines the characters used in a PRINT USING or PRINT# USING statement.

Format: PUDEF ***"abcd"***
Modes: Immediate and program
Token: 221 ($DD)
Abbreviation: P SHIFT-U
Not available in BASIC 2.0

PUDEF redefines any of the four main formatting characters for subsequent PRINT USING statements:

Character	Use
a	filler character (default is a space)
b	separator, for use within numbers (default is a comma)
c	decimal point (default is a period)
d	monetary symbol (default is dollar sign)

It must be followed by a literal string containing from one to four characters. Consider the example PUDEF "-@*!". The first character within quotation marks redefines the filler character used by PRINT USING (ordinarily a space) as a dash (-). The second character redefines the comma as an at sign (@). The third replaces the period with an asterisk, and the fourth replaces the dollar sign with an exclamation point. You need not redefine all four characters. The following example shows the output from PRINT USING before and after PUDEF:

```
10 A=1234.56
20 PRINT USING "$###,###.##";A
30 PUDEF "-@*!"
40 PRINT USING "$###,###.##";A
```

```
$ 1,234.56
!--1@234*56
```

RCLR

Graphics command
Reads the color setting for the color source specified.

Format: RCLR(*color source*)
Modes: Immediate and program
Token: 205 ($CD)
Abbreviation: R SHIFT-C
Not available in BASIC 2.0

RCLR tells you what color is held in any color source. To change the colors, see the COLOR statement.

Source	Reads from
0	40-column background (text screen color)
1	Hi-res foreground (pixel color)
2	Multicolor 1 (text or hi-res)
3	Multicolor 2 (text or hi-res)
4	40-column border
5	Character color (40 or 80 column text)
6	80-column background

The following program prints the number of the background, border, and character colors of a text screen.

```
10 PRINT "BACKGROUND COLOR "; RCLR(0)
20 PRINT "BORDER COLOR     "; RCLR(4)
30 PRINT "TEXT COLOR       "; RCLR(5)
```

RDOT

Graphics function
Returns information about the current state of the hi-res pixel cursor.

Format: RDOT(*n*)
Modes: Immediate and program
Token: 208 ($D0)
Abbreviation: R SHIFT-D
Not available in BASIC 2.0

If the number *n* in parentheses is 0, RDOT reads the X coordinate of the pixel cursor. When *n* is 1, RDOT gives you the Y coordinate of the pixel cursor. If *n* equals 2, the color source at the pixel cursor is returned. Note that the color source is not the same as the actual color (see Chapter 2). To find the color of the pixel cursor, use the RCLR function as in the statement RCLR(RDOT(2)). The following program sets the location of the pixel cursor, then uses the RDOT function to print the location.

```
10 GRAPHIC 2,1
20 LOCATE 100,40
30 PRINT "THE X COORDINATE IS "; RDOT(0)
40 PRINT "THE Y COORDINATE IS "; RDOT(1)
```

READ

Control over variables
Pulls values sequentially out of DATA statements.

Format: READ *variable*
Modes: Immediate and program
Token: 135 ($87)
Abbreviation: RE SHIFT-A
Same as BASIC 2.0

READ is always associated with DATA statements. If the items in a DATA statement are separated by commas, they're considered separate pieces of data. The first time READ is performed, the computer searches for the first DATA statement in the program and copies the string or number there into the variable following the READ. The next READ does the same with the second DATA item, and so on. READ and DATA are often used in combination to POKE machine language programs into memory, define a series of array variables, and so on.

The following program reads two numbers, multiplies them, and then reads several strings.

```
10 READ A,B: PRINT A;"TIMES";B;"EQUALS" A*B
20 FOR J=1TO3: READ T$(J): NEXT
30 FOR J=3TO1 STEP-1: PRINT T$(J): NEXT
90 DATA 5,7
100 DATA "TO TOP, WITH AN EMBEDDED COMMA"
110 DATA BOTTOM, FROM
```

Note that READ does not treat commas inside quotation marks as delimiters. The string in line 100 is printed in its entirety, but since the comma in line 110 is not inside quotes, it acts as a delimiter and separates two DATA items from each other.

RECORD

Disk command

Sets the relative file pointer prior to reading a record.

Format: RECORD #*logical file number, record number, byte number*

Modes: Immediate and program

Tokens: 254 18 ($FE $12)

Abbreviation: RE SHIFT-C

Not available in BASIC 2.0

RECORD positions a relative file pointer to select a certain byte within a record in a relative disk file. The logical file number refers to the file number used when you first opened the file with DOPEN or OPEN. The record number can be any number between 0–65535, though few if any relative files approach this size. The byte number can range from 1–254, but cannot exceed the record length established when the file was first created. To read from or write to an existing relative file you must: OPEN a logical file, position the pointer with RECORD, perform a read (GET# or INPUT#) or write (PRINT#) operation, reposition the pointer to the beginning of the record, and CLOSE the file when all read/write operations are complete. Chapter 4 discusses relative file handling in detail.

REM

Programming aid
Lets you include comments in a BASIC program.

Format: REM *comments about the program*
Modes: Immediate and program
Token: 143 ($8F)
Abbreviation: None
Same as BASIC 2.0

REM, short for REMark, lets you include descriptive text in a program without affecting what happens when it runs (apart from a slight increase in execution time). You can outline what the program does (easy to forget after a couple of months), what the variables mean, when you wrote it, or whatever else you want. Here are some examples:

```
10 REM THIS PROGRAM WRITTEN BY JOSEPH JOHNSON
20 REM
30 REM ************* SECTION 1 **************
40 GOSUB 5000: REM INITIALIZE VARIABLES
```

RENAME

Disk command
Changes the name of a program or file on disk.

Format: RENAME *"old filename"* **TO** *"new filename",Ddrive number,Udevice number.*
Modes: Immediate and program
Token: 245 ($F5)
Abbreviation: RE SHIFT-N
Not available in BASIC 2.0

RENAME changes a disk file name without affecting the file's contents. You may not rename a file that is currently open. This command renames the file ALPINE.V15 as ALPINE on the disk in drive 0, device 8:

```
RENAME "ALPINE.V15" TO "ALPINE"
```

This command renames ALPINE.V15 as ALPINE on the disk in drive 1, device 9:

```
RENAME "ALPINE.V15" TO "ALPINE",D1,U9
```

RENUMBER

Programming utility
Changes the line numbers of the BASIC program currently in memory.

Format: RENUMBER *first line, increment, middle line*
Mode: Immediate only
Token: 248 ($F8)
Abbreviation: REN SHIFT-U
Not available in BASIC 2.0

The RENUMBER command renumbers some or all lines of the current BASIC program, including internal line references such as GOSUB 2000, GOTO 10, or IF A=1 THEN 100. If you simply type RENUMBER and press RETURN, the computer renumbers the entire program in increments of 10 beginning with line 10 (10, 20, 30, etc.). The optional parameters let you change the first new line number, use a different increment between line numbers, or begin renumbering at a designated line within the program. If you choose to start renumbering at line 1000, every line in the old program from 1000 to the end is renumbered. RENUMBER always works from the designated line number (or the first if none is specified) to the program's end. RENUMBER stops with an error (without harm to your program) if the renumbered program would include a line greater than 63999 or if an internal line reference points to a nonexistent line.

RESTORE

Control over variables
Resets the pointer to DATA statements, so they can be read again.

Format: RESTORE *line number*
Modes: Immediate and program
Token: 140 ($8C)
Abbreviation: RE SHIFT-S
Enhanced BASIC 2.0 statement

When READ (see above) is used to read sequentially through a list of DATA statements, a pointer in the 128 keeps track of which lines have already been read. After you reach the last item in the list, further attempts to READ will yield an OUT OF DATA error, meaning the program contains no more information in the form of DATA statements.

But RESTORE resets the pointer, so DATA statements can be reused as many times as you wish. The line number is optional; RESTORE defaults to the beginning of the program—effectively to the first DATA line in the program.

```
10 DO: READ A$: PRINTA$
20 LOOP
100 DATA FIRST, SECOND
110 DATA THIRD, LAST
```

Without an exit condition (WHILE, UNTIL, or EXIT), the DO-LOOP should continue forever. But the READ in line 10 runs out of data after four passes. Try adding the line 15 IF A$ = "LAST" THEN RESTORE 110. The DATA pointer is set back to line 110, and the program continues.

RESUME

Program control
Used within an error-trapping routine, restarts the program after an error has occurred.

Formats: **RESUME** *line number*
RESUME *NEXT*
Mode: Program only
Token: 214 ($D6)
Abbreviation: RES SHIFT-U
Not available in BASIC 2.0

RESUME tells the program where to restart after a TRAP statement has detected an error condition and sent the program to an error-handling routine. You may use it with or without a line number, and may optionally follow the command with NEXT. Here are some typical uses.

```
100 RESUME : REM RE-EXECUTE THE LINE THAT CAUSED
    THE ERROR
110 RESUME NEXT : REM GO TO STATEMENT AFTER THE
    ONE THAT CAUSED THE ERROR
120 RESUME 1000 : REM GO DIRECTLY TO LINE 1000
```

RESUME cannot be used in immediate mode, nor is it permissible to replace the line number with a variable. This command combines some features of RETURN and GOTO, since it can either return the program to the place from whence it came, or jump to an entirely new destination.

RETURN

Program flow
Ends execution of a subroutine and returns to the main program.

Format: RETURN
Mode: Program only
Token: 142 ($8E)
Abbreviation: RE SHIFT-T
Same as BASIC 2.0

RETURN has only one purpose: It sends the program back to the statement after the most recent GOSUB command.

```
10 PRINT "GO HERE,"
20 GOSUB 50
30 PRINT "AND EVERYWHERE."
40 END
50 PRINT "AND THERE, IN THE SUBROUTINE"
60 RETURN
```

Note line 40, where the END statement prevents the computer from falling through to the subroutine at line 50. If you delete the END, the program would run line by line from 10 to 20 (to the subroutine at 50 to 60) back to 30 to 50 and finally to 60. You would then see an error message, RETURN WITHOUT GOSUB. In this program, END marks the division between the main program (10–30) and the subroutine (50–60). GOSUB and RETURN are useful only in program mode, while the computer still remembers the location of the most recent GOSUB.

Every GOSUB in a program should be balanced with a matching RETURN statement. If the computer encounters RETURN without having previously executed GOSUB, the program stops with a RETURN WITHOUT GOSUB error. And if a program performs several GOSUBs without terminating RETURNs, the program may eventually stop with an OUT OF MEMORY error.

It's possible for several subroutines to share a RETURN statement. For example, you might have a subroutine at line 560 that does a SLEEP 5 and then clears the screen, followed by RETURN. Adding a line 550 to calculate a sum would give you two subroutines: GOSUB 550 (which does a sum, pauses five seconds, and clears the screen) and GOSUB 560 (to pause five seconds and clear the screen). By entering the subroutine at different spots, you can accomplish different tasks.

RGR

Graphics function
Returns the current graphics mode.

Format: RGR(*n*)
Modes: Immediate and program
Token: 204 ($CC)
Abbreviation: R SHIFT-G
Not available in BASIC 2.0

RGR determines what graphics mode the computer is currently using. The value *n* is a dummy argument (it doesn't matter what the value is). After switching to the multicolor hires screen by using GRAPHIC 3, you could test the graphics mode with PRINT RGR(0), which should return a 3. The primary value of RGR is that it lets you find out if the user has a 40-column (mode 0) or 80-column (mode 5) monitor. Once this is known, your program can adjust the screen display accordingly. The following program displays the current graphics mode.

```
10 PRINT "YOU ARE NOW IN GRAPHICS MODE "; RGR(0)
```

RIGHT$

String function
Defines a substring from the right of the main string.

Format: RIGHT$(*string$,n*)
Modes: Immediate and program
Token: 201 ($C9)
Abbreviation: R SHIFT-I (includes the $)
Same as BASIC 2.0

RIGHT$ takes two arguments, a string and a number. It returns a substring consisting of the rightmost *n* characters of the specified string. Thus, this function performs the same job as LEFT$, but starts at the opposite end of the string. The value for the number of characters in the substring must be in the range 1–255, or an ILLEGAL QUANTITY ERROR will result. If the string has not been defined or if it has been defined as a null string (two quotation marks with nothing inside, a string with a length of zero), the substring returned is the null string. If the original string has fewer characters than the number specified for the substring, then the substring will be the same as the original. For example, RIGHT$("ABC",6) returns ABC.

This program shows how RIGHT$ can align characters in neat columns:

```
10 FOR J=0 TO 15:N=INT(2↑J)
20 PRINT J,RIGHT$("{8 SPACES}"+STR$(N),8)
30 NEXT
```

RND

Numeric function
Returns a random number in the range 0–0.99999999.
Format: RND(*n*)
Modes: Immediate and program
Token: 187 ($BB)
Abbreviation: R SHIFT-N
Same as BASIC 2.0

This function produces a pseudo-random number, based on the sign and value of the argument. Since a computer is too logical to do anything truly random, it must generate the random number by performing multiplication and addition on a *seed* value. There are three classes of arguments: positive, zero, and negative. Each affects the seed value differently.

A negative argument can be used to establish a known seed value. No matter how many times you enter PRINT RND(−1), RND(−20), or RND(−1E5), the results are always the same. This can be used with positive arguments to produce a predictable (and hence nonrandom) sequence, which may be useful while you are debugging the program. Otherwise, you should avoid negative numbers in RND, unless you want a specific series of numbers to appear.

If the value of the argument is zero, the current value of the CIA chip's time-of-day (TOD) clock is used as a seed, which produces generally unpredictable numbers. But the random numbers generated fall into a certain regular pattern, which makes this option undesirable. The following program illustrates:

```
10 SCNCLR
20 R = INT(RND(0)*1000): POKE 1024 + R, 1: GOTO 20
```

A pattern of diagonal lines gradually fills the screen. If you change RND(0) to RND(1) in line 20, the pattern is distributed more evenly, indicating a wider variety of random numbers.

With positive arguments, the value in parentheses has no effect, so RND(1) does exactly the same thing as RND(50). In both cases, the previous RND value becomes the seed for the next. Thus, positive arguments always produce the same series of pseudo-random numbers (the numbers only appear to be random because the series is very long). When you first turn on the 128, the first seed is always the same, so powering on and then typing PRINT RND(1) will always return the same number. The solution is to randomize the seed, with either RND(0) or RND(−TI), at the beginning of the program and then use RND(1) thereafter. The following example simulates the rolling of dice.

```
10 R=RND(−TI/101)
20 FOR J = 1 TO 6: D = RND(1): PRINT D, INT(D*6+1): NEXT
```

The negative argument in line 10 puts a definite seed in the random number generator, but TI changes every 1/60 second, so the seed varies according to how long the computer has been turned on. Chapter 3 explains how to obtain random values in machine language programs.

RREG

Machine language function

Reads the values in the 8502 registers after a SYS to a machine language program.

Format: RREG ***variable1, variable2, variable3, variable4***
Modes: Immediate and program
Tokens: 254 9 ($FE $09)
Abbreviation: R SHIFT-R
Not available in BASIC 2.0

After exiting a machine language program with RTS, it is sometimes necessary to find the last values held in one of the registers (A, X, Y, or P). Unlike most other functions, RREG does not return a numeric value. Instead, it assigns a value directly to a variable. This program demonstrates how to read the various registers:

```
40 SYS xxx: REM INSERT ADDRESS OF ML PROGRAM
50 RREG Z1, Z2, Z3, Z4
60 PRINT "ACCUMULATOR ="; Z1
70 PRINT "X REGISTER ="; Z2
80 PRINT "Y REGISTER ="; Z3
90 PRINT "PROCESSOR STATUS="; Z4
```

RSPCOLOR

Graphics function
Reads the contents of the color registers used by sprites.

Format: RSPCOLOR(*register*)
Modes: Immediate and program
Tokens: 206 7 ($CE $07)
Abbreviation: RSP SHIFT-C
Not available in BASIC 2.0

The RSPCOLOR (Read SPrite COLOR) function provides information about the colors currently assigned to sprites. Multicolor sprites can contain up to four colors. The first color is *transparent,* the same as the current screen background color. The second color is unique to each sprite (one sprite could be blue, another could be yellow, and so on). The other two available colors are shared by all eight sprites.

Including an argument of 1 returns the first color, and 2 gives you the second common color. See also RSPPOS and RSPRITE.

RSPPOS

Graphics function (sprites)
Returns information about the current location and speed of the sprites.

Format: RSPPOS(*sprite number,attribute*)
Modes: Immediate and program
Tokens: 206 5 ($CE $05)
Abbreviation: R SHIFT-S
Not available in BASIC 2.0

RSPPOS (Read SPrite POSition) determines the X coordinate, Y coordinate, and speed of any of the 128's eight sprites. The sprite number must be in the range 1–8. If the attribute is 0, RSPPOS returns the X coordinate of the specified sprite. If it is 1, RSPPOS reads the sprite's Y coordinate. When the attribute is 2, RSSPOS returns the speed (0–15) of the selected sprite. See also RSPCOLOR and RSPRITE.

RSPRITE

Graphics function (sprites)
Returns information about sprites: enabled/disabled, color, priority, and expansion.

Format: RSPRITE*(sprite number,attribute)*
Modes: Immediate and program
Tokens: 206 6 ($CE $06)
Abbreviation: RSP SHIFT-R
Not available in BASIC 2.0

The first number in parentheses after RSPRITE selects a sprite number (1–8). The attribute controls which information is returned:

0 Enabled flag: 0 if turned off, 1 if turned on
1 Sprite color 1–16
2 Priority: 0 in front of screen objects, 1 behind
3 X expansion: 0 if not expanded, 1 if expanded (double width)
4 Y expansion: 0 if not expanded, 1 if expanded (double height)
5 Multicolored: 0 if single color, 1 if multicolor

RSPRITE is the complement of the SPRITE command, which sets the parameters shown above. See also RSPCOLOR and RSPPOS.

RUN

Program control
Runs a BASIC program.

Format: RUN *line number*
or
RUN *"program name"*, *Ddrive number,Udevice number*
Modes: Immediate and program
Token: 138 ($8A)
Abbreviation: R SHIFT-U
Enhanced BASIC 2.0 statement

RUN erases all variable definitions and causes the computer to execute the BASIC program currently in memory. If you add the name of a program, it first loads the program from disk and then RUNs it. RUN followed by a line number starts execution at that line. Typing RUN without any additional parameters makes the computer run the program beginning at its lowest line number. Here are some examples:

```
RUN : REM RUNS PROGRAM FROM LOWEST NUMBERED
  LINE
RUN 525 : REM RUNS PROGRAM STARTING AT LINE 525
RUN "PROGRAM NAME" : REM LOADS AND RUNS
  PROGRAM STORED ON DISK
```

RUN "PROGRAM NAME,"1,9 : REM SAME AS ABOVE FOR DRIVE 1 AND DEVICE 9

One new feature, not available in 64 mode, is that you may add a filename (and optional drive and device numbers) to load and run the specified program from disk with a single command. If you want to use a variable name, enclose it in parentheses: RUN (PN$). RUN is most commonly used in immediate mode, but may be employed in a program as well. Keep in mind that RUN normally clears all variables. However, you can DLOAD one program from within another without erasing variables (see DLOAD for more details).

RWINDOW

Screen function
Returns general information about the screen format.

Format: RWINDOW(*number*)
Modes: Immediate and program
Tokens: 206 9 ($CE $09)
Abbreviation: R SHIFT-W
Not available in BASIC 2.0

This function provides information about the current screen display window (see WINDOW). The statement PRINT RWINDOW(0) prints the number of columns in the current screen window, PRINT RWINDOW(1) shows the number of rows, and RWINDOW(2) indicates whether the active monitor has 40 or 80 columns.

```
10 PRINT "# OF SCREEN COLUMNS=";RWINDOW(0)
20 PRINT "# OF SCREEN ROWS =";RWINDOW(1)
30 PRINT RWINDOW(2);"COLUMN MONITOR IN USE"
```

SAVE

Input/output
Saves the program in memory to tape or disk.

Tape format: SAVE *"filename", device number, EOT flag*
Disk format: SAVE *"drive number:**filename**", **device number***
Modes: Immediate and program
Token: 148 ($94)
Abbreviation: S SHIFT-A
Same as BASIC 2.0

SAVE stores a BASIC program on tape or disk (but for owners

of disk drives, DSAVE is preferable). If you type SAVE without any other information, the computer assumes you want to save the BASIC program currently in memory on tape, and prints the prompt to press RECORD and PLAY (the program is saved without a filename). If you include a filename, but no device number, SAVE again defaults to tape. You should enclose any filename in quotes and use a comma to separate the filename from the device number (1 for tape, usually 8 for disk). Here are some typical uses of SAVE:

```
SAVE : REM SAVES PROGRAM TO TAPE WITHOUT FILENAME
SAVE "PROGRAM NAME":        REM SAVE "PROGRAM NAME" TO TAPE
SAVE "PROGRAM NAME",1:      REM SAME AS PRECEDING EXAMPLE
SAVE "PROGRAM NAME",1,1:    REM SAVE TO TAPE, WITH END OF TAPE
                                MARKER
SAVE "0:PROGRAM NAME",8:    REM SAVE "PROGRAM NAME" TO DISK
A$="1:PROGRAM NAME": SAVE A$,9: REM SAVE TO DRIVE 1, DEVICE 9
```

SCALE

Graphics command
Sets and resets the hi-res coordinate system to maximum values given.

Format: SCALE *flag,Xmax,Ymax*
Modes: Immediate and program
Token: 233 ($E9)
Abbreviation: SC SHIFT-A
Not available in BASIC 2.0

Since the hi-res graphics screen is 320 pixels wide and 200 deep, X coordinates range from 0–319 and Y coordinates are 0–199. In multicolor mode, the pixels are twice as wide, so the highest X coordinate allowed is 159.

SCALE allows you to vary the maximum size of the bitmap, to give you a wider variety of locations. It doesn't actually change the size of the screen and cannot provide better resolution. If the flag is zero, scaling is turned off. The highest permissible value for the *Xmax* and *Ymax* parameters is 32767; the lowest is one more than the normal maximum. If these numbers are omitted, the scale defaults to a size of 1024 horizontally (X values 0–1023) and 512 vertically (Y values 0–511).

The following program draws two boxes. Although both boxes are drawn with identical commands, the second is smaller because of the change in scale.

```
10 GRAPHIC 2,1
20 BOX 1,50,50,200,150
30 SCALE 1,1023,1023
40 BOX 1,50,50,200,150
```

SCNCLR

Graphics command
Clears the screen of any graphics mode.

Format: SCNCLR *graphics mode*
Modes: Immediate and program
Token: 232 ($E8)
Abbreviation: S SHIFT-C
Not available in BASIC 2.0

SCNCLR followed by a number from 0–5 clears the corresponding hi-res or text screen:

0 40-column text screen
1 hi-res graphics screen
2 hi-res/40-column split screen
3 multicolor graphics screen
4 multicolor/40-column split screen
5 80-column text screen

Used by itself, without a number, SCNCLR clears the screen currently displayed.

SCRATCH

Disk command
Deletes a file from disk.

Format: SCRATCH *"filename",Ddrive number,Udevice number*
Modes: Immediate and program
Token: 242 ($F2)
Abbreviation: SC SHIFT-R
Not available in BASIC 2.0

SCRATCH deletes a file from the disk directory. In direct mode, the computer asks "ARE YOU SURE?" If you do want to delete the file, type N and press RETURN. As with other disk commands, SCRATCH uses drive number 0 and device number 8 unless you specify otherwise. After performing this operation, the computer reports the drive status (1 FILES SCRATCHED means the operation was successful).

To delete two or more similarly named files, use one of

the wildcard symbols (? or *). For example, SCRATCH"BRAT*" deletes all files that begin with the letters BRAT. SCRATCH "??ALPINE" scratches all eight letter files ending with the letters ALPINE, including ABALPINE, SCALPINE, 01ALPINE, 02ALPINE, and so on. Be cautious when using wildcards with this command. SCRATCH"?" affects all files with one character names, while SCRATCH "*" (an exceedingly drastic command) deletes every file on the disk, just as if you had reformatted the disk without any ID.

To delete several files with dissimilar names, you can separate the names with commas. SCRATCH "AESOP,ROMULUS" would first scratch AESOP, and then scratch ROMULUS.

SCRATCH doesn't really erase programs from a disk, it simply marks the sectors previously used by a program as available for future use. It is sometimes possible to restore a scratched file with a special "unscratch" utility—the chances for recovery are especially good if you have not saved to the disk since the scratch.

Occasionally you will see a directory containing file types (PRG, SEQ, REL) followed by a less than (<) sign. These files have been *locked,* meaning you can't delete them with SCRATCH. Other directories may contain improperly closed files marked with an asterisk (*). *Do not use SCRATCH to get rid of such files* (you may damage other files on the disk). Use a COLLECT command instead.

SGN

Numeric function
Finds the sign (negative, zero, or positive) of a number or numeric variable.

Format: SGN(*number*)
Modes: Immediate and program
Token: 180 ($B4)
Abbreviation: S SHIFT-G
Same as BASIC 2.0

Returns a value which depends on the numeric sign of the argument. For negative arguments, the value returned is −1. For positive arguments, the result is 1. If the argument has a value of zero, the value returned is 0.

SGN is used where only the sign of the number—not its exact value—is important. The following simple number guessing game illustrates one possible use:

```
10 N=INT(RND(1)*10)+1
20 INPUT "GUESS MY NUMBER (1-10)";G
30 ON SGN(G-N)+2 GOTO 40,60,50
40 PRINT "TOO LOW":GOTO 20
50 PRINT "TOO HIGH":GOTO 20
60 PRINT "CORRECT"
```

SIN

Numeric function
Returns the sine of the angle specified.

Format: SIN(*angle*)
Modes: Immediate and program
Token: 191 ($BF)
Abbreviation: S SHIFT-I
Same as BASIC 2.0

The important thing to remember when using SIN is that the angle must be measured in radians, not in degrees. To convert from degrees to radians, divide by 180 then multiply by π.

```
10 PRINT "THE SINE OF 30 DEGREES IS"; SIN(30/180*π)
```

SLEEP

Program control
Causes the program to pause a specified number of seconds.

Format: SLEEP *seconds*
Modes: Immediate and program
Tokens: 254 11 ($FE $0B)
Abbreviation: S SHIFT-L
Not available in BASIC 2.0

SLEEP delays program execution for the specified number of seconds. For instance, SLEEP 10 creates a ten-second delay during which nothing else happens. This command is useful for giving the user some time to read a message, and in many other situations. The largest value SLEEP accepts is 65535, which at least in theory causes a delay of about 1,092 minutes (over 18 hours). Programmers who enjoy an occasional catnap could enter SLEEP 900 (15 minutes) followed by an endless DO-LOOP that prints CTRL-G (CHR$(7)).

```
10 PRINT "I'LL BE BACK IN A MINUTE"
20 SLEEP 60
30 PRINT "DID YOU MISS ME?"
```

In earlier versions of Commodore BASIC, it was common to create delays with "empty" loops such as (FOR DELAY=1 TO 2000:NEXT). Needless to say, SLEEP eliminates the need for such constructions.

SLOW

Timing control
Sets the internal clock to a speed of 1 MHz and enables the composite 40-column or hi-res screen.

Format: SLOW
Modes: Immediate and program
Tokens: 254 38 ($FE $26)
Abbreviation: None
Not available in BASIC 2.0

The 8502 chip which controls the 128 synchronizes its actions with a signal from a clock chip that can run at either one million or two million ticks per second. FAST sets the speed to 2 megahertz (MHz), SLOW reduces the speed to 1 MHz. While FAST mode is in effect, all calculations are performed twice as fast and disk access speeds up slightly. But FAST also turns off the 40-column screen. SLOW brings the screen back and slows down the system. The following program illustrates the difference between FAST and SLOW.

```
400 SLOW: TI$= "000000"
410 FORJ = 1 TO 1000: X = X + J: NEXT
420 PRINT TI/60;"SECONDS FOR 1000 SLOW ADDITIONS"
430 FAST: TI$= "000000"
440 FORJ = 1 TO 1000: X = X + J: NEXT
450 SLOW: PRINT TI/60;"SECONDS FOR 1000 FAST
    ADDITIONS"
```

SOUND

Sound and music
Plays a musical note or sound effect.

Format: SOUND *voice, frequency, duration,* *direction, minimum, step, waveform, pulse*
Modes: Immediate and program
Token: 218 ($DA)
Abbreviation: S SHIFT-O
Not available in BASIC 2.0

The SOUND statement requires at least three parameters: *voice* (1, 2, or 3), *frequency* (0–65535), and *duration* (0–32767 jiffies). A jiffy is 1/60 second.

The *direction* (0 = up, 1 = down, 2 = mixed) lets you make the sound sweep up, down, or oscillate (sweep up and down like a police siren). *Minimum* (0–65535) sets the bottom frequency for the sound sweep. *Step* (0–32767) sets the step value of the sweep. *Waveform* (0 = triangle, 1 = sawtooth, 2 = pulse, 3 = noise) lets you choose one of the 128's four waveforms. When the pulse waveform is selected, you must also specify the *pulsewidth* (0–4095), which controls the quality of the sound produced by the pulse wave. Here are a few examples:

```
10 VOL 12
20 SOUND 1,32767,60: SLEEP 5
30 SOUND 1,49152,440,1,30000,128,0: SLEEP 5
40 SOUND 1,32767,128,5000,1500,1,1024: SLEEP 5
50 SOUND 1,21983,256,1,10000,10000,3: SLEEP 5
60 VOL 0
```

Doubling the frequency raises the tone by an octave, so an octave above frequency 2000 would be 4000, and an octave above that is frequency 8000. Halfway between is a fifth, and halfway between a fifth and the base note is a third:

```
10 A1=2000: A2=4000: A3=8000: GOSUB 500: REM THREE
   OCTAVES
20 A1=2000: A2=3000: A3=4000: GOSUB 500: REM FIFTH
   INSIDE AN OCTAVE
30 A1=2000: A2=2500: A3=3000: GOSUB 500: REM MAJOR
   CHORD
499 END
500 SOUND1,A1,180:SLEEP1
510 SOUND2,A2,120:SLEEP1
500 SOUND3,A3,60:SLEEP3: RETURN
```

You can find more information about SOUND and related commands in chapter 3.

SPC

Cursor function
When printed, outputs a given number of spaces.

Format: **SPC(*number*)**
Modes: Immediate and program
Token: 166 ($A6)

Abbreviation: S SHIFT-P
Same as BASIC 2.0

This function can be used only with PRINT or PRINT#, where it causes the indicated number of spaces to be printed. The number must be in the range 0–255. If you're trying to align columns on a printer, SPC works correctly, but TAB does not. Note that the abbreviation S SHIFT-P includes the left parenthesis.

The following example uses SPC to center output on the 40-column screen:

```
10 INPUT TEXT$:RM=(40-LEN(TEXT$))/2-1
20 PRINT:PRINT SPC(RM);TEXT$: GOTO 10
```

SPRCOLOR

Graphics command
Sets the multicolor registers for sprites.

Format: SPRCOLOR *multicolor1, multicolor2*
Modes: Immediate and program
Tokens: 254 8 ($FE $08)
Abbreviation: SPR SHIFT-C
Not available in BASIC 2.0

By choosing multicolor mode for any given sprite (in a SPRITE statement) you can paint it in as many as four colors. One color must be transparent (the same as the screen background), another comes from the foreground color selected in SPRITE. The last two (multicolor 1 and multicolor 2) are shared by all eight sprites.

The values passed to SPRCOLOR should be in the range 1–16. To read the current multicolor values, see RSPCOLOR.

SPRDEF

Programming utility (sprites)
Turns on the sprite editor, which allows you to create sprite shapes.

Format: SPRDEF
Modes: Immediate and program
Tokens: 254 29 ($FE $1D)
Abbreviation: SPR SHIFT-D
Not available in BASIC 2.0

The 128 has a built-in sprite editor which you can activate

with the SPRDEF command (which works in immediate or program mode). In other words, SPRDEF is more like a mini-program built into BASIC, rather than a command proper. It lets you examine and change the definition of any of the eight sprites the 128 can display.

SPRDEF begins by asking which sprite you wish to edit. Press a number key from 1–8 to select the designated sprite (or press RETURN to exit to BASIC). The following keys are active:

- Cursor keys—move the cursor around the grid
- RETURN—moves the cursor to the start of the next line
- HOME—moves the cursor to the top left corner
- CLR—clears the grid and moves the cursor to the top left
- Color keys—change the foreground color
- 1–4—select the color source (1 turns off pixels, 2 turns them on); the 3 and 4 keys are active only in the multicolor mode
- A—turns the automatic cursor on/off
- C—copies a shape from one sprite to another
- M—turns the multicolor mode on/off
- X and Y—turn X and Y expansion on/off
- STOP—cancels changes
- SHIFT-RETURN—exits current sprite and prints prompt (press RETURN to exit to BASIC)

Chapter 2 contains additional information about SPRDEF and discusses sprite graphics in detail.

SPRITE

Graphics command (sprites)
Turns a sprite on/off and defines its characteristics.

Format: SPRITE *sprite number*, *on/off, color, priority, X expansion, Y expansion, multicolor*
Modes: Immediate and program
Token: 254 7 ($FE $07)
Abbreviation: S SHIFT-P
Not available in BASIC 2.0

SPRITE is primarily used to turn sprites on and off. If no other parameters are included, the sprite retains its previous shape and color. For example, SPRITE 3,1 turns on sprite 3 and SPRITE 3,0 turns it off.

Color is a number from 1–16. Sprites 1–8 default to colors 1–8. *Priority* (0–1) determines whether sprites will seem to pass in front of objects on the screen (priority 0) or behind them (priority 1). Turn on X *expansion* (double width) and Y *expansion* (double height) by placing a 1 in the appropriate position, turn off expansion by inserting a 0. The final parameter, *multicolor*, is also turned on with a 1, turned off with a 0.

Chapter 2 discusses sprites in detail.

SPRSAV

Graphics command (sprites)
Transfers sprite shapes between sprites and string variables.

Formats: SPRSAV ***sprite number, string$*** (saves sprite shape into a string)
SPRSAV ***string$,sprite number*** (saves string into a sprite shape)
SPRSAV ***sprite number1 ,sprite number2*** (copies the first sprite shape into the second)
Modes: Immediate and program
Token: 254 22 ($FE $16)
Abbreviation: SPR SHIFT-S
Not available in BASIC 2.0

Once you've defined a sprite shape with SPRDEF, you can transfer the shape into a string variable, or copy one sprite to another. The strings can be saved to a sequential file if you wish, or manipulated with MID$ and the other string functions. Saving several shapes to strings and switching back and forth is one way of animating sprite characters. You might define three or four shapes for a walking man: the first showing his knee moving forward, the second showing his foot in the air, the third showing his heel touching the ground in front, and so on. Sprite shapes saved in strings can also be used in a GSHAPE statement on the hi-res screen.

SQR

Numeric function
Returns the square root of the argument

Format: SQR(*number*)
Modes: Immediate or program
Token: 186 ($BA)
Abbreviation: S SHIFT-Q
Same as BASIC 2.0

SQR finds the square root of a number: the value that, when multiplied by itself, yields the original number.

10 X=1: A=1
20 DO UNTIL X>1000
30 PRINT A, X, SQR(X)
40 A=A+2: X=X+A: LOOP

The exponentiation function (↑) can substitute for SQR. X ↑ (1/2) is the same as SQR(X). And X ↑ (1/3) returns the cube root of X.

SSHAPE

Graphics statement
Stores a shape from the hi-res screen into a string variable, for use later as a type of rubber stamp.

Format: SSHAPE *string$, Xcoord1, Ycoord1,* *Xcoord2, Ycoord2*
Modes: Immediate and program
Token: 228 ($E4)
Abbreviation: S SHIFT-S
Not available in BASIC 2.0

If you create a shape you wish to copy to other sections of the hi-res screen, SSHAPE lets you save it in a string for later use by GSHAPE. For example, an American flag has 50 stars, so you could draw a single star, save the shape into a string, then use GSHAPE to put the other 49 stars into position. SSHAPE and GSHAPE can also be used for slow animation.

The coordinates defined by (*Xcoord1, Ycoord1*) and (*Xcoord2, Ycoord2*) set the opposite corners of the screen area which SSHAPE saves in a string. If you omit the second set of coordinates, the pixel cursor becomes the other corner. Since strings are limited to a maximum length of 255 characters, some shapes may have to be SSHAPED into several variables.

ST

Reserved variable
Returns the status of input/output operations.

Format: ST
Modes: Immediate and program
Token: None
Abbreviation: None
Same as BASIC 2.0

ST is a reserved variable used to check for serial input/output (I/O) errors. When ST is 0, no errors have occurred. If ST is not 0, its value indicates the type of error that occurred. The meanings of the various values of ST depend on the operation that was attempted (serial bus, tape, RS-232).

Value	Tape	RS-232	Serial
1		parity error	no response on write
2		framing error	no response on input
4	short block	buffer full	
8	long block	buffer empty	
16	read error	CTS missing	VERIFY error
32	bad checksum		
64	end of file	DSR missing	EOI (end of file)
−128	end of tape	break received	device not present

The following lines read a string from tape and test the success of the operation:

```
100 OPEN 1
110 INPUT #1,A$
120 IF ST<>0 THEN PRINT "TAPE READ FAILED"
```

This program reads through and prints the contents of a disk file called ADDRESSES. The DO-LOOP continues until bit 6 of the ST variable is set, indicating the end of the file has been reached.

```
500 DOPEN#1,"ADDRESSES"
510 DO UNTIL 64 AND ST
520 INPUT#1,A$:PRINT A$: LOOP
530 DCLOSE#1
```

STASH

Memory control

Copies a block of memory into expansion memory.

Format: **STASH** ***bytes, address1, bank, address2***
Modes: Immediate and program
Tokens: 254 31 ($FE $1F)
Abbreviation: S SHIFT-T
Not available in BASIC 2.0

STASH is followed by the number of bytes you wish to copy, the starting address (in the current bank), the bank you are copying to, and the starting address where the copy will be made. This allows you to treat expansion memory as a RAM disk for swapping programs or data in and out. See Chapter 7 for more information on the memory expansion module.

STEP

Program flow (loops)
Defines the increment in FOR-NEXT loops.

Format: FOR *index* = *start* TO *finish* *STEP increment*
Modes: Immediate and program
Token: 169 ($A9)
Abbreviation: ST SHIFT-E
Same as BASIC 2.0

Without a specified STEP size, a FOR-NEXT loop counts forward by ones. By including STEP, you can make a loop increment by fractions, by negative numbers, or both.

```
10 FOR J = 10 TO 1 STEP -1
20 PRINT J: SLEEP 1: NEXT
30 PRINT "BLASTOFF!"
```

Fractional STEP sizes sometimes lead to small rounding errors if the fraction cannot be expressed as sums of powers of two. Fractions such as 0.5, 0.25, 0.125, and so on will work fine, as will sums of binary fractions like 0.75 or 0.375. But other fractions (like .1) cannot be translated into exact powers of two and may eventually lead to slight errors of accuracy. See also FOR.

STOP

Program control
Halts program execution and puts computer into immediate mode.

Format: STOP
Modes: Immediate and program
Token: 144 ($90)
Abbreviation: S SHIFT-T
Same as BASIC 2.0

STOP makes a program stop running, just as if you had pressed the RUN/STOP key. The computer prints BREAK IN LINE (line number) and returns to immediate mode. STOP is usually put in a program for debugging purposes, since after it executes, you may PRINT the value of any suspect variables, then use CONT to restart the program at the next statement after STOP. Though this command does not generate an error in immediate mode, it has no practical use outside of a program.

The TRAP statement is sensitive to STOP and can divert the program to an error-handling routine when either the RUN/STOP key is pressed or a STOP is encountered.

STR$

Conversion function
Takes a number or numeric variable and converts it to a string.

Format: STR$(*number*)
Modes: Immediate and program
Token: 196 ($C4)
Abbreviation: ST SHIFT-R (includes the $)
Same as BASIC 2.0

String functions like MID$, LEFT$, RIGHT$, and INSTR require strings or string variables as input (and CHAR won't work on numbers, it prints only strings). STR$ allows you to change a number into a series of characters. For example, A=15: B$=STR$(A) defines a numeric variable A which holds the *number* 15. B$, a string variable, holds the characters "   15" (note the leading space, which holds a minus sign if the number is negative, a space if it's positive). To convert the other way, from strings into numbers, use the VAL function.

Here the contents of a memory location are printed from top to bottom instead of from left to right.

```
100 P$= STR$ (PEEK (65280))
110 FOR A=2 TO LEN(P$)
120 PRINT SPC (10);MID$ (P$,A,1)
130 NEXT
```

SWAP

Memory control
Exchanges the contents of two sections of memory.

Format: SWAP *bytes, address1, bank, address2*
Modes: Immediate and program
Tokens: 254 35 ($FE 23)
Abbreviation: S SHIFT-W
Not available in BASIC 2.0

SWAP allows you to trade the current contents of a chunk of memory with a section of expansion memory. The first two parameters are the number of bytes to be traded and the address where they start in the current bank. The next two are the bank number of expansion memory and the starting address there. See Chapter 7 for more information on the memory expansion module.

SYS

Machine language
Begins execution of a machine language program in current bank.

Format: SYS ***address****, accumulator, X, Y, status*
Modes: Immediate and program
Token: 157 ($9E)
Abbreviation: None
Enhanced BASIC 2.0 statement

SYS causes the computer to begin executing a machine language program in the current bank starting at the specified memory location in the range 0–65535.

SYS allows you to mix a machine language program with a BASIC program. Before using SYS, you must have a machine language program in memory. This can be done via BLOAD, a series of POKE statements, or the built-in machine language monitor. The machine language program must end either with an RTS instruction (to return to the BASIC program) or a BRK (to return to the ML monitor). After RTS, execution of the BASIC program resumes with the statement following the SYS statement.

One thing you must be careful about is the current bank. If you load a program into bank 0, then switch to bank 1 for some particular task, the SYS will jump to the address in bank 1 (not to the program in bank 0). It makes good sense to precede SYS with a BANK statement.

There are many built-in ROM routines you can access with SYS. These do not have to be loaded into memory, they're already there when you turn on the machine. For example, BANK 15: SYS 65341 performs a warm start (as if the computer had been turned off and then on).

If you follow the SYS address with numbers or numeric variables, these values are placed into specific 8502 registers—the accumulator, the X register, the Y register, and the processor status (which contains the status flags). Upon returning to BASIC, you can read the last values in these registers with the RREG function.

Chapter 6 contains additional information about machine language programming.

TAB

Screen control
Moves the cursor to the specified position on the screen.

Format: TAB(*number*)
Modes: Immediate and program
Token: 163 ($A3)
Abbreviation: T SHIFT-A
Same as BASIC 2.0

This function can be used as part of a PRINT statement. TAB makes the cursor move to the position (on the current line) given in parentheses. If the cursor is already past that screen position, it moves to the next line down. The number must be in the range 0–255. TAB has a couple of quirks. It doesn't work correctly in PRINT# statements, so it's not reliable for aligning columns on a printer (use the SPC command instead). Also, the abbreviation T SHIFT-A, like almost no other function, includes the opening parenthesis. Don't add a left parenthesis if you use the abbreviated form of TAB.

```
10 A$="COMMODORE": PRINT"{CLR}{RVS}";
20 FOR I=1 TO 80: PRINT" ";: NEXT: PRINT:
30 FOR I=1 TO 9: PRINT"{3 UP}"; TAB(5+I); MID$(A$,I,1);
   TAB(34-I); MID$(A$,10-I,1): NEXT
```

TAN

Numeric function
Finds the tangent of an angle measured in radians.

Format: TAN(*angle*)
Modes: Immediate or program
Token: 192 ($C0)
Abbreviation: None
Same as BASIC 2.0

TAN(A) returns the tangent of angle A, measured in radians. The tangent of an angle is equal to the slope of the line that defines the angle (in a right triangle, the Y axis divided by the X axis). The tangent of 90 or 270 degrees is undefined: PRINT TAN (π/2) results in a DIVISION BY ZERO error.

TEMPO

Sound and music
TEMPO X controls the time elapsed between tones during a PLAY statement.

Format: TEMPO ***time***
Modes: Immediate and program
Token: 254 5 ($FE $05)
Abbreviation: T SHIFT-E
Not available in BASIC 2.0

When TEMPO is performed, the computer assigns a value (from 0 to 255) to a time counter for notes that are PLAYed. It works like a delay loop: the larger the number, the slower the music plays. If TEMPO is not used, the speed defaults to 8. Changing the tempo can affect how much of the sound envelope you hear. At a very fast pace, the notes may be cut off in the middle of the attack or decay. Slow speeds allow you to hear the entire shape of the note.

```
10 TEMPO 32
20 PLAY "O4 E D C D E E E"
30 TEMPO 8
40 PLAY "D D E D C"
50 TEMPO 64
60 PLAY "C D E F G A B O5 C"
```

THEN

Program control (decisions)
Marks a statement that is executed only if a certain condition is true.

Format: IF ***condition*** **THEN** ***action*** *ELSE action*
Modes: Immediate and program
Token: 167 ($A7)
Abbreviation: T SHIFT-H
Same as BASIC 2.0

THEN is an integral part of the IF-THEN construction. The first part tests IF a condition is true and performs the statements after THEN accordingly. If the condition is false, everything after the THEN (up until an ELSE or the beginning of the next line) is ignored.

A block of statements can be defined with BEGIN and BEND. If the IF condition is true, every statement within the BEGIN/BEND block is executed. But if it's false, the program proceeds to the next command on the other side of the BEND. An ELSE (even another BEGIN/BEND block), to be executed if the condition was false, can follow the BEND.

Inside IF-THENs, true statements are evaluated to a value of −1, false statements are 0. Any nonzero value also counts as true, so it is possible to have a line like IF Z THEN PRINT "METEOR SHOWER." In this context, the variable Z is considered false if it equals zero, and true if it holds any other value. It's the same as IF Z<>0 THEN PRINT "METEOR SHOWER."

TI

Programming utility (reserved variable)
Returns a number which, when divided by 60, gives the number of seconds since the internal clock was reset.

Format: TI
Modes: Immediate and program
Token: None
Abbreviation: None
Same as BASIC 2.0

Both the 64 and the 128 have a realtime clock which can be read with the TI or the TI$ variables. The value returned by TI is the number of jiffies that have elapsed since the computer was turned on or reset. There are 60 jiffies in a second. You can never assign a value to TI (TI=15 won't work), you can only read its value. To reset the clock, enter TI$="000000".

```
100 T=TI
110 PRINT T;"JIFFIES =";T/60;"SECONDS"
120 GOTO 100
```

TI$

Programming utility
A reserved variable that returns the time in hours/minutes/seconds format.

Format: TI$
Modes: Immediate and program
Token: None
Abbreviation: None
Same as BASIC 2.0

The TI$ variable holds the value of the 128's built-in realtime clock, also known as the jiffy clock, interpreted as a six-digit string indicating hours, minutes, and seconds. When you first turn on your 128, the clock is set to "000000" and updates every second.

```
100 T$=TI$
110 PRINT MID$(T$,1,2);"HRS, ";
120 PRINT MID$(T$,3,2);"MINS, ";
130 PRINT MID$(T$,5,2);"SECS "
```

The clock can be set to any value by assigning the value, as a six-digit string, to TI$. This operation affects both TI$ and TI. The following test shows that you gain some speed by defining variables before using them in calculations.

```
100 TI$ = "000000":REM RESETS CLOCK TO 0
110 A=5: B=6.1
120 FOR J=1 TO 1000: C=A*B: NEXT: PRINT TI$ ": TIME FOR
    MULTIPLYING VARIABLES"
130 TI$ = "000000"
140 FOR J=1 TO 1000: C=5*6.1: NEXT: PRINT TI$ ": TIME FOR
    MULTIPLYING ACTUAL NUMBERS"
```

TO

Connector
Separates two parameters within FOR-NEXT loops, DRAW statements, or disk commands (BACKUP, COPY, RENAME).

Format: See related commands.
Modes: Immediate or program
Token: 164 ($A4)
Abbreviation: None
Same as BASIC 2.0

TO doesn't work as a stand-alone command. It is found in statements such as FOR J=1 TO 5, DRAW 1,160,100 TO 10,10, and so on. For examples and explanations, see FOR, DRAW, and the various disk commands.

TRAP

Program control
Prevents errors from stopping a program by allowing them to be handled in a special routine.

Formats: TRAP *line number* (turns on error-trapping)
TRAP (turns it off)
Modes: Immediate and program

Token: 215 ($D7)
Abbreviation: T SHIFT-R
Not available in BASIC 2.0

TRAP gives you full control over what happens when an error occurs. Earlier versions of Commodore BASIC stop the program completely and display a message describing the error.

TRAP followed by a line number tells the computer to GOTO that line if an error should happen. A TRAP statement without any line number turns error-trapping off. It is helpful to use the reserved variables EL, ER, and ERR$(ER):

```
10 TRAP 1000
20 J=J+1:PRINT J;
30 GOTO 20
40 END
1000 PRINT "ERROR OCCURRED IN LINE:";EL
1010 PRINT "SYSTEM ERROR NUMBER IS:";ER
1020 PRINT "USUAL ERROR MESSAGE IS:";ERR$(ER)
1030 SLEEP 5
1040 RESUME 20
```

Try pressing RUN/STOP while this program is running. The system variables EL, ER and the function ERR$ contain information about what caused the error. A RESUME statement is used to return from the error-trapping routine. Note that since RESUME may take any line number, it is not necessary to return to the program line with the error. TRAP is not affected by certain INPUT errors (EXTRA IGNORED and REDO FROM START), nor can it handle errors within the trapping routine itself.

TRON

Programming utility
Turns on trace mode, which prints the current line being executed.

Format: TRON
Modes: Immediate and program
Token: 208 ($D8)
Abbreviation: TR SHIFT-O
Not available in BASIC 2.0

The 128's program trace facility is a great aid in debugging BASIC programs. Each time BASIC begins executing a new program line while tracing is active, it prints the number of the new line on the screen. Since TRON and its counterpart, TROFF, can be included in the program being debugged, you can limit tracing to only those parts of the program that you need to test.

```
100 TRON:REM THIS LINE NUMBER ISN'T DISPLAYED
110 REM THIS ONE IS
120 TROFF:REM SO IS THIS ONE
130 REM BUT THIS ONE ISN'T
```

Note that the line number of line 120 will be displayed, since the trace function prints the number when the line is entered. Only after the line number is printed will the TROFF command turn the tracing off.

To prevent the lines from being printed all over the screen, you can define a text window with ESC-T and ESC-B (or use the WINDOW command). The traced line numbers will print only within the window you created.

TROFF

Programming utility
Turns off trace mode.

Format: TROFF
Modes: Immediate and program
Token: 217 ($D9)
Abbreviation: TRO SHIFT-F
Not available in BASIC 2.0

The TROFF command turns the 128's BASIC program tracing off. See TRON above for examples.

UNTIL

Program flow (loops)
Defines the exit condition for a DO-LOOP. The loop will not end UNTIL the expression is true.

Formats: DO UNTIL *condition* ... LOOP
DO ... LOOP UNTIL *condition*
Modes: Immediate and program
Token: 252 ($FC)
Abbreviation: U SHIFT-N
Not available in BASIC 2.0

A DO-LOOP defines a block of lines that are executed repeatedly. DO and LOOP by themselves define an endless loop, one that never stops. But UNTIL allows you to provide an exit condition. The loop continues UNTIL the condition is true.

The following program inputs names into an array. The loop continues for the specified number of names or until the user enters an asterisk.

```
300 INPUT "HOW MANY NAMES ON THE LIST?";NN
310 DIM LN$(NN): S=0
320 DO UNTIL (S=NN) OR (D$="*")
330 S=S+1: PRINT "NAME #";S;"(* TO QUIT)"
340 INPUT D$: LN$(S)=D$: LOOP
350 PRINT "THE NAMES YOU ENTERED ARE:"
360 FOR J=1 TO S: PRINT J;LN$(J): NEXT
```

See DO for more examples.

USING

General output

Sets the format for strings or numbers within a PRINT or PRINT#.

Format: PRINT USING ***"format";expression***
Modes: Immediate and program
Token: 251 ($FB)
Abbreviation: US SHIFT-I
Not available in BASIC 2.0

Commodore BASIC truncates unnecessary zeros to the right of the decimal point. PRINT 32.00, for example, would print 32 without the decimal point or trailing zeros. PRINT USING "##.##";32 forces the zeros to be printed. Formats can also include commas, plus or minus signs, and so on (see PUDEF). Strings can be centered or printed flush right. For more information, see PRINT and PRINT USING.

USR

Machine language function

Executes a user-defined machine language function.

Format: USR(number)
Modes: Immediate and program
Token: 183 ($B7)
Abbreviation: U SHIFT-S
Same as BASIC 2.0

USR allows you to define your own custom function, for use

in BASIC programs, if you know how to program in machine language. Before calling USR, you must have a machine language program in memory. You can use the built-in monitor to write it, BLOAD a previously written program, or POKE the numbers into memory. Then use POKE to store the starting address of the machine language program into locations 4633–4634 in low-byte/high-byte format.

When USR is executed, the number in parentheses is stored in floating point accumulator 1. Control is then passed to the machine language program which processes the number and stores the result back into floating point accumulator 1. The machine language program must end with an RTS instruction to return to BASIC. The number returned by the USR function is the number in floating point accumulator 1. Execution will then resume with the statement following the USR statement. Chapter 6 provides more information about how USR works.

VAL

Conversion function
Returns the numeric value of a string.

Format: VAL(*string$*)
Modes: Immediate and program
Token: 197 ($C5)
Abbreviation: V SHIFT-A
Same as BASIC 2.0

The VAL function finds the numeric value of the string expression within its parentheses. If the string starts with a nonnumeric character, VAL returns 0. If a user's input to a program is a command containing both character and numeric fields, VAL can be used to convert the numeric fields to numeric values. Here's a program to demonstrate how to read a user's response to a menu using VAL.

```
100 PRINT "WHICH ITEM?(1-9)"
110 DO:GET A$: N=VAL(A$): LOOP WHILE N=0
120 PRINT "YOU CHOSE NUMBER";N
```

VERIFY

General input/output
Compares the program in memory to a program on tape or disk.

Tape Format: VERIFY *"program name",1*
Disk Format: VERIFY *"drive number:**program name"**,**device number***
Modes: Immediate and program
Token: 149 ($95)
Abbreviation: V SHIFT-E
Same as BASIC 2.0

VERIFY compares the program currently in memory with a program stored on disk or tape, signaling an error if they are not the same. The format for VERIFY is the same as for SAVE. The program name and device number are optional for tape users; VERIFY by itself checks the next program it finds on tape. Disk users must specify a filename and device number (however, DVERIFY does not require a device number). If you own a dual drive, the drive number can be 0 or 1. Disk device numbers usually range from 8–15. Here are some examples of VERIFY:

```
VERIFY :REM VERIFY NEXT PROGRAM ON TAPE
VERIFY "PROGRAM NAME" :REM FIND AND VERIFY
  "PROGRAM NAME" ON TAPE
VERIFY "0:PROGRAM NAME",8 :REM VERIFY "PROGRAM
  NAME" ON DISK
A$="1:PROGRAM NAME" :VERIFY A$,9 :REM VERIFY FROM
  DRIVE 1, DEVICE 9
```

If the two programs are identical, the computer prints OK; if they are not, the computer displays a VERIFY ERROR message. Note that graphic memory allocations affect the internal linkage of BASIC programs; thus, VERIFY may signal a false error if you have just allocated or deallocated a graphics memory area. See also DVERIFY.

VOL

Sound and music
Sets the volume of the 128's musical voices.

Format: VOL *n*
Modes: Immediate and program
Token: 219 ($DB)
Abbreviation: V SHIFT-O
Not available in BASIC 2.0

VOL sets the volume for the SOUND command, in the range 0–15. If you don't turn up the sound chip's volume with VOL,

SOUND probably won't produce any sound at all. This command is not needed for PLAY, which sets volume with a separate control character (U).

WAIT

Machine language
Pauses a BASIC program until a specified memory location contains a certain value.

Format: WAIT *memory location, test bits,* *off bits*
Modes: Immediate and program
Token: 146 ($92)
Abbreviation: W SHIFT-A
Same as BASIC 2.0

WAIT is rarely used except for advanced input/output operations. It takes the value in the designated memory location, ANDs it with the second parameter, and exclusive ORs it with the third parameter. It waits as long as the result is zero: As soon as the result is not zero, execution resumes with the statement following the WAIT statement.

The third parameter is optional. The on bits in the second parameter select the bits that will be tested. If no third parameter is specified, the WAIT statement waits until the corresponding bits in the memory location are on. The third parameter allows you to test for an off condition. If the corresponding bits in the third parameter are on, the WAIT statement waits until the bits in the memory location are off.

WHILE

Program flow (loops)
Defines a condition for continuing a DO-LOOP. The loop runs as long as (WHILE) an expression remains true.

Formats: DO WHILE *condition* .... LOOP
DO .... LOOP WHILE *condition*
Modes: Immediate and program
Token: 253 ($FD)
Abbreviation: W SHIFT-H
Not available in BASIC 2.0

The condition following WHILE is generally a comparison of two things, DO WHILE A<B for example would make the loop continue as long as variable A is less than variable B. DO WHILE means the condition is tested *before* the loop begins: If

the statement is false, the program skips over the loop. If you place WHILE at the end of a loop, the commands within the loop are executed at least once.

The following program fragment might be valuable in a simple football simulation. The variable DN, in this case, would be 1, 2, 3, 4 (for first, second, third, or fourth down):

```
550 DO WHILE DN<4
560 GOSUB 1000 :REM SUBROUTINE TO RUN A PLAY, 1ST
    DOWN RESETS DN TO 1
570 LOOP
580 GOSUB 1200 :REM PUNT OR KICK FIELD GOAL ON 4TH
    DOWN
```

See the entry under DO for more details.

WIDTH

Graphics command
Sets the width, in pixels, of any point plotted on the hi-res screen.

Format: WIDTH ***n***
Modes: Immediate and program
Token: 254 28 ($FE $1C)
Abbreviation: WI SHIFT-D
Not available in BASIC 2.0

WIDTH controls the thickness of lines on the hi-res screen. The value of *n* can be either 1 or 2. Width 2 provides more clarity and prevents artifacting (which distorts the color of points on a hi-res screen). Width 1 is more suitable for precise, delicate work. The following program draws two circles, one in single width, and the other in double width. The circle drawn in double width suffers less color loss than the circle drawn in single width.

```
10 GRAPHIC 2,1
20 WIDTH 1
30 CIRCLE 1,100,100,40,40
40 WIDTH 2
50 CIRCLE 1,200,100,40,40
```

WINDOW

Screen control
Defines a screen window.

Format: WINDOW ***X top, Y top, X bottom, Y bottom,*** *clear*

Modes: Immediate and program
Tokens: 254 26 ($FE $1A)
Abbreviation: W SHIFT-I
Not available in BASIC 2.0

The WINDOW command lets you define any portion of the current display screen as the window in which text activity occurs. WINDOW is followed by at least four values to define the four corners of the window in terms of screen columns (X coordinates) and rows (Y coordinates). The first two values set the column and row location of the window's top left corner. The next two values set column and row locations for the window's bottom right corner.

```
10 WINDOW 5,6,20,21
```

This example redefines the text window within the current screen, locating its upper-left corner at column 5, row 6 and putting its lower-right corner at column 20, row 21. After this statement executes, the cursor moves to its new home position, and all subsequent printing is confined to the window. You may include an optional fifth value, *clear,* to clear the screen. WINDOW 5,6,20,21,1 creates a window and clears the screen. WINDOW 5,6,20,21,0 does not clear the screen. Be sure to use values that make sense within your current screen configuration: For instance, column 70 does not exist on a 40-column screen and causes an ILLEGAL QUANTITY error.

ESC-T and ESC-B can also be used to create a window. ESC-T sets the top left corner; ESC-B sets the bottom right corner.

XOR

Logical operator
Exclusive OR two numbers in the range 0–65535.

Format: XOR(*number1,number2*)
Modes: Immediate and program
Tokens: 206 8 ($CE $08)
Abbreviation: X SHIFT-O
Not available in BASIC 2.0

XOR performs an exclusive OR operation on the individual bits of each number. Exclusive OR is similar to OR except that when both bits are on, the resulting bit is off.

```
10 FOR A=1 TO 3:FOR B=1 TO 3
20 PRINT A, B, XOR (-(A=2),-(B=3)), XOR(A,B)
30 NEXT B, A
```

Chapter 2

Graphics

Graphics

Hardly a day goes by when you're not confronted with some evidence of computer graphics in television, motion pictures, or the printed media. What does the term *graphics* include? Anything from intricate high-resolution drawings to rapidly moving sprites, custom-defined characters, or ordinary text on a 40-column or 80-column screen. Some graphics modes even let you combine two different kinds of graphics on a split screen.

Regardless of which mode you choose, graphics can add greatly to any program's appeal. Of course, sprites and similar graphic features are handy for arcade-style games, but they're effective in more utilitarian applications as well. Instead of displaying a lackluster table of numbers, why not create a bar graph or a pie chart? After all, most programs communicate to you chiefly through the display screen. The more effectively you can use that screen, the greater the impact your programs will have.

This chapter doesn't require that you learn a lot of jargon. However, there's one term we'll be using frequently. As you may know, the picture on your TV or monitor screen is actually composed of thousands of separate dots called *pixels* (short for "picture elements"). By lighting up certain dots and leaving others dark, the monitor creates everything you see on the screen. When we use the term *pixel,* just remember that it amounts to a single screen dot—like an atom, the pixel is the basic unit from which everything else is formed.

Graphics Modes

The Commodore 128 offers six different graphics modes as shown in Table 2-1.

Table 2-1. Graphics Modes

Number	Description
0	40-column text
1	Standard hi-res
2	Split-screen standard hi-res
3	Multicolor hi-res
4	Split-screen multicolor hi-res
5	80-column text

Let's look briefly at what each different mode offers. Later in the chapter, we'll examine each mode in detail.

40-column text. Text mode is what you see when you turn the computer on. In this mode you can use ordinary text and graphic characters, custom-defined characters, and sprite graphics. Characters can be displayed in any of 16 different colors.

Standard high resolution. This mode offers the highest resolution, 320 × 200 pixels. Each pixel can be one of two colors, and several drawing commands (DRAW, BOX, CIRCLE, and so on) are available for creating complex designs. Sprites are available in this mode, and you may also print characters on the hi-res screen with the CHAR command.

Split-screen high resolution. This mode is the same as standard hi-res, but provides an adjustable text window at the bottom of the screen. The text window is handy for typing commands in immediate mode, or for any application that requires text in addition to a hi-res display.

Multicolor high resolution. Multicolor hi-res mode offers four color choices (twice as many as standard hi-res), but has only half the resolution: 160 × 200 pixels. Each pixel can be one of three foreground colors (or the background color). Sprites and hi-res drawing commands are available, but any character printed with CHAR looks distorted.

Split-screen multicolor high resolution. This mode provides an adjustable text window at the bottom of a multicolor hi-res screen. The sample game program in this chapter uses this mode to permit colorful hi-res shapes at the top of the screen and display information like the total at the bottom.

80-column text. Since 80-column text mode provides twice as much onscreen text space as 40-column mode, it is ideal for word processing, spreadsheets, CP/M, and similar applications. Though it provides certain features available nowhere else, this mode is limited largely to text. Sprites and hi-res drawing commands are not available.

Finding Your Way Around the Screen

Graphics programming requires that you pay close attention to where you are on the screen. In text modes, this is relatively simple: Just think of what the blinking cursor does when you're typing in direct mode. Each time you type (or PRINT) another character, the cursor automatically moves one space to the right. Since you're dealing with characters, text mode commands affect the screen space in character-sized chunks. And certain characters (like certain keys in direct mode) move the cursor or perform another control function rather than put a character on the screen. For instance, PRINT CHR$(147) clears the screen just as if you had pressed SHIFT–CLR/HOME.

In high-resolution modes, your control is much finer. Each pixel on the screen can be turned on (lit) or off (dark), and you can locate any pixel by specifying its vertical and horizontal coordinates. Just as in elementary geometry, the vertical coordinate is called Y, and the horizontal coordinate is called X. Coordinate 0,0 stands for the upper-left dot on any high-resolution screen. The Y coordinate becomes larger as you move downward on the screen, and the X coordinate increases as you move to the right. For instance, coordinate 15,10 is below and to the right of coordinate 0,0.

Up to this point, we've described the *absolute* method of fixing coordinates on a high-resolution screen. To take a simple example, the command GRAPHIC 1:DRAW 1,15,10 lights up a pixel with an X coordinate of 15 and a Y coordinate of 10. Absolute coordinates refer to fixed locations. That is, each pair of X,Y coordinates refers to one and only one pixel on the screen.

Some hi-res commands also accept *relative* coordinates. Using relative coordinates is much like using PRINT commands on the text screen. The place where you end up depends on where you started. Just as the blinking cursor shows your text screen position in direct mode, so the *pixel cursor* identifies your location for relative hi-res commands. The difference between the two is that the pixel cursor doesn't move automatically after completing the most recent hi-res command. For instance, if you draw a line from coordinate 15,10 to coordinate 100,100, the pixel cursor remains at 100,100. It doesn't go anywhere after it lights up the last pixel.

How can you move the pixel cursor in relative terms? Put a plus (+) or minus (−) sign before a coordinate. A plus sign *adds* the specified coordinate value to the present position, and a minus sign *subtracts* from the present location. For instance, the following statements plot a point at coordinate 45,60.

GRAPHIC 1:LOCATE 50,50:DRAW 1,−5,+10

(At least, that's the way it's supposed to work. At the time of this writing—admittedly in the 128's infancy—BASIC 7.0 stops with an ILLEGAL QUANTITY error when you attempt to use negative relative coordinates. Commodore has assured us that this problem will be remedied as soon as practically possible.)

You can also specify relative coordinates by supplying a distance and angle. This method of locating a point always uses a semicolon. The angle must be in the range 0–65535 degrees, and is relative to the present position of the pixel cursor. An angle of 0 degrees points straight to the top of the screen. A semicolon indicates this method of plotting. This line plots a point at 75,50:

GRAPHIC 1:LOCATE 50,50:DRAW 1,25;90

There's another easy way to make the 128 use relative coordinates: Simply omit the coordinates from a hi-res graphics command. For instance, the following command draws a circle whose center is located at the most recent pixel position:

GRAPHIC 1:CIRCLE 1,,,10,10

Look at the places where one comma follows another. If you put values between the commas, the 128 would use them as X and Y coordinates. When those coordinates are absent, the computer (which "remembers" the last pixel position) begins drawing where it previously left off.

Hi-Res Graphics

We'll resist the temptation to tell you how many words a picture is worth. Instead, type in and save Program 2-1, then run it to see what the 128 can do with hi-res graphics. As short as it is, the program demonstrates a full library of hi-res graphics commands. The screen will blank for about ten seconds. After that, you can press any key to see how lucky you are.

Program 2-1. Slot Machine

```
5 TRAP 500
100 FAST:GRAPHIC 4,1:COLOR 1,3:COLOR 0,2:COLOR 2,6
    :COLOR 3,8:T=200
110 CIRCLE 1,20,20,7,10:CIRCLE 1,23,16,1,2:WIDTH 2
    :CIRCLE 2,15,15,7,10,0,60:PAINT 1,20,20,1:WIDT
    H 1:SSHAPE A$(1),9,5,30,30
120 CIRCLE 3,35,35,9,15,75,210:CIRCLE 3,29,29,14,2
    0,100,175:PAINT 3,42,43,1:SSHAPE A$(2),26,31,5
    0,53
130 CIRCLE 2,60,60,7,10:PAINT 2,65,65,1:SSHAPE A$(
    3),49,49,67,70
```

```
140 BOX 1,80,84,92,98,,1:CHAR 1,20,11,"BAR",1:SSHA
    PE A$(4),76,80,92,98
150 CIRCLE 3,110,110,7,10:PAINT 3,115,115,1:SSHAPE
     A$(5),99,99,117,120:SCNCLR
160 BOX 1,40,20,120,150:FOR A=50 TO 95 STEP 21:BOX
     1,A,40,A+19,70:NEXT:BOX 1,125,20,126,85,,1:BO
    X 1,120,82,125,85,,1:PAINT 1,41,21:SLOW
170 WINDOW 0,20,39,24,1:PRINT SPC(15);"{3}TOTAL $"
    T:PRINT:PRINT SPC(14);"{BLU}{RVS}PRESS ANY KEY
    {OFF}";:GETKEY A$:T=T-5
180 FOR A=20 TO 60:DRAW 0,125,A TO 126,A:NEXT:BOX
    {SPACE}1,125,20,126,85,,1
190 FOR A=1 TO 3:GSHAPE A$(S(A)),27+21.5*A,43,4:NE
    XT:FORA=1TO5:Q(S(A))=0:NEXT
200 S$="":FOR A=1 TO 3:FOR B=1 TO RND(1)*1400+700:
    NEXT:S(A)=5*RND(1)+1:Q(S(A))=Q(S(A))+1:GSHAPE
    {SPACE}A$(S(A)),27+21.5*A,43,4:NEXT
210 IF Q(4)=3 THEN T=T+200:ELSE IF Q(4)=2 OR Q(1)=
    3 THEN T=T+50:ELSE IF Q(1)=2 OR Q(2)=3 THEN T=
    T+25:ELSE IF Q(3)=3 THEN T=T+20
220 GOTO 170
500 SLOW:GRAPHIC 0:PRINT"{CLR}";ERR$(ER),EL:END
```

Anatomy of a Program

While abstract explanations are helpful, most people find a concrete example easier to follow. Let's walk through the sample program step by step, examining each hi-res command in detail. In addition to learning about hi res, you'll see how other BASIC commands like FAST and SLOW can help maximize the impact of any graphics program.

If you've ever used a Commodore 64 or VIC-20, the first thing you'll notice about Program 2-1 is that it doesn't use a single POKE or PEEK statement. Programming hi-res graphics on the 128 does not require that you memorize a multitude of numbers or keep a library of reference books at your side.

Take a look at the TRAP and FAST statements in lines 5 and 100. Because hi-res commands take you out of the normal text screen, it's always a good idea to start hi-res programs with a TRAP command directed to a statement that puts you back in graphics mode 0. If an error occurs, TRAP kicks you back into a screen that lets you see what went wrong. The FAST statement makes the computer run roughly twice as fast as normal (it also blanks the screen in 40-column mode). Since a hi-res shape contains many pixels, it can take a long time to draw. It's more dramatic—and much quicker—to draw the shape while the screen is blank and then suddenly present the finished image. The SLOW command resets the computer to normal speed and brings the screen back.

Every graphics program should begin by putting the computer in the right graphics mode with a GRAPHIC command. Here's the general format for such commands:

GRAPHIC ***mode number***, *clear, split line*

The first number after the keyword chooses the graphics mode. Supply a number from 0 to 5 as illustrated in Table 2-1. The second value (clear) indicates whether you want to clear the graphic screen upon entry. If this value is 1, the screen is cleared; if it's 0, the computer displays the selected screen without altering its contents (useful when you've already drawn something on the screen and want to bring it into view). The third parameter (split line) is needed only if you choose a split-screen graphics mode. This value can range from 0 to 25; it selects the screen line where the text window should begin. If you omit this parameter when a split screen is enabled, the text window begins at line 20 (five lines above the bottom of the screen).

The GRAPHIC command takes another form as well:

GRAPHIC CLR

Whenever you enter a hi-res mode with GRAPHIC, the 128 allocates (reserves) a section of memory from 7168 to 16383 ($1C00–$3FFF) to hold information for the hi-res screen. Among other things, this steals 9K of the memory space available for your BASIC program—and the hi-res allocation remains in effect even after you return to text mode. GRAPHIC CLR lets you recover the lost memory space after you've finished using the graphics screen. (The details of this process are quite interesting. Since BASIC programs normally start at 7168, the computer actually moves the entire program 9K bytes higher in memory when you enter a graphics mode, and moves it back down to the normal location when you deallocate the graphics screen with GRAPHIC CLR.)

After the graphics mode is set, line 100 sets the game colors with a COLOR command. Here's the general format for COLOR:

COLOR *source, color*

The first value (source) can be a number from 0 to 6. The value you supply here determines which part of the screen

COLOR affects. Here are the choices for the source parameter:

Source	Controls
0	40-column background color
1	Foreground color of the hi-res screen
2	Foreground color 1 of the multicolor hi-res screen
3	Foreground color 2 of the multicolor hi-res screen
4	40-column border color
5	Text color in 40 and 80 columns
6	80-column background color

The second parameter picks a color number, which can range from 1 to 16:

Code	Color	Code	Color
1	Black	9	Orange
2	White	10	Brown
3	Red	11	Light red
4	Cyan	12	Dark gray
5	Purple	13	Medium gray
6	Green	14	Light green
7	Blue	15	Light blue
8	Yellow	16	Light gray

Our program sets the foreground color to red (COLOR 1,3), the background color to white (COLOR 0,2), and the multicolor values to green and yellow (COLOR 2,6:COLOR 3,8). The variable T in line 100 keeps track of the total amount of money.

Now it's time to draw the shapes on the screen. To see the shapes being drawn, remove the FAST command from line 100 and rerun the program. The cherry is the first shape to be drawn, using a CIRCLE command (line 110). Here are the parameters for CIRCLE:

CIRCLE *color source, X, Y, X radius, Y radius, starting angle, ending angle, rotation, degree increment*

The first parameter (color source) tells CIRCLE which of the previously defined color sources you want to use. That may sound confusing at first, but remember that you've already defined four possible color sources in line 100. Since you want to draw the cherry in red, and color source 1 is already set to red, the correct source value is 1. In other words, you choose a color indirectly, by referring to the color source defined in a previous command.

The next two parameters (X and Y) set the horizontal and

vertical coordinates for the center of the circle, defining its screen location. These coordinates can be either absolute or relative, as explained earlier.

After locating the center, you must supply X-radius and Y-radius values to define the circle's shape. That might seem unnecessary—after all, a circle is always perfectly round—but CIRCLE can draw many different shapes in addition to circles. By changing the radius parameters, you can draw any sort of *ellipse* (regular, rounded shape). A circle is just an ellipse whose height and width happen to be equal. (To obtain a circle that looks perfectly round, you must make the Y radius somewhat larger than the X radius. This is necessary because multicolor screen pixels are slightly wider than they are tall.)

The next two parameters, starting angle and ending angle, are used to draw an arc (a segment of an ellipse). These values must be specified in degrees. For instance, if you choose a starting angle of 0 degrees (straight up) and an ending angle of 90 degrees (directly to the right), CIRCLE draws a quarter-circle arc. This program forms the banana shape by drawing two arcs (line 120).

The rotation parameter lets you rotate the whole circle; the angle of rotation is also specified in degrees.

Strictly speaking, CIRCLE does not draw circles, but regular polygons (multisided shapes). The final parameter (degree increment) determines how many sides your polygon has. To calculate the number of sides, divide 360 (the number of degrees in a circle) by the degree increment. The default value for this parameter is 2, meaning that most of the "circles" drawn by the 128 are actually 180-sided polygons. To draw a more precise circle, specify a degree increment of 1. By supplying a larger degree increment value, you can make CIRCLE draw regular, nonrounded shapes. The following command draws an equilateral triangle:

CIRCLE 1,80,100,20,20,,,,120

Now it's time to draw the cherry's stem. Since we want the stem to curve naturally, we'll draw a small, circular arc with CIRCLE, and thicken the arc with WIDTH. The WIDTH command can take a value of 1 or 2. Most hi-res drawing is done in width 1, which gives you thin, precise lines, one pixel in width. When you select width 2, every line is two pixels wide.

Painting

Now you have nothing but the outline of a cherry. Let's fill it with color to make it look solid. The PAINT command can fill any closed figure on the hi-res screen. Its general form is

PAINT *color source*, X, Y, *mode*

Again, the color source value picks a painting color by referring to a previously defined source. The X and Y coordinates tell PAINT where to start painting, and may be defined in relative or absolute terms. Since PAINT begins at the designated pixel and paints outward in all directions, you must take care to specify a point inside the shape you want to fill. It's also important that the shape's outline be closed: If there's a hole anywhere in the outline, the paint "spills" out of the shape and may cover the entire screen.

It's also important to select the right painting mode. If the mode is 0, PAINT doesn't recognize a boundary unless it is drawn in the *same* color selected by the source in the PAINT command. If the mode is 1, painting stops when you hit *any* nonbackground color.

The mode isn't critical when we're filling the fruit shapes in this program. In each case we simply want to fill a simple shape with the same color it was drawn in. For instance, either mode 0 or mode 1 would fill the red-outlined cherry with red. In mode 0, the paint stops when it hits red pixels; in mode 1, the paint stops when it hits pixels of a nonbackground color (which happen to be red). However, mode 0 wouldn't work if we had outlined the cherry in black. PAINT would recognize only red pixels as boundaries, and would fill outward until it hit a red-outlined shape or covered the entire screen. Incidentally, you'll notice a small area inside the cherry that doesn't get filled. We inserted a tiny circle there to give a reflection effect.

Saving Hi-Res Shapes

Since the cherry shape is one of the slot machine symbols, it needs to be displayed many times in the course of each game. While you could do that by repeating the CIRCLE and PAINT commands described above, that would be slow and inefficient. It's much faster to save the entire shape with an SSHAPE command and use GSHAPE to redraw it quickly whenever it's needed. SSHAPE, as the name implies, lets you save a shape drawn on a hi-res screen:

SSHAPE ***shape string, X1, Y1,*** *X2, Y2*

The *shape string* parameter must be a string variable of some kind. The following values define two sets of X,Y coordinates, which define opposite corners of the screen area you want to save. For instance, the first two coordinates (X1,Y1) might define the upper-left corner of the saved area, and the second two (X2,Y2) might define the bottom right. Since only two corners can be defined, the saved area is always a rectangle.

Though you can store a hi-res shape in any sort of string variable, it's often most convenient to put it into an array, which can be referenced by a simple element number. No matter which type of variable you use, it's impossible to save a shape that contains more than 255 bytes (the maximum size of a string in Commodore BASIC). If an SSHAPE command stops with an ILLEGAL QUANTITY error, it's probably because you tried to save too big a shape. Line 110 of the program stores the cherry shape in the array element A$(1) with the following statement:

SSHAPE A$(1),9,5,30,30

Printing Text in Hi-Res

The very same techniques are used to draw and store the banana, lime, and lemon shapes, leaving only one more shape: the BAR symbol. Since it contains the characters B-A-R, this figure looks difficult at first. On the Commodore 64, you'd need a fairly elaborate (and slow) routine to draw each character pixel by pixel. The 128 can do the job with a single CHAR command. Here is the basic syntax for CHAR:

CHAR ***color source, column, row, string,*** *reverse*

CHAR works the same way in every graphics mode, even 40-column text mode. The column and row values locate the character on the screen and must be in the ranges 0–79 and 0–24, respectively. Choosing a column value greater than 39 in 40-column mode makes the printing "wrap around" to the next line below. The string may be either a literal ("HELLO") or a variable (A$). CHAR prints normal characters when the *reverse* parameter is 0, or reverse-video characters when it is 1.

Because the computer interprets character definitions

somewhat differently in multicolor modes, these modes distort characters to a certain extent. In this case the distortion makes the characters a bit wider than normal. If you select a split-screen graphics mode (mode 2 or 4), CHAR can print on the hi-res portion of the screen, but not inside the text window. Use ordinary PRINT commands to put text in the window.

Text Windows

Line 170 of the program defines a text window to simplify the positioning of text within the text window. Here is the syntax for WINDOW:

WINDOW ***X1, Y1, X2, Y2, clear***

To define a text window within a hi-res screen, you must specify two sets of X,Y coordinates. The first set (X1,Y1) defines the upper-left corner of the window, and the second set (X2,Y2) defines the bottom-right corner. Once the window is defined, all printing to the screen occurs within that space. If the *clear* parameter is 1, the computer clears the window when you first set it up; when it is 0, the previous contents of the window area are not disturbed.

Drawing Boxes

If we stopped at this point, the BAR symbol would consist of the letters B-A-R. Let's improve its appearance by drawing boxes above and below the characters. The 128 has a special command (BOX) designed specifically for the job. Here is its general format:

BOX ***color source, X1, Y1,*** *X2, Y2, angle, fill*

Again, the color source refers to a previously defined color, and the two sets of coordinates (X1,Y1 and X2,Y2) define the opposite corners of the area you want to box in. As in most other cases, you can define the corners with either relative or absolute coordinates. The *angle* parameter serves the same function here as it does for CIRCLE. An angle of 0 specifies no rotation. Larger values rotate the shape and can be used to make diamond shapes, and so forth.

The final parameter (fill) lets you choose whether to paint in the box while it's being drawn. When this value is 0, the box is drawn in outline; when it's 1, the box is filled automatically. Though you could fill the box with a separate PAINT command, it's much faster to do it this way.

Now that you've seen how to create all the game shapes, you may want to watch them being drawn. Remove the FAST command from line 100 and rerun the program. As you'll see, once each shape has been drawn and saved, we clear the screen with SCNCLR and draw the slot machine itself with BOX and PAINT commands. Then a SLOW command sets the computer to normal speed, making the screen visible again.

Because this program blanks the screen for only a few seconds, no warning message is given. However, if you need to blank the screen for a longer period, it's a good idea to warn the user in advance (if you don't, he or she may assume the system has crashed). You could also blink the border colors periodically, to signal that something is going on.

DRAW

The next part of the program actually puts the slot machine to work. After printing a money total on the screen, we prompt the player to press any key (line 170). As soon as you press a key, the slot machine's handle appears to be pulled down. This is done in line 180, which draws a series of shorter and shorter handles. DRAW takes the following general form:

DRAW *color source, X1, Y1* **TO** *X2, Y2*

If you have followed the previous explanations, these parameters should all be familiar. The first set of coordinates (X1,Y1) defines the point where you want to start drawing, and the second set (X2,Y2) defines the point where you want to stop. Translated into plain English, this simple form of DRAW means "draw a line in the specified color from point (X1,Y1) to point (X2,Y2)." Either relative or absolute coordinates are acceptable (see explanation above). If you supply additional coordinates (and another TO), you can draw several lines with a single DRAW command. These statements draw a fat bow-tie shape on the screen. Notice how each new line begins where the last line ended.

GRAPHIC 4:SCNCLR:COLOR 2,4:WIDTH 2:DRAW 2,10,50 TO 150,150 TO 150,50 TO 10,150 TO 10,50

To create the illusion of a moving handle, the program simply draws over portions of the handle with the background color. This is an easy way to erase a specific shape on the hires screen.

Placing Shapes with GSHAPE

Once you have stored a shape in a variable with SSHAPE, GSHAPE lets you display it at any time:

GSHAPE ***string***, *X, Y, mode*

The *string* parameter identifies which shape you want to display, and should match the variable name you used when saving the shape. The X,Y coordinates locate the shape on the screen and may be either relative or absolute. The final parameter (mode) can be any value from 0 to 4; it determines what happens when GSHAPE draws a new shape where another shape already exists.

The various GSHAPE modes are much easier to illustrate than they are to explain. Say that you already have a circular shape onscreen and wish to draw a triangular shape in the same screen area. Figure 2-1 shows you the shapes we'll use.

Figure 2-1. Circle and Triangle

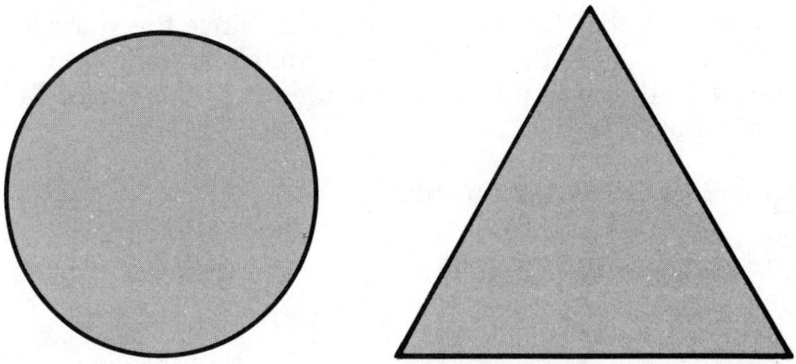

Mode 0 is the easiest mode to understand. Assume that both shapes contain exactly the same number of bytes, and that we'll use GSHAPE to place the triangle precisely over the circle. Figure 2-2 is the mode 0 result:

Figure 2-2. GSHAPE Mode 0

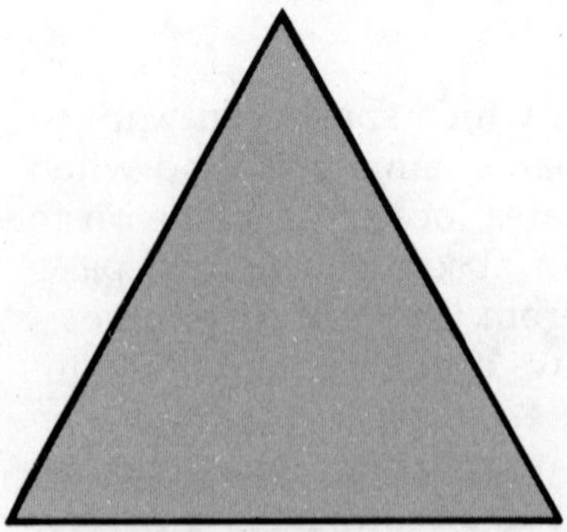

In mode 0, every part of the new shape replaces whatever previously occupied the same space. Keep in mind that every shape definition is rectangular and includes unlit pixels as well as the lit ones that form the shape itself. Since the triangle definition is exactly the same size as the circle definition, displaying it with mode 0 erases all evidence of the circle. Take a look at Figure 2-3.

Figure 2-3. GSHAPE Mode 1

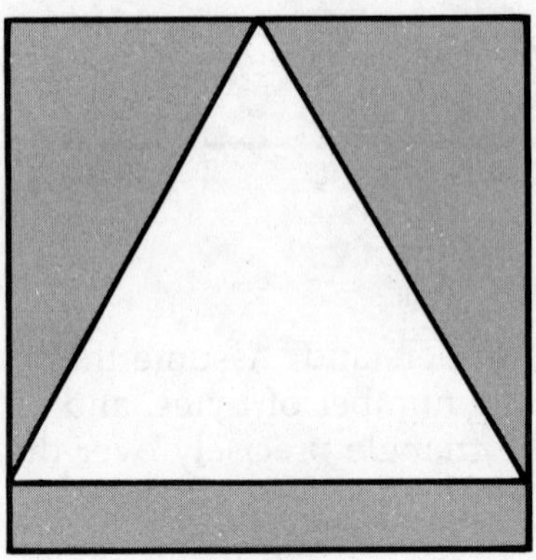

In mode 1, all underlying data is erased, just as in mode 0, but the new shape is inverted: Every lit pixel is turned off, and every unlit pixel is turned on. Mode 2 (Figure 2-4) performs a logical OR operation between existing data and the new shape.

Figure 2-4. GSHAPE Mode 2 with OR

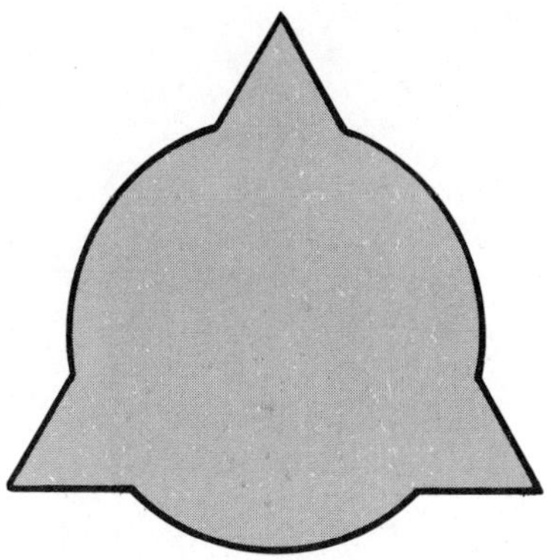

Since an OR operation preserves every lit pixel in both shapes, the final result is a combination of both shapes. Mode 3 (Figure 2-5) performs a logical AND operation between the two shapes.

Figure 2-5. GSHAPE Mode 3 with AND

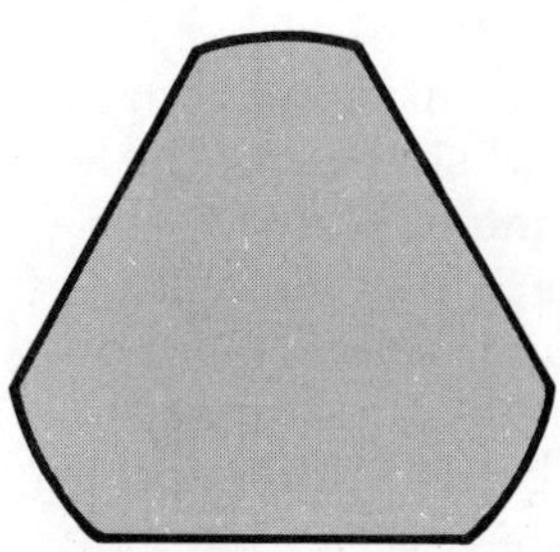

Mode 3 preserves only those pixels which were lit up in *both* shapes. Every pixel that appears only in one shape is turned off. Mode 4 (Figure 2-6) performs an *exclusive OR* (XOR) operation on the shapes.

Figure 2-6. GSHAPE Mode 4 with XOR

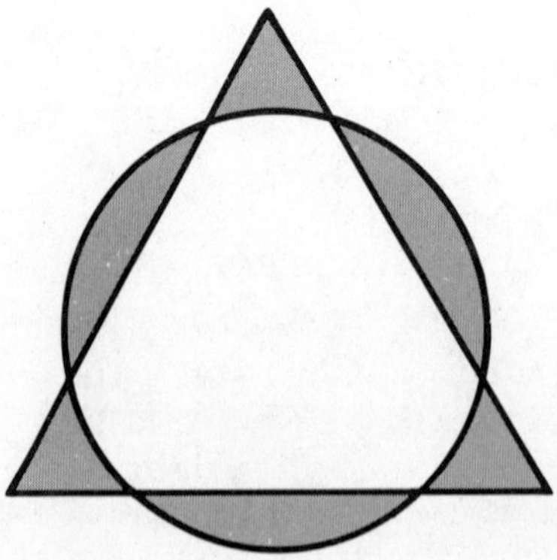

This mode is simply the inverse of mode 3. Every pixel that's common to both shapes (the middle, intersecting area) is turned off, leaving only those pixels that are unique to one shape or the other. Mode 4 is useful for animation, since it allows you to erase an existing shape by drawing it a second time in the same place. This is the method used in the sample game. Once the shapes have been drawn on the screen (line 200), the remainder of the program calculates the amount won or lost (line 210) and repeats the whole process (line 220).

Sprite Graphics

As you saw in the preceding sections, hi-res drawing commands let you create complex, multicolored shapes on the computer's screen. But they're not really intended for high-speed animation. A *sprite* is a graphic shape that you can move quickly to any part of the screen (and beyond) without it having to be constantly erased and redrawn in every new position. Sprites can move in front of or behind other sprites or graphic shapes, can be expanded vertically or horizontally, may contain as many as four different colors, and even have built-in collision detection. In short, sprites are an arcade-game programmer's dream come true. For former Commodore 64 owners, the best news of all is that BASIC 7.0 includes several powerful new commands for programming sprites.

Creating a Sprite

Before you can use a sprite, you must define its shape. This can be done the hard way—by plotting every pixel of the sprite on graph paper, converting the shape to numeric form, and storing it in DATA statements—or the easy way—by using the 128's built-in sprite editor. Let's design a sprite with the editor, which is more like a mini-program within BASIC than an actual command. Type SPRDEF and press RETURN (this does not disturb any BASIC program in memory).

The first thing the sprite editor asks you to do is to enter a number from 1 to 8. This tells the editor which sprite you want to work on. Choose sprite 1. You'll see a large grid on the left side of the screen, the current sprite on the right. Since you haven't defined the sprite's shape yet, it will probably look like garbage (disorganized memory). Clear the sprite box by pressing SHIFT–CLR/HOME.

Now move the cursor to the upper-left corner of the drawing grid, using the cursor keys just as you would in BASIC. The number keys 1 and 2 let you draw and erase any point within the grid (keys 1–4 are used for multicolor sprites). Go ahead and draw a shape in the grid, using the number keys and cursor keys. Notice that the sprite takes shape at the right of the screen while you are drawing. Though you don't have to produce an elaborate sprite (this is just for practice), draw something that's big enough to be clearly visible. You'll be using this sprite in some of the examples that follow.

Table 2-2 (on the following page) lists all the commands that the built-in sprite editor accepts. The best way to become familiar with each command is to experiment while drawing your sprites. Note that to select different colors, you must hold down either CONTROL or the Commodore key and press one of the number keys from 1 to 8.

Once your shape is finished, press SHIFT–RETURN. The 128 displays the same sprite number prompt as when you began. While you could enter a new sprite number to define another sprite, let's return to BASIC; press RETURN. Before you can do anything useful with a sprite, you must call the sprite into existence with a SPRITE command:

SPRITE ***number***, *on/off, color, priority, X-expand, Y-expand, multicolor*

Table 2-2. SPRDEF Commands

Key	Action
Cursor keys	Move cursor inside drawing grid
HOME	Moves cursor to upper-left corner of drawing grid
RETURN	Moves cursor to beginning of next row
X	Turns horizontal expansion on or off
Y	Turns vertical expansion on or off
M	Turns multicolor mode on or off
C	Copies shape data from one sprite to another
RUN/STOP	Cancels sprite definition and asks for new sprite number
CONTROL + 1–8	Select sprite foreground color (colors 1–8)
Commodore + 1–8	Select sprite foreground color (colors 9–16)
A	Turns cursor advance mode on or off

As you've probably gathered from using the sprite editor, the 128's eight sprites each have a number from 1 to 8. The first value in a SPRITE command tells the computer which sprite you want to work with. Since you just drew a shape for sprite 1, this parameter should be 1. The second value (on/off) turns the sprite on (1) or off (0). Turn the sprite on by supplying a 1. The priority controls whether the sprite moves in front of other objects on the screen (1) or behind them (0). The last three parameters, X-expand, Y-expand, and multicolor, also take a 1 or 0. In each case a 1 turns the special feature on, and a 0 turns it off. Turn the sprite on by typing the following statement:

SPRITE 1,1,2,1

This command turns on sprite 1, colors it white, and gives it priority over (makes it move in front of) other graphics on the screen. What happens when two sprites move into the same screen space? The 128 always gives lower numbered sprites higher priority than higher numbered ones. This built-in pecking order means that sprite 1 moves in front of all other sprites, sprite 8 moves behind all others, and so on.

Move the cursor to the area near the sprite, then type some letters on the screen. As you'll see, the sprite remains in front of any character data within its own space. Enter the following line to double the sprite in size:

SPRITE 1,1,2,1,1,1

Locating a Sprite

You've nearly reached the best part—moving the sprite around the screen. Before you can set a sprite in motion, however, you must learn how to put it on the screen. As it happens, the 128 uses a single command to do both jobs. MOVSPR can either place a sprite in a certain screen position or move it around. Here is the form it takes:

MOVSPR ***sprite number***, *X, Y*

If you supply MOVSPR with three numbers separated by commas, the 128 assumes you want to position a sprite somewhere on the screen. The X and Y values define horizontal and vertical locations, respectively, using a coordinate scheme similar to hi-res drawing commands. X coordinates can range from 0 to 511, and Y coordinates can range from 0 to 255, with coordinate 0,0 being the extreme upper-left position.

Figure 2-7 illustrates the sprite coordinate system in relation to the screen. Note that sprites are not limited to the normal boundaries of the screen. They can move far off the screen, disappearing behind any border. This is important to consider when dealing with collisions, since collisions can take place even when sprites are not visible.

Figure 2-7. Sprite Coordinates

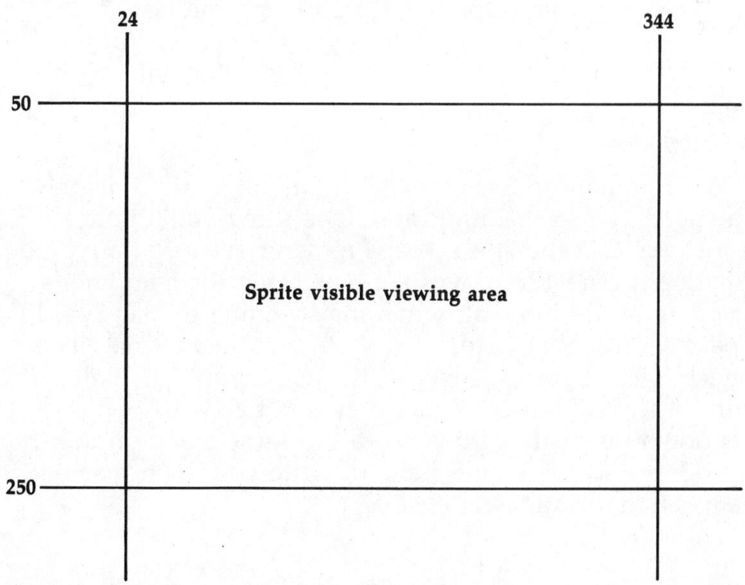

If you supply MOVSPR with two coordinate numbers (without any prefixes), the computer uses them as *absolute* coordinates—that is, it puts the sprite at the exact location you specify. Like hi-res drawing commands, MOVSPR also accepts *relative* coordinates. If you add a plus sign (+) in front of a coordinate value, the 128 computes the new position by adding that number to the most recent coordinate used for that sprite. If you supply a minus sign (−) in the same position, the 128 subtracts that value from the most recent coordinate. For instance, the command MOVSPR 1, +10, +10 puts sprite 1 at a location ten pixels below and ten pixels to the right of its last screen position.

Sprite Movement

To set a sprite in motion, use the following form of MOVSPR:

MOVSPR ***sprite number, angle#speed***

The first number, of course, tells the 128 which sprite to move. Notice the number sign (#) between the *angle* and *speed* values. This informs the computer that you want to move the sprite rather than place it at a fixed location. The angle can range from 0 to 360, and is expressed in degrees, just as in ordinary geometry. An angle of 0 degrees points straight up, 90 degrees points directly to the right, and so on. The speed value can range from 0 to 15, with 15 being the fastest. If you've been following the previous examples, your sprite should still be on the screen. Type in this statement to set it in motion:

MOVSPR 1,45#7

This command moves sprite 1 at an angle of 45 degrees and a speed of 7 (a medium rate). One thing you'll notice right away is that the sprite keeps moving even if you type on the keyboard. The 128 moves sprites during the computer's *hardware interrupt* interval, when it's scanning the keyboard and performing other automatic, system-related tasks. Since the mechanics of sprite movement consume only a small amount of the computer's time, they don't slow BASIC programs down noticeably. To achieve the same effect on the Commodore 64, you would have to write your own machine language sprite routines.

Saving and Recalling Sprite Shapes

Sprite shape definitions are very easy to save. To save a sprite shape to disk, type the following line and press RETURN:

BSAVE "SPRITE",B0,P3584,P4096

The BSAVE command lets you save any section of the computer's memory, using the last numbers specified (3584 and 4096, in this case) as starting and ending addresses. BSAVE is explained more fully in Chapter 1. How did we know which memory area to save? SPRDEF always puts sprite shapes in the memory area from 3584 to 4095 ($0E00–$0FFF), which is reserved exclusively for this purpose. Whether you're saving one sprite shape or eight, you use the same starting and ending addresses.

Since all sprite definitions are erased from memory when you turn the computer off, each sprite program must begin by putting the sprite shapes it needs into memory. If you have already BSAVEd the shapes to disk as shown above, you can use a BLOAD command to bring them back into memory. This program begins by loading a shape file named SPRITESHAPE from disk:

```
10 BLOAD "SPRITESHAPE"
20 REM THE REST OF THE PROGRAM STARTS HERE
```

You can also create sprite shapes in a program by drawing them on a hi-res screen, then saving the shape in a string variable with SSHAPE (see "Saving Hi-Res Shapes" above). The SPRSAV command can transfer sprite shape data from the string into the section of memory reserved for sprite definition or vice versa. Use this form of SPRSAV to move the definition from a string variable into the correct memory area:

SPRSAV ***string,sprite number***

Note that the string variable name comes first, followed by a number to identify the sprite. To perform the same operation in reverse, switch the two parameters around:

SPRSAV ***sprite number,string***

This command moves the shape data from its normal memory location into the string variable you designate. When saving a sprite shape with SSHAPE, you must take care to save a memory area of exactly the same width as a sprite: 24

pixels. If you use any other size, the sprite shape becomes distorted. This program shows how to use SSHAPE and SPRSAV with sprite shapes:

```
10 GRAPHIC 2,1
20 FOR B=1 TO 4:C=B*11:SCNCLR
30 CIRCLE 1,50,50,9,9
40 FOR A=C TO 360+C STEP 45:DRAW 1,50,50 TO 9;A
50 NEXT A:SSHAPE A$,38,40,61,64:SPRSAV A$,B
60 SPRITE B,1,8
70 NEXT B:SCNCLR:FOR A=0 TO 300
80 FOR B=1 TO 4:IF B<>SP THEN SPRITE B,0:ELSE SPRITE B,1
90 NEXT:SP=SP+1+3*(SP=4)
100 MOVSPR SP,A,100:NEXT
```

Multicolor Sprites

Multicolor sprites behave exactly like normal sprites, but may have as many as four different colors. To switch to multicolor mode in SPRDEF, simply press the M key. In this mode the sprite cursor is twice as wide as normal. In order to get four colors, the computer has to use two pixels for each dot in the sprite shape. The BASIC command to set the colors of a multicolor sprite is SPRCOLOR. Its syntax is

SPRCOLOR *multicolor1, multicolor2*

The first SPRCOLOR parameter selects the color for the parts of the sprite drawn with color 2 in SPRDEF; the second selects a color for the parts corresponding to color 4. As you've certainly noticed, that doesn't add up to four colors. How are the other two selected? One of them is defined as part of the SPRITE command that calls up the sprite. Remember, the third number in a SPRITE command selects a sprite's foreground color. The fourth "color" may or may not qualify as a color in your book. It's simply the screen background color; any part of the sprite defined with this color is transparent.

Because a multicolor sprite has limited horizontal resolution, it inevitably looks coarser than a regular sprite. If you find the coarseness unacceptable, there's a simple way to emulate the multicolor effect without sacrificing any detail. Overlay two or more single-color sprites—put them in the same screen space—and move them together as if they were one. By matching up solid areas of the underlying sprite with "holes," or transparent areas of the sprite in front, you can achieve quite satisfying multicolor effects.

One side advantage of the arrangement is that it can improve collision detection. Ordinarily, when a sprite collides with some other object, there's no simple way to tell what *part* of it has suffered the collision. When a complex shape is made of two or more sprites, you can at least identify which of those sprites was involved in the collision.

When Sprites Collide

Though it's fun to make sprites zoom about the screen, you'll often want something more than mere motion. Virtually every arcade-style game demands that you detect collisions. Of course, the term *collision* merely connotes contact, not necessarily of a violent nature. In a juggling clown game, for instance, you might need to detect collisions between the clown's hands and the objects being juggled. BASIC 7.0 has two commands which detect sprite collisions. The first, aptly named COLLISION, takes this form:

COLLISION ***type**, line number*

The first parameter (type) calls for a value from 1 to 3 and tells the computer to watch out for one of the following types of collisions:

Number	Type
1	Sprite/sprite collision
2	Sprite/character collision
3	Light pen

When the computer detects a collision of the designated type, it finishes performing the current BASIC command, then does a GOSUB to the line number specified as the second number in the COLLISION statement. (Since the RENUMBER command does not change COLLISION line number references, you should note them down before renumbering the program.) To disable the collision routine, execute the same COLLISION statement, but omit the line number from the end. It's a good idea to begin every sprite program with this kind of COLLISION statement to make sure the computer won't be confused by the results of previous sprite collisions.

COLLISION has some built-in drawbacks which are due chiefly to the slowness of BASIC itself. Since the computer always finishes performing the current command before doing a

GOSUB to your collision routine, considerable time may elapse between the time you detect a collision and the time you can actually respond to it. By the time the computer gets to your collision routine, the sprite may have moved far beyond the place where the collision occurred.

Paradoxically, this problem is exacerbated by the interrupt-driven feature of MOVSPR that makes sprites so convenient to use. Once you set a sprite in motion with MOVSPR, it is the system which keeps it going, not your BASIC program. And the computer can move the sprite many times faster than you can respond in BASIC.

Say that you want two balls to move randomly about the screen, rebounding whenever they collide. You write a collision routine that reverses the direction of a sprite whenever it contacts another sprite. But because of the inevitable delay, the balls will probably travel well into one another before your routine can reverse them. As soon as you reverse direction, the program immediately detects another collision, which occurs because the balls are still overlapping. Another reversal follows, then another collision, and so on. In the worst case the balls end up stuck together, unable to free themselves.

The following section introduces some machine language techniques you can use to alleviate this problem. If you're not interested in using machine language, you'll just have to accept the limitations of COLLISION.

The 128 has a second collision statement that tells you which sprites have collided:

BUMP (*type*)

The BUMP function tells you which sprites have been involved in a collision. If you put a 1 inside the parentheses, BUMP indicates which sprites have hit other sprites; if you replace the 1 with a 2, BUMP tells you which sprites have collided with character data. This statement generates a number in the range 0–255. Each bit of the BUMP number represents the collision status of a single sprite, as outlined in Table 2-3.

By referring to Table 2-3, you can tell which sprites have collided. The BUMP number is the sum of the numbers for each sprite involved in the collision. For instance, when sprites 1 and 4 collide, BUMP returns a value of 9 (1 + 8).

However, BUMP has a significant limitation. Let's take the bouncing ball example one step further and imagine that

Table 2-3. BUMP Collision Values

Sprite Number	BUMP Value
1	1
2	2
3	4
4	8
5	16
6	32
7	64
8	128

you want to write a simple billiards game. You want to move several balls around the screen, causing each of them to rebound naturally whenever it strikes any other ball. But what happens if two pairs of balls strike together at separate points on the screen? BUMP tells you that four balls have suffered a collision, but not which balls were involved in each collision.

Despite these limitations, COLLISION and BUMP work well in most cases where you're likely to need them. Here is a program that demonstrates both commands, followed by a line-by-line explanation:

```
10 SCNCLR
20 FOR A=3584 TO 3711:POKE A,255:NEXT
30 SPRITE 1,1,7:SPRITE 2,1,8
40 MOVSPR 1,50,100:MOVSPR 2,300,100:COLLISION 1
50 COLLISION 1,80
60 MOVSPR 1,90#2:MOVSPR 2,270#2
70 GOTO 70
80 PRINT "BANG!":MOVSPR 1,0#0:MOVSPR 2,0#0
90 PRINT BUMP(1)
```

Line	Description
10	Clears the screen
20	Defines two sprites as solid blocks
30	Turns on sprites 1 and 2 and sets their colors to yellow and blue
40	Puts sprites on the screen and clears the effect of any previous collisions
50	Enables sprite/sprite collision detection and diverts execution to line 80 when a collision occurs
60	Starts both sprites moving at the same speed in opposite directions
70	Repeats until a collision occurs
80	Prints a collision message and stops both sprites
90	Prints the BUMP value for collision

Animating Sprite Figures

True animation requires more than merely moving a shape across the screen. Imagine how you might create the image of a flying bird. If you simply draw a bird shape with SPRDEF and set it in motion with SPRMOV, the effect will be no more realistic than dragging a drawing of a bird across a table. To bring the bird to life, you need some method of flapping its wings. In other words, you need to change the sprite's shape along with its position.

Fortunately, sprites use a pointer at the end of the current video matrix (screen memory) to designate which block of shape data defines the sprite. By changing this pointer, you can flip the sprite from one shape to another almost immediately. Although BASIC 7.0 contains no command to change the sprite shape pointer, this is easily done with POKE.

Before you can control the sprite shape pointer, you must know its address. Sprite pointers are always located in the highest eight bytes of the current video matrix. The first (lowest) pointer controls sprite 1, with the others following accordingly. In text mode the video matrix is located from 1024 to 2047 ($0400–$07FF), so in this mode sprite 1's shape pointer is at location 2040 ($07F8), sprite 2's pointer is at 2041 ($07F9), and so on. In hi-res graphics modes, the video matrix stretches from 7168 to 8191 ($1C00–$1FFF), and the eight sprite pointers are located at 8184–8191 ($1FF8–$1FFF).

Now that you know where to find the sprite pointers, what values do you put in them? Since each block of sprite shape data is 64 bytes long, this part is comparatively easy. Find the address where the shape data begins and divide it by 64, then POKE that value into the pointer location. Remember, sprite shape definitions usually start at location 3584, so to point sprite 1 at the first block of shape data, POKE 56 (3584/64) into its pointer.

Before you decide that this method isn't worth the trouble, let's look at a demonstration. In a previous program we drew four hi-res wagon wheels and saved them as sprites (see "Saving And Recalling Sprite Shapes" above), then made the wheel spin with SPRITE commands that activated each sprite in sequence. While reasonably effective, that program created a certain amount of flicker when changing from one shape to the next. The flicker results from the animation method. All four sprites move across the screen together; to change from one shape to the next, we turned one sprite off and turned the other on.

In this case we can get much better results by moving only one sprite across the screen and changing its shape by flipping the pointer. The instant that the pointer is changed, a new shape replaces the old one, allowing a flicker-free transition between shapes. Replace the following lines in the wagon wheel program, then run it again. You'll see a distinct improvement in the quality of animation.

```
60 SPRITE 1,1,8
90 SP=SP+1+3*(SP=4):POKE 8184,SP+55
100 MOVSPR 1,A,100:NEXT
```

Sprites and Machine Language

If you are convinced that the sprite commands in BASIC 7.0 will satisfy your programming needs, then by all means use them. But there are certain jobs that BASIC just can't do efficiently. For this reason, nearly all commercial graphics programs are written in machine language (ML), and a good many noncommercial programs use ML as well. If you are familiar with machine language sprite programming on the Commodore 64, you will be pleased to know that all of your knowledge translates directly to the Commodore 128. All the sprite control registers are in the same places and serve the same purposes. The sprite shape pointers, as explained above, can move around as a result of graphics allocations, but otherwise work just as they do on the 64.

For ML purposes, you can create a sprite shape any way that is convenient, using SPRDEF or any other sprite editor. If you have saved one or more sprite shapes to a disk file with BSAVE, they should be loaded into memory when your program begins, either by performing a BLOAD (if your program begins with some BASIC lines) or by calling the Kernal LOAD routine mentioned in Chapter 6. Another option is to read the sprite shape data from a section of your program code and store it in the proper memory locations.

It requires several separate ML operations to perform the equivalent of a SPRITE command in BASIC 7.0. Each sprite is activated by setting its control bit in location 53269 ($D015). To turn on sprites 1 and 8, store the value 129 in 53269, and so on. Turning a sprite's control bit off makes it disappear. Locations 53287–53294 ($D027–$D02E) set the color for each sprite. The color values range from 0 to 15 and correspond to the values used in a COLOR statement minus one. Vertical and horizontal expansion is controlled by locations 53271 ($D017) and 53277 ($D01D), respectively. Each bit in an expansion register controls the expansion of a single sprite.

ML Sprite Movement

The first 16 registers of the VIC-II chip, locations 53248–53263 ($D000–$D00F), control the horizontal and vertical coordinates of all eight sprites. A sprite can have a vertical position from 0 to 255, and a horizontal position from 0 to 511. Since a single byte cannot hold a number greater than 255, it is necessary to use part of another byte as a ninth bit for horizontal positioning. Location 53264 is used as a ninth bit of the horizontal position for all eight sprites. Bit 0 (the least significant bit) is the ninth bit of sprite 1's horizontal position, and so on. When a bit in this location is set, the computer adds 256 to the horizontal position of that sprite. The following statement reads the position of sprite 0:

```
PRINT PEEK(53248)+256*(PEEK(53264) AND 1)
```

While it works just fine, this system is confusing to many people (as evidenced by the large number of Commodore 64 games that don't even attempt to move sprites onto the right part of the screen). Handling the high bit of the sprite's horizontal position is indeed cumbersome. The following BASIC statements could be used to move sprite 1 across the screen:

```
FOR A=0 TO 320:POKE 53248,A AND 255:POKE
  53264,PEEK(53264) AND 254 OR INT (A/256): NEXT
```

Moving sprites in ML is much easier if you treat the sprite's horizontal position as a two-byte value. Viewed in this way, all it takes is a simple two-byte addition or subtraction to move a sprite right or left. Here's a very efficient way to handle all eight sprites. First, set aside 16 free memory locations for the horizontal sprite position (a low byte and high byte for each of the eight sprites). Whenever you want to move a sprite, perform the position arithmetic on the appropriate register, then use an interrupt-driven routine to copy the contents of the *shadow* position registers into the actual control registers.

Sound confusing? Here's a program that does it all. Before you type it in, note that the 128 uses shadow registers of its own for sprite movement. The contents of these registers are automatically copied into the VIC-II control registers every 1/60 second, during the very brief interval when nothing changes on the screen. Since the sprites change position only when the screen is stable, all flicker is eliminated. To take advantage of this setup, the following routine copies our shadow registers into the 128's shadow registers rather than directly into the VIC-II chip control locations.

This routine assumes that you will put the low byte of each sprite's horizontal position in locations $0D00–$0D07, the high bytes in $0D10–$0D17, and the vertical position bytes in $0D20–$0D27. Since the routine is driven by the computer's hardware interrupt, it does not have to be called directly by your program. All you need to do is put the correct position values in the shadow registers.

```
0C00  SEI
0C01  LDA #$0D
0C03  STA $0314
0C06  LDA #$0C
0C08  STA $0315
0C0B  CLI
0C0C  RTS
0C0D  LDA #$00
0C0F  STA $A3
0C11  LDX #$07
0C13  LDY #$0E
0C15  LDA $0D00,X
0C18  STA $11D6,Y
0C1B  LDA $0D20,X
0C1E  STA $11D7,Y
0C21  LDA $0D10,X
0C24  LSR
0C25  ROL $A3
0C27  DEY
0C28  DEY
0C29  DEX
0C2A  BPL $0C15
0C2C  LDA $A3
0C2E  STA $11E6
0C31  JMP $FA65
```

Once this routine is in place, you can move any sprite horizontally with ordinary two-byte arithmetic. For instance, the following fragment of code moves sprite 1 one pixel to the right. (The semicolons and the comments which follow them are merely for explanation; *do not type them in* if you enter this code with the monitor.)

```
LDA $0D00  ;get low byte of sprite 1 horizontal position
CLC        ;prepare to add
ADC #$01   ;add 1 to low byte
STA $0D00  ;store result in low byte
LDA $0D10  ;get high byte of sprite 1 horizontal position
ADC #$00   ;increase high byte if needed
STA $0D10  ;store result in high byte
```

Similarly, moving a sprite to the left requires a two-byte subtraction. Use the same code shown above, substituting an SEC for the CLC and replacing the ADC instructions with SBC.

Machine Language Collision Detection

Detecting sprite collisions in ML is much the same as in BASIC. The contents of location 53278 ($D01E) contain the same value that the BUMP(1) function generates. Reading location 53279 ($D01F) gives you the same information as BUMP(2). Unfortunately, because the system updates these registers only once every 1/60 second, collision detection is just as big a problem in machine language as in BASIC (see "When Sprites Collide" above). At ML speeds, two sprites can pass completely through one another before the system gets around to updating the collision registers. The only foolproof detection method is to ignore the collision registers and compare the absolute position of every sprite on the screen before permitting any movement.

Custom Characters on the 128

Although sprites and hi-res drawing commands are flashy and easy to use, do not overlook the potential of character graphics. Custom-defined characters have long been used to create arcade-style games—you can redefine a single character into an alien shape, a bird, and so forth, or combine several custom characters into one big shape. Since every pixel is under your control, detailed effects are easy to achieve. Tired of seeing the same old characters on the screen? Why not replace them with characters of your own design? By redefining a few custom characters, you can also add special scientific symbols or foreign language characters to a screen display.

Character-based graphics have two distinct advantages over hi-res drawing. First, a hi-res screen takes up eight times as much memory as a text screen. This can be critical when you're writing a program that needs to flip amongst many different screens. Secondly, a text screen can be updated in a fraction of the time it takes to update an 8K hi-res screen. Thus, character graphics are often more suitable for high-speed applications such as driving or flying games that scroll the screen.

Where Do Characters Come From?

Though character displays might seem automatic to you—press a key, and a letter appears on the screen—the computer has to perform a considerable amount of work just to display one character. Before putting anything on the screen, the 128 looks up the internal pattern, or *character definition,* for that particular character. Creating custom characters is largely a matter of making the computer use your own custom character definitions in place of the normal ones.

Every displayable character on the Commodore 128 has a definition composed of eight bytes. For example, the bytes which form the definition for the letter A are 48, 60, 102, 126, 102, 102, 102, and 0. By translating these numbers to binary form we can see the definition itself:

```
 48 00011000
 60 00111100
102 01100110
126 01111110
102 01100110
102 01100110
102 01100110
  0 00000000
```

Whenever it needs to display an A, the 128 refers to this definition, lighting up one screen pixel for every 1 in the binary number and turning off a pixel for every 0. As you can see, there's an exact, one-to-one relationship between the binary form of the character definition and what ultimately appears on the screen.

Since each character definition takes up eight bytes, an entire set of 256 characters requires 2048 (256*8) bytes of memory. The Commodore 128 has two complete character sets, stored in ROM (Read-Only Memory). When you turn the computer on, it automatically chooses the uppercase/graphics character set; the definitions for these characters begin at location 53248 ($D000) of memory bank 14. If you hold down the Commodore key and press SHIFT, or type PRINT CHR$(14), the computer switches to the lowercase/uppercase graphics set; these definitions are found immediately after the first set, beginning at location 55296 ($D800). The definitions within each set are arranged in the same order as screen codes (see Appendix A).

Pointing to RAM

By changing the bytes that make up a character definition, you can change the appearance of any character. Though there's no way to change the ROM character set, it's a simple matter to move the definitions into RAM (programmable memory) where you can alter them at will. Let's walk through the process from beginning to end, writing a program as we go. The first step is to tell the 128 to look at RAM instead of ROM. This is done by setting bit 2 of location 217 ($D9) as shown here:

```
10 POKE 217,4
```

After instructing the 128 to fetch its character information from RAM, you must tell it *where* to look. Location 2604 ($A2C) is a double-purpose register which controls the location of the text screen and also tells the 128 where to look for a character set. The computer finds the starting address of the current text screen by multiplying the four highest bits of this location by 1024. The four *lowest* bits in location 2604 are multiplied by 1024 to find the starting address of the current character set.

When you turn the computer on, location 2604 contains 20. In this case the high four bits—(PEEK(2604) AND 240)/16—contain the value 1, meaning that the text screen starts at location 1024 (1*1024=1024). The low four bits—PEEK(2604) AND 15—contain a 4, so the character set starts at location 4096 (4*1024=4096).

At this point you may well wonder what the number 4096 signifies, since we told you a moment ago that ROM character definitions start at 53248. The VIC-II graphics chip can only "see" a single 16K section of memory at any given time. Since the text screen, hi-res screen, and sprite definitions are all in the first 16K of memory, the 128 performs some internal memory management tricks to make the VIC-II chip think the ROM characters are at 4096, when in fact they're at 53248. This is strictly an internal feature of the computer which you needn't worry about for ordinary programming. Just remember that the ROM characters start at 53248, and let the system manage itself.

Putting Custom Characters in Memory

Before you create a custom character set, you must decide where to put it. One excellent spot to start is location 8192 ($2000), a RAM area normally used as BASIC program space or for hi-res screens. To prevent BASIC from storing program lines here (which would destroy the character set), call one of the hi-res graphics modes. Whenever this is done, the computer moves BASIC program space up to location 16384 ($4000). After that, the space at 8192 is free from interference, even if you return to a text mode (note, however, that a GRAPHIC CLR statement moves BASIC down to its normal location at 7168). Here's the statement we'll use to move BASIC out of the way:

```
20 GRAPHIC 2,1
```

Now you have 8K of protected RAM. Let's tell the 128 where to find the new character set. Since you'll be starting the new definitions at 8192, the low four bits of location 2604 ($A2C) must be set to 8 (8192/1024). The text screen does not need to move, so we'll leave the high bits alone:

```
30 POKE 2604,PEEK (2604) AND 240 OR 8
```

If you've followed this entire discussion, you're probably anxious to see something happen on the screen. Go ahead and run the program. The hi-res portion of the screen is blank, of course. If you move to the text window, you'll see that the computer has no character set, either. We've told the computer to fetch its character definitions from the hi-res screen area, but that zone doesn't contain any definitions yet. Press RUN/STOP–RESTORE to reset the screen, add the following line, and rerun the program:

```
40 CHAR 1,0,0,"@ABCDEFGHIJKLMNOPQRSTUVWXYZ":CHAR
   1,0,4," ",1
```

Now move to the text window again. Part of the normal

character set (A–Z plus the @ character and reverse space) has been written into the custom definition area. Conveniently, the hi-res screen is mapped in eight-byte chunks that correspond exactly to the eight-byte arrangement of each character definition. Let's customize the new character set by DRAWing an underline beneath each character. Press RUN/STOP–RESTORE again, add line 50, and rerun the program:

```
50 DRAW 1,0,7 TO 216,7
```

In many cases it's convenient to copy an entire character set from ROM to RAM before making any changes. Replace line 40 with this line:

```
40 FAST:FOR A=0 TO 2047:BANK 14:B=PEEK (53248+A):BANK
   0:POKE 8192+A,B:NEXT:SLOW
```

The FAST command lets the computer perform this tedious job about twice as fast as normal. Since character ROM is in memory bank 14, but the hi-res screen is in bank 0, we use BANK 14 to switch banks before each PEEK, and BANK 0 to switch back for every POKE. When the whole set has been copied, SLOW resets the computer to normal speed and turns the screen back on.

You can also use BSAVE and BLOAD to save character sets and bring them back into memory. For instance, this command saves the ROM character set to disk in a file named CHRSET:

```
BSAVE "CHRSET",B14,P53248,P55296
```

Of course, you can save custom character sets with BSAVE as well. Once you have saved a character set, it's easy to load it back into memory. This command loads the CHRSET definition file into memory beginning at location 8192:

```
BLOAD "CHRSET",B0,P8192
```

Note that BLOAD lets you designate a load address if you want to load a character set into a memory area different from the area it was saved from.

Once you have the character set in RAM, you can make any changes you like. This can be done in various ways, the easiest of which is to use a character editor program. If you previously owned a Commodore 64, chances are good that you already have such a program. Since both computers use the same VIC-II chip, the 128 can use any custom characters created for the 64.

If you don't have an editor, you can design the characters on graph paper. Mark off an 8 × 8 grid on the paper, then put a 1 in every space where you want a dot and a 0 in every other space. Here's an example (an alien shape) to help you get started:

```
00111100
01111110
01011010
01111110
01111110
00100100
00100100
01000010
```

As explained above, each row of 1's and 0's represents an eight-bit binary number. The next step is to change these into decimal form. Decimal numbers have a base of 10, meaning that each digit is multiplied by a power of 10. For example, the number 124 can be thought of as (1 × 10↑2) + (2 × 10↑1) + (4 × 10↑0). The ↑ sign is the symbol for exponentiation. Remember that any number raised to the zero power is 1.

Binary numbers have a base of 2, meaning that each digit is multiplied by a power of 2. In this scheme the first line of binary values in the alien shape is interpreted as (0 × 2↑7) + (0 × 2↑6) + (1 × 2↑5) + (1 × 2↑4) + (1 × 2↑3) + (1 × 2↑2) + (0 × 2↑1) + (0 × 2↑0). The decimal value works out to 60.

Once you have converted all eight binary numbers to decimals, you can put them in a DATA statement, then POKE them into memory starting at 8192 with a FOR-NEXT loop. After you run the following lines, the @ symbol (the first character definition in a normal set) is converted into an alien shape.

```
50 FOR A=8192 TO 8199: READ B: POKE A,B:NEXT
60 DATA 60,126,90,126,126,40,40,66
```

80-Column Graphics

In addition to the VIC-II chip, which handles sprites, hi-res graphics, and the 40-column text screen, the 128 has an 8563 chip for 80-column graphics. The 8563 has its own 16K of RAM which cannot be accessed in quite the same way as other memory. Here is the basic layout of the 8563's RAM:

Location	Contents
$0000–$07CF	80-column text screen
$0800–$0FCF	Screen attributes
$2000–$3FFF	Character definitions

The 80-column chip has 37 control registers which you can manipulate for a variety of interesting effects. However, accessing these registers is a bit more involved than simply PEEKing or POKEing a location. To change the contents of one of these registers or to read what it contains, you must put a register number from 0 to 36 into location 54784 ($D600), then wait for the high bit of this location to be set by the system (this can be checked with a BIT instruction in machine language). Once the high bit has been set, you may write to or read from location 54785 ($D601) to affect the control register in question. In effect, locations 54784–54785 act as intermediaries between you and the 8563 control registers.

The following machine language program makes it easy to access the control registers from BASIC. Since every other program in this section relies on this program, type it in now, using the 128's ML monitor. Note that the semicolons and the comments which follow them are *not* part of the program, so don't try to type them in. We've simply included them for extra information.

```
0C00  LDY #$00    ;register write routine starts here
0C02  STY $FF00   ;select bank 15
0C05  STA $D600   ;store register number in $D600
0C08  BIT $D600   ;wait for high bit to be set
0C0B  BPL $0C08
0C0D  STX $D601   ;store data in $D601
0C10  RTS
0C11  LDA #$00    ;register read routine starts here
0C13  STA $FF00
0C16  JSR $AF0C   ;convert FAC1 to $16 and $17
0C19  LDA $16     ;get register number
0C1B  STA $D600   ;store register number in $D600
0C1E  BIT $D600   ;wait for high bit
0C21  BPL $0C1E
0C23  LDY $D601   ;read data from $D601 into Y register
0C26  LDA #$00
0C28  JMP $AF03   ;convert Y and A to FAC1 and exit
```

Once the preceding ML program is in memory, you can write to any 8563 control with a SYS command in this form:

SYS 3072, *register number, data*

The *register number* should be a number from 0 to 36, corresponding to the register you want to affect, and *data* should be the number you want to put in that location. For example, this command puts a 1 in register 11 (cursor end scan line control) to change the cursor from a box to an overscore:

SYS 3072, 11, 1

To read an 8563 register with this ML routine, use the command

A=USR (*register number*)

Before issuing a USR command, however, you must change the vector at locations 4633–4634 ($1219–$121A) to point to the right part of the ML routine, as shown in line 10 of the next program. The rest of the program reads and displays all the 8563 registers.

```
10 POKE 4633,17:POKE 4634,12
20 FOR A=0 TO 36
30 PRINT USR(A)
40 NEXT
```

This routine also makes it possible to read or write directly to the 8563's 16K RAM area. To do this, put the high byte of the target address in register 18 and the low byte in register 19 (note that the high byte must be written first). After the address has been set, you may write or read data from register 31. For example, this program puts a value of 6 into RAM location 1.

```
10 SYS 3072,18,0: REM HIGH BYTE OF ADDRESS
20 SYS 3072,19,1: REM LOW BYTE OF ADDRESS
30 SYS 3072,31,6: REM WRITE A VALUE OF SIX
```

Reading a RAM location is just as easy. To read the contents of RAM location 1, substitute this line and rerun the program:

```
30 A=USR(31): REM READ LOCATION 31
```

Locations 18–19 are auto-incrementing, meaning that the two-byte address they contain is increased by one whenever you read or write to them. As you'll see in the next section, this feature is very convenient when dealing with large chunks of 8563 RAM.

Custom Characters in 80 Columns

When you turn the computer on, it automatically copies the normal character set from bank 14 ROM into the 8563's RAM. This is done by a routine called INIT80, which you can also call at location 65378 ($FF62). Each 80-column character definition takes up 16 bytes of memory as compared with 8 bytes for a 40-column character definition. However, the last 8 bytes of each character definition are normally unused, so INIT80 puts zeros into these locations. The character definitions normally go into locations 8192–16383 ($2000–$3FFF). Since this area is RAM, we can redefine any 80-column character simply by writing a new definition in the appropriate spot. The following program redefines the @ symbol. (Note that this program calls the ML routine listed at the beginning of the previous section.)

```
10 SYS 3072,18,32:SYS 3072,19,0:REM WRITE TO LOCATION
   8192 HEX $2000
20 FOR A=1 TO 8:READ B
30 SYS 3072,31,B
40 NEXT A
50 PRINT "{CLR}@{DOWN}@{DOWN}@"
60 DATA 24,60,90,126,126,36,195,0
```

It's important to keep in mind that between each character definition are eight bytes of zeros. Thus, to redefine the character A (the next definition), you must store data in the eight bytes from 8208 to 8215 ($2010–$2017). Though you can always restore the normal 40-column characters by pressing RUN/STOP–RESTORE, the same is not true of an 80-column character set. To copy the ROM characters back into 8563 RAM, enter SYS 65378. During program development you may want to redefine a function key to enter the statement for you:

```
KEY 1,"SYS 65378"+CHR$(13)
```

Hi-Res Graphics in 80 Columns

Although the 80-column chip provides a high-resolution (640 × 200 pixels) graphics mode, the Commodore 128 offers no commands to activate this mode or plot points on the screen. Nevertheless, it is possible to access hi-res graphics in 80 columns. Bit 7 of register 25 in the 8563 chip controls whether the screen is text or graphics. When this bit contains a 1, hi-res mode is enabled.

The hi-res screen requires 16,000 bytes of memory, nearly all of the 8563's 16K of RAM. Because of this, there is no room for an attribute table (normally an integral part of 80-column graphics). This means you're limited to monochrome graphics. In fact, if you leave the attribute table enabled, it will interfere with the hi-res screen. Bit 6 of 8563 register 25 disables or enables screen attributes. Set it to 0 (disable screen attributes) whenever you enter hi-res mode.

While it's possible to clear the hi-res screen by writing zeros to all 16,000 locations, it's much faster to use the 8563's built-in memory-fill command. Set registers 18 and 19 to the beginning address of the area you want to fill, set register 30 with the number of bytes you want to fill (plus one), and put the value you want to fill with in register 31. Setting register 30 to zero fills an entire page (256 bytes) of memory. The following program calls the built-in fill routine until all 64 pages of memory are cleared.

```
10 FAST:AD=3072
20 SYS AD,25,128 :REM TURN ON GRAPHICS, TURN OFF
   ATTRIBUTES
30 SYS AD,18,0:SYS AD,19,0 :REM SET THE STARTING
   ADDRESS TO 0
50 FOR A=0 TO 63:SYS AD,31,0:SYS AD,30,0:NEXT :REM FILL
64 PAGES OF MEMORY WITH ZEROS
60 FOR L=0 TO 9:FOR X=0 TO 63.9 STEP .1:Y=INT(90+80*
   SIN(X*/32)):GOSUB 80 :NEXT: NEXT
70 GETKEY A$:SYS AD,25,64:END :REM TURN OFF GRAPHICS,
   TURN ON ATTRIBUTES
80 Q=X+L*64
82 P=Y*80+INT(Q/8)
85 SP=2↑(7-(QAND7)):HB=INT(P/256):LB=P-HB*256
90 SYS AD,18,HB:SYS AD,19,LB
100 SYS AD,31,SP
110 RETURN
```

The formula in lines 82–85 determines the address of any point in the hi-res screen. The variable Q represents the horizontal coordinate of a point, and Y represents the vertical. Note that the 80-column hi-res screen uses the same coordinate system as any other hi-res mode: Coordinate 0,0 is the upper-left corner, and so on.

Moving the 80-Column Screen

Registers 2 and 7 of the 8563 chip control the screen's horizontal and vertical sync positions, respectively. The sync position tells the chip where to start drawing the screen. By changing the values in these registers, you can move the screen up, down, left, or right. This program lets you push the screen around with the cursor keys. As you'll see, the picture loses sync and begins to roll whenever you make the sync value too large or too small.

```
10 X=102:Y=29:AD=3072
20 GETKEY A$:IF A$="{DOWN}" THEN Y=Y+1:GOTO 60
30 IF A$="{UP}" THEN Y=Y-1:GOTO 60
40 IF A$="{RIGHT}" THEN X=X+1:GOTO 60
50 IF A$="{LEFT}" THEN X=X-1:ELSE 20
60 SYS AD,2,X:SYS AD,7,Y:GOTO 20
```

Moving the Underline

The low five bits of 8563 register 29 control which line the underline cursor occupies. When you turn the computer on, these bits contain the value 7, which places the underline directly underneath each character. This program changes the underline register to produce a scrolling underline effect.

```
10 SCNCLR:FOR A=1 TO 10:PRINT "{B}ISNT THIS
   STRANGE?":NEXT
20 FOR A=7 TO 0 STEP-1
30 SYS 3072,29,A
40 NEXT:GOTO 20
```

Oversize Characters

A normal 80-column screen contains 25 lines of characters; each line is 8 bytes tall. As mentioned earlier, each 80-column character definition uses 16 bytes of memory, but 8 of these bytes are not used. This program displays double-height characters which use all 16 bytes of each character defintion.

```
10 AD=3072:BANK 15:FAST
20 SYS AD,9,15
30 SYS AD,6,12
40 SYS AD,4,15
50 SYS AD,5,6
60 SYS AD,7,15
70 SYS AD,23,16
80 SYS AD,18,32:SYS AD,19,0
```

```
90 FOR A=53248 TO 53759
100 BANK 14:AC=PEEK(A):BANK 15
105 SYS AD,AC,31:SYS AD,31,AC
110 NEXT
120 SYS AD,11,14:SCNCLR
130 POKE 228,11
```

Chapter 3

Sound and Music

Sound and Music

The term *computer music* seems contradictory to many people. Music is often perceived as something emotional, organic, and flowing—the essence of human creativity—while computers are seen as rigid, inhuman, and mechanical. But in fact, a computer is simply a tool, which you may use creatively or uncreatively according to your skills and inclinations. After all, every musical instrument (even the human voice) is a mechanical device of some sort. Like other musical tools, a computer does certain jobs better than others, and may take some time to master fully. As you gain familiarity with how it works, you'll be able to devote more attention to the business of making music, and less to the details of programming.

This chapter looks at computer music in a variety of ways. First, it explains all the BASIC commands involved in sound and music programming and provides a library of ready-to-use sound effects. In later sections we'll explore some fundamentals of music theory and look at a variety of BASIC programming methods. For the advanced programmer, we've included a discussion of filtering, some useful machine language programming techniques, and a detailed memory map of the 128's sound chip.

BASIC 7.0 Sound and Music Commands

Like its predecessor the Commodore 64, the 128 contains a powerful sound chip called SID (Sound Interface Device). While the 64 has no sound or music commands, the 128's advanced BASIC has several, making it possible to create music and sound effects without the complex POKEs required on the 64. BASIC 7.0 contains seven new sound and music statements: VOL, SOUND, ENVELOPE, TEMPO, PLAY, and FILTER. Let's see how each of these works.

VOL

You can think of the VOL command as the master volume control for SOUND statements. Until you turn up the SID chip's volume with VOL, SOUND doesn't produce any sound at all. This command accepts any value from 0 to 15: VOL 0 turns the volume off, and VOL 15 selects maximum volume. In most cases you need to use VOL only once, at the very beginning of a program. Since drastic volume changes create a distinct "pop" sound, don't use VOL to turn sounds on or off.

SOUND

The SOUND command is designed for sound effects rather than conventional music. As mentioned above, you must set the SID chip volume to a nonzero value with VOL before using SOUND. Here is the general format of the command:

SOUND *voice, frequency, duration*, *direction, minimum frequency, step, waveform, pulsewidth*

Every SOUND command must be followed by at least three parameters (controlling values) to choose a voice, frequency, and duration for the sound. Additional parameters are optional. Here is what each parameter does.

Voice assigns the sound to one of the 128's three separate voices (tone generators). Use the value 1 to select voice 1, 2 for voice 2, and so on. Since each voice works independently, you can create as many as three simultaneous sound effects with SOUND.

Frequency sets the pitch of the sound and may have any value from 0 to 65535.

Duration determines how long the sound is heard. This value is measured in jiffies (1/60 second). Thus, a duration value of 60 causes the sound to be generated for one second, a duration of 300 results in a sound that lasts five (300/60) seconds, and so on. Note that the duration value is absolute: As soon as the specified time has elapsed, the sound stops, whether or not the sound sweep you specify (see below) has completed its cycle.

To create a simple, unchanging tone, you need only supply SOUND with three parameters. For example, you might use SOUND 1,2000,10 to signal an error in a program. By supplying additional SOUND parameters you can create more interesting sounds that change frequency in realtime.

Direction makes the sound's frequency sweep up, sweep down, or oscillate (sweep up and down repeatedly). Using a 0 for this parameter sweeps the sound upward, 1 sweeps it downward, and 2 makes it oscillate.

Minimum frequency sets the bottom of the range for the sound sweep. This can be any value *lower than the frequency chosen for the second parameter*. For instance, say that you choose a main frequency of 12000, a downward sweep, and a minimum frequency of 2000. The sound sweeps downward in frequency from 12000 to 2000.

Step controls how fast the sound sweeps between the main frequency and minimum frequency. It works much like the familiar STEP value in a FOR-NEXT loop. A small step value like 1 or 5 creates a slow sweep, while larger step values create faster sweeps. Note that the step value must be less than the difference between the main frequency and the minimum. For instance, if the main frequency is 4000 and the minimum is 3000, the step value can be no greater than 1000 (4000−3000).

Waveform selects one of the four SID waveforms for the sound. Each waveform has a different sound quality. The *triangle* wave (use 0) sounds soft and mellow. The *sawtooth* wave (1) is louder and more strident. The *pulse* wave (2) can generate a variety of different sounds, most of them louder than the triangle. And the *noise* waveform (3) creates a rushing or hissing sound, useful for nonmusical effects.

Pulsewidth is relevant only when you select the pulse waveform. This parameter affects the quality of the sound produced by the pulse wave, and may be anything in the range 0–4095. By changing these values, you can make the pulse wave sound rich and full or thin and reedy.

Keep in mind when working with SOUND that its various parameters (particularly frequency, duration, direction, minimum frequency, and step) work interactively, each contributing to the final result. Enter the following lines to see how much difference results from changing only one or two parameters at a time:

```
SOUND 1,9999,10   ,0,2000,3
SOUND 1,9999,1000,0,2000,3
SOUND 1,9999,110  ,2,2000,300
SOUND 1,9999,110  ,1,2000,1500
```

A SOUND Effects Library

Here is a collection of different SOUND routines for your use. If you find one you like, go ahead and put it in your own programs. You can learn a lot about SOUND by studying the techniques used here and observing what happens when you change one or more of the SOUND values.

UFO

```
10 VOL 12:J=1024:K=8192:X=10
20 DO UNTIL X=25
25 X=X+1
50 SOUND 1,K,X,0,J,340,1,0
55 LOOP:END
```

Explosion 1

```
10 VOL4:J=2096:K=32767:X=15
50 SOUND 1,65000,480,1,K,1,3,0:SOUND 2,49152,240,0,0,100,1,0
55 SOUND 2,49152,240,1,0,100,1,0
57 FOR T=15 TO 1STEP-1:VOL T
60 SOUND 1,4992,60,1,K,1,3,0
70 NEXT T
```

Explosion 2

```
10 VOL 12:J=1024:K=8192:X=49152
20 DO UNTIL X=8192
25 X=X-1
50 SOUND 1,X,K,0,J,340,3,0
55 LOOP:END
```

Rocket

```
10 V=15:VOLV:J=2096:K=32767
15 SOUND 1,J,300,1,K,1,3,0
20 DO UNTIL V=0
25 V=V-.5
50 SOUND 1,J-(.5*V),30,1,K,1,3,0
55 VOLV:LOOP
```

Laser

```
10 V=15:VOLV:I=24570:J=16378:K=32767
12 DO UNTIL X=100
13 X=X+1:IF FL=1 THEN IF X/2=INT(X/2) THEN V=V-1
15 IF V=1 THEN FL=0
17 IF V=15 THEN FL=1
18 IF FL=0 THEN IF X/2=INT(X/2) THEN V=V+1
20 SOUND 1,I,10,0,J,350,1:SOUND 2,I,10,1,J,350,1
30 SOUND 3,I,10,2,J,350,1
40 VOLV:LOOP:X=0:GOTO 12
```

Busy

```
10 V=15:VOLV:I=2780:J=30
20 SOUND 1,I,J:SOUND 1,0,J:GOTO 20
```

Pong

```
10 V=15:VOLV
15 D=RND(0)*300+100
20 SOUND 1,9200,1,,,,2
25 FOR T=1 TO D:NEXT
30 SOUND 1,6900,1,,,,2
40 D=RND(0)*500+200
45 FOR T=1 TO D:NEXT
50 GOTO 15
```

Dial Session

```
10 V=15:VOLV:PRINT "DIAL YOUR NUMBER....":DO
   WHILE D<7:D=D+1
20 GETKEY R$:R=ASC(R$)
30 IF R<48 OR R>57 THEN 20
40 R=R-48:IF R=0 THEN R=10
50 GOSUB 80:SOUND 1,223,L,,,,2,1000:LOOP:PRINT
   "RINGING...."
60 IF C=5 THEN PRINT "NOT AT HOME!!!!":END
70 SOUND 1,642,120,,,,2,75:SOUND 1,1,220,,,,2:C=C+1:GOTO 60
80 L=INT(R*02/2)+INT((R↑2)/2):RETURN
```

Mania

```
10 V=11:DIM A(V),B(V):VOLV
20 FOR T=0TOV-1:READ A(T):NEXT
30 FOR T=0TOV-1:READ B(T):NEXT
40 FOR X=1 TO V
50 SOUND 1,A(X),B(X),1,10000,100,1
60 NEXT:GOTO 40
70 DATA 49152,37288,29831,19283,45023,53102,30923,20013,
   10029,39032,11102,49586
80 DATA 2,1,5,6,4,7,8,2,1,4
```

Computer

```
10 VOL12:FOR X=1 TO 7:READ F(X):NEXT
20 FOR X=1 TO 7
30 SOUND 1,F(X),6:IF X=3 THEN SOUND 2,45993,1,,,,3
40 IF X=6 THEN SOUND 2,58889,1,,,,3
50 IF X=7 THEN SOUND 3,745,2,,,,2,5
60 IF X=2 THEN SOUND 3,566,2
70 IF X=5 THEN SOUND 3,4566,2,,,,2,1000
80 NEXT:GOTO 20
90 DATA 32767,36060,32767,46869,32767,57869,37560
```

Seekers

```
10 VOLV
20 SOUND 3,295,540,,,,3
30 FORV=0 TO 10:VOLV:FORD=1TOV*75:NEXTD,V
40 SOUND 2,33333,540,0,3,62,3
50 SOUND 3,33333,540,0,3,62,3
60 SOUND 2,33333,540,2,3,62,3
70 SOUND 1,299,4040,,,,3:SOUND 3,1111,4020,,,,3
80 SOUND 2,33333,540,2,3,62,3
90 FORP=1 TO 5000:NEXT:VOL 11
100 FOR V=12 TO 0 STEP -1:S=S+1:VOLV:FOR D=1 TO
    200*S:NEXT D,V
```

Heliport

```
10 V=15:I=49252:J=32767:VOLV
20 FOR X=820 TO 0 STEP-1
30 SOUND 1,X,2,1,J,I,2,100
40 NEXT
```

Crickets

```
10 VOL 15
20 SOUND1,53000,10000,0,49152,3256,2,450
```

Surf

```
10 SOUND 1,52000,20006,,,,3
20 SOUND 2,989,20006,,,,3
30 X=INT(RND(0)*12)+6
40 IF X<7 THEN GOSUB 70
50 IF X>7 THEN GOSUB 80
60 GOTO 30
70 FORV=X TO 15:VOLV:FOR D=1 TO V*9:NEXT
   D,V:J=X:RETURN
80 FORV=15 TO X STEP-1:VOLV:FOR D=1 TO V*9:NEXT
   D,V:J=X:RETURN
```

Tick-Tock

```
10 SOUND 1,11534,1,,,,2
20 FOR T=1 TO 292:NEXT
30 SOUND 1,10009,1,,,,2
40 FOR T=1 TO 292:NEXT
50 GOTO 10
```

ENVELOPE

This command is used to create custom-defined instrument voices for use with PLAY statements (see below). Since PLAY always provides ten predefined instrument voices, you do not need to use ENVELOPE unless you want to create different instruments.

ENVELOPE *instrument number*, *attack, decay, sustain, release, waveform, pulsewidth*

Every ENVELOPE statement must be followed by an instrument number in the range 0–9 to tell the 128 which of the ten instrument voices you are dealing with. If you execute ENVELOPE with nothing but an instrument number, the 128 selects one of the ten predefined instruments, which use the parameters in Table 3-1.

Table 3-1. Predefined Instrument Voices for ENVELOPE

Envelope	Waveform	Pulsewidth	Attack	Decay	Sustain	Release	Instrument
0	2	1536	0	9	0	0	Piano
1	1	—	12	0	12	0	Accordion
2	0	—	0	0	25	0	Calliope
3	3	—	0	5	5	0	Drum
4	0	—	9	4	4	0	Flute
5	1	—	0	9	2	1	Guitar
6	2	512	0	9	0	0	Harpsichord
7	2	2560	0	9	9	0	Organ
8	2	512	8	9	4	1	Trumpet
9	0	—	0	9	0	0	Xylophone

By supplying additional parameters, you can define a custom instrument voice of your own. The new voice is assigned to the instrument number selected by the first number in the ENVELOPE statement. The next four parameters (attack, decay, sustain, release) all accept values in the range 0–15, and work together to form the instrument's sound envelope.

Attack determines how quickly the instrument's sound rises from silence to its peak volume. For instance, the sound of hands clapping reaches maximum volume more quickly than a soft violin sound. *Decay* controls how fast a sound falls from its maximum to its sustained volume. *Sustain* sets the volume at which the sound is held for the middle part of its cycle, and *release* controls how quickly it falls back into silence. Figure 3-1 depicts a typical sound envelope.

Figure 3-1. Typical Sound Envelope

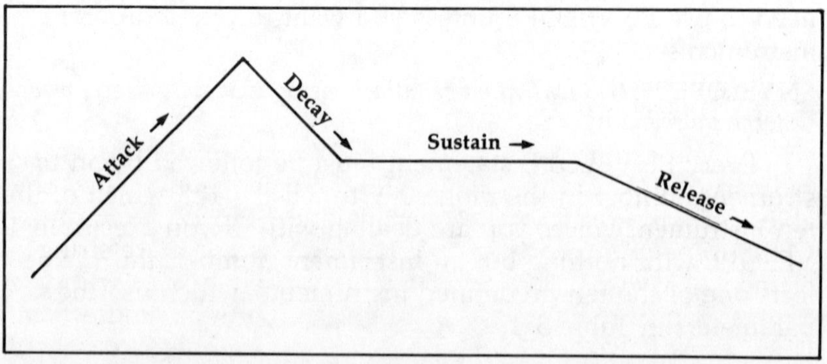

The *waveform* parameter selects one of the 128's four basic waveforms. Use a 0, 1, 2, or 3 to select the triangle, sawtooth, pulse, or noise waveforms, respectively. A value of 4 in this parameter enables a ring-modulated triangle wave. *Pulsewidth*, as noted earlier, need not be defined unless you have also selected the pulse waveform; any value in the range 0–4095 is acceptable.

TEMPO

Like VOL, the TEMPO command takes one parameter:

TEMPO *speed*

TEMPO has only one purpose: to set the overall speed at which PLAY statements produce notes. The default tempo (used unless you specify otherwise) is 8. By supplying TEMPO with another value in the range 1–255 you can make PLAY perform slower or faster. For instance, TEMPO 50 makes PLAY perform much faster than usual.

PLAY

Though technically a single command, the PLAY statement is more like a mini-language within BASIC. Using a syntax somewhat similar to PRINT, it allows you to play multipart music in realtime, with an almost limitless variety of different voices. The basic format of PLAY is very simple:

PLAY *string*

Before explaining everything a PLAY string might contain, let's look at some simple examples. Enter the following statements in direct mode (press RETURN after entering each line):

```
A$="C D E F G A B"
PLAY A$
PLAY "CDEFGABAGFEDC"
PLAY LEFT$(A$,3)
PLAY CHR$(67)+"DE"
```

As you can see, PLAY strings look and work much like ordinary PRINT strings. They can be literals ("CDE") or variables (A$), the result of a string function—LEFT$(A$,3) or CHR$(67)—or of concatenating (adding) two or more string elements (A$+"C"). PLAY is not fussy about spaces within strings. You can add spaces or leave them out, depending on your tastes. However, your other choices are limited to characters that PLAY recognizes as music symbols. Table 3-2 lists all the symbols PLAY can understand:

Table 3-2. PLAY Parameters

Symbol	Explanation
A–G	Note pitches
H	Half note
I	Eighth note
M	Measure
O	Octave (0–6)
Q	Quarter note
R	Rest
S	Sixteenth note
T	Tune (0–9)
U	Volume (0–15)
V	Voice (1–3)
W	Whole note
X	Filter (0=off, 1=on)
.	Dot (note or rest)
#	Sharp
$	Flat

That's more than 20 different characters—quite an impressive list. Let's look at each symbol in turn. As you would expect, PLAY interprets the characters A, B, C, D, E, F, and G as the corresponding musical notes. By preceding a note with a sharp (#) or flat ($), you can raise or lower its pitch one half tone, just as in ordinary music. For instance, #C plays a C-sharp (D-flat), and so on. Sharps and flats affect only the notes which they precede.

If you don't specify an octave, PLAY defaults to octave 4, the middle of the 128's seven-octave range. By including the letter O followed by a number in the range 0–6, you can select any other octave:

FOR J=0 TO 6:PLAY"O"+CHR$(J+48)+"SCDEFGAB":NEXT

Note that the octave setting persists until you change it with another O symbol, whether the computer is running a program or idling in BASIC READY mode.

The U symbol sets the SID volume for PLAY, using values in the range 0–15. If you don't specify a volume, PLAY uses a default value in the middle range. As noted above, VOL commands are ignored by PLAY, which sets its own volume level. Like other general settings, this one persists until you change it.

The symbols S, I, Q, H, and W select sixteenth, eighth, quarter, half, and whole note durations, respectively. For example, PLAY "S CD Q EF" plays two sixteenths followed by two quarters. Duration settings are also persistent.

Rests are inserted with R and follow the prevailing duration. That is, the statement PLAY "Q C R S D R" plays a C-natural quarter note followed by a quarter rest, then a D-natural sixteenth note followed by a sixteenth rest.

The dot (.) symbol has the same effect as in ordinary music, making any duration one and a half times longer than usual. For instance, PLAY "Q C .Q D" plays a quarter note and a dotted quarter note. Note that the dot precedes the duration symbol, not the note. Rests may be dotted just as durations are.

V stands for *voice*, and tells PLAY which of the SID's three voices you want to use. For example, PLAY "V1 C V2 E V3 G" plays a major chord with all three voices. When using more than one voice, you must make it clear at all times which voice should be used and pay careful attention to the durations involved. If you fail to specify a voice, the 128 uses voice 1.

The T symbol (think of *tune*) selects one of the ten available instrument voices (refer to Table 3-1). If no instrument is specified, the 128 uses instrument 0 (piano). For example, PLAY "T7 CD T9 EFG" plays the notes C-D with instrument 7 and E-F-G with instrument 9. If you redefine instrument 1 with an ENVELOPE statement, then select instrument 1 with

PLAY "T1", the 128 uses your custom instrument in place of the default.

Finally, X1 turns the SID filter on, and X0 turns it off. Since filter settings may persist even after a program has stopped, it's wise to insert a statement like PLAY "X0" near the beginning of every program that uses PLAY. If you don't, there's always a chance that residual filter settings from another program may prevent your music from being heard. Needless to say, X1 depends on your having executed an appropriate FILTER command at some earlier point. If you turn on the filter when all FILTER parameters are at zero, you will likely hear nothing at all.

FILTER

The SID filter offers the ability to fine-tune any SID tone to produce exactly the sound you want. While PLAY's default instruments are fine for simple music, and ENVELOPE gives you control over a sound's basic envelope, only FILTER gives you the control needed to emulate natural sounds with precision. This command takes as many as five parameters:

FILTER ***frequency,*** *lowpass, bandpass, highpass, resonance*

The *frequency* value can range from 0 to 2047, and sets the filter's cutoff frequency. As the name implies, a filter "strains out," or subtracts, certain frequencies from the range of possible frequencies. The cutoff frequency sets the point where maximum filtering occurs and causes different effects depending on which type of filter you select. The SID filter actually consists of three different filters which you control separately by supplying a 1 or 0 at the appropriate spot in a FILTER statement. For example, the statement FILTER 1000,1,0,0,15 sets the cutoff frequency at 1000, turns the lowpass filter on with a 1, turns the bandpass and highpass filters off with 0's, and selects a resonance of 15.

A *lowpass* filter permits frequencies significantly below the cutoff point to pass through, but suppresses those above the cutoff point. This program lets you hear a lowpass filter:

```
10 TEMPO 8
20 PLAY "O3 T0 U12 X0 HE F E D WC"
30 PRINT CHR$(147);"PRESS ANY KEY TO HEAR WITH
   FILTER"
40 FILTER 1024,1,0,0,7
50 PLAY "X1 HE F E D WC"
```

A *bandpass* filter passes a narrow range of frequencies near the cutoff point but suppresses those above and below.

```
10 TEMPO 8
20 PLAY "O3 T0 U12 X0 HE F E D WC"
30 PRINT CHR$(147);"PRESS ANY KEY TO HEAR WITH
   FILTER"
40 FILTER 1024,0,1,0,7
50 PLAY "X1 HE F E D WC"
```

A *highpass* filter suppresses frequencies significantly below the cutoff point (high frequencies pass through unchanged).

```
10 TEMPO 8
20 PLAY "O3 T0 U12 X0 HE F E D WC"
30 PRINT CHR$(147);"PRESS ANY KEY TO HEAR WITH
   FILTER"
40 FILTER 1024,0,0,1,7
50 PLAY "X1 HE F E D WC"
```

What does this mean in plain English? You may find it easier to think in terms of what's left rather than what's taken away. A lowpass filter leaves behind low sounds and cuts out high ones. Thus, music played through a lowpass filter tends to sound rich and full, but not particularly sharp. A highpass filter does the opposite: It leaves behind the sharp, high frequency components of a sound and takes away the low tones. Music played through a highpass filter tends to sound hollow, tinny, and rather distant. A bandpass filter leaves behind only a narrow range of frequencies near the cutoff point and suppresses everything else. By turning on the highpass and lowpass filters at the same time, you can create a bandstop, or "notch reject," filter which does the opposite of a bandpass filter: It suppresses a narrow range of frequencies near the cutoff point and lets everything else through.

The *resonance* value (0–15) controls the strength or peaking effect of the filter. Maximum resonance accentuates frequencies near the cutoff point, making the overall effect more pronounced.

Program 5-1 makes it easy to experiment with the 128's filter. When you run it, the program displays all the current FILTER parameters on the screen, letting you change any that you like. Press P to hear the default settings. The current FILTER statement is displayed on the screen while the 128 plays seven octaves of notes. Now you can press any key to return to the main display screen. Pressing L, B, or H lets you toggle the lowpass, bandpass, and highpass filters on or off. Press C to alter the cutoff frequency or R to change the resonance. In each case, the program prevents you from entering illegal values. By experimenting with different settings, you can hear the filter's effect on a wide variety of frequencies. Note that since the filter is enabled (with PLAY "X1" during the setup portion of the program), you will not hear any sound when all three filters are turned off.

Program 3-1. Filter Editor

```
1Ø CF=7ØØ:LP=1:BP=Ø:HP=Ø:RE=15:P$="CLBHRP":TEMPO2Ø
   :PLAY"XØU15T7S"                              :rem 2Ø6
2Ø PRINT"{CLR}{DOWN}{2 RIGHT}{RVS}FILTER EDITOR":P
   RINT"{DOWN}{2 RIGHT}{RVS}C{OFF}UTOFF{3 SPACES}"
   ;CF"{LEFT}{2 SPACES}"                        :rem 22
3Ø PRINT"{2 RIGHT}{RVS}L{OFF}OWPASS{3 SPACES}";:IF
   LP=1THENPRINT"{RVS}ON ":GOTO5Ø               :rem 2Ø8
4Ø PRINT"OFF"                                   :rem 16
5Ø PRINT"{2 RIGHT}{RVS}B{OFF}ANDPASS{2 SPACES}";:I
   FBP=1THENPRINT"{RVS}ON ":GOTO7Ø              :rem 237
6Ø PRINT"OFF"                                   :rem 18
7Ø PRINT"{2 RIGHT}{RVS}H{OFF}IGHPASS{2 SPACES}";:I
   FHP=1THENPRINT"{RVS}ON ":GOTO9Ø                :rem 2
8Ø PRINT"OFF"                                   :rem 2Ø
9Ø PRINT"{2 RIGHT}{RVS}R{OFF}ESONANCE";RE"{LEFT} "
                                                :rem 1Ø5
1ØØ PRINT"{2 RIGHT}{RVS}P{OFF}LAY{5 SPACES}"
                                                :rem 118
* 11Ø GETKEY A$:IF(A$<>"C"ANDA$<>"L"ANDA$<>"B"ANDA$<
    >"H"ANDA$<>"P"ANDA$<>"R")THEN11Ø            :rem 71
12Ø FORJ=1TO6:IFA$=MID$(P$,J,1)THENA=J           :rem 3
13Ø NEXT                                        :rem 211
14Ø ON A GOSUB15Ø,17Ø,18Ø,19Ø,2ØØ,22Ø:GOTO2Ø
                                                :rem 43
15Ø PRINT"FILTER CUTOFF FREQUENCY":INPUT"(Ø-2Ø47)"
    ;CF:IFCF<ØORCF>2Ø47THEN15Ø                  :rem 171
16Ø RETURN                                      :rem 119
17Ø LP=1-LP:RETURN                              :rem 133
18Ø BP=1-BP:RETURN                              :rem 114
19Ø HP=1-HP:RETURN                              :rem 127
2ØØ PRINT"RESONANCE (Ø-15)";:INPUT RE:IFRE<ØORRE>1
    5THEN2ØØ                                    :rem 26
21Ø RETURN                                      :rem 115
22Ø PRINT"{CLR}FILTER"CF"{LEFT},"LP"{LEFT},"BP"
    {LEFT},"HP"{LEFT},"RE:FILTER CF,LP,BP,HP,RE
                                                :rem 11Ø
23Ø FORJ=1TO6:PLAY"X1O"+CHR$(J+48)+"CDEFGAB":NEXT
                                                :rem 187
24Ø PRINT"PRESS ANY KEY":GETKEYA$:RETURN        :rem 71
```

Music Fundamentals

Here is a short discussion of basic music theory for those whose musical skills could stand some refreshing. As you may know already, conventional music is written on a series of lines and spaces called a *staff*. While a musical staff is theoretically limitless (or bounded only by the range of human hearing), Western musicians have agreed to limit a single staff to five lines and four spaces. Each line and space represents a different pitch on the musical scale. These pitches or notes are represented with the letters A, B, C, D, E, F, and G. Figure 3-2 is a typical staff.

Figure 3-2. Musical Staff

Most written music uses two *staves*, with higher notes shown in the upper staff and lower notes shown in the staff below. Each staff uses a different *clef* symbol to show whether it is treble (higher) or bass (lower).

The staff in Figure 3-2 also contains two numbers resembling a fraction. This, the *time signature*, shows what rhythms are used in the piece. The upper number indicates how many *beats* are contained in each measure, and the lower value shows what sort of note constitutes one beat. When the specified number of beats has elapsed, a *bar line* is drawn vertically across the staff to mark the end of one measure and the beginning of the next. For instance, if you see a 4 in the top of a time signature, you know that each measure must contain four beats. If the top number is 3, each measure needs three beats, and so on.

In many songs a quarter note equals one beat, or basic unit of time, and other notes are a fraction or multiple of the time taken up by a quarter. An eighth note lasts half as long as a quarter, and a sixteenth lasts one-quarter as long. A half note last twice as long as a quarter, and a whole note lasts four quarters.

The actual time elapsed between one note and the next depends on the lower number in the time signature. Since this value controls which note equals one beat, music with a 4/8 time signature plays considerably faster than music with a 4/4 time signature. Within a given time signature, however, the relative note durations are always constant. An eighth note always lasts half as long as a quarter note, and so on.

A *rest* indicates an interval during which no sound is heard. Rests follow the same duration scheme as ordinary notes, and look like those in Figure 3-3 in written music:

Figure 3-3. Rests

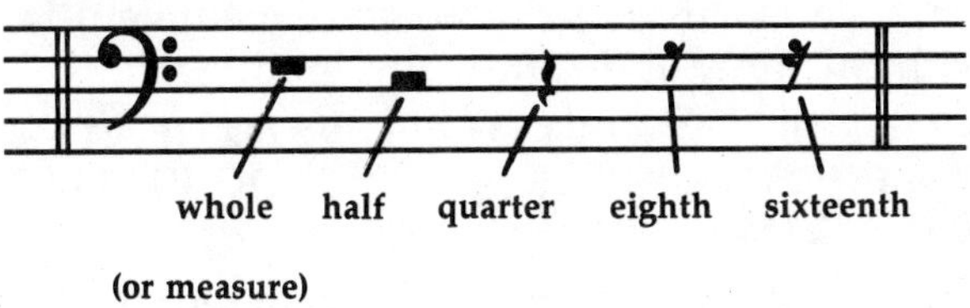

Putting a *dot* (.) in front of any note makes that note last half again as long as its normal duration. For instance, a dotted quarter note lasts one and a half beats, while a dotted eighth lasts three-fourths of a beat. Dots affect rests exactly like notes: A dotted quarter rest lasts one and a half beats, and so on.

Occasionally, you will see a *fermata* (some call it a *bird's eye*) symbol above a note. This means the performer should emphasize the note by holding it somewhat longer than its indicated duration.

BASIC Programming Techniques

Written music contains many more specialized symbols, but let's proceed to a real example. The first step is to set tempo at an average rate. That's not absolutely necessary, since the computer assigns a default tempo if none is specified. But it's a good habit to develop. After all the notes are in place, you can return to line 30 (which we'll mark with a REM for now) and insert a FILTER statement to further refine the sound.

```
10 TEMPO 21
20 ENVELOPE 5,0,9,2,1,1,255
30 REM FILTER
```

Here is the basic melody line for the song "Oh, Susanna" by Stephen Foster:

```
40 PLAY "V1 O4 IF G A O5 C .QC ID C O4 A"
50 PLAY ".QF IG A A G F .HG IF G"
60 PLAY "A O5 C .QC ID C O4 A .QF"
70 PLAY "IG QA A G G WF"
```

Like many other popular songs, "Oh, Susanna" is structured in A-A-B-A form, with A being the verse (the part you just typed in) and B a refrain or chorus. If you run the program at this point, you'll notice that we have all of the melody. That's fine for a start, but we have no accompaniment. Replace line 40 with this line, and run the program again:

```
40 PLAY "V2 O3 QC O2 $B A V2 G V1 O4 IF G V2 O2 QF V1 O4
   A V2 O3 C V1 O5 C V2 O2 C V1 O5 .QC V2 O3 QC V1 O5 ID
   V2 O2 QF V1 O5 C V2 O3 C V1 O4 A"
```

You will hear the beginning of the accompaniment. Now reenter lines 50–70 as shown here:

```
50 PLAY "V2 O2 QC V1 O4 .QF V2 O3 QC V1 O4 IG V2 O2 QF
   V1 O4 A V2 O3 C V1 O4 A V2 O2 D V1 O4 G V2 O2 B V1 O4
   F .HG V2 O3 QC O2 $B A V2 G V1 O4 IF G"
60 PLAY "V2 O2 QF V1 O4 A V2 O3 C V1 O5 C V2 O2 C V1 O5
   .QC V2 O3 QC V1 O5 ID V2 O2 QF V1 O5 C V2 O2 #C V1 O4
   A V2 O2 QD V1 O4 .QF V2 O2 QB V1 O4"
70 PLAY "IG V2 O3 QC V1 O4 QA V2 O2 QC V1 O4 A V2 O2
   D V1 O4 G V2 O2 E V1 O4 G V2 O2 QF V1 O4 WF V2 O2 QG
   A F"
```

Now enter these lines, which constitute the refrain and recap:

```
80 PLAY "V1O4H$BV2O2HDV1O4$BV2O2FV1O5QDV2O2$BV1O
   5HDV2O3FV1O5QDV2O3$BV1O5CV2O3AV1O5CV2O3AV1O4
   AV2O3FV1O4FV2O3DV1O4.HGV2O3QCO2$BAV2GV1O4IFIG"
90 PLAY "V2 O2 QF V1 O4 A V2 O3 C V1 O5 C V2 O2 C V1 O5 .Q
   C V2 O3 QC V1 O5 ID V2 O2 QF V1 O5 C V2 O2 #C V1 O4 A V
   2 O2 QD V1 O4 .QF V2 O2 QB V1 O4"
100 PLAY "IG V2 O3 QC V1 O4 QA V2 O2 QC V1 O4 A V2
    O2 D V1 O4 G V2 O2 E V1 O4 G V2 O2 HF V1 O4 HF V1 O5 IF V
    2 O1 IF"
```

The song is complete. Compare what you have with Program 3-2. Before doing anything else, save the program to disk or tape, then run it. If you like the way it sounds, nothing more needs to be done. But don't be afraid to experiment with different tempo, envelope, and filter settings in lines 10–30.

Program 3-2. Oh, Susanna

```
10 TEMPO 21
20 ENVELOPE 5,0,9,2,1,1,255
30 FILTER 1024,0,0,1,10
40 PLAY "V2 X1 O3 QC O2 $B A V2 G V1 O4 IF G V2 O2
   QF V1 O4 A V2 O3 C V1 X1 O5 C V2 O2 C V1 O5 .Q
  C V2 O3 QC V1 O5 ID V2 O2 QF V1 O5 C V2 O3 C V1
   O4 A"
50 PLAY "V2 O2 QC V1 O4 .QF V2 O3 QC V1 O4 IG V2 O
  2 QF V1 O4 A V2 O3 C V1 O4 A V2 O2 D V1 O4 G V2
   O2 B V1 O4 F .HG V2 O3 QC O2 $B A V2 G V1 O4 I
  F G"
60 PLAY "V2 O2 QF V1 O4 A V2 O3 C V1 O5 C V2 O2 C
  {SPACE}V1 O5 .QC V2 O3 QC V1 O5 ID V2 O2 QF V1
  {SPACE}O5 C V2 O2 #C V1 O4 A V2 O2 QD V1 O4 .QF
   V2 O2 QB V1 O4"
70 PLAY "IG V2 O3 QC V1 O4 QA V2 O2 QC V1 O4 A V2
  {SPACE}O2 D V1 O4 G V2 O2 E V1 O4 G V2 O2 QF V1
   O4 WF V2 O2 QG A F"
80 PLAY "V1O4H$BV2O2HDV1O4$BV2O2FV1O5QDV2O2$BV1O5H
  DV2O3FV1O5QDV2O3$BV1O5CV2O3AV1O5CV2O3AV1O4AV2O3
  FV1O4FV2O3DV1O4.HGV2O3QCO2$BAV2GV1O4IFIG"
90 PLAY "V2 O2 QF V1 O4 A V2 O3 C V1 O5 C V2 O2 C
  {SPACE}V1 O5 .QC V2 O3 QC V1 O5 ID V2 O2 QF V1
  {SPACE}O5 C V2 O2 #C V1 O4 A V2 O2 QD V1 O4 .QF
   V2 O2 QB V1 O4"
100 PLAY "IG V2 O3 QC V1 O4 QA V2 O2 QC V1 O4 A V2
    O2 D V1 O4 G V2 O2 E V1 O4 G V2 O2 HF V1 O4 H
   F V1 O5 IF V2 O1 IF"
```

Here are some more examples of how the elements of traditional music can be realized on the computer. Whether it's opera or pop music, there's usually one part of a piece that stands out—the part that everyone recognizes. Run the following program and see if you recognize the song:

10 TEMPO 12
20 PLAY "V2 O3 T0 U12 X0 IG F E G O4 QC O3 G HG"
30 PLAY "IG E D F QA G HE"
40 PLAY "IG F E G O4 QC O3 A G .HF"
50 PLAY "IG F QE G G WE"

No? If you felt there was something missing, you're absolutely right. What's missing from this song is the *melody* line. Try running Program 3-3.

Program 3-3. Happy Birthday

```
100 TEMPO 12:PLAY "V1 O4 T0 U12 X0 IG V2 O3 G V1 O
    4 G V2 O3 F"
110 PLAY "V1 O4 QA V2 O3 IE G V1 O4 QG V2 O4 C"
120 PLAY "V1 O5 QC V2 O3 G V1 O4 HB V2 O3 QG"
130 PLAY "V1 O4 IG V2 O3 G V1 O4 G V2 O3 E"
140 PLAY "V1 O4 QA V2 O3 ID F V1 O4 QG V2 O3 A V1
    {SPACE}O5 QD V2 O3 G"
150 PLAY "V1 O5 HC V2 O3 E"
160 PLAY "V1 O4 IG V2 O3 G V1 O4 G V2 O3 F"
170 PLAY "V1 O5 QG V2 O3 IE G V1 O5 QE V2 O4 C V1
    {SPACE}O5 C V2 O3 A"
180 PLAY "V1 O4 B V2 O3 G V1 O4 .HA V2 O3 F"
190 PLAY "V1 O5 IF V2 O3 G V1 O5 F V2 O3 F V1 O5 Q
    E V2 O3 E"
200 PLAY "V1 O5 QC V2 O3 G V1 O5 D V2 O3 G V1 O5 W
    C V2 O3 E"
```

The melody *is* important, isn't it? The previous examples point out two important concepts. First, the melody line is usually more important than any other part of a song. Second, most music requires that you use more than one of the SID's three voices. Program 3-4 gives just the melody.

Program 3-4. Mozart Melody

```
10 TEMPO 30
20 PLAY "V1 O5 T0 U12 X0"
30 PLAY "O5 I#D D"
40 PLAY "QD I#D D QD I#D D"
50 PLAY "O5 QD H#A I#A A"
60 PLAY "O5 QG IG F Q#D I#D D"
70 PLAY "O5 QC HC ID C"
80 PLAY "O5 QC ID C QC ID C"
90 PLAY "O5 QC HA IA G"
100 PLAY "O5 Q#F I#F #D QD ID C"
110 PLAY "O4 Q#A H#A"
```

Do you recognize the melody? Let's try writing the same song with an accompanying bass line. Type in Program 3-5.

Program 3-5. Mozart with Bass

```
10 TEMPO 30
20 PLAY "V1 O5 T0 U12 X0"
30 PLAY "V2 O3 T0 U12 X0"
40 PLAY "V1 O5 I#D D QD I#D D QD I#D D"
50 PLAY "V1 O5 QD V2 O3 WG V1 O5 H#A I#A A"
```

```
60 PLAY "V1 O5 QG V2 O3 WG V1 O5 IG F Q#D I#D D"
70 PLAY "V1 O5 QC V2 O3 W#D V1 O5 HC ID C"
80 PLAY "V1 O5 QC V2 O3 W#D V1 O5 ID C QC ID C"
90 PLAY "V1 O5 QC V2 O3 WC V1 O5 HA IA G"
100 PLAY "V1 O5 Q#F V2 O3 WD V1 O5 I#F #D QD ID C"
110 PLAY "V1 O4 Q#A V2 O2 WG V1 O4 H#A"
```

The PLAY symbols V1 and V2 switch the computer from one voice to another. How do we know where to insert notes for the second voice? Remember, in conventional music the number of beats in each measure must equal the top number in the time signature. Here's an example you can listen to. LIST line 50 from the last program , move the cursor over the P in PLAY, then press INST/DEL three times to erase the line number. You should see this:

PLAY "V1 O5 QD V2 O3 WG V1 O5 H#A I#A IA"

Now press RETURN. This line constitutes one measure. The time signature is 4/4, meaning there are four beats per measure, with a quarter note being equal to one beat. Voice 1 plays one quarter note, one half, and two eighths. To keep the voices synchronized, we must give the second voice four beats as well. In this particular measure, voice 2 plays one whole note, precisely equal in duration to the number of beats played by voice 1. By using a separate PLAY string for each measure of a song, you can simplify the task of keeping correct time. Note how every PLAY string in the program contains exactly four beats for each voice.

Of course, the 128 doesn't really care whether you keep correct time. Whether your music makes rhythmic sense or not, the computer will do its best to play it correctly. But multipart music always requires some attention to rhythm. Program 3-6 is also written in 4/4 time.

Program 3-6. Habeñera

```
10 TEMPO 13
20 PLAY "V1 O5 T4 U12 X0 QD Q#C ..IC ..IC ..IC O4
   {SPACE}QB Q$B"
30 PLAY ".QA IA Q#G QG IF SG SF IE IF QG QF HE"
40 PLAY "V1 O5 QD Q#C ..IC ..IC ..IC O4 QB Q$B"
50 PLAY ".QA IA QG QF IE SF SE ID IE QF QE HD"
99 FOR X=1 TO 1000:NEXT X
100 PLAY "V2 O3 T5 U12 X0 .QD IA O4 QF O3 QA"
105 PLAY ".QD IA O4 QF O3 QA"
```

```
110 PLAY ".QD IA O4 QF O3 QA"
115 PLAY ".QD IA O4 QF V1 O5 QD V2 O3 QA V1 O5 Q#C
    "
120 PLAY "V2 O3 .QD V1 O5 ..IC ..IC ..IC V2 O3 IA"
125 PLAY "V1 O4 QB V2 O4 QF V1 O4 Q$B V2 O3 QA"
130 PLAY "V1 O4 .QA V2 O3 .QD V1 O4 IA V2 O3 IA"
140 PLAY "V1 O4 Q#G V2 O4 QF V1 O4 QG V2 O3 QA"
150 PLAY "V2 O3 .QD V1 O4 IF SG SF IE IF V2 O3 IA
    {SPACE}O4 QF V1 O4 QG"
160 PLAY "V2 O3 QA V1 O4 QF V2 O3 .Q#C V1 O4 HE"
170 PLAY "V2 O3 IA V1 O5 QD V2 O4 QE V1 O5 Q#C V2
    {SPACE}O3 QA"
180 PLAY "V2 O3 .Q#C V1 O5 ..IC ..IC ..IC V2 O3 IA
    "
190 PLAY "V1 O4 QB V2 O4 QE V1 O4 Q$B V2 O3 QA"
200 PLAY "V1 O4 .QA V2 O3 .Q#C V1 O4 IA V2 O3 IA"
210 PLAY "V1 O4 QG V2 O4 Q#C V1 O4 QF V2 O3 QA"
220 PLAY "V2 O3 .Q#C V1 O4 IE SF SE ID"
230 PLAY "V2 O3 IA V1 O4 IE V2 O4 QE"
240 PLAY "V1 O4 QF V2 O3 QA V1 O4 QE V2 O3 WD V1 O
    4 WD"
```

Program 3-7 is a Scott Joplin ragtime piece in 2/4 time. It uses all three voices as well as rests and dotted notes.

Program 3-7. Entertainer

```
10 TEMPO 6
20 PLAY "V1 O4 T0 U12 X0 SD S#D V2 T6 U12 X0 V3 T5
    U12 X0"
30 PLAY "V1 O4 SE V2 O4 IR V3 O3 IC V1 O5 IC V2 O4
    IE V3 O3 IG V1 O4 SE"
40 PLAY "V1 O5 IC V2 IR V3 O2 I#A V2 O4 IE V3 O3 I
   G V1 O4 SE O5 .QC"
50 PLAY "V2 IR V3 O2 IA V2 O4 IF V3 O3 IA V2 IR V3
    O2 I$A V1 O5 SC"
60 PLAY "V2 O4 IF V3 O3 I$A V1 O5 SD S#D"
70 PLAY "V2 IR V3 O2 IG V1 O5 SE SC V2 O4 E V3 O3
   {SPACE}IG V1 O5 SD IE"
80 PLAY "V2 IR V3 O2 IG V1 O4 SB ID V2 O4 IF V3 O3
    IG"
90 PLAY "V2 O4 HE V1 O5 HC V3 O3 IC O2 IG QC"
```

Program 3-8 is a rendition of a piece by Domenico Scarlatti.

Program 3-8. Scarlatti Piece

```
10 DIM B$(22),C$(22),D$(22):TEMPO 12
20 READ A$:PLAY A$
30 FOR X=1 TO 22:READ A$:B$(X)=A$:C$(X)=A$:D$(X)=A
   $:NEXT:C$(2)="V1T4V2T9V3T5"+C$(2):D$(2)="V1T6V2
   T0V3T8"+D$(2)
40 FOR X=1 TO 20:PLAY B$(X):NEXT
50 FOR X=2 TO 20:PLAY C$(X):NEXT
60 FOR X=2 TO 20:PLAY D$(X):NEXT:TEMPO 22
70 PLAY B$(21):TEMPO 20:PLAY B$(22)
80 FOR T=1 TO 1000:NEXT:FOR X=54272 TO 54276:POKE
   {SPACE}X,0:NEXT:END
90 DATA "V1T6X0V2T6X0V3T6X0U8"
100 DATA "V1WRV2WRV3O4QD"
110 DATA "QCO3Q$BIAIG"
120 DATA "QFIEIDI#CO2IAIRO3IA"
130 DATA "I$BIGO4I#CO3IAO4IDIEIFIG"
140 DATA "V3O4IFV2O4QAV3O4IDV2O4QGV3O4IEI#CV2O4QFV
    3QDV2IEV3ICV2IDV3O3IB"
150 DATA "V2O4QCV3O3QAV2O3IBV3IGV2IAV3IFV2I#GV3QEV
    2IEV3QCV2IRO4IE"
160 DATA "V3O3QDV2O4IFIDV3O4QDV2I#GIEV3ICV2IAV3O3I
    BV2O4IBV3O3IAV2O5ICV3O3SGV2O5IDV3O3SF"
170 DATA "V2O5ICV3O3IEV2O4IBV3O4QEV2O4IAV3IDV2I#GV
    3I#CV2QAV3O3IAV2O4IGV3O3IBO4IC"
180 DATA "V3O4IDV1O5QDV2O4IRV2IFV3O3IDV1O5QCV2O4IG
    V3O3IEV2O4IAV3O3IFV1O4QBV2IRV3O3QGV2O4IDV1O4IA
    V2Q#CV3O3QAV1O4IG"
190 DATA "V1O4QFV2O4QDV3O3H$BV1O4IEV2QRV1IDV3QAV1O
    4I#CO3IAV3O3QFV2O4QDV1IRO4IA"
200 DATA "V2O4QDV1O4IBV3O3QGV1O4IGV3O4QGV1O5I#CO4I
    AV3O4IFV1O5IDV3O4IEV1O5IEV3O4IDV1O5IFV3O4SCV1O
    5IGV3O3S$B"
210 DATA "V1O5IFV3O3IAO4QAV1O5IEIDV3O4IGV1O5I#CV3O
    4QFV1O5QAV2IRO4IAV3O4QEV2O4IBV1O5QGV2O5IC"
220 DATA "V1O5QFV2O5IDV3O4IDV2O4IAV1O5IEV2O4Q#GV3O
    4QEV1O5IDV2O4QAV1O5QCV3O4HFV1O4IBIA"
230 DATA "V3O4QEV2O4I#GIEV3O4QCV2O4HAV1IRO5IEV3O4Q
    DV1O5IFIDV2O5QDV1I#GIE"
240 DATA "V2O5ICV1O5IAV2O4IBV1O5IBV2O4IAV1O6ICV2O4
    SGV1O6IDV2O4SFV1O6ICV2O4IEV1O5IBV2O5QEV1IAV2ID
    V1I#G"
250 DATA "V2O5I#CV1QAV2O4IAV1O5QGV2O4IBO5ICV2O5IFV
    1O5IFV3O4IDV1O5IGV2IEV3O4IEV1O5QAV2O5IDV3O4IFV
    2O5ICV3O4ID"
260 DATA "V2O4IBV3IGV2O5ICV3O4IAV1O5MIGV2HDV3O4IBV
    1O5IFV3O4IGVV1O5IEV3O4ICV1O5IFV3O4IDV1O5QGV2O5
    ICV3O4IEV2O4IBV3IC"
```

```
270 DATA "V2O4IAV3IFV2IBV3IGV2HCV1O5IFV3O4IAV1O5IE
    V3O4IFV1O5IDV3O3I$BV1O5IEV3O4ICV1O5QFV2O4I$BV3
    O4IDV2IAV3O3I$B"
280 DATA "V2O4IGV3IEV2IAV3IFV1O5MIEV2O4HBV3IGV1O5I
    DV3O4IEV1O5I#CV3O3IAV1O5IDV3O3IBV1O5QEV2O4IAV3
    O4#CV2IGV3O3IA"
290 DATA "V1O5QDV2O4QFV3O4QD"
300 DATA "V1O5QFV2O4QAV3O4QFV1O5HCV2O4T5QGV3O3T5HD
    V2QEV3O2........WDV1O4H$BV2QFQDV1O4HAV2O4QEQCV
    1"
310 DATA "......WGV2O3QFO4QDO3HEO4H#CSDS#CSDS#CSDS
    #CSDS#CSDS#CSDS#CSDS#CO3HBO4..W#CMV3O2WDV1O4W#
    FV2T6WD"
```

The last selection demonstrates another useful technique. By storing PLAY strings in arrays, you make them accessible at any time—to implement repeats as shown here, and other effects as well. By changing tempo at appropriate points, you can create dynamic effects such as *rallentando* (gradual slowing) or add trills and other embellishments.

If you add an M symbol to a PLAY string, the 128 waits until all three voices finish their current notes before beginning any new ones. This can be handy when dealing with complex rhythms. Of course, there's a limit to what this command can do. Don't expect it to repair music that doesn't add up in the first place.

Transcribing Sheet Music to the 128

Even if you have little or no musical experience, it's still possible to create "real music" by transcribing written music into program statements the computer can understand. While at first that might seem a complicated task, the 128's powerful BASIC makes it quite simple. Figure 3-4 is some music written in conventional form.

The piece we've chosen is an excerpt from the "Paragon Rag" by Scott Joplin. One of the first items of interest is the time signature. As noted earlier, this determines the overall speed and rhythm of the piece. A time signature of 2/4 means there are two beats per measure, with a quarter note being equal to one beat. To simplify matters, we'll assign voice 1 to notes in the top (treble) clef, and voices 2 and 3 to the bottom (bass) clef.

Figure 3-4. Paragon Rag

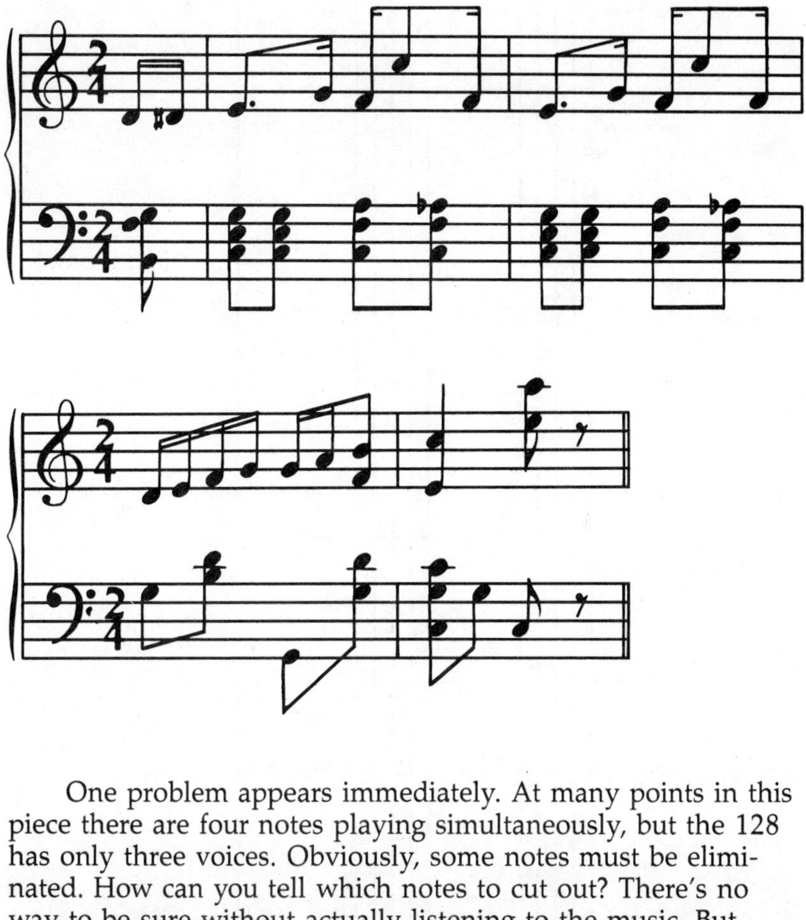

One problem appears immediately. At many points in this piece there are four notes playing simultaneously, but the 128 has only three voices. Obviously, some notes must be eliminated. How can you tell which notes to cut out? There's no way to be sure without actually listening to the music. But here's a trick you can use. If any chord (vertically aligned set of notes) contains a note that is doubled—played in more than one octave at once—chances are you can eliminate one of the doubled notes without serious damage to the music.

For instance, look at the second chord in this piece. The bottom note is a C, the next higher note is an E, the next is a G, and the highest note (on the treble clef) is an E. Now that you know the E is doubled, which one do you eliminate? In many compositions the highest note of a chord contains the melody—too important to eliminate under any circumstances. So we'll guess that the lower E is less important and exclude it.

Figure 3-5. Octave Ranges

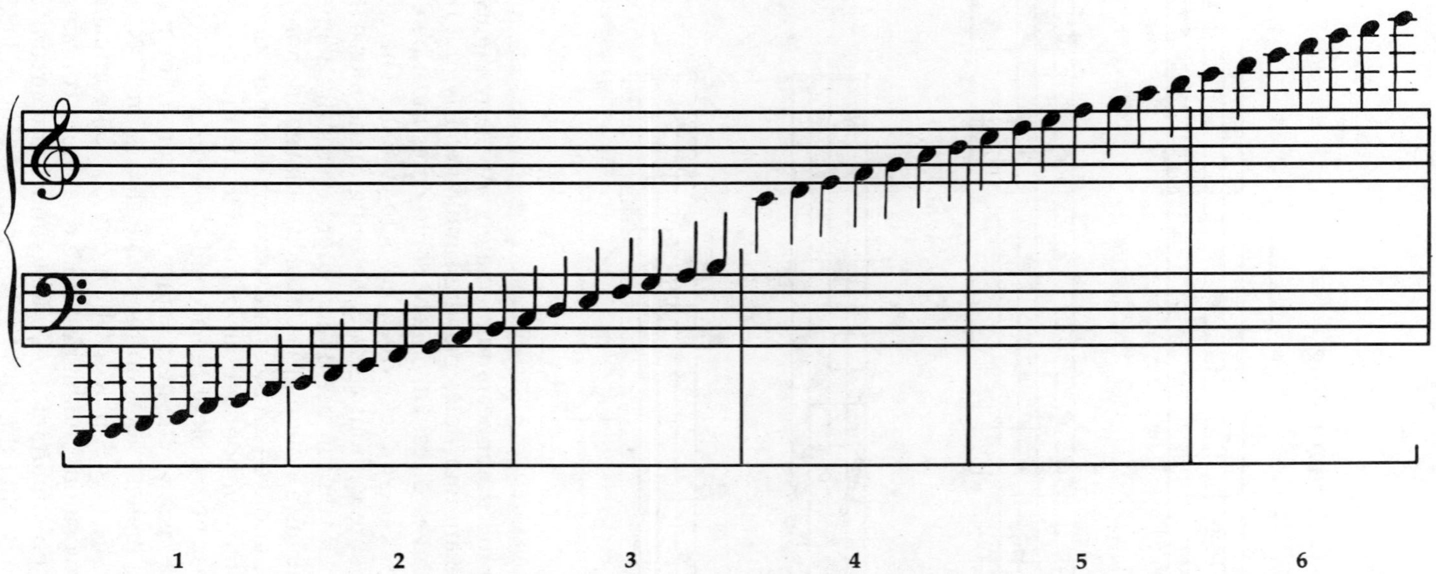

Without making it a hard-and-fast rule, we'll plan to leave out the lower note of any doubled pair.

Let's transcribe the first measure. The first note for voice 1 is a D. Given that the 128 provides seven octaves, how do we know which D it is? Look at Figure 3-5.

As you can see, this note belongs in the fourth octave. Figure 3-6 tells you what duration value to use.

Figure 3-6. Duration Values

𝅘𝅥𝅯 = Sixteenth (S)

𝅘𝅥𝅮 = Eighth (I)

𝅘𝅥 = Quarter (Q)

𝅗𝅥 = Half (H)

𝅝 = Whole (W)

At this point you know the voice assignment, pitch, and duration of the note—enough to write the first program line:

10 PLAY "V1 O4 SC"

The bass notes we've chosen are G in the third octave and B in the second octave, both with an eighth note duration. Here's another useful tip: When playing notes of different durations all at the same time, begin the longer note(s) first. In this case, for instance, you need to hold two eighth notes (the bass) under two successive sixteenths (the treble). By putting the eighth notes at the beginning of the PLAY string, you can assure that all the durations work out correctly. Here is what the first measure looks like.

10 PLAY "V2 O3 IG V3 O2 IB V1 O4 SD S#D"

Program 3-9 is the 128 equivalent of the sheet music above.

Program 3-9. Paragon Rag

```
1 TEMPO 8
1Ø PLAY "V2 O3 IG V3 O2 IB V1 O4 SD S#D"
2Ø PLAY "V1 .IE V2 O3 IG V3 O3 IC V2 IG V3 IC V1 O
   4 SG"
3Ø PLAY "V2 O3 IA V3 IC V1 O4 SF O5 IC V2 O3 I$A V
   3 IC V1 O4 SF"
4Ø PLAY "V1 .IE V2 O3 IG V3 O3 IC V2 IG V3 IC V1 O
   4 SG"
```

```
50 PLAY "V2 O3 IA V3 IC V1 O4 SF O5 IC V2 O3 I$A V
   3 IC V1 O4 SF"
60 PLAY "V3 O3 IG V1 O4 SD SE M V2 O3 ID V3 IB V1
   {SPACE}O4 SF IG"
70 PLAY "V3 O2 IG V1 O4 SA M V2 O3 ID V3 IG V1 O4
   {SPACE}IB"
80 PLAY "V1 O5 QC V2 O4 QE V3 O3 IC O2 IG V1 O6 IC
    V2 O5 IE V3 O2 IC"
```

Machine Language Programming Techniques

Programming sound and music in machine language requires a different set of skills from in BASIC. The 128's BASIC sound commands are designed for easy access—you can create satisfying effects without understanding a thing about how the SID chip works. But there are a number of things the built-in commands can't do. For example, SOUND provides no means for using the filter or ring modulation. And advanced effects such as envelope following are completely beyond BASIC's scope. Here are some examples to help you get started. They're all listed in monitor format. If you're not familiar with how to use the 128's built-in machine language monitor, see "How to Type In Machine Language Programs" in the Introduction.

Note that in order to access the SID chip, you must set the computer to one of the memory banks in which it can "see" SID. This is easy to do: Type BANK 15 and press RETURN. Be sure to do this before trying any of the following examples.

Clearing the SID Chip

Every machine language program (and every BASIC program, for that matter) should begin by clearing all SID chip registers to zero. This insures that your sounds won't be affected by, for example, residual filter settings from previous programs. Here is a fast, simple way to clear the entire chip:

```
0C00  LDX #$18
0C02  LDA #$00
0C04  STA $D400,X
0C07  DEX
0C08  BPL  $0C04
```

Location $D400 (54272) is the first SID chip register and $D418 (54296) is the highest one you can write to. The BPL instruction at $0C08 in this example causes the program to branch back as long as X has not decremented to zero.

Loading the SID Chip

After clearing the SID chip, it's often useful to preload certain registers. While you could do this with a series of LDA and STA instructions, it's more efficient to do it inside a loop as in the first example. First, let's store the data we'll need. Enter the following bytes with the monitor > command:

```
>0D00 00 07 00 07 20 0B 00 00
>0D08 0F 00 07 40 0A 00 00 03
>0D10 00 07 40 0A 00 00 00 00
>0D18 3F
```

Now our table of data is stored safely in one of the RS-232 buffers, starting at location $0D00. Here is the code that loads the data into the SID chip. Since this would ordinarily be done immediately after clearing the chip, we'll continue where the last routine left off.

```
0C0A  LDX #$18
0C0C  LDA $0D00,X
0C0F  STA $D400,X
0C12  DEX
0C13  BPL $0D0C
0C16  RTS
```

That completes the setup routine. To try it out, exit the monitor, type SYS 3072, and press RETURN. You're rewarded with three notes—not much, but it's a start.

Background Routines

Some of the most exciting SID effects—like "wah-wah" and other dynamic sounds—can be achieved only from machine language. In many cases the simplest way to produce these effects is with an *interrupt-driven* machine language routine. Though the term sounds a bit intimidating, such routines are actually quite simple to write. They work by wedging into the computer's hardware interrupt routine, which normally does background jobs like reading the keyboard and updating internal timers. Once you have set up an interrupt routine, the computer performs it automatically in the background, 60 times every second.

The first step in creating a background routine is to change the computer's interrupt vector as follows:

```
0C00  SEI
0C01  LDA #$0D
```

```
0C03  STA $0314
0C06  LDA #$0C
0C08  STA $0315
0C0B  CLI
0C0C  RTS
```

The SEI instruction at the beginning of the routine is critical. It turns off the computer's interrupts so that nothing happens while you're redirecting the routine to your own code. Before writing the setup routine, you must know where your code is going to go. In this case, we'll put it at $0C0D, right after the setup routine. Put the low byte of the code address in $0314 and the high byte in $0315, then exit the routine with CLI (to turn interrupts back on) and RTS (to return to BASIC). Now we're ready to write the interrupt routine itself:

```
0C0D  LDA $FC
0C0F  CLC
0C10  ADC #$18
0C12  STA $FC
0C14  STA $D401
0C17  JMP $FA65
```

Once everything is ready, you can start the interrupt routine (before doing so, load the SID chip as explained above). Exit the monitor and enter BANK 15:SYS 3072. Whereas before all three voices produced a constant tone, now voice 1's frequency changes very rapidly. Location $D401 is the high byte of voice 1's frequency register. The interrupt routine simply stores rapidly increasing values in that register, using location $00FC (a free zero page register) as a counter. Sixty times every second, this routine adds 24 ($18) to the value in $00FC, and transfers that value to $D401 to increase the pitch. While you're still in BASIC, enter this line and press RETURN:

BANK 15:POKE 54276,64:POKE 54276,65

This restarts voice 1 so that you can hear the sound again. The interrupt routine keeps working, even after the sound has faded out (on some computers you can hear the tone continuing very faintly; this is a "crosstalk" effect caused by electronic leakage within the 128's circuits). The fading effect is automatic, caused as the sound completes its natural attack/decay cycle.

Why use an interrupt routine? For one thing, it's automatic. Once you start it up, it performs the whole job on its own, regardless of what the computer is doing. Notice that after typing the last BASIC line, the cursor returned immediately. If you wanted to use this sound in a game, for instance, you'd need only one SYS to start the interrupt routine. After that, all it takes is a simple BASIC statement like the one above to make the sound; while it's completing its attack/decay cycle, your program can continue with other things.

Jump to the Interrupt

You may already have noticed that the interrupt routine doesn't end with RTS or BRK like most of the ML examples in this book. Remember, when you set up an interrupt routine, you're diverting the computer from a critical task. The hardware interrupt is particularly important because it scans the keyboard (if the computer can't read the keyboard, you can't type anything and might as well shut the machine off). After an interrupt routine is finished, it must always end with a JMP to the address of the computer's normal interrupt routine ($FA65, in this case). Don't leave out this important step—the result is invariably a system crash.

Disabling an interrupt-driven routine can be done in one of two ways. During program development, the simplest method is to press RUN/STOP–RESTORE. If you want to modify these routines (and that's the best way to learn about them), don't make any changes while the interrupt wedge is active; first set things back to normal with RUN/STOP–RESTORE. This not only restores the normal interrupt routine, but also clears the SID chip. Here is a routine that restores the interrupt under program control:

```
0C00  SEI
0C01  LDA #$65
0C03  STA $0314
0C06  LDA #$FA
0C08  STA $0315
0C0B  CLI
0C0C  RTS
```

Dynamic Filtering

The SID chip offers four different waveforms, but those basic tones can quickly lose their glamour. The SID filter lets you shape the basic waveforms in many different ways, to emulate a banjo's nasal twang, the soft tones of a harp, or the full sound of a pipe organ. Though BASIC is fine for static or slowly changing effects, truly dynamic filtering requires the speed of machine language. Here is an example (note that this must be used in conjunction with a setup routine like the one described above).

```
0C0D  LDA $FC
0C0F  SEC
0C10  SBC  #$18
0C12  STA  $FC
0C14  STA  $D416
0C17  JMP  $FA65
```

We're using location $00FC as a counter again, just as in the last example. But this time we're decreasing the value held there (with SBC) rather than increasing it. Location $D416 (54294) is the high byte of the filter cutoff frequency register. The effect of this routine is to sweep the filter's cutoff frequency downward from 255 to 0, over and over as the tone fades into silence. Before using the routine, exit to BASIC and set up the filter by entering the following line:

BANK 15:POKE 54295,241:POKE 54296,31

Now SYS to the routine that sets up the interrupt, and enter the following line:

BANK 15:POKE 54276,64:POKE 54276,65

You can modify the rate of the filter's sweep by changing the value following SBC in the example routine. Larger values create a faster sweep, and smaller ones slow the sweep down.

Envelope Following

Up to now we've been using our own counter to control dynamic effects. But the SID chip itself provides the means for similar effects. Locations $D41B (54299) and $D41C (54300) are two special-purpose "read-only" registers within the chip. Read-only means you can read their contents, but can't change them directly (with a POKE, for example). Both registers are controlled with voice 3.

Location $D41C is voice 3's envelope register. As you've seen in the preceding examples, sounds have a natural attack/decay cycle, or sound envelope, which determines how quickly they fade into silence. This envelope, like other sound features, is programmable. Location $D41C permits you to read the envelope cycle in realtime and use the resulting values to control other effects. Sound confusing? Never mind—it's easier to demonstrate than it is to explain. Enter the following code (keep in mind that you must activate this with an interrupt setup routine as shown above).

```
0C0D  LDA $D41C
0C0F  STA $D416
0C12  JMP $FA65
```

After that's done, exit the monitor and press RUN/STOP–RESTORE to reset the interrupt vector, then start the routine with a SYS. Now enter the following lines:

```
BANK 15:POKE 54286,0:POKE 54287,0:POKE 54273,10
POKE 54277,12:POKE 54291,12
POKE 54290,64:POKE 54276,64:POKE 54276,65:POKE 54290,65
```

The POKEs give both voices the same sound envelope and activate both at once. Voice 1 is filtered and voice 3 is inaudible (its frequency is zero). As the sound from voice 1 goes through its natural envelope cycle, the filter's cutoff frequency is changed in accord with voice 3's envelope. Since both envelopes are the same (or nearly so), the interrupt routine creates a more natural, integrated effect than is usually the case with computer sound effects. By changing voice 3's sound envelope, you can control the rate at which the filter changes.

Note how the cutoff frequency changes dynamically, right along with voice 3's envelope. This is the origin of the term "envelope following." One sound parameter follows another. Though we've used location $D41C to change the filter, you can use it to change any other SID register that you like. For example, try substituting $D401 (frequency high byte) or $D403 (pulsewidth high nybble) for $D416 in the example routine. Of course, by setting voice 3's frequency register to something higher than zero, you can hear that voice as well. But it's often preferable to keep it silent so that you can fully appreciate the modulating effect it has on the other voice.

Multipurpose Number Generator

Another SID register useful to the ML programmer is location $D41B (54299). This programmable register outputs changing values controlled by the frequency and waveform settings of voice 3. In fact, voice 3 is so valuable as a number generator that many ML programmers reserve it exclusively for that purpose. Here's an example to try:

```
0C0D  LDA $D41B
0C0F  STA $D416
0C12  JMP $FA65
```

Activate this routine as described above, then exit to BASIC and enter the following lines:

```
BANK 15:POKE 54286,25:POKE 54287,0:POKE 54273,7
POKE 54277,15
POKE 54276,64:POKE 54290,0
POKE 54276,65:POKE 54290,16
```

Note that voice 3 is set to the triangle waveform, but not gated. The number generator runs continuously whenever you set 54290 to one of the four waveforms. When the triangle waveform is chosen (54290 contains 16), the number generator oscillates between 0 and 255. The noise waveform (128) generates random values in the same range, a very useful feature. When the sawtooth wave (32) is chosen, the values sweep upward. The pulse wave (64) creates an on/off effect: The output switches between 0 and 255, again at a rate determined by the voice's frequency.

SID Architecture

The 128's SID (Sound Interface Device) chip is like no other chip in the computer. Supply it with the right information, and it provides you with sounds. The SID contains 28 separate registers, or addressable locations. The lower 24 locations are all write-only, meaning you can change their contents with POKE (or a machine language store instruction), but can't PEEK them to discover what they contain. The highest four registers are read-only. You can PEEK them, but you can't directly change their contents.

The 128's SID chip is exactly the same as the SID chip found in the Commodore 64. This means that any 64 sound or music program runs perfectly on the 128 in 128 mode. Of course, the 128's BASIC sound and music commands make most 64 sound techniques unnecessary. However, you will still need to know about the SID chip in order to create sound and music in machine language or to use advanced effects such as ring modulation and envelope following from BASIC. Here is a brief description of the function of each SID register.

Since the SID chip provides three independent voices (tone generators), the lowest 21 registers are divided into three sets, with seven control registers for each of the three voices. Locations 54272–54278 ($D400–$D406) control voice 1, with 54279–54285 ($D407–$D40D) and 54286–54292 ($D40E–$D414) controlling voices 2 and 3, respectively. Let's look at each of the control registers in turn.

54272–54273 ($D400–$D401) Frequency
These two registers control the frequency or pitch of the tone produced by voice 1. The first register is the low byte of the 16-bit frequency number, and the second is the high byte. Appendix E lists the values you may POKE into these registers to obtain standard musical notes in all eight octaves. Of course, you may use values other than those listed in the Appendix. Note that the frequency must be set to some nonzero value in order to make the voice produce a tone.

54274–54275 ($D402–$D403) Pulsewidth
The contents of these two registers are treated as a 12-bit number which controls the width of the pulse waveform. Location 54274 contains the low eight bits of the pulsewidth value, and the four low bits of 54275 contain its high nybble. These locations are not used by waveforms other than pulse.

54276 ($D404) Waveform and Gate
Each bit of this register serves a different purpose. It allows you to select the waveform to be produced by the voice, turn the voice on or off, select ring modulation and/or synchronization, or disable the voice completely. The lowest bit (bit 0) is the gate bit which turns the voice on or off. When this bit is set to 1 at the same time a waveform is selected, the voice begins the attack/decay portion of its envelope cycle. When this bit is set to 0 (if the sound is in progress), the voice begins the release portion of the cycle.

Bits 4, 5, 6, and 7 select one of the four SID waveforms for the voice. In order to hear a sound you must enable a waveform and gate the voice. For instance, POKE 54276,16 selects the triangle wave and turns off (ungates) the voice. POKE 54276,17 selects the triangle wave and turns on (gates) the voice. Note that the pulse wave produces no sound unless the pulsewidth is set to some nonzero value.

Bits 1 and 2 of this register are used to select synchronization and ring modulation, respectively. Synchronization mixes the frequency of voice 3 into the output of voice 1. Ring modulation also mixes the frequencies of voices 3 and 1, but accentuates the resulting overtones and suppresses the fundamental frequency of the modulated voice. Bit 3, the test bit, is rarely used. When set to 1, this bit disables the voice completely.

54277–54278 ($D405–$D406) Envelope Control
These two registers define the sound envelope for voice 1 in terms of four different parameters: attack, decay, sustain, and release. Attack defines how quickly the sound rises from silence to maximum volume. Decay determines how quickly it falls from its peak to the volume at which it will be sustained. Sustain defines the volume level for the middle portion of the sound's brief life. And release controls how quickly the sound fades from its sustain level back to silence again. The high nybble of 54277 controls attack, and its low nybble controls decay. Similarly, the high and low nybbles of 54278 determine sustain and release, respectively.

54279–54285 ($D407–$D40D) Voice 2 Control
These seven registers perform the same function for voice 2 as the registers described above except that when synchronization or ring modulation is selected, voice 1 modulates voice 2.

54286–54292 ($D40E–$D414) Voice 3 Control
Same functions for voice 3 as those described above except that when synchronization or ring modulation is selected, voice 2 modulates voice 3.

54293–54294 ($D415–$D416) Filter Cutoff Frequency
The contents of these two registers form an 11-bit number controlling the SID filter cutoff frequency. Location 54294 is the high eight bits, and bits 0–2 of location 54295 form the lower three bits of the value.

54295 ($D417) Filter Control
The four high bits of this register set the resonance (peaking effect) of the SID filter. Maximum resonance accentuates frequencies near the cutoff point, making the filtering more noticeable. Low resonance tones the filter down. The three low

bits of 54295 determine which of the voices are filtered. Setting bit 0 routes voice 1 through the filter, and bits 1 and 2 perform the same function for voices 1 and 3. If you connect an external sound source to the SID chip (be careful not to exceed safe voltage levels—you'll have difficulty getting a damaged SID chip replaced), its input is filtered when bit 3 is set.

54296 ($D418) Volume and Filter Type
The four low bits of 54296 set the volume for the entire chip. Nothing is audible unless this location contains a nonzero value. Setting bits 4, 5, and 6 turns on the lowpass, bandpass, and highpass filters, respectively. The SID chip is designed so that you may activate more than one filter at a time. The high bit of 54296 completely disables the output of voice 3, convenient when that voice is used as a modulator or number generator.

54297–54298 ($D419–$D41A) Paddle Inputs
These registers can be read to determine the current position of game paddle controllers connected to the joystick ports. This isn't an inherently musical function, but since the SID already contained the required analog-to-digital conversion circuity, tacking this feature onto SID eliminated the need for separate components to read paddles. The paddle inputs could also digitize an analog signal (audio output, and so on) from the external world. The input must be a dc voltage in the range 0–5 volts; the result will be a register value in the range 0–255, where a 0 register value indicates a 5-volt input and a register value of 255 indicates a 0-volt input. These locations can also be read with the BASIC function POT.

54299 ($D41B) Number Generator
This read-only location generates various series of numbers determined by the frequency and waveform settings of voice 3. The voice 3 frequency setting determines how rapidly the output changes, and the type of output depends on which waveform you select. When the triangle wave is enabled, the output oscillates, sweeping up and down in the range 0–255. The sawtooth wave generates a repeated upward sweep within the same range. Selecting the pulse wave causes the output to flip back and forth from 0 to 255, and the noise waveform generates random numbers in an identical range.

Random numbers are useful in games and many other applications. You can obtain an excellent distribution by setting the high byte for voice 3's frequency at 255.

54300 ($D41C) **Envelope Output**

When voice 3 is gated and its envelope cycle is in progress, this location returns a changing value in the range 0–255 which reflects the state of the envelope. Just as you can control the output of 54299 by setting voice 3's frequency and waveform, this register's output is controlled by voice 3's attack/decay/sustain/release configuration. When using this register to modulate others, it is often advisable to disable voice 3's output by setting bit 7 of location 54296.

Chapter 4

Peripherals

Peripherals

A *peripheral device* is any device that connects to your computer, letting the computer perform jobs that it couldn't manage on its own. A disk or tape drive, for instance, lets you store programs in permanent form. A printer lets you make hardcopy program listings, print word-processing documents, and so on. This chapter looks at the major peripherals used by the 128—disk and tape drives, printers, monitors, modems—as well as smaller devices such as the joystick, mouse, and game paddles.

Disk Drive

The Commodore 128 can use both the 1541 disk drive, designed for the Commodore 64 and VIC-20, and the new 1571, designed specifically for the 128. The 1571 is really three drives in one: In 64 or 128 mode, it can emulate a 1541; in 128 mode, it can also operate in fast serial mode; and in the even faster CP/M mode, it can read several different disk formats. Chapter 5 contains additional information about CP/M.

Since the 1541 has only one read/write head, it uses single-sided, single-density disks. Double-sided, double-density disks—which can store roughly twice as much information—are used on the 1571, which has two read/write heads, one above and one below the disk. This permits the 1571 to read some MFM (non-Commodore format) CP/M disks as well, a facility not available with the 1541.

The software that lets the computer communicate with the disk drive is called DOS, for Disk Operating System. In most other computers, DOS is loaded from disk into RAM when the computer is booted (turned on). However, in Commodore systems, DOS is stored permanently in ROM inside the disk drive. This means that DOS doesn't require large amounts of the computer's memory, as is the case with most non-Commodore machines. However, it also means that DOS cannot easily be changed or customized.

BASIC 2.0 (used in 64 mode) provides very limited support for DOS. For any disk operation other than loading, saving, or reading and writing files, you must open the command channel to the drive, send the command, and close the channel. This procedure still works in BASIC 7.0, but is unnecessary since BASIC 7.0 provides a supporting statement for every disk command except INITIALIZE. The following is a list of all the DOS commands available in each version of BASIC. You can find a complete explanation of each command in Chapter 1 and the user's manual for your disk drive:

BASIC 2.0 DOS Commands

DOS command	Corresponding BASIC statement
NEW	OPEN 15,8,15,"N0:*disk name,id*":CLOSE 15
COPY	OPEN 15,8,15,"C0:*new file*=0:*old file*":CLOSE 15
RENAME	OPEN 15,8,15,"R0:*new name*=*old name*":CLOSE 15
SCRATCH	OPEN 15,8,15,"S0:*filename*":CLOSE 15
VALIDATE	OPEN 15,8,15,"V0":CLOSE 15
LOAD	LOAD "*filename*",8
SAVE	SAVE "*filename*",8
VERIFY	VERIFY "*filename*",8

BASIC 7.0 DOS Commands

(You may also use any BASIC 2.0 commands)

NEW	HEADER "*disk name,Iid*"
COPY	COPY "*old file*" TO "*new file*"
RENAME	RENAME "*old file*" TO "*new file*"
SCRATCH	SCRATCH "*filename*"
VALIDATE	COLLECT
INITIALIZE	OPEN 15,8,15,"I0":CLOSE 15
LOAD	DLOAD "*filename*"
	BLOAD "*filename*",*Bbank*,*Pstart address*
	BOOT "*filename*"
SAVE	DSAVE "*filename*"
	BSAVE "*filename*",*Bbank*,*Pstart address* TO P*end address*
VERIFY	DVERIFY "*filename*"

What Is a File?

A *file* is simply a collection of information—the electronic equivalent of a manila file folder. What you put into a file is up to you: It may contain a BASIC program, a word processing document, numeric data from a spreadsheet, or whatever. The disk directory shows you all the files contained on a disk (use DIRECTORY or CATALOG in BASIC 7.0 or LOAD"$0",8 followed by LIST in BASIC 2.0). (Note that although a 1541 drive can read all the filenames from a double-sided 1571 disk, it cannot access any file stored on the second side.) To slow the listing of a directory, press CTRL (BASIC 2.0) or the Commodore key (BASIC 7.0); you may pause a BASIC 7.0 directory listing by pressing CTRL-S or NO SCROLL.

A Commodore disk may contain several different types of files. BASIC programs are ordinarily saved as *program* files, indicated by PRG after the filename in the directory. Other types include *sequential* (SEQ), *relative* (REL), *user* (USR), and *deleted* (DEL) files. Of these five types, only the first three—program, sequential, and relative files—are widely used. User files can be accessed only with advanced techniques, and DEL is actually an error condition rather than a file type.

The most common way to access a disk file is to load or save a program from BASIC or the machine language monitor. LOAD, BLOAD, DLOAD, and BOOT (or L from the monitor) usually bring a program from the disk into the computer's memory. SAVE, BSAVE and DSAVE (or S from the monitor) usually move a program from memory to a disk file. One feature common to all these commands is that they work with program files.

However, you must be careful not to confuse the format of a file with its contents. In many cases, a program (PRG) file contains a program which you can load into memory and run. But program files can just as easily contain other sorts of data (a word processing document, etc.). And you will sometimes see programs (usually machine language) stored in a sequential file. For the purpose of general file-handling, sequential and program files have a virtually identical structure. With the exception of append operations in BASIC 2.0 (see below), you can do anything with a program file that can be done with a sequential file, and vice versa. Though DOS distinguishes between the two file types, the difference is largely one of name alone.

Talking to the Drive

Before you can access a disk file, you must open a channel of communication between the computer and the drive. The *command channel* (channel 15) is reserved for sending commands to the drive and reading its error status. This channel is most often used to find out what caused a disk error (when the drive's busy light flashes). BASIC 7.0 makes this very easy to do: Simply type PRINT DS$ and press RETURN. Reading the error status in BASIC 2.0 requires a short program:

```
10 OPEN 1,8,15
20 INPUT#1, ER, EM$, TR, SE
30 PRINT ER, EM$, TR, SE
40 CLOSE 1
```

In both cases, the result is the same. The computer displays an error number and message, followed by the disk track and sector associated with the error (the track and sector are irrelevant to certain errors). The message 00, OK, 00, 00 means that no errors were detected. The variables DS and DS$ provide the same information in BASIC 7.0. DS returns the disk error number, and is very useful within a program. For instance, after trying to find a particular disk file, you might call a subroutine like this:

```
500 IF DS<>0 THEN PRINT DS, DS$:PRINT "PRESS ANY KEY
    TO CONTINUE":GETKEY A$
510 RETURN
```

When an error condition exists, line 500 prints the error message and waits for you to press a key. We'll return to the command channel later in this chapter.

Reading and Writing to Disk

Many people find disk programming difficult at first. Like any other procedure, what seems complex at first becomes simple when you break the process down into individual steps. Let's look at a typical program that opens a sequential disk file, writes data into the file, then reads it back into memory. The first step is to open the file. Remember, the BASIC 7.0 version works only in 128 mode; the second version of line 10 works in 128 or 64 mode.

BASIC 7.0

```
10 DOPEN#1,"SEQFILE",W
```

BASIC 2.0

```
10 OPEN 1,8,2,"SEQFILE,S,W"
```

Both versions use the same logical file number (1) and filename (SEQFILE). Since the D in DOPEN stands for *disk*, the 128 assumes you want to use device 8 when that command is used. BASIC 2.0 requires that you specify the device number and secondary address. In both cases, the ,W stands for Write, meaning you want to prepare for writing data to disk. If you replace the W with an R, the computer prepares for a read operation. The BASIC 2.0 version requires ,S to signal that a sequential file is desired. By replacing the S with a P, you could create a program file instead. Unless you specify otherwise, DOPEN assumes you want to create a sequential file.

The secondary address is very important: Although its use is anything but self-evident, the drive uses the secondary address internally to identify which incoming commands apply to the file. It can be any number from 0–30 (except for 15, which has a special meaning), but *each file you open must have a unique secondary address*. This is not a problem when using DOPEN, since that statement automatically selects an unused secondary address for each new file it opens. However, if you OPEN 1,8,5,"FILE1" then OPEN 2,8,5,"FILE2", both files become unavailable when either is closed. If either file were opened for writing, this could lead to an improperly closed (splat) file. Because you cannot easily tell what secondary addresses DOPEN has chosen, you should not mix OPEN and DOPEN statements within a program. Use one or the other form exclusively, or perform all OPENs before the first DOPEN.

Note that you may substitute variables for any of the parameters following DOPEN or OPEN. For instance, A$="SEQFILE":OPEN 1,8,2,A$+",S,W" works just as well as the previous examples. DOPEN requires that variables be placed in parentheses, so the equivalent BASIC 7.0 statement would be A$="SEQFILE":DOPEN#1,(A$),W. Variables become very useful when you want a program to handle more than one option. By replacing line 10 as shown here, you can let the user specify the filename and type:

```
10 INPUT "FILENAME, TYPE (S/P)";F$,T$:DOPEN#1,(F$+","+
   T$),W
```

Sequential files are called sequential for a very good reason. Every piece of data in the file must be written or read in order, from beginning to end. There's no way to jump into the middle of a sequential file and start reading or writing. If you want to change data somewhere in the middle of the file, you must read the whole file into memory, make the desired changes, then write it all back to disk again. The same is generally true of program data files. As we'll learn later on, relative files do not have this restriction.

The PRINT# command is most often used to write data to disk. Like its close relative PRINT, PRINT# is very flexible.

You can use it to output numeric or string data, in the form of literals (123, "ABC," and so on) or variables such as X%, X(21), A$, A$(50). Let's add some lines to the example program for writing data to disk:

20 FOR J=1 TO 20
30 PRINT#1,J
40 NEXT J

Note that PRINT# uses the same logical file number (1) used when opening the file. The data (J in this case) is separated from the file number by a comma. Just as with PRINT, you can use commas or semicolons to insert spaces between data items or cause them to be written without any separating characters. The SPC and TAB functions are also permissible, though less often seen. After writing to a disk file, you must always take care to close it properly:

BASIC 7.0
50 DCLOSE#1

BASIC 2.0
50 CLOSE 1

Again, CLOSE and DCLOSE refer to the logical file number. If you omit this important step, the file will probably remain on the disk as an unclosed file. Such files are marked with an asterisk (*) before the file type in the disk directory. The 1571 manual refers to these as splat files, although a more common name in older Commodore literature is poison files. Whatever the name, you should never save a program on a disk containing a splat file until that file has been removed. Furthermore, you should never scratch a splat file; instead, remove the offending file by validating the disk. Use COLLECT in BASIC 7.0, or OPEN 1,8,15,"V0:":CLOSE 1 in either 64 or 128 mode.

Closing a file also ensures that all the data sent to the drive actually ends up on the disk. Though you may think of the serial cable as a direct pipeline between your computer's memory and the disk itself, that's not really true. The drive stores data in its own internal memory prior to writing it out to the disk. If you interrupt the writing process before the file is closed, the drive may not get a chance to transfer all the data from its memory to the disk.

If the command channel (specified with a secondary address of 15) is also open during read or write operations, you should not close it until after all other disk files are closed. As a general rule, the command channel should be the first channel opened and the last to be closed.

Reading a File

Of course, a disk file is of no use unless you can read its contents back into the computer's memory. The general procedure is very similar to the writing process. You must open the file, bring in the data with GET# or INPUT# commands, then close it. These commands open a sequential file for reading:

BASIC 7.0
DOPEN#1,"SEQFILE"

BASIC 2.0
OPEN 1,8,1,"SEQFILE,S,R"

If you supply nothing but a filename, DOPEN assumes you want to read a sequential file from disk, using device 8. In this case, the BASIC 7.0 version does not require you to specify the file type (sequential) or the operation (reading). Here is a BASIC 7.0 program that reads the file we created in the previous example.

```
10 DIM A$(20)
20 C=0
30 DOPEN#1,"SEQFILE"
40 C=C+1
50 INPUT#1,A$(C)
60 IF ST<>64 THEN 40
70 DCLOSE#1
80 FOR J=1 TO C
90 PRINT A$(J)
100 NEXT
```

Line 10 creates a string array (A$) large enough to hold all 20 data items, and line 20 sets the counter C to zero. Line 30 opens the file for reading. In BASIC 2.0, you substitute OPEN 1,8,1,"SEQFILE",S,R for the DOPEN in line 30. The INPUT# command in line 50 brings in one piece of data at a time. Line 60 tests the status variable ST to check if we've read all the data. Since the system automatically sets ST to 64 when it finds an end-of-file marker, this is a convenient way to check for the end of a file. In this case, you know that the file contains only 20 data elements, but in many circumstances there is no way to know the file's exact length in advance.

Line 70 closes the file (replace DCLOSE#1 with CLOSE 1 for BASIC 2.0), and lines 80–100 display the data. Used without a file number, DCLOSE has the effect of closing all open disk files; if no device number is specified, DCLOSE assumes you are working with device 8.

INPUT# and GET#

INPUT# works much like the familiar INPUT statement. Both commands stop input after a comma or colon and reject data which is too large to fit in BASIC's input buffer. Neither lets you store nonnumeric data in a numeric variable. Here is the general format for INPUT#:

INPUT#*logical file number, variable(s)*

Again, the logical file number identifies which file you want to read. After the file number comes the variable or variables used to store the data. INPUT# can bring in several data items at once if you separate different variables with commas:

INPUT#1, A$, B$, C$

The single statement shown here brings in three pieces of data, storing them in the string variables A$, B$, and C$. Because INPUT# causes a FILE DATA ERROR if you try to read nonnumeric data into a numeric variable, it is common to read all data into string variables, then convert to the desired variable type with a function like VAL.

Where sequential and program files are concerned, reading the file brings the data back in the same order as it was written. You couldn't write NAME$, ADDRESS$, CITY$ to the disk file, then expect to read it back correctly with INPUT#1,CITY$,NAME$,ADDRESS$. The variable CITY$ would contain the name, NAME$ would hold the address, and ADDRESS$ would contain the city. This restriction does not apply to relative files.

One disadvantage of INPUT# is that it may cause a STRING TOO LONG error, halting your program with an error message. Though a BASIC string may contain up to 255 characters, the length of the BASIC input buffer limits the size of a string that INPUT# can bring in from disk. The input buffer is 88 characters long in BASIC 2.0 and 160 characters in BASIC 7.0. When the buffer overflows with an overly long piece of data, BASIC invariably stops the program and signals an error.

For this reason, GET# is often preferred to INPUT# when working with files that contain data of unknown length. Like GET, the GET# command brings in one character or byte of data at a time. Here's one way to read our example file with GET#:

```
10 DIM A$(20)
20 C=0
30 DOPEN#1,"SEQFILE"
40 C=C+1
50 G$=""
60 GET#1,T$
70 IF T$<>CHR$(13) THEN G$=G$+T$:GOTO 60
80 A$(C)=G$
90 IF ST<>64 THEN 40
100 DCLOSE#1
110 FOR J=1 TO C
120 PRINT A$(J)
130 NEXT
```

Line 70 builds the input string one character at a time, testing for the carriage return (CHR$(13)) which PRINT# placed at the end of each data item. GET# correctly reads control characters such as the carriage return and cursor controls. But when you read CHR$(0), GET# converts it to an empty string (""). Because BASIC 2.0 generates an ILLEGAL QUANTITY error if you try to perform ASC(""), constructions such as A=ASC(A$+CHR$(0)) appear frequently in Commodore 64 file-reading routines. This bug does not exist in BASIC 7.0.

Append Operations

The APPEND command in BASIC 7.0 simplifies the process of adding new data to the end of an existing file. The following statement simultaneously opens the sequential file SEQFILE as logical file number 1 and prepares the drive to add new data at the point where the old data ends:

```
APPEND#1,"SEQFILE"
```

Note the similarity between APPEND and DOPEN in BASIC 7.0. If you supply only the logical file number and filename, both commands assume you are working with a sequential file and device number 8. Different operations require additional parameters (see Chapter 1). Here is the BASIC 2.0 version of the same statement:

```
OPEN 1,8,1,"SEQFILE",A
```

In this case, A appears where W (write) would otherwise be used. Keep in mind that append operations merely paste a new chunk of data onto what already exists. If you need to delete or modify existing data items, it is still necessary to read the entire file into memory, make the changes, delete the old file, and write the modified data back to disk again.

Relative Files

If you're familiar with BASIC 2.0, you may have gotten the impression that relative files are difficult to use. This largely unwarranted reputation is due to a lack of correct information about relative files and the fact that BASIC 2.0 has no specific commands for handling them. Happily, BASIC 7.0 has reversed this situation, making this powerful file type quite convenient to use. Since there is no compelling reason to use BASIC 2.0 for relative file programming, the following discussion applies exclusively to BASIC 7.0. We will not mention the oddities of BASIC 2.0 any further, and recommend that you avoid using it for relative files whenever possible.

What is a relative file? As explained above, sequential and program data files must be read in beginning-to-end order: Even though the file may be internally divided into individual elements (usually called records), there's no way to access an individual record midway through the file without reading in everything that comes before it. And you can't make any change without reading the whole file into memory. This slows down every file operation and limits files to a size that can fit into available memory.

Relative files, on the other hand, let you access any individual record without reading the whole file into memory. This saves a tremendous amount of time and lets you handle files that are much bigger than available memory. One limitation built into the system is that you can have only one relative file open at a time. However, you may open a sequential file along with a relative file, and this combination is often used: Typically, a small, ancillary sequential file provides an index into the main body of data held in a much larger relative file.

Records

As noted in the earlier discussion of sequential and program files, those file types let you create any internal file structure that you like. You can divide the file internally into separate *records*—distinct data areas—by inserting a carriage return, null character, or whatever else you intend to represent the end of one record and the beginning of another. The point is that you are the one who imposes an internal structure on the file (if indeed it has any at all).

Relative files, on the other hand, have a predetermined record structure. In this context, a record is simply a distinct data area on disk which you can access by means of its *record number*. It may be as short as one character, or as long as 254, depending on what you specify. In many cases, a programmer will further subdivide each individual record into internal *fields*—just as you might subdivide a sequential file in a certain way—but any internal field structure is strictly a creation of the programmer, not a consequence of using relative files. If you want to put one chunk of data in each record, there's nothing to prevent you from doing so.

Though in many cases computers begin counting with the number zero, relative files do not follow this convention. The first record in every file is record number 1, and the first character in every record is character number 1. Since DOS limits every disk directory to 144 filenames, you may put no more than 144 separate relative *files* on a disk. However, a disk can hold as many as 65,535 separate *records*, many more than are needed for ordinary purposes.

Creating a Relative File

DOPEN is used to create a relative file, and the format is very similar to that used in opening sequential or program files. Consider this example:

DOPEN#1,"RELFILE",L20

As you probably recognize by now, the 1 after DOPEN sets the logical file number associated with this file, and quotation marks surround the filename (RELFILE). The L after the filename stands for *length*, and tells DOS you want to create a relative file. After the L is a value (20 here) that sets the *record length* for every record in this file. The length determines how many characters a record in this file can hold, and must be some value in the range 1–254. Note that the length sets the size of each individual record; it has no effect on how *many* records you put in the file.

You must specify the record length in order to create a relative file. The length must also be specified when you expand a file by adding new records. If you leave off the L parameter, DOS assumes the file already exists and generates an error when that file is not found. It is not necessary to specify the record length for read/write operations on existing records. For instance, if RELFILE already exists on the disk, you can open it with this command:

DOPEN#1,"RELFILE"

In this case, you don't need to tell DOS what type of file this is or how long its records are. The drive discovers the file type and record length for itself. Nor is it necessary to indicate whether you want to read or write to the file. You may perform *either* operation on a relative file at any time, without special commands. By way of contrast, consider how much work it takes to change just one data item in a sequential file: You must open it for reading, read the whole file into memory, close the read file, and delete it from the disk, then open a new file, write the entire file back to disk, and close it. Once opened, a relative file is simultaneously open for reading and writing, a feature which greatly simplifies the programmer's task.

Note that although it's not necessary to specify record length when handling an existing record, specifying the length does no harm either. Some programmers include the length in every DOPEN command as a reminder of the maximum number of characters that can be put in each record.

At this point, it's often helpful to decide (or at least estimate) the total number of records you'll need in the file. Though you can always create additional records as needed, it takes time for DOS to make each record, and you may save time in the long run by starting out with the right number. When large files are involved, this also helps you gauge how much disk space will be left for other files. On the other hand, if you're sure you'll never need more than a certain number of records, don't create any extras. Since there's no practical way to delete individual records from a relative file, this simply wastes precious disk space. As we'll see in a moment, creating many files at once is very easy.

The Record Pointer

Before you can read or write relative files, there's one more command you need to learn. The RECORD command lets you position a pointer at any place within the record, to read or write only the character(s) you are interested in. Say you've already created RELFILE and want to read data from record number 2, beginning with the third character in that record. Assuming you have opened RELFILE as logical file number 1, you can set the record pointer with this command:

```
RECORD#1,2,3
```

Here the 1 signifies the logical file number, the 2 sets the record number, and the 3 points the drive to the third character in the record. To point the pointer at the first character in record number 3, use RECORD#1,3,1, and so on. Once the pointer is set, you can read or write to the file as you would in any other case, relying on DOS to advance the pointer from one character to the next as needed.

Once you understand how to create and open a relative file and position the record pointer, you know the basics of relative file-handling. Let's put these commands together in a practical example. The following program creates a relative file of 50 records—each 30 characters in length—then writes data to each record and reads it back, displaying the results on the screen.

```
10 PRINT"MAKING "CHR$(34)"RELFILE"CHR$(34)
20 DOPEN#1,"RELFILE",L30
30 RECORD#1,50,1
40 PRINT#1,CHR$(255)
50 PRINT"WRITING TO "CHR$(34)"RELFILE"CHR$(34)
60 FOR J=1 TO 50
70 RECORD#1,(J),1
80 PRINT#1,"THIS IS RECORD #";(J)
90 NEXT
100 PRINT"READING "CHR$(34)"RELFILE"CHR$(34)
110 FOR J=1 TO 50
120 RECORD#1,(J),1
130 INPUT#1,A$
140 PRINT A$
150 DCLOSE
```

Line 20 opens the file for the first time, specifying a record length of 30 characters. Since we have planned in advance to use 50 records, lines 30–40 create all 50 at once. The

RECORD command in line 30 points the record pointer at the first character of the last record (number 50), and line 40 writes one character to that position. This causes the drive to create records 1–49 in addition to record 50. Lines 60–90 write a simple text message in each record. Again, don't forget to position the pointer with RECORD before reading or writing to the file. Like some other file-handling commands, RECORD requires that you enclose variables within parentheses (line 70). Once the write operation is finished, lines 110–150 read the contents of every record in turn, closing the file with DCLOSE when no further operations are desired.

Note that we left RELFILE open during the entire process, from beginning to end. It bears repeating that relative files, once open, are open either for reading or for writing. It's not necessary to close and reopen the file to switch from one mode to the other.

An Error That's Not an Error

The DOS message RECORD NOT PRESENT occurs only when working with relative files, and may or may not signify an error. Like certain other DOS messages, it's really a status message, not necessarily a signal that something went wrong. Look at the example program again. If you end the program with DCLOSE immediately after line 40, the drive's busy light will flash to indicate a pending DOS message. If you read the message by typing PRINT DS$, you'll see the message RECORD NOT PRESENT.

Though the text sounds a bit ominous, in this case RECORD NOT PRESENT means that you wrote to a record (number 50) that was not in existence *before the write operation.* Rather than indicate a problem, it simply tells you that there was no such record before. DOS generates the same message whenever you add a new record to an existing file. For instance, say that after running the example program you write to record number 51. That's very easily done: Execute DOPEN#1,"RELFILE",L30 followed by RECORD#1,51,1. Now the pointer is positioned at the first character in record 51. Writing data to the record with PRINT# creates the record and puts your data into it. Again, since record 51 didn't exist before you wrote to it, DOS tells you RECORD NOT PRESENT.

When should you worry about the RECORD NOT PRESENT error? One case is when you DOPEN a file without specifying a record length, for the purpose of working on an existing file. Obviously, if DOS can't find a file which you believe to exist, something has gone wrong.

Changing a Record

Existing records can be changed in one of two ways. The simplest method is to write new data directly into the record. For instance, try running this program after creating RELFILE with the example shown above:

```
10 DOPEN#1,"RELFILE"
20 RECORD#1,50,9
30 PRINT#1,"NEW RECORD #";50
40 RECORD#1,50,1
50 INPUT#1,A$
60 PRINT A$
70 DCLOSE
```

Line 20 sets the pointer at the ninth character in record number 50, and line 30 writes new data beginning at that position. Since we want to read back the entire contents of this record, line 40 repositions the pointer at the first character. As you'll see, record 50 now contains THIS IS NEW RECORD #50. Record 50 now contains more data than it did before. When replacing a long piece of data with a shorter piece, you should pad out the record with extra spaces.

If your records contain more complex data (perhaps divided into several fields) or you don't know in advance exactly what they contain, the simple technique shown here will not yield correct results. In such cases, you must read the entire record (not the entire file, of course) into memory, make the necessary changes, then rewrite the record in full.

In all but the simplest cases, it's a very good idea to position the pointer to the beginning of a record *after* every write operation as well as beforehand. The reasons for this are fairly involved, having to do with whether a record fits evenly into a disk sector or spills over from one sector into another. It doesn't matter whether you understand why the problem may occur. Just position the pointer before and after rewriting a record, and the problem will never occur.

Disk Organization

Ordinary data file programming does not require that you know exactly how your disk files are stored, or even where they are located on the disk. DOS manages those details for you, finding the best place to put your files and maintaining a directory that lets you access them at will. However, DOS also offers advanced commands that give you access to any individual sector on the disk.

In order to use advanced commands, you must understand something about how Commodore disks are organized. Though the following discussion may involve some new concepts and unfamiliar terms, do not feel as if you must master it all in one reading or even the first several (few people do). You can benefit from learning something about disk organization even if some parts remain unclear. After gaining some practical experience, you will find more of the details falling into place.

One case when you might find this knowledge handy is when you have inadvertently deleted an important file or scrambled an entire disk. By reading and editing individual sectors, you can often retrieve information that would otherwise be lost forever. Of course, advanced disk commands are integral to high-level disk programs such as "turboloaders" or "fast copy" programs that perform ordinary disk operations at accelerated speeds, as well as virtually all copy protection schemes.

Large-Scale Organization

When you format a disk for the first time, the drive divides it into a certain number of *tracks* or concentric circular areas. Though no change is visible to the naked eye, the disk is now segmented into electromagnetic zones which the drive can use for data storage. A disk formatted by the 1541 drive has 35 tracks, numbered 1–35, while a double-sided 1571-format disk has 70 tracks (numbered 1–35 on the first side and 36–70 on the second). Note that the bottom side of the disk is the one used in 1541 mode, and for tracks 1–35 in 1571 mode.

Each track is further subdivided into distinct *sectors* or 256-byte data areas (also called *blocks*). The number of sectors found in any given track depends on the track's physical location. Lower-numbered tracks are located toward the disk's outer perimeter and thus contain room for more sectors than the smaller, higher-numbered tracks near the center. Figure 4-1 illustrates the general layout of tracks and sectors on a disk, and Table 4-1 indicates which sectors are present on each disk track.

Figure 4-1. General Disk Organization

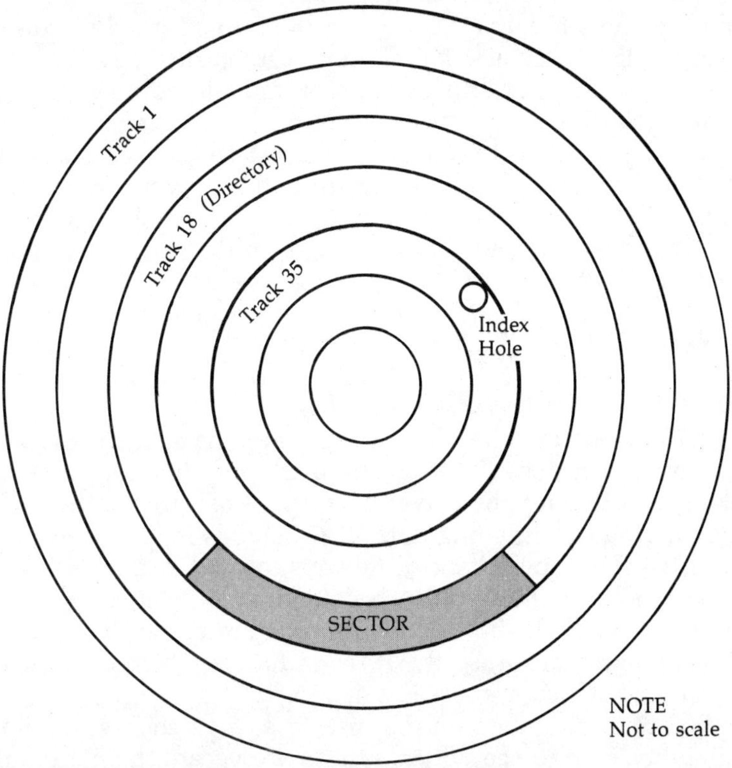

Table 4-1. Tracks and Sectors

Track No.	Sector No.	Total Sectors	
1–17	0–20	21	
18–24	0–18	19	
25–30	0–17	18	
31–35	0–16	17	(last track for 1541 mode)
36–52	0–20	21	
53–59	0–18	19	
60–65	0–17	18	
66–70	0–16	17	

The amount of information you can store on a disk is limited by two factors. A 1571-format disk contains 1366 sectors in all, while a 1541 disk has 683. However, not all of these sectors are free for file storage. DOS itself uses some of them for storing the disk's directory and BAM (Block Availability Map, a bit-mapped record of which sectors are currently in use). After subtracting those tracks, you are left with 664 usable sectors on a 1541 disk or 1328 sectors for a 1571 disk. Since the disk directory is limited to 144 entries regardless of format, a Commodore disk can accommodate no more than 144 separate files.

Though each sector consists of 256 bytes, in ordinary circumstances only 254 of these are free to hold your data: The first two bytes in a sector usually contain a pointer that tells the drive where to find the next sector in that file. Thus, the true number of bytes free for your use is either 168,656 (664*254) on a 1541 disk or roughly twice that number for a double-sided disk.

Block Availability Map (BAM)

Track 18, located in the disk's central area, is always reserved for a special purpose. It stores the BAM and directory that make it possible for the drive to find its way around the disk when storing or retrieving data. BAM stands for *Block Availability Map*. This special sector (always located at track 18, sector 0) works something like a hotel manager's daily logbook. Just as the logbook shows which rooms are currently occupied and which are vacant, so the BAM indicates which disk sectors are free and which are already in use.

Before storing data on the disk, the drive checks the block availability map to see which sectors are vacant, taking pains not to put data in any sector that's already allocated (in use). After filling an empty sector with new data, the drive automatically updates the BAM to protect the data from being overwritten. Table 4-2 shows the meaning of each byte within the BAM sector on a single- or double-sided disk.

Of all the sectors on a disk, the BAM is unquestionably the most important, since it alone controls whether other sectors are treated as empty or full. DOS updates the BAM automatically as needed, so you will rarely have occasion to worry about it under ordinary circumstances. Until you have gained considerable experience, it is best to avoid operations that may

Table 4-2. BAM Organization

1541 BAM Contents, Track 18, Sector 0

Byte	Contents	Explanation
0	18	Track of next directory block. (usually 18)
1	1	Sector of next directory block. (usually 1)
2	65	ASCII character A indicating 1540/1541/1551/1571/4040/2030 format
3		Double-sided flag (ignored in 1541 mode)
4–143		Bitmap of free and allocated blocks. 1 = free, 0 = allocated (in binary form)
144–159		Disk name padded with shifted space character, CHR$(160)
160–161	160	Shifted space character, CHR$(160)
162–163		Disk ID
164	160	Shifted space character, CHR$(160)
165–166	50 65	ASCII codes for 2A (DOS Version 2 and format type A)
167–170	160	Shifted space character, CHR$(160)
171–255	0	Nulls, not used, CHR$(0)

1571 BAM Contents, Track 18, Sector 0

Byte	Contents	Explanation
0	18	Track of next directory block. (usually 18)
1	1	Sector of next directory block. (usually 1)
2	65	Character A indicating 1540/1541/1551/1571/4040/2030 format
3		Double-sided flag: 128 = double-sided, 0 = single-sided
4–143		Bitmap of free and allocated blocks. 1 = free, 0 = allocated (in binary form)
144–159		Disk name padded with shifted space character, CHR$(160)
160–161	160	Shifted space character, CHR$(160)
162–163		Disk ID
164	160	Shifted space character, CHR$(160)
165–166	50 65	ASCII codes for 2A (DOS Version 2 and format type A)
167–170	160	Shifted space character, CHR$(160)
171–220	0	Nulls, not used, CHR$(0)
221–237		Number of sectors available on tracks 36–52
238	0	Number of sectors available on track 53, always marked as full, but some are available. DOS does not support use of track 53
239–255		Number of sectors available on tracks 54–70

(Table 4-2 cont.)

1571 BAM Contents, Track 53, Sector 0 (second side of double-sided disk)

Byte	Contents	Explanation
1–104		Bit map of free and allocated blocks. 1 = free, 0 = allocated (in binary form)
105–255	0	Nulls, not used

directly change the contents of the BAM. If you inadvertently mark used sectors as free, DOS may overwrite existing files the next time you save a program on that disk.

There are two BAM bytes in particular which should never be casually altered: If you change the contents of bytes 165–166 (DOS version and format) to anything other than the characters 2A, you will never again be able to write to *any* sector unless the disk is completely reformatted. Though useful as a means of permanently write-protecting a whole disk, this is obviously undesirable for ordinary use.

Disk Directory

A disk directory serves much the same purpose as a library card catalog. Just as each card in a library catalog tells you what a book contains and where to find it, the directory tells the drive where to find any file on the disk. It also records the name and ID of the disk, its total number of free sectors, and three items of information about each file (name, file type, and size in terms of sectors). Figure 4-2 illustrates a typical disk directory.

Figure 4-2. Typical Disk Directory

```
0    "WORK DISK"           10 2A
19    "TURBODISK MAKER"    PRG
11    "DISK AUTOLOAD"      PRG
5     "DISK DATAMAKER"     PRG
1     "COPYFILE"           PRG
628 BLOCKS FREE.
```

Sectors 1–19 in track 18 contain a file entry for each file on the disk. Table 4-3 shows the general format of a sector in the directory: The first two bytes of a directory sector always point to the next sector in the directory, and the remaining bytes in the sector store information for as many as eight files.

Table 4-3. Directory Sector Format

Byte	Explanation
0,1	Track and sector of next directory block
2–31	File entry #1
34–63	File entry #2
66–95	File entry #3
98–127	File entry #4
130–159	File entry #5
162–191	File entry #6
194–223	File entry #7
226–255	File entry #8

Within any sector of the directory, you may find entries for as many as eight individual files. These entries are often of interest, since by changing their contents you can immediately alter the way DOS treats the file. For instance, by adding 64 ($40) to the file type byte you can mark it as locked, preventing DOS from deleting or rewriting the file. Many copy-protected disks have cosmetically doctored directories which permit DOS to access the files, but prevent casual users from learning anything meaningful by LISTing the directory. To take one example, with a disk editor program you can easily change bytes 28–29 of the file entry to zeros, concealing the file's true size.

If you have accidentally scrambled the BAM of a disk (but not yet written over existing files), you may be able to retrieve the entire disk, using the directory as a guide. Bytes 1–2 of a directory entry show the track and sector where the file begins; and the first two bytes of each file's data sector usually point to the track and sector where the next sector for that file is located. So with patience and a good disk editor it is possible (though tedious) to remap the contents of the disk and salvage it by reconstructing the BAM. Table 4-4 shows the structure of an individual directory entry.

File Storage Format

As noted earlier, DOS recognizes the difference between various types of files, and insists that you use commands consistent with a file's type. If you try to LOAD a sequential file from BASIC, the drive generates a FILE TYPE MISMATCH error, and so on. Tables 4-5, 4-6, and 4-7 show the internal structure of the commonly used file types (PRG, SEQ, USR, and REL).

Table 4-4. Structure of Individual File Entry

Byte	Explanation
0	File type (OR with $40 (64) to lock the file) File Types: $80 (128) = DELeted $81 (129) = SEQuential $82 (130) = PRoGram $83 (131) = USeR $84 (132) = RELative
1–2	Track and sector of first data block
3–18	File-name padded with shifted spaces, CHR$(160)
19–20	Relative file only: track and sector of first side sector block
21	Relative file only: record length
22–25	Unused
26–27	Track and sector of replacement file during a @SAVE or @OPEN operation
28–29	Number of blocks in file: stored as a two-byte integer, in low-byte, high-byte order

Note that Table 4-5 shows the format of a PRG file created with a BASIC SAVE, DSAVE, or BSAVE command (or an S command from the monitor). Such files are structurally unusual in two respects: The initial two bytes of the first data sector contain a load address used when loading the file back into memory. And the file data always ends with three zeros. PRG files created by other means ordinarily contain data, not executable programs, and have the same structure as sequential files. Though DOS distinguishes between SEQ and USR files, they are structurally identical.

Table 4-5. Program File Format

Byte	Explanation
First Sector	
0–1	Track and sector of next block in file
2–3	Load address of the program (high byte, low byte)
4–255	252 bytes of program information as stored in computer memory (BASIC keywords are tokenized)
Remaining Full Sectors	
0–1	Track and sector of next block in file
2–255	Next 254 bytes of program information as stored in computer memory (BASIC keywords are tokenized)

(Table 4-5 cont.)

Final Sector

0–1	Null (0), followed by the number of valid data bytes in sector
2–	Last bytes of program information as stored in computer memory. (BASIC keywords are tokenized.) The end of a BASIC file is marked by three zero bytes in a row. Any remaining bytes in the sector are garbage and may be ignored

Table 4-6. Sequential and User File Formats

Byte	**Explanation**
All But the Final Sector	
0–1	Track and sector of next data block in file
2–255	254 bytes of data
Final Sector	
0–1	Null (0), followed by number of valid data bytes in sector
2–	Last bytes of data

Table 4-7. Relative File Format

Byte	**Explanation**
Data Block	
0–1	Track and sector of next data block in file
2–255	254 bytes of data. Empty records contain $FF (255) in the first byte, followed by $00 to the end of the record. Partially filled records are padded with nulls ($00)
Side Sector Block	
0–1	Track and sector of next side sector block
2	Side sector number (0–5)
3	Record length
4–5	Track and sector of first side sector (number 0)
6–7	Track and sector of first side sector (number 1)
8–9	Track and sector of first side sector (number 2)
10–11	Track and sector of first side sector (number 3)
12–13	Track and sector of first side sector (number 4)
14–15	Track and sector of first side sector (number 5)
16–255	Track and sector pointers to 120 data blocks

Note: Relative files are unique in having *side sectors* which contain pointers to the records within data sectors. This feature accounts for the speed and flexibility of relative files, and also explains why only one relative file can be open at a time. The drive's internal memory is too small to service two relative files simultaneously.

Direct Access Commands

Armed with a basic understanding of Commodore disk structure, you are ready to begin using advanced DOS commands, called *direct access* commands because they permit you to read and write to any individual sector on the disk. You can manipulate anything on a disk, free of the limitations (and safeguards) normally provided by BASIC and DOS. But with this freedom comes a certain amount of risk. If you accidentally scramble the BAM, replace a directory sector with garbage, etc., you may destroy everything that a disk contains. For this reason, *exercise extreme caution when using these commands.* Until you have gained more experience, it is best to practice on a disk that does not contain important data.

Since these commands address the drive directly, you must always open the command channel with OPEN 15,8,15 before using them. Once this is done, PRINT#15,*command* sends the command to the drive. Reading or writing an entire block also requires that you open a second channel to force the drive to allocate enough internal memory space to hold the block. Note that the B-R and B-W forms of the Block-Read and Block-Write commands are defective and should never be used. Substitute the alternate *user* commands (U1 or UA for Block-Read, and U2 or UB for Block-Write) instead. Tables 4-8 and 4-9 list the format for all of the direct access and user commands.

Table 4-8. Direct Access Commands

Command	Format
Block-Allocate	"B-A";0;track number;sector number
Block-Execute	"B-E";channel number;0;track number;sector number
Block-Free	"B-F";0;track number;sector number
Buffer-Pointer	"B-P";channel number;byte
Block-Read	"U1";channel number;0;track number;sector number
Block-Write	"U2";channel number;0;track number;sector number
Memory-Execute	"M-E"CHR$(low byte of address)+CHR$(high byte of address)
Memory-Read	"M-R"CHR$(low byte of address)+CHR$(high byte of address)
Memory-Write	"M-W"CHR$(low byte of address)+CHR$(high byte of address)+CHR$(data byte)
User	(see Table 4-9)
Utility Loader	"&0:filename"

Only three of the user commands are commonly used. The UA and UB commands are always preferred for reading or writing a disk sector. The UJ command resets the drive as if you turned the power off and on. Since only the four lower bits of the second character are significant, each command has an alternate form (U1 for UA, U2 for UB, and so on) which functions identically.

Table 4-9. User Commands

User Command	Function
U0	restores default user jump table
U1 or UA	Block read replacement
U2 or UB	Block write replacement
U3 or UC	Jump to $0500
U4 or UD	Jump to $0503
U5 or UE	Jump to $0506
U6 or UF	Jump to $0509
U7 or UG	Jump to $050C
U8 or UH	Jump to $050F
U9 or UI	Jump to ($FFFA) reset tables
U: or UJ	Power up vector

All but the simplest direct-access operations require some knowledge of the drive's internal memory structure. There are two books which explore this subject in detail: *Inside Commodore DOS*, published by Sybex, Inc. and *The Anatomy of the 1541*, published by Abacus Software. Both books predate the 1571, but contain extensive information about the 1541's DOS and memory organization. Table 4-10 is an abbreviated 1541/1571 memory map. Both drives are similar in architecture, the major difference being that locations $1C10–$BFFF are unused in the 1541. The 1541 and 1571 are both *intelligent* units, meaning they contain their own microprocessors, RAM, ROM, and I/O chips. In effect, your drive is a separate, highly specialized computer system.

Table 4-10. 1541/1571 Memory Map

Location	Description
$0000–$00FF	Zero page work area, system variables
$0100–$01FF	Stack (1571 mode: BAM for side one)
$0200–$02FF	Command buffer, parser, tables, variables
$0300–$07FF	Five 256-byte data buffers, 0–4 (one used by BAM)
$1800–$180F	VIA I/O chip for serial bus communications
$1C00–$1C0F	VIA I/O chip for drive control and read/write
$C000–$FFE5	1541: 16K ROM (DOS and controller routines)
$8000–$FFE5	1571: 32K ROM (DOS and controller routines)
$FFE6–$FFFF	User command vectors, 6502 hardware registers

Disk Autoboot

When you turn the 128 on, its operating system automatically checks the disk in the drive. If it finds the proper codes on disk, a designated program on the disk loads and runs automatically. This ability to *autoboot* a program, while common on other systems, is a new feature for Commodore computers. Here's a short program that lets you create autoboot files on any disk.

Program 4-1. Autoboot Maker

```
10 REM READ NAME OF DISK
20 PRINT"{CLR}"
30 OPEN15,8,15:REM OPEN COMMAND CHANNEL
40 OPEN1,8,2,"#":REM OPEN DATA CHANNEL
50 PRINT#1"U1 2 0 18 0":REM SEND BLOCK-READ TO C
   OMMAND CHANNEL
60 PRINT#15,"B-P 2 144":REM SET BLOCK POINTER AT B
   YTE NUMBER 144
70 FOR I=1TO16:REM MAXIMUM LENGTH OF NAME
```

```
80 GET#1,A$:IFA$=CHR$(16Ø)THEN11Ø :REM GET A BYTE,
    CHECK FOR SHIFTED SPACE CHAR
9Ø DN$=DN$+A$:REM CONCATENATE DISK NAME
1ØØ NEXT
11Ø CLOSE1:CLOSE15:REM CLOSE CHANNELS
12Ø PRINT"DISK NAME: ";DN$
13Ø DIRECTORY
14Ø PRINT"{DOWN}ENTER NAME OF BASIC PROGRAM TO BOO
    T:":INPUTBN$
15Ø PRINT"{DOWN}PREPARING DISK.....WAIT"
16Ø OPEN15,8,15:REM OPEN COMMAND CHANNEL
17Ø OPEN1,8,2,"#":REM OPEN DATA CHANNEL
18Ø PRINT#15,"U1 2 Ø 1 Ø"
19Ø PRINT#15,"B-P 2 Ø":REM SET BLOCK POINTER AT Ø
    {SPACE}BYTE
2ØØ PRINT#1,"CBM"+CHR$(Ø)+CHR$(Ø)+CHR$(Ø)+CHR$(Ø)+
    DN$+CHR$(Ø)+BN$+CHR$(Ø)+CHR$(76)+CHR$(153)+CHR
    $(175)
21Ø PRINT#15,"U2 2 Ø 1 Ø":REM SEND DATA FROM BUFFE
    R OF CHANNEL 1 TO DISK T-1 S-Ø
22Ø CLOSE1:CLOSE15
23Ø PRINTDS$
24Ø IFDS=ØTHEN PRINT"DISK WILL AUTOBOOT"
25Ø IFDS<>ØTHENPRINT"DISK WILL NOT BOOT"
```

The autoboot process is actually quite simple. When you power up the 128, it reads bytes 0–2 of sector 0 from track 1 on the disk to see whether those bytes contain the codes for the characters CBM. If the signature bytes are present, the system then looks at the bytes following the signature for the filename of a program to load and run. Program 4-1 writes the signature bytes to disk along with the filename of any program you wish to autoboot. While it's not absolutely necessary to use a freshly formatted disk, that will make it easier for DOS to find the autoboot program (the first program saved on a disk always comes first on the directory). Since this program writes directly to track 1, sector 0, you should at least make sure that that sector is free.

When using "Autoboot Maker," enter the filename of the desired program exactly as it appears in the disk directory. Any deviation causes the autoboot to fail. Once the process is complete, turn off the computer, wait a few seconds, then turn the computer on and watch your program autoboot. If you'd like to autoboot a machine language program, use a BASIC loader like the one shown here. This two-line example loads MLPROG from disk and starts it with SYS. Of course, you should replace MLPROG and 3072 with the filename and starting address of your ML program. When answering the filename prompt in "Autoboot Maker," supply the name you used when saving the BASIC loader program to disk.

```
10 IF A=0 THEN A=1:LOAD "MLPROG",8,1
20 SYS 3072
```

How Autobooting Works

Here are some additional details about autobooting for advanced programmers. When you turn on the 128, it calls the Kernal BOOT_CALL routine. This routine tries to read track 1, sector 0 (the *boot sector*) from disk into the 128's cassette buffer (located at $0B00 in bank zero). If no disk drive is attached, or the drive contains no disk, or the first three bytes in the buffer aren't the character codes for the letters CBM, BOOT_CALL terminates, and the 128 transfers control to BASIC.

Once track 1, sector 0 has been read into the buffer, the 128 looks there for additional information. If the buffer contains the autoboot signature code (CBM), the 128 checks to see if any more sectors have to be loaded. As shown in Figure 4-3, the seventh byte in the boot sector contains a *block count*. If this byte is not zero, the computer will read more blocks from the disk, starting at track 1, sector 1. The bytes at $0B03–0B05 show the address and bank of the memory area where these additional blocks should be stored. If the count byte is zero, then these bytes can have any value. This effectively provides a load address for the contents of the additional blocks.

Next, the 128 prints BOOTING and looks for a name to add to this message, starting at the eighth byte in the buffer ($0B07). If this byte isn't a zero, the 128 prints every succeeding character on the screen as the disk's name, ending when it hits a zero byte. The next byte after this zero starts another name field, this one indicating a program (PRG) file that should be loaded from the disk. If this field contains nothing but a zero, the computer does not perform a load. Otherwise, the 128 tries to load a file of that name from the disk. Note that this is a conventional load: The first two bytes in the file are used as a load address, and you can only load the file at that address within bank zero.

Figure 4-3. Format of an Autoboot Sector

$00	$01	$02	
$43	$42	$4D	("CBM")

$03	$04	$05	$06
Addr. Low	Addr. Hi	Bank	No. of blocks

$07	$07+$L_1$
Name displayed in "BOOTING" message	$00

$08+$L_1$	$08+$L_1$+$L_2$
Name of PRG file to load	$00

$09+$L_1$+$L_2$	$FF
Boot program, 8502 machine language	

Track 1, Sector 0
L_1—length of disk name
L_2—length of PRG filename

When all requested disk reads have taken place, the 128 transfers control to the *boot program,* which comes immediately after the zero byte terminating the filename field. Again, keep in mind that the computer is looking at the contents of the cassette buffer, which it originally loaded from track 1, sector 0. Since the entire autoboot process takes place before the 128 activates BASIC, the boot program must be written in machine language.

In the simplest case—a CP/M boot sector—with no disk name and no additional load operations, the boot program starts at the tenth byte in the buffer ($0B09). What happens after that is up to the boot program. The CP/M boot program simply selects RAM bank zero and calls a routine (left at $FFD0 by the Z80 microprocessor during the cold-start process) to jump into CP/M mode. The boot program created by Program 4-1 jumps to the BASIC run-a-program routine; the name of the BASIC program to be run is contained in the second name field and loads from disk before the boot program gains control.

Split Personality

As you probably know, the 1571 drive has two separate operating modes. It can be either a fast, double-sided drive (1571 mode) or a slower single-sided drive (1541 mode). In ordinary circumstances, DOS automatically uses 1571 mode when the computer is in 128 mode, and 1541 mode when you switch the computer to 64 mode with GO 64. However, it's possible to switch the drive from one mode to another under program control. The following program switches from 1571 mode to 1541 mode.

```
10 OPEN 15,8,15
20 PRINT#15,"U0>M0"
30 CLOSE 15
```

After you run the program, the drive will read and write to the top side of the disk alone, just like a 1541. To return to 1571 mode, replace line 20 as shown here and rerun the program:

```
20 PRINT#15,"U0>M1"
```

You can also switch from one read/write head to another in a program. Switch your drive to 1541 mode, then format a new disk using the disk name SIDE ZERO. Now replace line 20 as shown here and rerun the program:

```
20 PRINT#15,"U0>H1"
```

Now format the disk again using the disk name SIDE ONE, then read the disk directory. It should look like Figure 4-4.

Figure 4-4. Disk Directory

```
0 "SIDE ONE        " ZX 2A
664 BLOCKS FREE.
```

Replace line 20 with this line and rerun the program:

```
20 PRINT#15,"U0>H0"
```

At this point, the disk directory should show SIDE ZERO. You now have a disk formatted on both sides in 1541 mode. Either side may be accessed by changing disk heads as shown above. If you have old single-sided disks around, this is one way to extend their usefulness. Note, however, that the second side cannot be read in a 1541 drive. It is only readable by a 1571 drive, which has two read/write heads rather than one.

Utility Commands

The M and H commands shown in the previous section are two of the 1571's *utility* commands. This program shows the general format for such commands, which are listed in Table 4-11.

```
10 OPEN 15,8,15
20 PRINT#15,"U0>command"
30 CLOSE 15
```

Table 4-11. DOS Utility Commands

Command	Meaning
S	DOS sector interleave
R	DOS retries
T	ROM signature analysis
M	Mode select (0 = 1541 mode, 1 = 1571 mode)
H	Head select (0 = side zero, 1 = side one)

It is very easy to change the device number of a 1571 drive. The simplest method is to flip the switches in back of the drive as explained in your disk drive manual. This can also be done with the following command. Replace *device number* with any number from 8–30, then type the command in direct mode (without a line number) and press RETURN.

OPEN15,8,15:PRINT#15,"U0>"+CHR$(*device number*):CLOSE 15

Why the 1571 Is Faster

A 1541 disk drive can read a disk pretty quickly. That is, it can copy data from the surface of the disk to its internal memory fast enough. But it transfers data to the computer at a much slower rate. The problem lies in the 1541's communication protocol, which Commodore has fittingly dubbed "slow mode." There are now an abundance of Commodore 64 programs which increase the speed of the 1541 drive. Such utilities reprogram both the drive and the computer to accelerate the data transfer rate, at the risk of less reliable communications. The 1571 offers much faster transfer modes, and we'll show you how to access them under program control. But you first need to understand some simple facts about serial data transfer. Even if you don't have any interest in this subject, you may want to try the example machine language program at the end. Once you see how speedy fast mode really is, you may be inspired to learn more about it.

Most Commodore peripherals, including 1541 and 1571 drives, attach to the computer through a serial communication bus. The term *bus* is a jargon name for "group of wires," and *serial* means that only one bit (logical 1 or 0) of data can move along the bus at a time. To send a byte of data over the serial bus, a device first has to break the data down into its eight component bits. This sounds slower than it really is. Some serial communication systems—the Ethernet local-area network, for instance—are very fast. But there's one reason why Commodore's serial bus is so slow. Commodore computers built before the 128 don't use any special-purpose hardware for serial bus communications. Instead, the computer's microprocessor executes a program to convert a byte to bits and send both the data and associated control signals (like "Here's another bit" and "I'm done, now it's your turn to talk") down the bus. Since the microprocessor isn't specifically designed for such operations, it can't do them as fast as a special-purpose serial device.

The 128 and 1571 use a new system called *fast serial mode* to relieve the microprocessor of most serial communication chores. In the original serial protocol, one wire in the serial bus cable was named—Service Request (SRQ)—but never used. Now this wire has been put to work carrying a high-speed clock signal to accompany data sent at a faster rate. Since the clock signal and the data move faster than the microprocessor can follow, the Complex Interface Adapter chip at location $DC00 (CIA #1) assumes more responsibility for communications. The CIA's serial data register (SDR) at location $DC0C was unused on the 64. But in the 128 it reads and writes to the serial bus's data line. Thus, in the 128's fast serial mode the most speed-critical tasks are done by hardware that was unused (or underused) on the 64.

The Nuts and Bolts of Fast Mode

Here are some details about fast serial transfer. To read the serial bus in fast mode, the SDR collects eight bits of data and then signals the microprocessor that a new byte has arrived. To send data, the microprocessor waits for a signal to indicate that the SDR is empty, then stores a whole byte in the SDR. This data is sent, one bit at a time, down the serial bus's data line. The CIA's timer A provides the high-speed pulses which tell both the SDR and the device at the other end of the bus—

through the SRQ line—when another bit of data should be on the data line. One additional bit of handshaking takes place as well: Before it sends a byte of data, the 128 toggles the state of the serial bus's CLK line. This signal, called Acknowledge and Ready For Data (ARFD), is accomplished by exclusive-ORing CIA #2 data port A ($DD00) with 16.

Before a disk operation can begin, the 128 needs to know if the disk drive at the other end of the serial bus can handle fast serial mode. Older serial devices not only don't understand fast serial communication, they *can't even tell that it's going on,* since they ignore the SRQ line. The 128 takes advantage of their ignorance by sending a secret signal down the serial bus at the beginning of each disk command. This signal, called Host Request Fast (HRF), consists of eight pulses of the SRQ line while the data line is held at its high level. The 1571 recognizes this signal and sends its own secret signal, Device Request Fast (DRF), when its time comes to talk back. By holding the data line low for eight pulses of the SRQ line, it identifies itself as a fast serial device. From then on, the rest of the transaction takes place in fast serial mode.

When a Kernal I/O routine recognizes a device that can communicate in fast serial mode, it sets bit six of location $0A1C. Once that's done, other routines can test this bit to find out how the disk drive will be communicating. Any routine which directly accesses the SDR to communicate with the serial bus can use two new Kernal routines, SPIN and SPOUT, to change the direction that data flows on the serial bus. Calling the vector at $FF47 with the carry bit clear calls SPIN, which configures the serial bus for fast input, including setting up timer A for the proper speed of data transfer. If the carry bit is set when the vector is called, the SPOUT routine does everything necessary to set up the serial bus for output. Most programs call SPIN and SPOUT directly only when the direction of data transfer changes in the middle of a command, since CHKIN and CHKOUT make these calls for them.

Why Learn About Fast Mode?

Some people—Commodore's programmers, for instance—have to know the details of serial communication backward and forward, but you can ignore all the bits and bytes and three-letter words and still benefit from fast serial mode. Every serial input/output routine in the 128's operating system has been written to use fast mode whenever it can. Whenever a serial device is active, the 128 checks to see if it can handle fast mode. Whether you access the device from BASIC or machine language, fast mode will be used if you have a 1571 connected to your 128.

For some disk operations, the 1571 is even faster because of new *burst mode* disk access commands. In conventional disk access, each request for data from the drive only returns one byte. When you're loading a large file, the computer spends most of its time saying "next byte, please" over and over again. Burst commands, on the other hand, tell the disk drive to pass many *blocks* (256-byte packages) of data without any further instruction. These commands can operate on as many as 256 blocks of disk data at a time. There is also a new fastload command that reads a complete disk file in one operation. As CP/M users will be glad to learn, burst mode is also available with any command that relates to MFM-formatted (non-Commodore CP/M) disks.

Since the computer's LOAD routine knows about fastload, ordinary BASIC commands like LOAD, DLOAD, and BLOAD (as well as ML routines which call Kernal LOAD) use burst mode if it's available. Unfortunately, since there is no corresponding fastsave command, all save operations transfer data at the normal byte-by-byte rate.

An Impressive Example

Program 4-2 shows how to use the fastload command and direct fast serial communications for your own purposes. In addition to showing off the speed of the system, it demonstrates one way to do a task which the operating system doesn't support: reading an entire sequential file into memory. It can read a 120-block sequential file (30,720 bytes of data) into memory in just eight seconds. That's about 3,840 bytes per second—several times faster than ordinary serial communications. Even if you have no use for this particular application, it's an excellent example of how to handle the command channel, filenames, and such from machine language. You must enter and save this program with the machine language monitor as explained in the Introduction:

Program 4-2. Burst Mode Example

```
0C00  LDA #$00
0C02  STA $FF00
0C05  STA $FA
0C07  LDA #$20
0C09  STA $FB
0C0B  LDA #$0F
0C0D  LDY #$0F
0C0F  LDX #$08
0C11  JSR $FFBA
0C14  LDA #$00
0C16  JSR $FFBD
0C19  JSR $FFC0
0C1C  BCS $0C8A
0C1E  LDX #$0F
0C20  JSR $FFC9
0C23  BCS $0C8A
0C25  LDA #$BF
0C27  AND $0A1C
0C2A  STA $0A1C
0C2D  LDY #$00
0C2F  LDA $0CF1,Y
0C32  JSR $FFD2
0C35  INY
0C36  CPY $0CF0
0C39  BNE $0C2F
0C3B  JSR $FFCC
0C3E  BIT $0A1C
0C41  BVC $0C84
0C43  SEI
0C44  BIT $DC0D
0C47  JSR $0C7E
0C4A  JSR $0C77
0C4D  STA $0CEF
0C50  CMP #$02
0C52  BCS $0C8A
0C54  LDY #$00
0C56  JSR $0C77
0C59  LDX #$3F
0C5B  STX $FF00
0C5E  STA ($FA),Y
0C60  LDX #$00
0C62  STA $FF00
0C65  INY
0C66  CPY #$FE
0C68  BNE $0C56
```

```
0C6A  TYA
0C6B  CLC
0C6C  ADC $FA
0C6E  STA $FA
0C70  BCC $0C74
0C72  INC $FB
0C74  JMP $0C4A
0C77  LDA #$08
0C79  BIT $DC0D
0C7C  BEQ $0C79
0C7E  LDA $DD00
0C81  EOR #$10
0C83  STA $DD00
0C86  LDA $DC0C
0C89  RTS
0C8A  CLI
0C8B  LDX #$0F
0C8D  JSR $FFC9
0C90  BCS $0CA0
0C92  LDY #$00
0C94  LDA $0CAA,Y
0C97  JSR $FFD2
0C9A  INY
0C9B  CPY $0CA9
0C9E  BNE $0C94
0CA0  JSR $FFCC
0CA3  LDA #$0F
0CA5  JSR $FFC3
0CA8  RTS
>0CA9 02 49 30
>0CF0 0C 55 30 FF 4C 4F 4E 47
>0CF8 20 54 45 58 54
```

The program starts by enabling Kernal ROM and the I/O chips. First it stores a zero in the Memory Management Unit (MMU) configuration register ($FF00) to choose memory bank 15. Then it stores the address $2000 in locations $FA and $FB, which are used as a pointer to the file buffer. The next four lines call the Kernal SETLFS routine ($FFBA) to open the 1571's command channel as logical file 15. SETNAM ($FFBD) is called with zero in the accumulator to signal that no filename is associated with this channel. The file is then opened by calling OPEN ($FFC0). If the carry flag is set after OPEN executes, we know the operation caused an error, and abort with a branch to $0C8A. Otherwise, we call CKOUT ($FFC9) with 15 in the X register to direct output to the drive's command channel.

To make sure that later tests of the fast serial flag at location $0A1C will be valid, the next three instructions (starting at $0C25) clear bit 6 of this byte. If the next operation sets this flag, we'll know for sure that fast serial mode is OK.

The disk command string "U0πLONG TEXT" tells the 1571 to perform a fastload for the file named LONG TEXT. The length of this string is stored at $0CF0 and the string itself begins at $0CF1. BSOUT ($FFD2) sends each character of the command string to the drive over channel 15. After sending the command, we call CLRCHN ($FFCC) to restore normal output to the screen.

The BIT operation at $0C3E tests bit 6 of the fast serial flag, setting or clearing the overflow flag according to its state. If the overflow flag is clear, we branch to the error routine and give up. Otherwise, the interrupt disable flag is set. Since the SDR normally indicates the arrival of a new byte by interrupting the processor, it's easier for us to wait in a loop until bit 3 of the CIA's Interrupt Control Register (ICR) at $DC0D goes high than it would be to recover from an interrupt. We have nothing else to do in the meantime, anyway.

The first time we BIT the ICR (see the instruction at $0C44) we're just resetting all the ICR's flags, which happens with any kind of read access. Then we call $0C7E, the second entry point in the subroutine that handles direct serial bus access. This entry toggles the CLK line on the serial bus—the AFRD signal—to request data, then returns. The next instruction calls $0C77, the main entry point for this subroutine, which waits for the SDR to fill before sending ARFD and reading the newly received byte. The first byte read is a status byte, sent before each block in burst operations. If this byte isn't a zero or a one, something dreadful has happened—perhaps the file wasn't found—so we quit immediately.

If the drive signals no errors, the instruction at $0C54 loads the Y register (which will count the number of data bytes received) with zero. A call to $0C77 reads the first data byte, and we switch in memory bank 0 just long enough to store the byte in the buffer using Y-indexed indirect addressing. Then bank 15 is restored and the Y register is incremented to reflect the newly received byte. If Y is not equal to 254 (the number of data bytes in a block minus two pointer bytes), we branch back to $0C56 to read the next byte.

At the end of each block, we add 254 to the buffer pointer at $FA–FB and jump back to $0C4A to read the next status byte. If the disk drive has read the whole file, the status byte contains $1F (the End Or Identify (EOI) signal) which qualifies as an error in this context and terminates the load. If EOI is not found, we load the next block. The error routine at $0C8A first clears the interrupt disable bit to restore the normal keyscan interrupt, then calls CKOUT ($FFC9) to reconnect the disk command channel. If this routine is successful, the disk drive is reinitialized with the "I0" command string, stored at $0CAA. The program ends with calls to CLRCHN ($FFCC) and CLOSE ($FFC3) to close the command channel and restore normal input/output.

Datassette

The 128 uses a special tape drive, called the Datassette, which has been a feature of all Commodore computers since the original Commodore PET made its debut in 1977. It's similar to a standard cassette recorder, but specially optimized for data storage. Most microcomputers use an analog tape data storage format—bits of data are represented on the tape as audio tones. A certain number of cycles of a given tone represent a 1 bit, and number of cycles of another tone represent a 0. Commodore uses a much more elaborate digital system, where 0 and 1 bits are represented by specific magnetization patterns on the tape. Moreover, the system is able to compensate for speed variations and to detect and correct errors. As a result, while the Datassette is somewhat slow, it is also extremely reliable. If you've experienced the frustration of trying to load a balky program from tape on another brand of computer, you'll be relieved to discover that Commodore tape programs almost always load without error.

The principles of tape and disk data storage are quite similar. Tapes and disks are made from the same magnetic material, and the recording heads of tape drives and disk drives are closely related. Tape drives are much cheaper because they are much simpler—the tape is pulled past a fixed read/write head—and because the components of the system (tapes, motors, recording heads, etc.) are produced in large volumes for the audio market. Disk drives are more complex—the movable read/write head must be positioned very precisely (to within hundredths of an inch)—and the components of the system (disks, recording head positioners, etc.) are more highly specialized products.

The types of files available with tape reflect the sequential nature of the tape drive. To get from one point on a tape to another, you have to wait for all the intervening length of tape to wind past. And the tape winds in only one direction—you can't go backwards without rewinding. (In contrast, a disk drive can move its read/write head immediately to any point on the disk.) As a result, the tape drive supports only program and sequential data files.

Tape program files are handled very much like disk program files. The device number for tape is 1, and LOAD and SAVE operations assume device 1 if no other number is specified. To load a BASIC program from tape, simply enter:

LOAD *"program name"*

To save a BASIC program to tape, enter:

SAVE *"program name"*

Actually, for tape you don't even have to specify a program name. If you enter SAVE alone, the program is saved with no name. If you enter LOAD alone, the computer simply loads the next program it finds on the tape, regardless of its name. The only way to load a "nameless" program from tape is with LOAD alone. LOAD can also load the first program with a name that matches all the characters in the specified program name. Thus, LOAD "DO",1 will load the first program it finds on the tape with a name beginning with DO, whether the program's full name is DO, DOT, or DOGFIGHT.

Machine language programs are usually written to run at a certain address within the computer, and should be loaded at the address from which they were saved. This is called a nonrelocatable load, and can be accomplished by entering:

LOAD *"program name"*,1,1

Tape also has several SAVE formats not available with disk. If you add an extra ,1 after the SAVE statement, the program cannot be relocated when loaded. That is, the program always loads at the same address from which it was saved, regardless of whether or not you follow the LOAD statement with ,1,1. The syntax is

SAVE *"program name"*,1,1

If you follow the SAVE with an additional ,2 after the statement, then the computer writes an end-of-tape marker following the program: This is a special pattern placed on the tape to tell the computer not to search beyond that point when searching for programs on the tape. You should use the 2 parameter only when you are sure you want the program to be the last one stored on the tape. The syntax is

SAVE *"program name"*,1,2

Actually, the end-of-tape marker only stops the computer's automatic search for programs. You can, of course, search for programs farther along the tape by manually advancing the tape past the marker position.

Finally, adding a ,3 to SAVE combines the two previous functions: The program will be nonrelocatable and terminate with an end-of-tape marker:

SAVE *"program name"*,1,3

With the disk drive, you can OPEN program files, read data from them with GET#, and write data with PRINT#. *This is not true of tape program files.* Program files on tape can be accessed only with LOAD and SAVE.

Using Sequential Files with Tape

To illustrate how sequential tape files are handled, let's look at a typical program that opens a sequential file, writes data into the file, then reads it back into memory. The first step is to open the file.

10 OPEN 1,1,1,"DATAFILE"

The first number after the OPEN is the logical file number, which can take any value from 1–255. However, each open file must have a unique number. The second number is the device number, and 1 specifies that the Datassette will be used. The third number is the secondary address; it's very important to use the proper value here. For tape, the secondary address serves the function that the ,R and ,W filename suffixes serve for disk files. A 0 in this position specifies that the file is being opened for reading. A 1 here specifies that the file is being opened for writing, and a 2 specifies that the file will terminate with an end-of-tape marker. Refer to the section above on special SAVE formats for information on end-of-tape markers.

Note that you may substitute variables for any of the parameters following OPEN. For instance, A$="DATAFILE":OPEN 1,1,1,A$ works just as well as the previous examples.

The PRINT# command is used to write data to tape. PRINT# can be used to write numeric or string data, in the form of literals (123, "ABC" and so on) or variables such as X%, X(21), A$, A$(50). Let's write some data to tape:

```
20 FOR J=1 TO 20
30 PRINT#1,J
40 NEXT J
```

Of course, PRINT# uses the same logical file number used when opening the file. The data (J in this case) is separated from the file number by a comma. Just as with PRINT, you can use commas or semicolons to insert spaces between data items or cause them to be written without any separating characters. The SPC and TAB functions are also permissible, though less often seen. After writing to a file, you must always take care to close it properly:

```
50 CLOSE 1
```

Again, CLOSE refers to the logical file number. If you omit this important step, some data may never get written properly onto the tape.

Reading a File

A file is of no use unless you can read its contents back into the computer's memory. The general procedure is similar to the writing process. You must open the file, bring in the data with GET# or INPUT# commands, then close it. These commands open a sequential file for reading:

```
OPEN 1,1,0,"DATAFILE"
```

The filename can be omitted in the OPEN statement, just as the program name can be omitted during a tape load or save. The following statement opens the next file on the tape for reading regardless of its filename:

```
OPEN 1,1
```

The following example program shows one way to read back the data file written with the previous example:

```
10 DIM A$(20)
20 C=0
30 OPEN1,1,0,"DATAFILE"
```

```
40 C=C+1
50 INPUT#1,A$(C)
60 IF ST<>64 THEN 40
70 CLOSE 1
80 FOR J=1 TO C
90 PRINT A$(J)
100 NEXT
```

Line 10 creates a string array (A$) large enough to hold all 20 data items, and line 20 sets the counter C to zero. Line 30 opens the file for reading. The INPUT# command in line 50 brings in one piece of data at a time. Line 60 tests the status variable ST to check if we've read all the data. Since the system automatically sets ST to 64 when it finds an end-of-file marker, this is a convenient way to check for the end of a file. In this case, you know that the file contains only 20 data elements, but in many circumstances there is no way to know the file's exact length in advance. Line 70 closes the file, and lines 80–100 display the data.

Modems, RS-232, and the User Port

Another popular peripheral is the telecommunications interface, or *modem*. The telephone system was designed to carry human voices, not the high-speed digital signals that are the language of computers. A modem converts the digital signals from a computer into an audio format that can be transmitted over phone lines—a process known as modulation. The modem also converts signals received over the phone lines back into a digital format which can be understood by the computer—a process known as demodulation. Hence the name modem, for *mo*dulator-*dem*odulator.

The interface standard for connecting modems to computers is known as RS-232, since it was defined by Electronic Industries Association (EIA) Revised Standard 232. The 128 provides support for RS-232 communications in all three operating modes—128, 64, and CP/M. RS-232 is a serial communications standard; data is passed back and forth through the RS-232 interface one bit at a time, rather than in eight-bit byte-sized chunks. However, you should not confuse the RS-232 serial interface with the 128's serial data bus for disk drives and printers. The two use entirely different signal formats, and are not at all compatible.

All RS-232 communications—and hence all modem communications—are handled through the user port, located at the back left corner of the computer. Commodore modems, and some others, plug directly into the port. However, most modems from other manufacturers require an adapter to work with the 128. The RS-232 standard specifies a particular type of connector, which is different from the user port. Also, the RS-232 standard calls for voltage levels which are different from those available at the user port.

Briefly, RS-232 signals consist of high or low voltage pulses on a wire between the two devices. The higher voltage level (3–12 volts according to the RS-232 standard, 5 volts in the Commodore 128 implementation) is called a *space* and represents a 0 bit. The lower level (−3 to −12 volts according to the standard, but 0 volts in the 128 implementation) is called a *mark* and represents a 1 bit. The length of the pulse depends on the data transfer rate, measured in *baud*, or bits per second (bps) being sent or received. At the common rate of 300 baud (300 bps), each pulse lasts 1/300 second.

To send a character, the transmitting device pulls the data line, which normally rests at the mark (low) state, to the space (high) state for one baud. This is called the start bit, and indicates that data is to follow. The start bit is followed by mark and space pulses—each one baud long—corresponding to the bits that represent the character being sent. The number of bits varies depending on the *word size*—the number of bits in the character. Seven or eight bits are the most common word sizes.

Next a *parity bit* may be added for error-checking. The additional bit will be set to whichever state (1 or 0) is required to make the total number of 1 (mark) bits in the character either even (for *even parity*) or odd (for *odd parity*). The receiving device can then check the number of mark bits it receives and detect an error when the total does not agree with the parity being used. The parity bit can also be ignored, always set to 1 (*mark parity*), or always set to 0 (*space parity*). Finally, the data and parity bits are followed by one or two mark bits called *stop bits*, which indicate the end of the character. After the stop bits, the line remains low until the next start bit is sent. Figure 4-5 illustrates this graphically:

Figure 4-5. RS-232 Signals

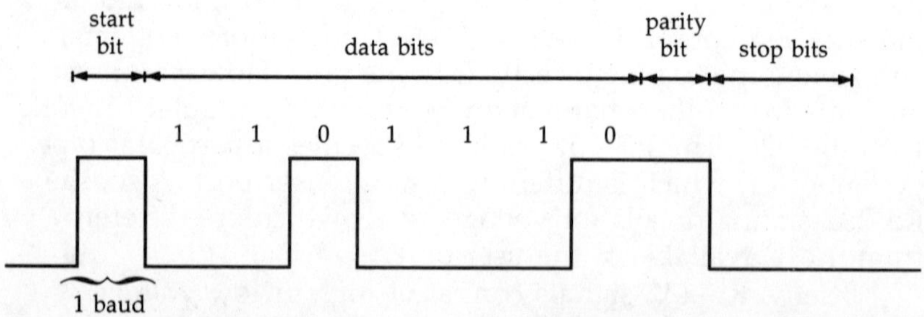

In 128 and 64 modes, the operating system supports the RS-232 interface as device 2. From a programming perspective, telecommunications are handled in essentially the same manner in both 128 and 64 modes (see Chapter 5 for details of CP/M's RS-232 support). In both modes, you prepare for RS-232 communications by opening a channel (also called a *logical file*) to device 2. In BASIC, you can read the characters being received from the RS-232 interface with the GET# statement, and you can send characters to the interface with PRINT#, just as with disk files.

Because of the precise timing requirements for RS-232 communications, the computer sets aside two 256-byte buffers (reserved areas of memory), one for characters waiting to be sent and another for characters which have been received from the modem but not yet read by the computer. In 64 mode, these buffers are established at the highest 512 bytes of available RAM. The establishment of these buffers—which is automatic when an OPEN for device 2 is performed—includes execution of the BASIC CLR routine, which erases all variables and closes all other files. Thus, for RS-232 communications in 64 mode, *you must open the channel to the modem before opening any other file and before defining any variables.*

Generally, the OPEN statement will be the first statement in any program involving RS-232 communications. The CLR is performed again when BASIC reclaims the buffer area, so closing a file to device 2 also wipes out all variables and closes all other files, and should thus be done only at the end of the program. These rules do not apply in 128 mode. In that mode, two 256-byte areas of memory are always reserved for RS-232 buffers—$0C00–$0CFF for characters received and $0D00–$0DFF for characters waiting to be sent—so no CLR is performed.

The general format for opening a channel to the RS-232 interface is

OPEN ***channel number,2,secondary address, control register, command register,*** *user baud rate low, user baud rate high*

The channel number can be any value from 1–255, although if you specify a number greater than 127 the computer will automatically add a line feed (CHR$(10)) after each RETURN (CHR$(13)). The secondary address can be any number in the range 0–255. The value is irrelevant—it's not used in any way—but it must be present to satisfy the syntax of the OPEN statement.

The other parameters require a bit more explanation. A special integrated circuit called a UART (Universal Asynchronous Receiver-Transmitter) is generally used to generate the required RS-232 signals. The companion UART for the 8502/6502 family of microprocessors is a device called the 6551. However, the 128 does not actually contain a 6551. Instead, the operating system software emulates the functions of the 6551. The emulation is complete to the point of requiring that you specify the operating parameters as if they were to be placed in the hardware registers of a 6551. That is, you must provide single-byte values rather than numbers for the parameters. This is usually accomplished by using CHR$ to create a character with the desired value.

The control register value determines the number of stop bits, the word size, and the data transfer (baud) rate. Tables 4-12–4-17 show how values for the parameter are calculated.

The high bit of the parameter specifies the number of stop bits to be used. For word sizes of seven or eight bits, it's common to use only one stop bit.

Bits 5 and 6 of the parameter specify the word size. For computer-to-computer communications, only seven- or eight-bit word sizes are used. Five- and six-bit words, holdovers from the earliest days of Teletypes, are now largely obsolete. Note that you must use eight-bit words to send character codes greater than 127 or transfer tokenized BASIC programs. Bit 4 of this register is unused.

Bits 0–3 of the control register specify the data transfer rate. Although the 128 gives you a wide variety of choices, you'll find that only two or three of these rates are commonly used. The speed you're likely to use most often is 300 baud.

Control Register Parameters

Table 4-12

Control Register

Stop Bits		
Bit: 7	Value to add to control register	For:
0	0	1 stop bit
1	128	2 stop bits

Table 4-13

Word Size		
Bit: 6 5	Value to add to control register	For:
0 0	0	8-bit words
0 1	32	7-bit words
1 0	64	6-bit words
1 1	96	5-bit words

Table 4-14

Baud Rate		
Bit: 7 2 1 0	Value to add to control register	For:
0 0 0 0	0	user-defined rate
0 0 0 1	1	50 baud
0 0 1 0	2	75 baud
0 0 1 1	3	110 baud
0 1 0 0	4	134.5 baud
0 1 0 1	5	150 baud
0 1 1 0	6	300 baud
0 1 1 1	7	600 baud
1 0 0 0	8	1200 baud
1 0 0 1	9	1800 baud
1 0 1 0	10	2400 baud

Most microcomputer telecommunications are currently conducted at this rate for the simple reason that 300 bps modems are the least expensive and most widely available. The two original Commodore modems, the 1600 VICmodem and the 1650 Automodem, as well as the new Modem/300, are all 300 bps units. Also, most faster modem models are also capable of operating at the 300 bps speed. The next most popular rate is 1200 baud. Advances in modem technology have recently cut the cost of 1200 bps modems like Commodore's new 1665 Modem/1200 significantly. Finally, enough 2400 bps modems are now in use that some bulletin boards and other services are providing 2400 baud access. For now, however, the 2400 bps units are still comparatively expensive.

The transfer rate you choose is determined by two factors: your modem and the capability of the system you are communicating with. First, you can't specify a rate faster than your modem can handle—you can't send data at 2400 bps from a 300 bps modem (although most 2400 bps modems *can* send data at 300 bps). Secondly, you must set your system for the same rate as the system you are calling. You can't simultaneously send at 1200 bps and receive at 300 bps.

The command register is used to specify parity and two other options called duplex and handshaking. Tables 4-15–4-17 show how values for the parameter are calculated.

Bits 5–7 determine whether parity is used and, if so, what type. With eight-bit words, it's most common to use no parity. If you choose to use parity with seven-bit words, even parity is common.

The duplex setting determines whether or not the computer is expected to echo characters on the screen. In *half-duplex* mode, each computer is responsible for displaying the characters it sends on its own screen. In *full-duplex* mode, the computer does not immediately display the characters it sends. Instead, it expects the system on the other end of the link to echo those characters, which are displayed when they are received. Many modems also have a full/half duplex switch. You should be careful not to set both your telecommunications program and your modem for half duplex, otherwise you may get two copies of each character you type. It's usually best to leave the modem set for full duplex; then the telecommunications program can be used to switch between the duplex modes.

Bits 1–3 of the command register are unused. Bit 0 deter-

Command Register Parameters

Table 4-14
Command Register

Parity		
Bit: 7 6 5	Value to add to control register	For:
- - 0	0	parity ignored
0 0 1	32	odd parity
0 1 1	96	even parity
1 0 1	160	mark parity
1 1 1	224	space parity

Table 4-16

Duplex		
Bit: 4	Value to add to control register	For:
0	0	full duplex
1	16	half duplex

Table 4-17

Handshaking		
Bit: 0	Value to add to control register	For:
0	0	3-line handshaking
1	1	x-line handshaking

mines which of the signal lines of the RS-232 interface are used. The simplest configuration is the three-line interface, which uses only the absolute minimum number of lines: one for data being transmitted, one for data being received, and one which is the ground required to complete the electrical circuit for the other two. In three-line mode, the computer assumes that the modem is always ready to send data, and the modem assumes that the computer is always ready to receive data. In x-line mode, a number of *handshaking* signal lines become available which can be used to control the data flow. For example, the computer and modem can use the RS-232 DTR (Data Terminal Ready) and DSR (Data Set Ready) lines to inform each other about their respective readiness to send or receive data. Commodore modems use three-line handshaking, the simpler mode.

As an example, suppose you wanted to communicate at 1200 baud using seven-bit words, even parity, one stop bit, and full duplex, and that your modem only used three-line handshaking. The parameters for your statement would be

Control Register:	**1 stop bit**	=	**0**
	7 data bits	=	**32**
	1200 baud	=	**8**
			40
Command Register:	**even parity**	=	**96**
	full duplex	=	**0**
	3-line handshake	=	**0**
			96

Remember that the parameters must be single-byte values, so we use CHR$ to create characters with the desired values. Thus, your OPEN statement might look something like the following:

OPEN 11,2,0,CHR$(40)+CHR$(96)

The final two parameters of the OPEN statement, the user baud rate low and high bytes, are optional and rarely used. They allow the interface to operate at nonstandard baud rates. If you specify 0 for the baud rate portion of the control register—if bits 0–3 in that register are 0—then the computer uses these two characters as the low and high bytes of a delay factor used to calculate the baud rate timing. The formula is

baud rate = clock frequency/(2 * (high byte * 256 + low byte +100))

(The system clock frequency is 1.02273E6 Hz for U.S. NTSC-video 128's and 0.985265E6 Hz for European PAL-video 128's.) Since the control register settings allow for all standard baud rates, there's almost never a reason to bother with calculating the rate factors.

There's one other feature of modems to be considered before you begin telecommunicating. Modems can transmit and receive data simultaneously. To accomplish this, the modem uses two separate sets of audio frequencies, called the answer set and the originate set. For telecommunications to work, one modem must be set to send data out using tones from the originate set of frequencies while interpreting incoming tones in the answer set as data and ignoring any originate tones it hears; this is called *originate mode*. The other modem must send data out using the answer set and be prepared to receive tones from the originate set, which is called *answer mode*. It doesn't really matter which modem is set in which mode, but the two modems must be in opposite modes for the link to be established. The convention is that the modem on the system making the call is set for originate mode while the modem on the system receiving the call is set to answer mode.

Telecommunications Software

Telecommunications programs are frequently called terminal programs because they allow the computer to emulate dedicated terminal units like those connected to mainframe computers. Terminals are classed according to their "intelligence"; *dumb terminals* do no more than send and receive text, while *intelligent terminals* allow for fancy formatting and editing. Program 4-3 is short and simple, yet it includes all the basic functions required for a dumb terminal. (Unless otherwise indicated, all the following programs work in both 128 and 64 modes.)

Program 4-3. Dumb Terminal

```
10 OPEN 2,2,2,CHR$(6)+CHR$(0)
90 PRINT CHR$(14)"{CLR}{2 DOWN}"TAB(12)"{RVS} DUMB
   TERMINAL ":PRINT
100 GET#2,A$:IF A$="" THEN 120
110 PRINT A$
120 GET A$:IF A$="" THEN 100
130 PRINT#2,A$;:PRINT A$;:GOTO 100
```

Line 10 opens a channel to the modem (device 2). The CHR$(6) and CHR$(0) set up the RS-232 interface for communication at 300 bps, with eight-bit words, one stop bit, no parity, and full duplex. In this case, we actually want a half-duplex program, but we'll set the interface for full duplex and use the program itself to provide the half-duplex character echo. Leave the modem set for full duplex or you'll get two copies of each character you type. Change these values if you need another configuration. For example, to use seven-bit words change the CHR$(6) to CHR$(38). Refer to Tables 4-12–4-17 for more information on these parameters.

At line 100, the program checks whether a character has been received from the modem. If so, that character is displayed in line 110; otherwise, the program checks whether anything has been typed on the keyboard (line 120). Any character typed is sent to the modem, and also displayed on the screen—in half duplex, each computer is responsible for echoing its own characters to the screen. If you wish to use full duplex (or if you set the modem's duplex switch for half-duplex mode so that it provides its own character echo), you should remove the PRINT A$; in line 130. Otherwise, you'll get double characters on the screen when you type.

In this simple example you must press the RUN/STOP key to exit the program. To provide for a more graceful way out, add these two lines:

```
125 IF A$="£" THEN 140
140 CLOSE 2:END
```

Now pressing the British pound symbol (£) key will take you out of the terminal program and close the channel to the modem.

This simple program works well enough if you are communicating with another Commodore computer. However, if you try to communicate with another type of computer—for example, a mainframe computer at one of the big information services like CompuServe—you may get some unexpected results. For example, all the lowercase letters in the text you receive may appear as uppercase on the screen, and vice versa. This is because different computers represent characters differently. Appendix A explains this in more detail.

If you are having character incompatibility problems, one solution is to set up a pair of translation tables, one for characters going out and one for characters coming in. Entries in the tables provide substitute values for any characters that differ between the systems. To add translation tables, make the following additions and changes to Program 4-3.

```
20 DIM IN%(255),OU%(255):FOR J=0 TO 255:IN%(J)=J:O
   U%(J)=J:NEXT
30 FOR J=65 TO 90:IN%(J)=J+32:OU%(J)=J+32:NEXT J
40 FOR J=97 TO 122:IN%(J)=J-32:OU%(J)=J-32:NEXT J
50 FOR J=193 TO 218:OU%(J)=J-128:NEXT J
110 PRINT CHR$(IN%(ASC(A$)));
130 PRINT#2,CHR$(OU%(ASC(A$)));:PRINT A$;:GOTO 100
```

Lines 20–50 show how translation tables can be set up to account for the differences between Commodore's codes for uppercase and lowercase letters and the common ASCII standard (explained in Appendix A). Note the use of integer arrays, which use less memory than normal floating point arrays like IN() and OU(). The new lines 110 and 130 show how characters are looked up in the tables (again, for full duplex operation remove the PRINT A$; in line 130).

Now that you have the basic translation tables set up, you can begin to customize the tables for your own needs. For example, printing some characters with codes 0–31 and 128–159 can have undesired effects, such as changing the color of printing, moving the cursor, or clearing the screen. Lines 60 and 70 below show how to render these characters harmless when they are received. Remember, however, that some of the characters in these groups are important. For example, the final statement in line 60 restores the essential RETURN character. Line 80 corrects for two other differences: the ASCII delete is character 127 while the Commodore delete is character 20, and the ASCII backspace, character 8, can be replaced with Commodore's cursor left, character 157.

```
60 FOR J=0 TO 31:IN%(J)=0:NEXT J:IN%(13)=13
70 FOR J=128 TO 159:IN%(J)=0:NEXT J
80 IN%(8)=157:IN%(127)=20:OU%(20)=127:OU%(157)=8
```

Uploading and Downloading

So far, the terminal program only allows data to be typed or received one character at a time. For computer telecommunications to be truly useful, you need the capability to send and receive whole sets of data, or *files.* For example, many bulletin board systems offer a variety of public domain programs.

Rather than just view the program listings on your screen, you'll probably want to load them into your computer.

The process of receiving a file is known as *downloading*. The converse process, sending a file to another computer, is called *uploading*. (Of course, the direction depends on your perspective. In any file transfer, one computer is uploading and the other is downloading.) Uploading is a relatively simple process. Instead of sending the modem a series of characters which you type on the keyboard, you send it characters which you read from a disk or tape file (or perhaps out of memory). Add the following lines to the terminal program to provide a primitive upload capability:

```
95 PRINT"{2 SPACES}(PRESS: {RVS} ↑ {OFF} TO UPLOAD
   {2 SPACES}{RVS} £ {OFF} TO QUIT)":PRINT
126 IF A$?="↑" THEN 2ØØ
2ØØ PRINT"{2 DOWN}{RVS} UPLOAD ":F$="":INPUT"
    {2 DOWN}FILENAME";F$:IF F$="" THEN 1ØØ
21Ø SS=Ø:EE=Ø:OPEN 15,8,15:OPEN 1,8,8,"Ø:"+F$:INPU
    T#15,EE,EE$:IF EE THEN 25Ø
22Ø IF SS THEN 24Ø
23Ø GET#1,A$:SS=ST:PRINT#2,CHR$(OU%(ASC(A$)));:GOT
    O 22Ø
24Ø IF SS=64 THEN CLOSE 1:CLOSE 15:PRINT "{2 DOWN}
    ** UPLOAD COMPLETE **":GOTO 1ØØ
25Ø CLOSE 1:CLOSE 15:PRINT"{2 DOWN}{RVS} DISK ERRO
    R ";:IF EE THEN PRINT EE;EE$
26Ø PRINT"READING FROM ";F$:GOTO 1ØØ
```

With this addition, the terminal program can upload both sequential and program files from disk. This program should upload sequential text files just fine, but it may not be reliable for BASIC program files. First of all, BASIC program files can only be uploaded to another Commodore computer. When a BASIC program is stored in memory or on disk or tape, the keywords like PRINT and POKE are not spelled out. Rather, they are represented in memory by a single character called a *token*. For example, the token for PRINT is CHR$(153). The token is expanded to the full keyword only when the program is listed. Different versions of BASIC use different tokens, so only a Commodore computer can understand a Commodore BASIC program file. (All BASIC tokens have values greater than 128, so an eight-bit word size must be used. A seven-bit code can only send characters with codes less than 128.) Also, BASIC program files contain character 0 as a line separator, and some terminal programs at the other end of the line may ignore character code 0.

The usual solution is to convert the BASIC program to a text file, a simple process. First, load the BASIC program to be converted, then type:

OPEN 1,8,8,"0:*filename*,S,W":CMD1:LIST

When the cursor reappears, you know that the file is done listing. Close it with the following commands:

PRINT#1:CLOSE 1

It's important to add that final PRINT#; otherwise you might lose the last part of the file. Note that this is very similar to the syntax you use to list a program on a printer. What you are doing, in effect, is listing the program onto the disk. The resulting text file can usually be uploaded with fewer problems.

Downloading is a bit more complicated. It's not possible—at least not in BASIC—to download directly to disk. Even using 128 fast mode and limiting modem communications to 300 bps, the computer cannot write characters to the disk fast enough to keep up with the data coming in from the modem, so some of the incoming characters will be lost or garbled. The standard solution is to set aside an area of memory to hold the data as it is received, then to save the contents of this reserved area (called a buffer) to disk or tape. For communications at 300 bps, BASIC can POKE data into memory fast enough to keep up with the modem. Add the following lines to provide the terminal program with a simple download routine (unlike the other portions, this routine will work only in 128 mode):

```
5 BANK Ø:POKE 58,96:CLR:BS=24576:BE=6528Ø
96 PRINT"{2 SPACES}(PRESS {RVS} ← {OFF} TO OPEN DO
   WNLOAD BUFFER)"
127 IF A$="←" THEN 3ØØ
3ØØ PRINT"{2 DOWN}{RVS} DOWNLOAD {OFF} (";BE-BS;"B
    YTES AVAILABLE)"
31Ø PRINT"{DOWN}PRESS {RVS} ← {OFF} TO CLOSE BUFFE
    R":BP=BS:BANK 1
32Ø GET#2,A$:IF A$<>"" THEN A=IN%(ASC(A$)):PRINT C
    HR$(A);:POKE BP,A:BP=BP+1:IF BP=BE THEN PRINT"
    {DOWN}** BUFFER FULL **":GOTO 34Ø
33Ø GET A$:IF A$<>"←" THEN 32Ø
34Ø INPUT"{2 DOWN}SAVE BUFFER CONTENTS [Y/N]";A$:I
    F A$<>"Y" THEN 1ØØ
```

```
350 F$="":INPUT"{2 DOWN}FILENAME";F$:IF F$="" THEN
    100
360 OPEN 1,8,8,"0:"+F$+",S,W":IF DS THEN 390
370 FOR J=BS TO BP-1:PRINT#1,CHR$(PEEK(J));:IF ST
    {SPACE}THEN 390
380 NEXT J:CLOSE 1:PRINT"{2 DOWN}** BUFFER SAVED *
    *":GOTO 100
390 PRINT"{2 DOWN}{RVS} DISK ERROR: ";DS$;DS:PRINT
    "WRITING FILE ";F$:CLOSE 1:GOTO 100
```

Line 5 reserves the upper 40K (40960 bytes) of bank 1 of RAM as a buffer. This must be done *before* the channel to the modem is opened (in line 10), since the BASIC statement CLR, used to reset the memory pointer, has the side effect of closing all open files. Characters received are simply POKEd into memory until the buffer is full, or until the back arrow (←) key is pressed. Then you are offered the option to save the contents of memory.

If you are going to download programs you may want to avoid translation, since it can introduce errors. If so, change the A=IN%(ASC(A$)) in line 320 to the simpler statement A=ASC(A$). As noted earlier in the discussion of uploading, BASIC programs are often converted to text files before they are transferred. To be able to use a BASIC program downloaded as a text file, you must have some method of converting it back into a program. The conversion process is usually referred to as *tokenization*. The following one-line program converts downloaded files back into BASIC programs:

1 INPUT"{2 DOWN}NAME OF TEXT FILE";F$:DOPEN#1,(F$) BANK 15:SYS DEC("FFC6"),0,1

When you run this program, the screen display will scroll as the file is converted, then the program will end with a SYNTAX ERROR message. Don't worry; this is normal. After the error message, type CLOSE 1, then type LIST to see your tokenized program. The tokenizer line will be attached, so you'll need to delete line 1. If you don't get the error message, only a continuously scrolling screen and a blinking light on the drive, then a disk error has occurred. Press RUN/STOP–RESTORE to regain control.

Telecommunicating in Machine Language

The procedure for telecommunicating in machine language is essentially the same as for BASIC. You must open a channel to device 2 and set the word size, baud rate, and other parameters, then look for a character arriving from the modem and display the character if one is received. Next, you must check the keyboard and, if a key is pressed, echo the character on the screen (for half duplex), and send the character out to device 2. Program 4-4, which can be entered with the 128 monitor (see the instructions in the Introduction), is the machine language equivalent of the initial BASIC terminal program given above. The routine makes extensive use of the 128's Kernal ROM routines. (See Chapter 6 for more information on the Kernal.)

Program 4-4. Dumb Terminal in Machine Language

```
F0BB8 LDA #$02   ; code at $0BB8–$0BCA performs
F0BBA TAX        ; the equivalent of OPEN 2,2,2
F0BBB TAY
F0BBC JSR  $FFBA ; Kernal SETNAM
F0BBF LDA #$02
F0BC1 LDX #$FC   ; RS-232 parameters are at $0BFC
F0BC3 LDY #$0B
F0BC5 JSR  $FFBD ; Kernal SETNAM
F0BC8 JSR  $FFC0 ; Kernal OPEN
F0BCB LDA #$0E
F0BCD JSR  $FFD2 ; equivalent to PRINT CHR$(14)
F0BD0 JSR  $FFB7 ; Kernal READSS
F0BD3 AND #$08   ; was status bit 3 set?
F0BD5 BNE  $0BE2 ; if so, character was not vaild
F0BD7 LDX #$02
F0BD9 JSR  $FFC6 ; Kernal CHKIN
F0BDC JSR  $FFE4 ; Kernal GETIN (now from device 2)
F0BDF JSR  $FFD2 ; Kernal BSOUT (to screen)
F0BE2 JSR  $FFCC ; Kernal CLRCH
F0BE5 JSR  $FFE4 ; Kernal GETIN (from keyboard)
F0BE8 BEQ  $0BD0 ; branch if no key was pressed
F0BEA PHA        ; store character temporarily
F0BEB JSR  $FFD2 ; Kernal BSOUT (to screen)
F0BEE LDX #$02
F0BF0 JSR  $FFC9 ; Kernal CKOUT
F0BF3 PLA        ; retrieve character
F0BF4 JSR  $FFD2 ; Kernal BSOUT (now to device 2)
F0BF7 JSR  $FFCC ; Kernal CLRCH
F0BFA BEQ  $0BD0 ; loop back for another character
F0BFC 06 00
```

Activate the program by typing J F0BB8 from the monitor, or BANK 15:SYS DEC("0BB8") from BASIC 7.0.

The code at $0BD0–$0BD6 shows the primary additional requirement of receiving characters in machine language. When using the Kernal GETIN routine to read from RS-232, you cannot simply check for a zero value returned to indicate that no character is available, as you can when reading from the keyboard. You must check the RS-232 status register, either by calling the Kernal READSS routine, or by directly reading the register at location 2874 ($0A14) (location 659 ($0293) in 64 mode). Bit 3 of the status register is the receiver-buffer-empty indicator. When this bit is set, there are no characters available to be read from the buffer.

Many of the machine language examples in this book have use locations $0C00–$0DFF. Keep in mind that these locations are the RS-232 input and output buffers, and thus are not available for use during telecommunications.

There's no particular advantage to using machine language to open the channel to the modem. In fact, it's easier to do this cumbersome task in BASIC. The extra speed of ML is important only when transmitting and receiving characters. You can omit lines $0BB8–$0BCF in the program above and call the send/receive routine with the following one-line BASIC program:

```
10 BANK 15:OPEN 2,2,2,CHR$(6)+CHR$(16):PRINT CHR$(14):SYS
   DEC("0BD0")
```

Video Displays

Like virtually every other microcomputer, the Commodore 128 communicates with you, the programmer, chiefly through a *monitor* or some type of display screen. Several options are available to accommodate a wide variety of needs. (The use of the term *monitor* to describe a dedicated video display should not be confused with the use of the same word to describe the built-in machine language control program. It's an unfortunate quirk of computerese that monitor has two different uses, but both stem from the same idea: Video monitors let you monitor (watch) the output of your programs, while machine language monitor programs let you "see" machine language.)

The least expensive alternative is to connect the computer to an ordinary TV, using the cable and switch box supplied by the manufacturer. The RF (Radio Frequency) modulated output of the computer contains both audio and video signals, which the TV receives through its antenna input like an ordinary broadcast signal. Though it has the advantage of low cost, a TV hookup rarely provides as clear a display as using a dedicated monitor. The RF cable acts as an antenna of sorts, picking up stray signals from the general vicinity—including the radio frequency waves generated by the chips in your computer and associated peripherals. In the past few years, an increasing number of combination TV/monitor devices have appeared on the market. These are essentially televisions with extra connections for direct input from a home computer or video-recording device. In monitor mode, the device bypasses the TV circuits that receive broadcast signals, usually providing a display equal to that of a dedicated monitor.

If you have owned or used another Commodore computer before purchasing your 128, chances are good that you're familiar with the most popular type of dedicated monitor—the *composite* monitor. This type includes the Commodore 1701 and 1702 monitors (and many similar non-Commodore devices), which display an excellent image in 40-column mode. These monitors are connected to the computer through the eight-pin video connector at the computer's rear. Commodore composite monitors usually produce the best picture through the rear connectors, which split the color portion of the signal into separate chroma (color) and luma (brightness) signals, rather than those in the front of the device.

A monochrome monitor, though it provides no color (and often no sound), offers another inexpensive alternative. For a 40-column display, simply connect the luma output plug of the video output cable to the monitor's input (luma is essentially the video signal stripped of its color information). A diagram of the pins in the video output appears in your *128 System Guide*. If you're not sure which plug is luma, go ahead and experiment. You can't harm either device by momentarily connecting the wrong plug to the monitor. Monochrome displays are usually very sharp—more distinct than the best display produced by a composite monitor.

The third major type of monitor is the RGBI (Red/Blue/Green/Intensity), in which a separate signal is provided for each of the three primary video colors—red, green, and blue. The 128's 80-column display is in RGBI format. Since the nine-pin RGBI connector at the rear of the 128 is much like that on an IBM PC or PCjr, you should be able to use any color monitor compatible with those machines. Besides providing an extremely clear image, an RGBI monitor gives you 80 columns of characters on the screen—ideal for word processing, spreadsheets, and so on. The Commodore 1902 monitor, designed expressly for the 128, is a dual monitor: You can switch it from 40-column composite mode to 80-column RGBI mode simply by pressing a switch.

Though it requires making your own connector cable, you can get an acceptable 80-column monochrome display on a Commodore 1701 or 1702 monitor. The first step is to purchase a standard male nine-pin D connector (Radio Shack part #276-1537 is acceptable), a length of shielded coaxial cable and an ordinary RCA phono plug. As shown on page 352 of the *Commodore 128 System Guide,* pin 1 of the RGBI connector is ground, and pin 7 is monochrome output. (Note that the diagram on page 352 shows the pins as if you are *inside the computer looking out.* The pins of the plug you buy should be numbered; just look for pins 1 and 7.) To make an 80-column cable, you need only connect pin 7 of the D connector to the signal (inner) portion of the RCA plug and connect pin 1 to the ground (outer) portion of the plug (via the coaxial cable, of course). If you don't know how to do this yourself, any friend with a soldering iron and some electronics experience should be able to do it for you.

A homebrew cable of this type produces an excellent 80-column image on any monochrome monitor that accepts composite output, and an acceptable display on a Commodore 1701 or 1702 monitor. To use it with a Commodore composite monitor, turn the contrast down and plug the RCA connector end of the cable into the VIDEO connector on the front or the LUMA connector on the back. The ordinary light-on-dark display will probably not be very readable: Press ESC-R to switch to dark characters on a light background. Though it's not quite RGBI quality, the image is definitely usable, and gives you access to 80 columns at a cost of only a few dollars.

Programming the Monitor

Commodore computers address the display screen as device number 3. Though you may never have done so, it's possible to OPEN the screen for input or output like any other device.

For example, this program lets you input a string without the question mark prompt generated by the normal INPUT command.

```
10 OPEN 1,3
20 PRINT "TYPE ANYTHING"
30 GET A$:IF A$<>CHR$(13) THEN PRINT A$;:GOTO 30
40 PRINT:PRINT CHR$(145);
50 INPUT#1,X$
60 PRINT "YOU TYPED ";X$
70 CLOSE 1
```

Printers

A printer is an output device, just like the screen on your television or monitor. Anything that can be printed to the screen can also be sent to the printer. You only need to know a few BASIC commands to use your printer.

The first command, OPEN, tells the computer to create a channel for input or output. The format of the OPEN command is

OPEN ***logical file number, device,*** *secondary address*

You may use any number in the range 1–255 for the logical file number. This number is used to identify the channel. Printers—like all other serial devices—can theoretically have any device number in the range 0–30. However, since nearly all printers for the 128 use device 4, the second parameter is usually 4. Unlike disk drives, it's often impossible to change the device number of a printer, although some can be switched between device 4 or device 5.

The secondary address is used to send special codes to the selected device. Each printer or printer interface interprets the secondary address differently, so it is difficult to generalize; however, two secondary addresses are widely used: A secondary address of 0 usually sets the printer to print everything in uppercase/graphics mode. Setting the secondary address to 7 usually causes the printer to print in lowercase/uppercase.

OPEN 2,4,0 opens channel 2 to the printer and sets uppercase/graphics
OPEN 3,4,7 opens channel 3 to the printer and sets lowercase/uppercase

Once a channel is open, you can redirect any output to the printer with the CMD or PRINT# commands. The

PRINT# command sends any information in the PRINT# statement to the designated channel.

PRINT#3,"HELLO" sends the characters HELLO to channel 3

The CMD statement sends all output to the designated channel. Once this is done, all output goes to that channel until it is closed, although certain other statements like GET will cancel the effect of CMD.

You can list a BASIC program on a printer with the following statements:

OPEN 4,4,0:CMD 4:LIST

When the printer finishes listing, return output to the screen with the following:

PRINT#4:CLOSE 4

CMD can also be used to list a machine language disassembly to the printer:

OPEN 4,4,0:CMD 4:MONITOR
D ***start address end address***

When the disassembly is finished, type X to return to BASIC, then use the statement shown above to return output to the screen.

Special functions in the printer are controlled with character codes. The following is a table of some of the standard control characters for Commodore printers (codes for other printers may vary):

Character Code	Action
10	Line feed
13	Carriage return
14	Turn on double-width character mode
15	End double-width character mode
18	Turn on reverse characters
146	Turn off reverse characters
17	Turn on upper/lowercase characters
145	Turn on uppercase/graphics characters

To use these special codes, simply send them to the printer with PRINT#. The following statements turn on double-width character mode:

OPEN 4,4,0:PRINT#4,CHR$(14)

Here is a simple program that dumps an entire 40-column screenful of text to a Commodore printer. Since it's designed to handle ordinary text, do not expect this program to accommodate reverse video, graphic symbols, sprites, or high-resolution screens.

```
10 OPEN 2,4,−7*(PEEK(53272)=23):OPEN 1,3:PRINT CHR$(19);
20 FOR A=1 TO 25:B$="":FOR B=1 TO 40
30 GET#1,A$:IF A$<>CHR$(13) THEN B$=B$+A$
40 NEXT:PRINT#2,B$:NEXT:CLOSE 1:CLOSE 2
```

The OPEN statement in line 10 may look strange at first. What it does is PEEK location 53272 to determine whether the computer is currently in uppercase/graphics or lower/uppercase mode, and set the printer's secondary address accordingly.

Joysticks, Mice, Paddles, and Light Pens

The 128 has two controller ports on the side of the computer. These ports are used for the joysticks, paddles, mice, and light pen. The following table shows the pins in the ports and their functions:

Pin	Port 1	Port 2
1	Joystick 1 north	Joystick 2 north
2	Joystick 1 south	Joystick 2 south
3	Joystick 1 west/ Paddle 1 button	Joystick 2 east/ Paddle 3 button
4	Joystick 1 east/ Paddle 2 button	Joystick 2 west/ Paddle 4 button
5	Paddle 1	Paddle 3
6	Button 1/light pen	Button 2
7	+5 volts	+5 volts
8	Ground	Ground
9	Paddle 2	Paddle 4

BASIC 7.0 provides three different statements for reading these ports, depending on which device is connected. The JOY function lets you read a joystick connected to port 1 or port 2. The PEN function returns coordinates from a light pen (light pens can be connected to port 1 only), and POT (think of *potentiometer*, a variable resistor) returns values from game paddles. A mouse is read with JOY, just like a joystick. The following examples demonstrate the use of each function.

Paddle Reader

```
10 KEY 8,"{WHT}PRINTCHR$(147){BLU}"+CHR$(13):PRINT
   CHR$(147):COLOR 5,7:COLOR Ø,2:COLOR 4,4
2Ø PRINT "PRESS ANY KEY "
3Ø GETKEY R$
5Ø PRINT "{CLR}":REM TESTER
6Ø PRINT "1=";POT(1),"2=";POT(2),"3=";POT(3),"4=";
   POT(4):GOTO 6Ø
```

Joystick Reader

```
1Ø KEY 8,"{WHT}PRINTCHR$(147){BLU}"+CHR$(13):PRINT
   CHR$(147):COLOR 5,7:COLOR Ø,2:COLOR 4,4
2Ø FOR X=1 TO 9:READ D$(X):NEXT:PRINT "WHICH PORT?
   <1 OR 2>"
3Ø GETKEY R$
4Ø P=ASC(R$)-48:IF P<1 OR P>2 THEN 3Ø
5Ø PRINT "{CLR}":REM TESTER
6Ø X=JOY(P):IF X=128 THEN X=9:GOTO 8Ø
7Ø IF X>128 THEN C=X-128:X=9:PRINT D$(C);" AND ";
8Ø PRINT D$(X)
9Ø GOTO 6Ø
1ØØ DATA N,NE,E,SE,S,SW,W,NW,FIRE
```

Light Pen Reader

```
1Ø KEY 8,"{WHT}PRINTCHR$(147){BLU}"+CHR$(13):PRINT
   CHR$(147):COLOR 5,7:COLOR Ø,2:COLOR 4,4
2Ø PRINT "WHICH PORT? <1 OR 2>"
3Ø GETKEY R$
4Ø P=ASC(R$)-48:IF P<1 OR P>2 THEN 3Ø
5Ø PRINT "{CLR}":REM TESTER
6Ø PRINT "X=";PEN(Ø),"Y=";PEN(1):GOTO 6Ø
```

Chapter 5

CP/M Mode

CP/M Mode

If you are familiar with Commodore computers, but not with the CP/M operating system, you may be tempted to view this chapter as foreign, somewhat forbidding territory. On the other hand, if you already know CP/M, but the 128 is your first Commodore, you may enter these pages with a welcome sense of relief. The 128 provides a bridge between both worlds: It's every inch a Commodore, yet it gives you access to the extensive realm of CP/M programming.

Given the scope of what CP/M includes, it would be difficult to cover the subject fully in one book, let alone one chapter. This chapter presents an overview of CP/M, from the user's and the programmer's points of view. For those who are new to CP/M, we'll look at basic CP/M commands, show how to use the utility programs included on the 128 CP/M disk, and dicuss some fundamentals of CP/M machine language programming. For those who already know CP/M—but not this particular implementation—we'll point out some ways in which this implementation differs from others.

To get the most out of this chapter, you may want to acquire the CP/M documentation package which Commodore offers with a coupon in the *128 System Guide*. This includes the 600-page Digital Research CP/M reference manual and two utility disks, one of which is double-sided. On the double-sided disk you will find the MAC and RMAC assemblers, the SID debugger, the LINK and LIB utilities, and complete source code for the 128 BIOS and the Z80 ROM.

In Commodore documentation, hexadecimal numbers are ordinarily represented with a leading dollar sign ($1C00, for instance) or with no special symbol at all (when it's clear from context that hexadecimal is intended). CP/M programmers usually represent hex numbers with a trailing H (1C00H). Since the dollar sign is used throughout the rest of this book, we'll continue to use it here. However, because most CP/M assemblers demand the latter form, actual program examples will use 1C00H rather than $1C00 or 1C00.

What Is CP/M?

CP/M stands for Control Program for Microcomputers, one of the first truly successful operating systems for microcomputers. In the last decade, it has been used on hundreds of different types of small computers and has generated an enormous number of programs and programming languages.

Compared with more elaborate operating systems like MS-DOS and UNIX, CP/M is relatively simple. But all three systems share the same basic features: input/output operations to terminals, printers, and communication devices like modems; file-structured disk storage; and an interactive command interpreter for running programs from disk. In keeping with the universal nature of such systems, CP/M on the 128 does not specifically support the 128's sound and graphics abilities.

CP/M is a modular system, composed of three major parts: the Console Command Processor (CCP), an interactive program which dispatches applications; the Basic Disk Operating System (BDOS), which provides file-based disk operations and simple line editing and line printing; and the Basic Input/Output System (BIOS), the only system-specific part of CP/M, which performs the simplest I/O operations. The CP/M system prompt, A>, indicates that the CCP is waiting for you to enter a command.

CP/M also includes utility programs that aren't part of the CCP or BDOS. Called *transient commands,* these programs reside in disk files and are loaded into the Transient Program Area (TPA) when needed. Though in many programming languages the terms *command* and *program* signify very different entities, CP/M treats the two as virtually identical. In fact, the concept of transient commands is so deeply imbedded in CP/M that CCP, the command interpreter, is itself a transient program (it appears as CCP.COM on the system disk).

This scheme makes CP/M highly extensible. There's no practical limit to the number of transient commands that the system can use, and each new command increases the power of the system. The only limitations are that each transient command must be stored in a file whose name ends with .COM, and each must be able to fit in the transient program area of the computer.

Program Portability

As implied earlier, CP/M is transportable, meaning you can often run the same program on several different machines. All that a system needs to run CP/M is an 8080 microprocessor (or compatible subsitute, like the 128's Z80); adequate RAM to hold the BDOS, BIOS, and transient programs; and a disk drive. The BDOS and CCP (and nearly all utility programs) will be the same for every CP/M system; the BIOS, which handles I/O tasks, is the only part that needs to be system-specific. Because CP/M software is often transportable from one machine to another, it is available in great abundance.

However, not all CP/M programs are portable, nor should they be. Many computers have particular features (like the 128's advanced graphics and sound capabilities) that don't exist on other machines and aren't supported by CP/M. Programs that use system-specific features are limited to a particular system, but you can still use CP/M for generic tasks like getting keyboard input or accessing the disk drive.

The Commodore 128 comes with CP/M 3.0, sometimes called CP/M Plus, the latest release of this operating system. In older versions of CP/M, the entire system—including the operating system and the TPA—could occupy only 64K of memory, the maximum address range accessible by an 8080-family microprocessor. Since address space was limited, a programmer could expand the BDOS or BIOS only at the expense of the TPA, which limited the size and complexity of any given application. Some manufacturers skirted this limitation by producing computers with several 64K memory banks and a mechanism for selecting banks (*bank switching*). This technique allows larger transient programs, but forces each program to comply with the particular computer's bank-switching scheme.

CP/M 3.0 expects the computer-specific part of BIOS to include a bank-switching function and locates almost all of the BIOS and BDOS code in a different bank from the TPA, allowing each to be larger. The 128 reserves nearly an entire bank for its 59K TPA; the CP/M BDOS uses its extra space to provide improved input editing and some extra disk operations. Even the 128's BIOS benefits from bank switching, allowing a totally redefinable keyboard, simultaneous 40- and 80-column video output, emulation of various terminals, and several different disk formats. In short, CP/M on the 128 takes full advantage of the 128's powerful memory management capabilities.

Getting Started

Before you can use CP/M on the 128, you must load the operating system from a disk. This is easily done. Put a CP/M disk in the drive, then turn the computer on (or issue a BOOT command from BASIC 7.0). The CP/M boot program loads from the disk and turns on the 128's Z80 microprocessor. The Z80, in turn, loads CP/M from disk and starts up the operating system.

Table 5-1. Line Editing Commands

Command	Description
CONTROL-E	Moves the cursor to the start of the next line. The contents of the old line remain part of the line that is being edited.
CONTROL-F	Moves the cursor one column to the right. The CRSR-right key performs the same function.
CONTROL-G	Deletes the character under the cursor and moves the remainder of the line one column to the left.
CONTROL-H	Deletes the character to the left of the cursor and moves the rest of the line, including the cursor, one column to the left. The same function is perfomed by the INST/DEL key.
CONTROL-I	Moves the cursor to the next tab stop, just like the TAB key. CP/M assumes that tab stops exist at every eighth column.
CONTROL-J	Performs the same function as the RETURN key.
CONTROL-K	Deletes all characters to the right of the cursor.
CONTROL-M	Performs the same function as the RETURN key.
CONTROL-R	Types # at the cursor's position, moves down one line on the screen, and retypes the old line up to the cursor's position.
CONTROL-U	Types # at the cursor's position and moves down one line on the screen.
CONTROL-W	Recalls the last command entered. The same function is performed by the CRSR-up key. If CONTROL-U has been pressed since the last command was entered, CONTROL-W recalls the canceled line up to the former cursor position. If CONTROL-R has been pressed, CONTROL-W recalls the entire previous line.
CONTROL-X	Deletes all characters up to the cursor position. Moves the cursor to the beginning of the current line.

The CCP (Console Command Processor) is the main interface between you and CP/M; it offers a number of line editing features for entering CP/M commands (see Table 5-1). Since CP/M line editing facilities are also available to transient programs, you can probably use these functions whenever you need to enter a line of text.

Drive Codes, Filenames, and File Types

CP/M is designed to access as many as 16 disk drives. Each drive has a single-letter specifier between A and P. The BIOS for an individual computer determines how these letters relate to actual hardware. In the case of the Commodore 128, only drives A–E are used. Device 8 on the serial bus is called drive A, device 9 is B, 10 is C, and 11 is D. Drive E is a *virtual drive;* asking for a file on drive E actually causes a search on drive A, but you will first be prompted to change the disk in drive A. This feature is quite valuable for copying files from one disk to another on a single-drive system.

The CP/M BDOS always maintains a default drive. If you name a file for some operation, but don't designate a specific drive, CP/M assumes it can be found on the default drive. This applies to CCP commands which load transient programs as well as to filenames which are passed to the commands. The current default drive identifier is always part of the CCP's command prompt. To change the default drive, type the new drive's identifier followed by a colon at the CCP's prompt.

Each CP/M file has a name of up to eight characters and a file type of up to three characters. The following characters can't be used in filenames:

**! * ? & ( ) + − . , ; : _ [ ] = < > | / **

When referring to a file, you must separate the name and type with a period. Where multiple drives are involved, you can also add a drive specifier (and a colon) before the filename and type. Here's a complete example:

A:FILENAME.TYP

Certain file types have acquired common meanings. Transient commands are stored in .COM type files. The 128 keeps the CCP and the BDOS in .COM files as well. Assembly language source code files usually have the .ASM type, and some assemblers put their output in files with the .HEX type. Others, like the RMAC assembler, generate relocatable output with the

.REL type. The PIP command (described below) uses the type .$$$ for temporary files, which are normally deleted at the end of the command's operation. The ED command—a file editor—renames any file that it's currently editing with the file type .BAK. When it's finished editing, it saves the newly edited file with the original type.

CP/M lets you substitute the wildcard symbols (* and ?) for actual characters in a file's name or type. The question mark symbol can replace any single character. For instance, the filename BA??.COM includes every .COM file whose name begins with BA and has four characters. The asterisk is more general: It matches any string of characters. C*.COM matches any .COM file whose name begins with C, regardless of the name's length. Since the asterisk also replaces a null (the absence of a character), the name C*.COM matches C.COM as well. If you include wildcards in a filename, many CP/M commands will keep looking for files even after the first match is found. This feature is very useful when you want to process a large number of files. The filename *.* matches every file on the current disk.

Built-in Commands

CP/M is unlike operating systems which reside in a ROM chip or load into memory in their entirety. Since some commands are used infrequently, there's no reason to keep them in memory at all times. Instead, they are stored in disk files until you want them. When you request a disk-resident command via the CCP, the system loads the required code from disk. However, the most often used commands (DIR, DIRSYS, ERASE, RENAME, TYPE, and USER) load automatically. Thus, they're available as soon as you boot CP/M.

DIR, meaning *directory,* displays the names of the files on a disk, either from the default drive (if no identifier follows the command) or from the drive which you designate. Note that DIR doesn't recognize *system files,* which are special files you won't need to access for everyday operations. The DIRSYS command (see below) can find system files on the rare occasions when you'll need them.

You can use wildcard symbols in a DIR command to display only a selected group of files. For instance, DIR A:*.COM lists all the transient command (.COM) files on the disk in drive A. DIR MUN*.* lists every file that starts with MUN, and so on.

A DIR listing can contain a very large number of filenames. By concealing the names of files that you'll have on virtually every disk, you can cut down on the visual clutter. For instance, you may get tired of seeing CPM+.COM and CCP.COM on every disk directory. With the SET command (see below) you can change the *system attributes* of these files, changing them to system files which DIR does not display. Note that this operation doesn't change the actual file type (a .COM file remains a .COM file, and so on), but it does affect the way that CP/M treats the file. DIRSYS (abbreviated as DIRS) lists every system file on a disk.

The ERASE command (abbreviated as ERA) removes any file from a disk. Since ERASE is not reversible, use it with care. Though its contents aren't actually erased, the file can't be accessed any more, which amounts to the same thing. Wildcard symbols can be used to erase groups of similarly named files (be sure you understand the risks involved before you perform an ERASE with wildcards). Though Commodore CP/M has no UNERASE command, there are many public domain programs which can recover an ERASEd file *if* you have not written any new data in the disk areas where the erased file resides.

The RENAME command (abbreviated REN) changes the name of a CP/M file. The new and old names of the file are separated by an equal sign (=) on the command line, the new name coming first. For instance, REN IS.NOW=ONCE.WAS searches the default drive for files named ONCE.WAS and IS.NOW. If ONCE.WAS isn't found, the command aborts with a NO FILE error. If IS.NOW already exists on the disk, you see a FILE EXISTS error. If neither error occurs, ONCE.WAS is renamed as IS.NOW.

The TYPE command reads the contents of a disk file and displays it on the console (monitor screen). CP/M will attempt to TYPE any file you designate, but this output is useful only for files which contain printable text. As a rule, files with the types .PRN, .LST, and .SUB are usually printable, as are source code files for most languages (including .ASM files). The .HEX files created as output by an assembler are printable, but are not very easy to understand; .COM files are invariably unprintable. TYPEing a nontext file such as a .COM file does no harm—it simply prints an indecipherable mass of characters on the screen.

USER changes the *current user number,* which has to do with disk organization. The files on a CP/M disk can be divided into up to 16 subsets: Each subset is known as a *user area* and is identified with its own *user number* in the range 0–15. As with drive identifiers, CP/M maintains a current user number at all times. To change the user number, type USER followed by a number from 0 to 15. Whenever the current user number is not 0, the CCP prompt includes the user number ahead of the default drive identifier.

Though you'll rarely need to change the user number, here's what it does. When you create a new file, it is given the current user number; commands that refer to files always use the current user number as well. By storing different groups of files with different user numbers, you can segregate them into different *user areas* on the disk. This is chiefly a convenience feature, useful for disks that contain a very large number of files. When the user number is 0, you have access to the files in user area 0, but can't access files in user area 1, and so on.

Because transient commands are generally stored in user area 0, you can't access them from any other user area—which diminishes the usefulness of switching to other areas. You can get around this problem by changing the most useful commands, such as DIR and DIRSYS, to system files, which are accessible from any user area. However, unless you have a hard disk, you probably won't have enough files on a disk to warrant using anything but area 0.

Additional Features

Though commonly used commands like DIR do reside in memory, you'll also find files named DIR.COM, ERASE.COM, RENAME.COM, and TYPE.COM on the CP/M system disk. In fact, only the most frequently used portions of the built-in commands reside in memory. Each of them has additional, more powerful options stored as transient commands.

Some common options for the DIR command are ATT, which displays a file's attributes (system or directory, read-only or read-write); FULL, which gives all available information about a file; and SIZE, which displays the amount of space that each file occupies on the disk. CP/M command options must be enclosed in square brackets and must follow the filename paramenter without any intervening spaces. For instance, DIR B:[FULL] lists all available information about all the files on the disk in drive B.

ERASE[CONFIRM] displays a file's name and prompts you to enter Y or N before it erases anything. Since this (the transient version of ERASE) gives a chance to reconsider, it's obviously desirable when using wildcards to erase a group of files.

Only the transient version of RENAME supports wildcard file references. And even then, you don't have complete freedom: You must use the same number of wildcard characters in each filename, and the wildcard symbols must appear in exactly the same position within each name. For instance, RENAME *.BAK=*.BAS works correctly, renaming all files with the .BAS type to .BAK. However, RENAME PROG.*=*.COM is illegal because the asterisk appears in different positions.

The built-in TYPE command can handle only one filename, without any wildcards, and pauses the listing after each screenful is displayed. The transient extension to TYPE.COM lets you use wildcards to read more than one file in sequence. The [NO PAGE] option is also useful if you're sending console output to the printer (activated by pressing CONTROL-P).

Common Transient Commands

PIP, the name of CP/M's file copying command, stands for Peripheral Interchange Program. Though it might have made more sense to name this command COPY, the term PIP has been around so long that you're not likely to see it changed.

The simplest form of PIP duplicates a single file. PIP FILE.NEW=FILE.OLD copies the contents of FILE.OLD into a new file named FILE.NEW. If the source file (FILE.OLD) can't be found, a NO FILE message appears. However, if the disk already contains a file named FILE.NEW, PIP *erases* the existing file, replacing it with a copy of FILE.OLD. PIP ordinarily provides no warning before it erases an existing file. However, it's simple to add a yes/no option to PIP. Type SET *.*[RO] to set the read-only attribute of every file on the disk. Then create the new file with PIP. When this is done, use SET *.*[RW] to make every file a read/write file again.

You can also copy from one drive to another by preceding PIP filenames with drive identifiers. If you want the copied file to have the same name as the original, you can abbreviate the command. For instance, PIP B:=A:MUN.COM puts the file MUN.COM on the disk in drive B. To copy from one disk to another on a single-drive system, designate drive E (the virtual drive). For example, PIP E:=A:MUN.COM causes the computer to read MUN.COM from the disk drive, and then try to create a copy on drive E. Whenever you attempt to access drive E, the 128 prompts you to change disks. The next time it needs to access drive A, you're prompted to change disks again. Since CP/M isn't very observant about which is disk A and which is disk E, be careful when swapping disks.

PIP lets you use wildcard symbols in several different ways. The command PIP BAX.*=MUN.* copies every file that starts with MUN into a file of the same type that starts with BAX. The command PIP *.BAK=*.TXT copies all files of the .TXT type into a file of the .BAK type (retaining the original name of each file). PIP B:=A:*.COM copies all .COM files from drive A to drive B. The command PIP BAX.TXT=*.TXT concatenates all .TXT files into one large file named BAX.TXT. You can also concatenate several files by supplying more than one filename on the right side of the equal sign, as in the command PIP BIGFILE.TXT=FILE1.TXT,FILE2.TXT,FILE3.TXT.

Another use of PIP is to access various I/O devices as if they were disk files. To create a file and put some text in it, enter PIP FILE.TXT=CON:. When you hit RETURN, no prompt will be displayed. Type a couple lines of text, then press CONTROL-Z (this is CP/M's end-of-file symbol) to indicate that you're done. PIP copies the characters from the console (CON:) and stores them in the file FILE.TXT. Of course, since the normal line editing keys don't work when you're copying from CON:, this method isn't very practical if you're prone to typing mistakes or if you want to make anything more than a one- or two-line file.

Table 5-2 lists all the various PIP command options. Again, the option must be enclosed in brackets and must follow the filenames without intervening spaces. The C option tells PIP to ask for confirmation before copying any files. When copying more than one file, this option can be used to keep PIP from doing any unexpected copying. If you include the E option, PIP will echo—display on the screen—the contents of each file that it copies. Of course, this is desirable only when copying text files.

The G option, followed by a number *n*, tells PIP to read from or write to the user area designated by *n*, depending on whether the number follows the source or destination filename. If you include the V option, PIP verifies the file by reading it back from disk immediately after making the copy.

Table 5-2. PIP Options

Option	Meaning
A	Copy only those files that have been modified since they were last copied.
C	Ask for confirmation for each file to be copied.
D*n*	Copy only the first *n* characters of each line.
E	Type (echo) the contents of each file on the console screen as it is copied.
F	Remove (filter) all form-feed characters from the file being copied.
G*n*	Send file to or get file from user area number *n*.
H	Check the contents of the file for proper .HEX (assembler output) format.
I	Don't copy any :00 records in a .HEX file.
L	Make all output lowercase.
N	Number each line of the file.
O	Ignore all end-of-file characters (CONTROL-Z). This option is needed only for binary (nonprinting) files that don't have the .COM or .REL type.
P*n*	Insert a form-feed character after every *n* lines. If *n* is omitted, the page length is set to 60 lines.
Q*s*	Quit copying after the string designated by *s* is found. You should type a CONTROL-Z to end the string.
R	Search for and copy system (nondirectory) files.
S*s*	Begin copying when the string designated by *s* is found. You should type a CONTROL-Z to end the string.
T*n*	Replace tab characters (CONTROL-I) with enough spaces to move to a column divisible by *n*.
U	Make all output uppercase.
V	Verify the output file by reading and comparing it with the original.
W	If the output file already exists, erase it before copying, even if it is read-only
Z	Set the parity bit (bit 7) to zero.

CP/M has a transient command to format disks (FORMAT) which is a little unusual among CP/M commands. Since the format in which information is stored on a disk varies tremendously among models of computers, the FORMAT command is written by the computer's manufacturer—Commodore in this case—instead of Digital Research, the author of most other CP/M commands.

The 128's FORMAT command asks which of three formats you would like to use on the disk to be formatted. One of these, double-sided 128 format, is only available with 1571 disk drives, since 1541 drives have only one read/write head. Single-sided 128 format disks can be formatted, written to, and read by both 1541 and 1571 drives, but hold only half as much data as double-sided disks. Commodore 64 CP/M format disks hold even less data than single-sided 128 CP/M disks, but this format is available if the new disk must be readable by a Commodore 64 with a CP/M cartridge.

When a disk has been formatted, it is ready to accept files for storage. However, you can't boot the 128 into CP/M mode with the disk until you add two special files. Use PIP to copy CPM+.COM and CCP.COM onto the new disk.

Utility Commands

The KEYFIG utility lets you reprogram any of the 128's keys (and all its combinations with SHIFT, CONTROL, and the Commodore key) to generate any character or string of characters. The only keys you can't redefine are SHIFT, CAPS LOCK, 40/80 DISPLAY, CONTROL, RESTORE, and the Commodore key.

The DATE command displays and sets the time and date of the built-in clock. DATE by itself simply displays the current time. DATE C displays a running clock on the next screen line, which keeps continuous time until a key is pressed. If you supply a date and time after DATE, the built-in clock is set to that time. The command DATE SET does the same thing, but prints an appropriate prompt. This command is often seen in batch files (see SUBMIT), particularly the PROFILE.SUB file which executes when CP/M boots.

One new feature of CP/M 3.0 is that file directories can hold time and date information about the files they contain. To activate this feature, however, you must rewrite the disk's directory in a new, expanded format. The INITDIR command performs this task (without destroying any existing directory information).

The SHOW command displays information about the system's disk drives and the disks in the drives. SHOW by itself displays the current access mode (RW for read/write or RO for read-only) for each drive. To limit the display to a single drive, include a drive identifier in the command. The [SPACE] option of SHOW displays the same information. The [LABEL] option shows information about the disk's directory, including the label that has been assigned to the disk, whether or not the disk requires passwords for access, and whether time and date stamping should be done to the disk. SHOW[USERS] tells which user number is currently active and the number of files currently associated with each user number. The [DIR] option displays the number of free directory entries remaining on the disk. This, together with the free space remaining on the disk, determines how many more files the disk can hold.

The SET command changes some attribute of a file or disk directory. Table 5-3 details all the SET options.

Table 5-3. SET Options

Option	**Meaning**
DIR	Make this file a nonsystem file, displayed by the DIR command.
SYS	Make this file a system file, not displayed by the DIR command.
RO	Make this file or drive read-only.
RW	Make this file or drive read/write.
ARCHIVE=OFF	Indicate that this file has been altered since last copied.
ARCHIVE=ON	Indicate that this file has not been altered since last copied.
F1/F2/F3/F4=ON/OFF	Turn one of the user attribute bits on or off.
NAME=label	Assign a name to the disk.
PASSWORD=password	Set a password for a file or disk. If no password follows the equal sign, password protection is turned off. If the file or disk is already password-protected, CP/M will prompt for the current password.
PROTECT=ON/OFF	Enable/disable password protection for the disk and all files on the disk.
PROTECT=READ/WRITE/DELETE/NONE	Change the level of access requiring a password for a file.
DEFAULT=password	Set a default password to be used if you omit the password when accessing a file.

The SETDEF command controls the order in which CP/M searches disks when looking for a program file. An asterisk in the list of drives refers to the default device at the time of the search. On a 128 system, it is handy to include the virtual drive (E:) in the list. In that way, you 'll have a chance to swap disks if the desired command can't be found on a disk in the drive(s). For instance, SETDEF *,E: tells CP/M to begin looking for transient commands on the default drive. If the designated command can't be found there, CP/M will try to search drive E:, at which point you're prompted to swap disks.

Device-Related Commands

CP/M generalizes the hardware of a system with five logical devices (CONIN:, CONOUT:, AUXIN:, AUXOUT:, and LST:). CONIN: and CONOUT: are collectively referred to either as CON: or as CONSOLE:. KEYBOARD: is a synonym for CONIN:. You can refer to the AUXIN: and AUXOUT: devices with either AUXILIARY: or AUX:. The PRINTER: command means the same thing as LST:. The CCP and most application programs send their output to the CON: logical device, which is usually associated with the computer's keyboard and video screen. The AUX: device is used for other serial devices, especially modems.

The machine-specific portion of BIOS provides several physical devices, which can be connected with the logical devices. Table 5-4 shows the CP/M logical devices, the 128's physical devices, and the ordinary connections between the two. The DEVICE command can alter these connections or display the current connections. It can also display and alter the characteristics of a physical device. By itself, DEVICE displays all available information about physical and logical devices. Adding the keyword NAMES to DEVICE limits the information to the names and characteristics of all physical devices, while the VALUES keyword tells DEVICE to display only the current assignments of logical devices.

To list information about a specific device, supply its name after the DEVICE command. To change the assignment of a logical device, use a command of the form DEVICE *logical name*:=*physical name*. A command like DEVICE *physical name*: [*options*] changes the characteristics of a physical device.

Table 5-4. Logical and Physical Devices

CP/M Logical Devices and Default Connections
CONIN: KEYS
CONOUT: 40COL or 80COL
AUXIN: NULL*
AUXOUT: NULL*
LST: PRT1

Commodore 128 Physical Devices
KEYS
80COL
40COL
PRT1
PRT2
6551

*NULL is not a physical device; rather, it is a CP/M shorthand for "no connection."

Console Redirection

The GET command can tell CP/M to read from a disk file instead of taking input from the CON: device. Typing GET FILE INPUT.TXT tells CP/M to start reading from the file INPUT.TXT as soon as the next command starts executing. When the next command terminates, input from the physical device assigned to CON: will resume. If the [SYSTEM] option follows the filename, even the next command is taken from the disk file. Furthermore, input from the file doesn't terminate until either you reach the end of the file or the file executes a GET CONSOLE command. Note that there is some overlap in function between GET and the SUBMIT command (discussed below).

The PUT command can be used in similar fashion to redirect console and printer output to a file. Since this command operates on two logical devices, the first argument must designate the device to be redirected. For instance, PUT CONSOLE OUTPUT.TXT stores console output from the next command in a file named OUTPUT.TXT. As with GET, normal console or printer output resumes when the next command terminates. However, the [SYSTEM] option is also available for this command to keep the file output active until a PUT CONSOLE CONSOLE or PUT PRINTER PRINTER command is performed.

The SUBMIT command lets you store any number of CP/M commands in a text file (with the file type .SUB), then execute them all whenever you need them. The file can contain lines of input for programs that expect input in addition to command lines. When CP/M boots up, the CCP looks for a file called PROFILE.SUB. If this file exists, SUBMIT then executes the commands in the file. The PROFILE.SUB facility is handy for configuring the system in a certain way at boot time. For instance, the PROFILE.SUB file might change device assignments, control the order in which the system searches for .COM files, and so on.

The CP/M Text Editor

CP/M's text editor is contained in a file called ED.COM. This is a line-oriented editor, which can only be described as primitive in comparison with modern, full-screen editors like the one built into BASIC 7.0. While ED.COM is capable of doing anything you need to do, it's really too cumbersome for anything but the simplest tasks. There are many good CP/M text editors available. If you plan to do word processing or programming, you will probably want to get a better editor than ED.COM fairly soon.

Organizing Disk Storage

Each CP/M disk contains a directory, which records information about every file on the disk. DIR simply searches the directory and lists the name of each file that it finds. The directory entry for each file is 32 bytes in length. Although Commodore's disks have 256-byte sectors, CP/M handles file data in 128-byte chunks called *records,* then determines how many records it can fit into each of the disk's sectors.

On a larger scale, CP/M disks are also organized into *allocation blocks*. Whenever you create a new file, CP/M must assign that file a certain block or area of disk space. The size of this block varies from system to system, depending on the total number of bytes on the disk, but a common size for an allocation block is eight records, or 1024 bytes (1K). To keep a list of allocation blocks for each file, each allocation block must have a unique ID number. If this ID is to fit in a single byte, there can no more than 256 allocation blocks on a disk.

Combining all this information, we find that if a disk has allocation blocks 1K in length, and each of these has a one-byte ID number, the disk can store only 256K of data. That's no problem for single-sided Commodore CP/M disks, which hold no more than 170K. But double-sided disks can hold as much as 340K. There are two possible solutions: We could either use two bytes to hold the ID for each block or make each block larger so that fewer IDs are required. Commodore chose the second option, making each allocation block on a double-sided disk 2K in length.

One important consequence of this scheme is that it establishes a minimum size for each file. Since each file must be associated with at least one allocation block, even the smallest file takes 1K of space on a single-sided disk (2K on a double-sided disk).

Each 32-byte directory entry contains the file's user number, name, and type. It also contains a *data map,* a 16-byte-long list of the allocation blocks assigned to that file. As you increase the size of the file, sooner or later CP/M needs to assign another allocation block to it. Whenever a new allocation block is assigned, CP/M adds the ID for that block to the data map in the file's directory entry. When all 16 data map bytes contain an ID, that particular directory entry is full (it can't reference any more allocation blocks). Thus, a single directory entry can refer to a 16K file area on a single-sided disk, or a 32K file area on a double-sided disk.

Obviously, many files need to be greater than 16K or 32K in length. To circumvent this problem, CP/M lets a file use more than one directory entry. Although the user number, filename, and file type information will be the same in each entry, the data maps will point to different allocation blocks.

When a file has more than one directory entry, CP/M needs to know the correct order in which to read the entries (that is, which entry should be read first, which should be read second, and so on). This is done with an *extent number.* The first directory entry for a file always has an extent number of 0. The second directory entry has an extent number of 1, and so on. Note that this use of *extent* differs somewhat from general CP/M parlance, which often uses the term to refer to a certain number of bytes.

CP/M's Native Tongue

The CP/M operating system is written in the machine language of the Intel 8080 microprocessor, and CP/M requires that all transient commands must be executable by an 8080 as well. Though the 8080 set the standard for CP/M, you can no longer buy a new 8080-based computer. Present-day machines use newer, 8080-compatible processors. The Intel 8085 can perform 8080 instructions, but is much easier to build into electronic circuits. The Zilog Z80 processor used in the Commodore 128 can perform all 8080 instructions and a number of new ones as well. Though the Z80 is capable of doing things that an 8080 can't, CP/M programs written for the Z80 ordinarily use only 8080 instructions so that they can run on earlier 8080- and 8085-based systems.

An *assembler,* as you may know, is a program that simplifies the process of writing a machine language program. Like other CP/M command programs, CP/M assemblers are written in 8080 code. Since the assemblers accept only 8080 instructions, we'll begin by discussing the 8080's structure.

The 8080 has seven main processor *registers,* or internal locations—named A, B, C, D, E, H, and L—each of which can hold a byte (eight bits) of data. If you're familiar with 6502-based programming, you may see some similarities between these registers and the 6502's A, X, and Y registers (though there are significant differences as well).

The A register, sometimes called the *accumulator,* is the most powerful register. All mathematical operations take place in the A register, though another register often supplies an operand for the operation. For example, ADD B adds the contents of the B register to the value in the accumulator and puts the result back in the accumulator. In *immediate mode* addressing, the second operand is a constant value (the A register is always the first operand). For instance, the instruction ORI 80H performs a logical OR operation between the accumulator and the hexadecimal value $80 (128), setting the highest bit of A to 1. Keep in mind that in Z80 and 8080 ML programming, the trailing H in a number like 80H denotes hexadecimal.

The 8080 provides several instructions which can use any register. The MVI (*move immediate*) instruction moves an eight-bit value into any register. For instance, MVI C,9 puts the value 9 in the C register. The MOV instruction moves data between any two registers. MOV H,A transfers the contents of the accumulator to the H register. Note that the destination register—the one that receives the value—comes *before* the source register—the one that provides the value. Though this order of occurrence makes perfect sense for immediate instructions like MVI, it can be confusing when two registers are involved.

The ICR (*increment register*) and DCR (*decrement register*) instructions also work on any register. ICR increases the value in the designated register by 1, and DCR decreases it by 1.

Two by Two

Unlike the 6502, which can handle only 8 bits in a given operation, the 8080 has a limited repertoire of 16-bit operations. These instructions actually simulate the effect of a 16-bit register by treating two 8-bit registers as a *register pair*. The three register pairs are BC, DE, and HL. The first register of each pair (B, D, or H) holds the most significant byte of the 16-bit number (or *word* in this context). In 8080 machine language, 16-bit instructions always use the name of the register holding the high byte of the word. For instance, the LXI *(load index immediate)* instruction loads a 16-bit value into any register pair; thus, LXI H,0 puts zeros in the HL register pair. In this case H, the high byte of the pair, identifies the pair composed of H and L.

The INX and DCX instructions are also 16-bit operations, incrementing and decrementing a register pair, respectively. XCHG (think of *exchange*) is the only 16-bit register move instruction; it swaps the contents of the DE and HL register pairs. The DAD instruction adds any register pair (including HL) to the HL register pair. LHLD and SHLD can load or store the HL register pair from any pair of memory locations.

Since the 8080 can access 64K (65,536) bytes of memory, a memory address is 16 bits long, meaning that you can interpret the contents of a register pair as a memory address. In instructions that use the *register indirect* addressing mode, data is stored to, read from, or otherwise manipulated in a memory location addressed by a register pair.

STAX is one of these; it stores the contents of the A register at an address pointed to by either the BC or DE register pair. STAX D stores the contents of the A register in the location addressed by the DE register pair. Note that although the D and E registers act as a 16-bit register pair, only 8 bits of data are actually transferred from the A register to memory.

A Register That's Not a Register?

The 8080 has an eighth 8-bit register named M which isn't really a register at all. Though you can use M like any other register, it's actually contained in memory rather than in the microprocessor itself. Specifically, the M register is *a byte of memory addressed by the HL register pair*. That may sound peculiar at first, but it's actually quite convenient. The M register (some would call it a *virtual* register) lets you access any memory address with register indirect addressing, exactly as you would access one of the processor's own registers.

For instance, the following code adds the contents of two consecutive memory locations and stores the result in a third consecutive byte. We'll assume that HL already holds the address of the first byte.

```
MOV A,M
INX  H
ADD A,M
INX  H
MOV M,A
```

Note that the M register represents three different memory locations, controlled by the value in HL. It's like having a processor register that you can move anywhere inside the computer's address space.

The 8080 uses another special 16-bit register, called the stack pointer, for last-in, first-out (LIFO) data storage operations. The data zone it addresses, called the *stack*, can be located anywhere in memory. PUSH and POP are the chief stack instructions. PUSH first subtracts two from the contents of the stack pointer, then stores the contents of a register pair in the memory locations addressed by the pointer. POP does the same thing in reverse. First, it loads a register pair from the memory location addressed by the stack pointer, then it adds two to the contents of the stack pointer. One special register pair, called PSW (*program status word*), can be PUSHed and POPped; it is composed of the A register and all the condition flags.

As you PUSH more data onto the stack, it grows downward into lower memory locations. The stack pointer always points to the address of the most recently PUSHed word. Despite the fact that it seems backward to virtually everyone, this address—the lowest memory location in the stack—is usually called the *top* of the stack. One 8080 instruction, XTHL, operates on the top of the stack, exchanging the contents of the HL register pair with the value at the top of the stack.

Since the stack's location is restricted only by the amount of available RAM, it's common for an 8080 program (and even a subroutine within a program) to set up its own stacks. SPHL lets you set the stack pointer; it loads the stack pointer with the value in the HL register pair. You can also load the stack pointer with an immediate value, using the LXI instruction. To save the value of SP, you have to use the LXI instruction to set HL to 0, then add SP to HL with the instruction DAD SP.

Here's how a subroutine can set up its own stack and save the old stack pointer on the new stack. The label *newstack* is assumed to point to the highest address of a RAM area which can act as a stack.

```
LXI H,0
DAD SP
LXI SP,newstack
PUSH HL
.
.
(subroutine code goes here)
.
.
POP HL
SPHL
```

Of course, moving data and performing calculations are useless unless you have some way to make decisions based on those results. Like other processors, the 8080 records the results of arithmetic operations in a set of *flag bits*. These flags are called *zero, carry, negative, and overflow*.

The 8080's flag bits work much as they do on other processors, with one significant exception. On the 6502, an SBC (subtract) operation clears the carry flag if a borrow takes place, and sets the carry if no borrow occurs. The 8080, on the other hand, indicates that a borrow has occurred by *setting* the carry flag; it clears the carry flag if no borrow takes place.

Since both processors perform comparisons just like subtractions, the effect of a comparison on the 8080's carry flag is also reversed from the 6502's. For example, to find out if the contents of the 8080's A register are larger than $90, we would use the instruction, CPI 90H. If A is larger than $90, the carry flag will be *clear*, since no borrow takes place when subtracting $90 from a larger number.

The 8080 has four basic instructions for jumping to a different program address: JMP, CALL, RET, and PCHL. The first two are three-byte instructions which contain the target address in the instruction. The CALL instruction calls a subroutine. In addition to loading the program counter with a new value, CALL pushes the old contents of the program counter onto the stack, creating a link back to the calling program. The RET instruction ends a subroutine by popping the return address off the stack and putting it in the program counter. The PCHL instruction transfers the contents of the HL register pair to the program counter.

The JMP, CALL, and RET instructions can have conditional forms, where the program counter is changed only if a certain condition, always involving a flag bit, exists. The most important conditional instructions are JZ (jump if zero), JNZ (not zero), JC (carry), JNC (no carry), JM (negative), and JP (not negative). For the CALL instructions, the equivalent forms are CZ, CNZ, CC, CNC, CM, and CP. The RET instruction has the conditional forms RZ, RNZ, RC, RNC, RM, and RP.

Two special 8080 instructions, IN and OUT, are used for input and output operations. Peripheral devices are commonly addressed at one of 256 I/O ports, which are independent of memory addresses. The IN instruction loads the A register from a specific input port. For example, IN 3 loads A from input port 3; OUT 6 sends the contents of A to output port 6.

Z80 Extensions

Though compatibility is a hallmark of CP/M, there are some cases where compatibility with other CP/M systems is not a factor. For instance, since each CP/M computer must have its own custom-designed BIOS, there's no reason not to use Z80-specific instructions in the 128's BIOS. The same consideration applies to the Z80 code located in the 128's ROM. Since you can often replace several 8080 instructions with a single Z80 instruction, Z80 code can be significantly smaller (hence, usually faster) than pure 8080 code.

One of the most useful Z80 extensions is JR, the relative jump instruction. Rather than load an absolute address into the program counter, it adds a single signed byte, called an offset, to the program counter. JR with an offset of 10 jumps ten bytes forward (higher) in memory. JR with an offset of 250 jumps six bytes backward (lower), since 250 is interpreted as a signed value of −6. Relative jumps can also be conditional and, in this form, are useful for building loop structures. However, since CP/M assemblers generate only 8080 instructions, relative jumps must be hand-assembled.

Another Z80 extension increases the flexibility of the IN and OUT instructions. If the C register holds the address of the I/O port, any register can be loaded from or stored to that port.

Assemblers

There are three Digital Research CP/M assemblers, named ASM, MAC, and RMAC, all of which expect an .ASM file as input. The first of these, ASM, is not an official part of the CP/M 3.0 operating system, but is supplied with the Commodore 64 CP/M 2.2 package and works on the 128. Both ASM and MAC generate .HEX files as their output. These are printable ASCII files which can be converted to .COM files with the HEXCOM command (in CP/M 2.2, this command was called LOAD). The MAC assembler is included on one of the utilities disks in the CP/M "extras" package. It is similar to ASM, but allows the definition of macro instructions (user-defined pseudo-operations for frequently needed instruction sequences).

Like subroutines, macros let you use a name to represent an often-used block of code. But, where an instruction like CALL tells the assembler to generate the opcode for a subroutine call and the address of a particular subroutine, a macro causes the assembler to insert an entire block of code—which can be many instructions long—at the point where the macro name appears. Since the result is in-line code, macro-based programs can run somewhat faster than those which use many subroutines (no time is wasted PUSHing and POPping the return addresses). On the other hand, well-designed subroutines reduce a program's size by eliminating redundant code.

The same package includes RMAC, a macro assembler which generates relocatable code. The .REL files that it generates contain both the machine language equivalent of the assembler source code and the information needed to modify this code to run at any location in memory. The LINK command converts .REL files into ready-to-run .COM files. Although all CP/M transient programs execute at $0100 in bank 1, a relocatable object code file doesn't have to contain an entire program. LINK makes it easy to merge a previously assembled routine wherever it's needed, without having to reassemble the routine. It can also accept more than one .REL file as input, combining them into a single program.

It's convenient to have a big collection of separately assembled subroutines. But these files can be a nuisance to keep track of, and they waste considerable disk space as well. Keep in mind that every CP/M file occupies at least 1K of the disk, no matter how small its contents. The LIB command makes it much easier to manage the small *modules,* or blocks, of code. LIB can combine several .REL files into a single .REL file, display the names of all the program modules contained in a .REL file, and rename or delete individual modules. Since the LINK command can search through library files to find subroutines that are referenced in another program, you don't have to tell LINK the name of each subroutine, just the name of the library file that holds the routines that you need. Related code modules can be kept in a single library file. When you make LINK search a library file, it includes only those modules which it needs to complete the program.

The EXTRN directive identifies modules at the start of a program. This tells RMAC that each name following EXTRN will be found by LINK when the .COM file is built. The PUBLIC directive, as the name implies, marks labels in the program that will be needed by other programs. CSEG causes the assembler to generate relocatable object code.

```
        PUBLIC  PRG1,PRG2 ;NAMES THAT OTHERS MIGHT NEED
        EXTRN   SUB1,SUB2 ;NAMES THAT WE NEED
;
        CSEG    ;CODE STARTS HERE
;
PRG1    CALL    SUB1
        CALL    SUB2
.
.
.
PRG2    CALL    SUB1
        CALL    SUB2
.
.
.
```

DDT and SID

Although machine-level programming puts every capability of the computer at your disposal, it greatly increases the difficulty of debugging—finding and diagnosing program errors. DDT and SID are two interactive debugging programs which simplify the machine language programmer's task considerably.

When either DDT or SID is run, it loads as a transient program, then moves itself to the top of the TPA to make room for another transient program. If you included the name of a .COM or .HEX file when calling the debugger, it also loads that file into the TPA. The L command lets you disassemble a range of code in standard 8080 mnemonics. The A (assemble) instruction lets you assemble 8080 code directly in memory. This is handy for testing program changes or for writing short routines without going through the entire edit-assemble-load process.

The G (go) command lets you run any code in memory, beginning at the designated address. T (trace) executes the program one instruction at a time; X lets you examine the contents of internal flags and registers. You can also use D to examine the contents of memory locations and S to modify them.

SID is a symbolic debugger. It can read .SYM files, which relate program labels to actual memory locations (MAC, RMAC, and LINK all produce .SYM files). In the case of relocatable program files, both RMAC and LINK have to make symbol files because each program knows the actual values of only some of the program's symbols. SID lets you use a label name in place of an absolute memory address in any debugger command.

If you want to change the contents of a .COM file, save it with the SAVE program after making the desired changes. Type SAVE at the CCP prompt. SAVE installs itself at the top of the TPA, then restarts the CCP. Now run the application—usually DDT or SID—that you will use to modify the command file. When you've made the modifications, exit the debugger. SAVE will come out of hiding, ask you for the number of blocks you wish to save and the name to give the file, and then save the modified version.

Living in the TPA

The Console Command Processor performs several services for the transient programs that it loads. When a transient program takes control, the stack pointer points to a 32-byte stack set up for that program alone. A stack of this size is sufficient for small programs, but any large or stack-intensive program will need its own, larger stack.

As noted earlier, you issue a command to the CCP by typing the name of a built-in or transient command, sometimes following the command name with one or more additional arguments. These arguments are collectively known as the *command tail*. Before loading a transient program, the CCP copies the entire tail, beginning with the first space after the end of the command name, into a text buffer located at $0080. The first byte in this buffer contains the number of characters in the tail. The actual text starts at the next byte.

The CCP *parses* (analyzes) this command tail in an attempt to find one or two file references. If it finds any, the CCP isolates the drive names, filenames, and file types, and stores this information in a File Control Block below the start of the TPA. Information about the first file is stored beginning at $005C, and the second file's information is stored at $006C. If either filename is omitted, the first byte of information for that file is a zero byte. If either filename or file type contains an asterisk wildcard character, the CCP removes the asterisk and pads out the field with question marks. For example, PROG*.COM shows up as PROG????.COM. When requesting BDOS file operations, the only legal wildcard character is the question mark, but the CCP translates filenames in the command tail into valid form.

Program Termination

There are three ways a program can terminate in CP/M 3.0. The simplest method is to perform JMP 0, which loads the program counter with 0. Location 0 contains another JMP instruction, this one leading to the BIOS warm start routine which restarts the CCP. The other two methods of termination eventually lead to the warm start routine as well.

The BDOS function 0 ends a transient program. To call this function, load the C register with 0 (MVI C,0), then call the BDOS function request entry, located at memory address 5 (JMP 5). There is no difference between calling this function and jumping directly to location 0.

If the stack pointer still addresses the original stack and if an equal number of PUSH and POP operations have taken place, you can also end a program with an RET instruction. Since the CCP pushes a return address of 0 onto the stack when first setting it up, the final RET instruction is effectively a JMP 0 (and requires two fewer bytes). However, in some older versions of CP/M, the return address on the stack points to an entry in the CCP program instead of the warm start vector, and the CCP may be overwritten by a transient program or its data. Even if the CCP is intact, it probably won't do a true warm start on these systems. If compatibility is a factor, RET is the least desirable way to terminate a program.

BDOS Service Calls

In ordinary circumstances, you can perform nearly all of a program's I/O operations with BDOS service calls, which include device I/O, file operations, and system utilities. The basic procedure for calling a BDOS service is straightforward: Load the number of the desired function into the C register, then perform CALL 0005H. Location 5 always holds an instruction which jumps to the actual service dispatch routine. In most cases you'll also need to load other registers with data (the character to be printed, and so on) before performing the service call. Many BDOS functions involve more data than can be held in the microprocessor's registers, in which case the DE register pair should contain the address of a buffer or parameter block. For some operations, the parameter block will contain the name of a file to be accessed or a string to be printed. For others, the BDOS service will store information into the buffer.

Device I/O can be performed on any of the three logical devices: CON:, AUX:, or LST:. Three basic operations are available. You can get a character, send a character, or check the status of the device. BDOS function 2 sends the character in the E register to the CON: device; BDOS 4 is used for auxiliary output; and function 5 sends a character to the list device. Input operations, though, return the new character in A. BDOS 1 gets a character from the console, while service 3 reads AUXIN:. Since the LST: device can be used only for output, no input or status operations are provided for it.

Both input operations wait until a character is actually available before returning. CP/M also provides services that check the status of either of these devices to see if a character is waiting. BDOS function 11 checks the console status, and BDOS function 7 checks the auxiliary input. Both of these functions return with 0 in the A register unless a character is ready; if no character is available, your program can do something else until it's time to check again.

The AUX: device is often connected to a relatively slow serial device. To see if it's finished sending the last character you gave it, you can call BDOS 8, which checks auxiliary output status. This service returns with 0 in the A register if AUXOUT: isn't ready for another character yet.

CP/M also offers more sophisticated console I/O operations. BDOS function 9 prints a string to the console, starting with the character addressed by DE and ending with the first $ character that it finds. Service 111 prints a string containing any characters. When you call service 111, DE should point to a four-byte data block. The first two bytes of the block must contain the address of the string, and the last two must hold the string's length. BDOS 10 reads a whole line from the console, permitting all CP/M line editing functions for the line that's input. Before you call BDOS service 10, make sure that the DE register pair holds the address of a buffer area which can receive the line. The first byte in the buffer should hold the buffer's length; when the service terminates, the next byte will hold the length of the input line.

Here's a simple transient command called ECHO that prints to the console device. While it's not inherently very useful, it does illustrate several useful CP/M techniques. The command checks for a command tail and prints the contents if one is found. If no command tail exists, the command calls the console line input routine and prints the line until you enter a naked carriage return. You will need a CP/M assembler to enter this program.

```
;ECHO COMMAND: PRINT EITHER THE COMMAND TAIL
; OR SEVERAL LINES OF INPUT ON THE CON: DEVICE
;
BDOS     EQU   0005H     ;CP/M FUNCTION REQUEST
                          VECTOR
WARM     EQU   0000H     ;WARM START VECTOR
PMSG     EQU   0009H     ;CP/M PRINT-A-STRING
                          FUNCTION
GETLINE  EQU   000AH     ;CP/M GET-A-LINE FUNCTION
TAIL     EQU   0080H     ;ADDRESS OF COMMAND TAIL
;
         ORG   0100H     ;GOES AT START OF TPA
         LXI   D,TAIL    ;POINT TO STRING LENGTH
         LDAX  D         ;CHECK STRING'S LENGTH
         ORA   A         ; BY ORING A WITH ITSELF
         JNZ   TAILOUT   ;PRINT IT IF LENGTH ISN'T ZERO
```

```
;
        MVI     A,7EH       ;NUMBER OF CHARACTERS
                             BUFFER CAN HOLD
        STAX    D           ;PUT IT AT START OF BUFFER
;
LOOP    MVI     C,GETLINE   ;USE STANDARD CP/M INPUT
        CALL    BDOS        ;ASK FOR BDOS FUNCTION
;
        LXI     D,TAIL+1    ;POINT TO RECEIVED STRING
        LDAX    D           ;CHECK LENGTH OF RECEIVED
                             STRING
        ORA     A           ; BY ORING A WITH ITSELF
        JZ      EXIT        ;QUIT IF BUFFER IS EMPTY
;
        CALL    SHOWIT      ;DISPLAY STRING ON CONSOLE
        LXI     D,TAIL      ;POINT TO BUFFER AGAIN
        JMP     LOOP        ;DO IT AGAIN
;
TAILOUT CALL    SHOWIT      ;PRINT THE COMMAND TAIL
;
EXIT    JMP     WARM        ;EXIT TO CCP VIA WARM START
;
;SHOWIT: PRINT STRING
;DE HOLDS ADDRESS OF STRING
;A HOLDS LENGTH OF STRING
SHOWIT  INX     D           ;SKIP LENGTH
        MOV     H,D         ;LOCATE CHARACTER AFTER
        ADD     E           ; END OF STRING BY ADDING
        MOV     L,A         ; LENGTH TO ADDRESS OF
                             STRING
;
        MVI     A,'$'       ;PUT TERMINATOR CHARACTER
                             AT
        MOV     M,A         ; END OF STRING
        MVI     C,PMSG      ;PRINT THE STRING ON CON:
                             DEVICE
        JMP     BDOS        ;CALL BDOS AND RETURN
;
```

CP/M File Operations

In most CP/M file operations, the file being manipulated is described by a File Control Block, or FCB. An FCB is 36 bytes long, 4 bytes more than a directory entry, but contains much the same information. Figure 5-1 is the format of a file control block. The essential items to put in an FCB are the drive code, filename, and file type of the file that we wish to access. When the file is accessed for the first time, whether opened or created, CP/M will fill in the rest of the details from the disk directory.

Figure 5-1. File Control Block

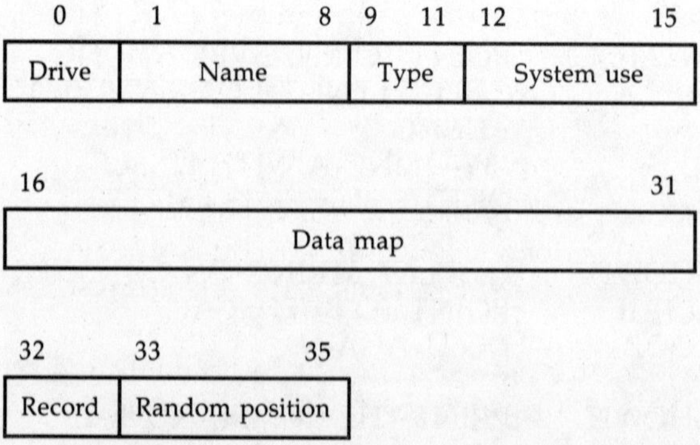

If the CCP left an FCB for us from the command tail, all we need to do to access that file is to load the DE register pair with $005C, the address of the default FCB, then call the BDOS open routine, service 15. If the function returns with the A register set to zero, the file was opened successfully. Otherwise, it was not found. However, if a second filename was included in the command tail, we have to copy its FCB at $006C to another part of memory first. CP/M puts the default FCB's data map—the list of allocation blocks that the first file owns—at that location. Closing the file is an identical process except that the BDOS code for this operation is 16.

If the file is not found by the open function, it can be created by using BDOS 22, which makes a new file. As in similar functions, the DE register pair should point to the FCB describing the file to be created. When a file is created, it is automatically opened, so no open call is needed before writing to the new file. If our program is supposed to create a new file, we would still try to open the file first to see if a file with the same name already exists. If so, the easiest way out is just to close the file, print an error message, and quit. Other options include deleting the file (service 19) or renaming it (service 23). The delete function requires the same register preparation as the open service. To rename a file, one additional piece of information is needed: The new drive code, filename, and file type for the file should be stored in the FCB, beginning at $006C.

BDOS 20, the sequential read service, can be called to read data from an open disk file. It puts one record (128 bytes) from the file into the current disk buffer. When the CCP loads a transient program, it sets the current buffer address to $0080, which is also where the command tail is stored. The address of this buffer can be changed with function 26. The first time that a newly opened file is read, we must tell CP/M to start reading from the beginning of the file. The thirty-second byte in the FCB—$007C in the default FCB—should be set to zero. From then on, this value will be updated by CP/M every time we do a read operation, so you don't need to worry about it unless you want to reread the file to its beginning.

The sequential write function, BDOS 21, works just like the read operation. The record of data in the disk buffer is stored in the file in the FCB pointed to by DE. As with the read service, you should set the current record field (the thirty-second byte in the FCB) to zero the first time you write to a file. After that, the system advances the pointer for you.

Other System Services

Filenames passed to a program on the CCP command line are parsed by the CCP. However, if your program asks the user for a filename directly, you need some means of obtaining the drive code, filename, and file type from the input line. Fortunately, BDOS service 152 converts a line of ASCII text into an FCB. To use the Parse Filename function, point the DE register pair to a four-byte block of data when calling the BDOS service. The first two bytes of this block should contain the address of the ASCII string to be parsed. The last two should have the address of the FCB to receive the information.

Direct BIOS Calls

CP/M programs rarely need to call the BIOS directly; almost every task can be performed better by the BDOS. However, certain programs that want to read absolute blocks of data from disk, for instance, would have to call the BIOS. CP/M 3.0 provides a service, number 50, for direct calls. Unlike the BDOS, which handles all its functions through a single entry address, the BIOS has a table of entries, one for each service, each separated by three bytes. In earlier versions of CP/M, a program had to calculate the address of the BIOS routine it was calling. This involved fetching the address of BIOS function 1 from the warm start vector at 0001H, then adding an offset of three times the number of the BIOS routine minus one. All this arithmetic is now performed by the BDOS service.

Since BDOS and BIOS both use the 8080's registers for their inputs, some special method is needed for sending parameters when using this service. The DE register pair should point to a parameter block, the first byte of which holds the number of the BIOS function that you wish to call. The following bytes should hold values for all the microprocessor registers, starting with the A register. Figure 5-2 shows the order in which to store the values for the registers. Before calling the BIOS, BDOS will load all the registers from this table.

Figure 5-2. BIOS Call Parameter Block

0	BIOS Function	A	1
1	C	B	3
4	F	E	5
6	L	H	7

CP/M Memory Usage

Table 5-5 is a map of CP/M on the Commodore 128. Bank 0 is for the exclusive use of the CP/M BIOS and BDOS, while most of bank 1 is available as the TPA. When the Z80 is active, all memory above $E000 is shared between banks. Both BIOS and BDOS have some code located up there, including the code that handles user calls. However, the top 3.5K of TPA is also located in common memory. If your program performs bank switching, the "executive" routine which controls the switching process should probably be located in this common area. The MMU is used to configure memory in CP/M mode, just as when the 8502 is running. However, a new address space is available, using the Z80's IN and OUT instructions. This appears to be the preferred method for accessing I/O chips and the 40-column screen's color memory.

Table 5-5. Commodore 128 CP/M Memory Map

Address	Contents
Bank 0	
$0000–$0FFF	Z80 ROM; code for reset and CP/M booting
$1000–$13FF	Keyboard definition tables
$1400–$1BFF	80-column screen storage
$1C00–$23FF	80-column display attributes
$2400–$25FF	Unused
$2600–$2BFF	BIOS85 code; 8502 ML
$2C00–$2FFF	40-column screen storage
$3000–$3C7F	CCP backup storage
$3C80–$5FFF	Unused
$6000–$9BFF	File buffers
$9C00–$C9FF	Bank 0 BDOS code
$CA00–$DFFF	Bank 0 BIOS code
$E000–$EDFF	Top of TPA (common memory)
$EE00–$F3FF	BDOS common code
$F400–$FBFF	BIOS common code
$FC00–$FCFF	Unused
$FD00–$FEFF	BIOS communication area
$FF00–$FF04	MMU registers
$FF05–$FF44	8500 interrupt handling code
$FF45–$FFCF	Unused
$FFD0–$FFDF	Interprocessor transfer code, 8502 ML
$FFE0–$FFEF	Interprocessor transfer code, Z80 ML
$FFF0–$FFF9	Unused
$FFFA–$FFFF	8502 IRQ, NMI, and RESET vectors
Bank 1	
$0000–$0002	Warm start—jump to BIOS entry
$0003	Current default drive
$0004	Current user number
$0005–$0007	BDOS function request vector
$0008–$005B	RST jump vectors; unused
$005C–$007F	Default FCB
$0080–$00FF	Default sector buffer; also holds command tail
$0100–$EDFF	TPA—59K long
$EE00–$FFFF	Common memory; same as bank 0
I/O Space	
$1000–$13FF	40-column display attributes
$D000–$D030	VIC chip
$D400–$D41C	SID chip
$D500–$D50B	MMU chip
$D600–$D601	8563 80-column chip
$DC00–$DC0F	CIA 1
$DD00–$DD0F	CIA 2

Accessing Input/Output Chips

Many of the 128's sound and graphics capabilities are not supported by CP/M, but there is no reason why 128-specific applications cannot take advantage of these features. To do so, the program must directly access the I/O chips involved.

Neither of the CP/M memory banks (Table 5-5) include these chips, but they can be addressed with the Z80's IN and OUT instructions. The Z80's specifications provide for 256 I/O ports. While there's no problem with interpreting these as just another memory bank, the 128's I/O space extends from $D000 to $DFFF when we're accessing it with the 8502. That's a 4096-byte range, so we need some way to expand the addressing range of the Z80.

As luck would have it, one oddity of the Z80 is that it really uses all 16 bits of its address bus when a certain I/O addressing mode is used. The instruction IN reg,(C) is intended to load a register from the location addressed by the C register. But in fact, the B register also shows up on the address bus, providing the high 8 bits of the address.

To write to the SID chip, for instance, you need to load the BC register pair with the address of a SID register between $D400 and $D41C, load another register with the byte that you're storing, and then perform a write operation with the OUT (C),reg instruction. Here's a macro for the MAC and RMAC assemblers that does the job in 8080 machine language.

```
SIDOUT  MACRO ?REG,?VALUE
        PUSH   B          ;DON'T ALTER ANY REGISTERS
        PUSH   D
        MVI    B,0D4H     ;THE HIGH BYTE OF SID'S
                           ADDRESS
        MVI    C,?REG     ;C HOLDS THE SID REGISTER
        MVI    E,?VALUE   ;E GETS THE BYTE THAT WE'RE
                          ;STORING
        DB     OEDH,79H   ;Z80 CODE FOR: OUT (C),E
        POP    D          ;RESTORE REGISTERS
        POP    B
        ENDM
```

Sharing the Work

An interesting feature of CP/M on the 128 is that it uses Kernal ROM routines for certain operations. Since the Kernal operating system—designed for 64 and 128 mode—is written in 8502 machine language, the Z80 processor must call the 8502 from its slumber for these tasks. Besides the Kernal, there is a small block of 8502 code located at $2600 in bank 0, called BIOS85, which CP/M loads while booting. Table 5-6 lists the specific functions this code provides. When you call BIOS85, a Z80 counterpart routine called BIOS80 stores the number of the desired service in location FD01, then calls a routine (located in RAM at $FFE0) to switch processors. The 8502 wakes up in the middle of the routine to transfer in the other direction, using the routine located at $FFD0 in RAM. This routine ends with a jump to BIOS80's dispatch routine.

Table 5-6. BIOS85 Functions

Name	Code	Description
Reset	−1	Reboot the 128 as though the RESET button had been pressed.
Init	0	Initialize the BIOS85. Reset all vectors, especially interrupts.
Read	1	Read one or more sectors from disk.
Write	2	Write to disk.
Fastread	3	Set up for fast serial read from disk.
Fastwrite	4	Set up fast serial disk write.
Testdisk	5	Check the status of the disk drive.
Querydisk	6	Determine the disk's format.
Print	7	Send a byte to a serial bus device.
Format	8	Format a disk.
User	9	Jump to user routine through address at FD05H. Warning: this routine has a bug.
Cmd	$FD01	Holds the number of the BIOS85 command.
Drv	$FD02	Contains the drive number for disk operations; serial device number for print.
Trk	$FD03	Indicates the track for disk read/writes; secondary address for print.
Sect	$FD04	First sector for disk operations.
Count	$FD05	Number of disk sectors to be read or written.
Data	$FD06	BIOS85 returns an error code here; also holds byte to be printed.
Buffer	$FE00	Data to be written or read is passed here.

Function 9, the user function, is intended to call the 8502 ML routine pointed to by $FD05 and $FD06. However, in the first release of 128 CP/M, a bug in the BIOS85 keeps this from working. The 8502 ML instruction at $262B should be JMP ($FD05), but it was assembled with the 8080 opcode for JMP ($C3) instead of the 8502 JMP ($6C). Before trying to call this function, your code should make sure that the correct value is stored there.

Chapter 6

Machine Language

Machine Language

The brain of the 128 is the 8502 microprocessor, a tiny computer capable of executing programs. But the programming language it uses is not BASIC. A microprocessor doesn't understand English words like PRINT. It understands only numbers, specifically, only integer numbers in the range 0–255. Each number is an instruction telling the 8502 what to do next. Thus, a machine language (ML) program is simply a series of numbers stored in computer memory.

While it's possible to write ML programs as a string of raw numbers, that method is slow and tedious. Fortunately, you can use a machine language monitor or an assembler to help you. These programming tools (which are themselves machine language programs) allow you to use three-letter mnemonics like LDA and BRK in place of the numbers that actually make up each instruction. Appendix C lists all of the 8502 instructions. Since a monitor is so important to machine language programming, the 128 has a built-in monitor. If you haven't already read the explanation of how to use the monitor (see the Introduction), please do so now. An assembler is a more powerful tool, which makes machine language programming almost as easy as BASIC programming.

Why bother to learn machine language when BASIC is much easier to understand? Primarily because an ML program can run hundreds of times faster than its BASIC equivalent. In fact, BASIC itself is a huge machine language program that starts running as soon as you turn the computer on. You don't have to learn ML to write good programs. But for some applications, BASIC is just too slow, and machine language is the only alternative. This chapter explains machine language techniques specific to the 128, and assumes that you already have some familiarity with the fundamentals of machine language programming on a 6502-based microprocessor. If you've never used ML before, there are many books which introduce the subject, including *Machine Language for Beginners,* available from COMPUTE! Publications.

Where to Put Machine Language Programs

Before you can write a machine language program, you must find a safe place in memory to put it. Unlike BASIC programs, machine language programs don't have an area of memory automatically set aside for their use. And unlike the Commodore 64, which automatically protects 4K of memory from BASIC, the 128 has no memory that's not used for other purposes at one time or another.

Nevertheless, in most cases it shouldn't be hard to find a safe haven for your ML. Think first about what your program does. For example, locations $0B00–$0BFF are used for the cassette buffer. A program stored here would be destroyed as soon as you operate the cassette drive, but it would otherwise be safe from virtually anything except a system cold start. The next 512 bytes at locations $0C00–$0DFF are reserved for RS-232 buffers. If your program doesn't use the RS-232 port, this area is free. Right above that area (at $0E00–$0FFF) is another 512-byte area which is used for storing sprite definitions. This is free if your program doesn't use sprites. Another large area which you'll often find free is $1300–$1BFF. This zone, reserved for foreign language systems and function key software, provides over 2K of free memory.

Of course, if your ML program is self-contained, not called from a BASIC program, you can use the entire BASIC text area at $1C01–$FEFF, almost 57K. However, you must be careful when loading your program into this area. If your program starts at $1C01 (the usual BASIC starting address) and you load it with a BASIC LOAD or DLOAD command, the 128 assumes it's a BASIC program file and tries to link it into a series of program lines—a process which garbles the ML code. While you could use BLOAD to bring the ML safely into memory, it's usually better to "paste" a pseudo-line of BASIC onto the front of the ML, which lets you start it up with LOAD and RUN. It's very easy to do: Simply begin your ML program at $1C0D, and put these hexadecimal numbers at $1C01:

0B 1C 0A 00 9E 37 31 38 31 00 00 00

Now save the entire program with BSAVE (or S from the monitor), then LIST the program from BASIC. The numbers at the beginning of the program form the BASIC line 10 SYS7181. The first two values are a BASIC program line link pointing to $1C0B. At that location are two zeros which mark the end of the BASIC program. The numbers 0A 00 form the low byte and high byte of the line number (10). The value 9E is the token for SYS, and the next four numbers are the character codes for decimal 7181. When you run the program from BASIC, it simply executes a SYS, passing control to your ML program at 7181 ($1C0D).

If you want your ML code to coexist with a BASIC program, you can put it in the free areas described earlier, or you can steal some of BASIC's program space. Like other Commodore computers, the 128 uses two zero page pointers to keep track of the top and bottom of BASIC program space. By raising the bottom-of-memory pointer, or lowering the top-of-memory pointer, or both, you can fool BASIC into thinking it has less memory than it actually has, thus freeing the extra memory for your ML.

Locations 45–46 (the bottom-of-memory pointer) normally contain values of 1 and 28, putting the start of BASIC at 28 * 256 + 1 = 7169 ($1C01). To raise the start of BASIC, POKE locations 45 and 46 with the low byte and high byte of the new starting address, and POKE a zero into the new starting address minus one (BASIC program area must *always* begin with a zero). For example, this line moves BASIC program space 1K above its normal starting point to location 8193:

POKE 45,1:POKE 46,32:POKE 8192,0

The drawback of this technique is that it can't be performed in program mode. You can't move the start of BASIC and expect a program to continue running. Here's an easier way to do the same job:

GRAPHIC 1:GRAPHIC 0

When you perform GRAPHIC 1, the 128 moves the entire contents of BASIC program space 9K higher in memory—up to $4000—to make room for the high-resolution screen. GRAPHIC 0 restores the text screen, but does not disturb the new memory configuration (GRAPHIC CLR would reset BASIC to its normal location, however).

All the preceding techniques reserve space in bank 0 of RAM. Another possibility is to lower the top of memory available for variable storage, which creates available space at the top of bank 1 (see Chapter 7 for more information on banks). Locations 57–58 (the top-of-memory pointer) normally contain values of 0 and 255, putting the end of variables at 255 * 256 + 0 = 65280 ($FF00) in bank 1. To lower the end of the variable space, POKE locations 57 and 58 with the low and high bytes of the new ending address. For example, this line moves the end of BASIC down 1K to location 64256:

POKE 57,0:POKE 58,251:CLR

The CLR is necessary to update other pointers to reflect the new value of top of memory.

This line *can* be used within a BASIC program, so it's entirely feasible to lower the end of variable storage, BLOAD an ML program into the newly protected zone, then proceed with the program. However, the CLR wipes out all variables, erases all function definitions, and disconnects (but does not really close) all open files. Thus, lowering the top of memory should be the first thing your program does, before any variables are defined or any files are opened.

The *zero page* of memory (locations $0000-$00FF) is very valuable in ML programming, and thus is heavily used by the computer itself. Zero page instructions work faster and take up less space than instructions that use higher addresses. And certain addressing modes are available only for zero page. For this reason, nearly all of this space is reserved for the 128's own internal use. Only locations $0012 and $00FA–$00FF are unused. However, depending on what your program does, you may be able to use certain other locations. For instance, locations $0002–$008F are used only by BASIC (not the Kernal operating system) and are free if your ML program doesn't call any BASIC routines. Similarly, locations $0090–$00F9 are used only by the Kernal. If your ML program doesn't rely on *any* BASIC or Kernal routines, locations $0002–$00FF are free. Locations 0–1 are special I/O configuration bytes and should not be used for any other purpose. Appendix D provides a description of each zero page location.

Interfacing with BASIC

BASIC offers three commands for communicating with ML programs: SYS, RREG, and USR. SYS transfers control from BASIC to an ML program. The starting address of the ML is specified immediately following the command. For example, SYS 3072 jumps to a machine language program beginning at location 3072. Of course, you must put an ML program at that location before performing the SYS. Otherwise, the computer may lock up, forcing you to press the RESET button to regain control. An ML program can be put into memory using BLOAD or a series of POKE statements. To return to BASIC, the machine language code must end with an RTS instruction. When this is done, the BASIC program resumes with the statement following the SYS.

By supplying additional parameters after the SYS address, you can specify the initial values of the accumulator, X register, Y register, and status register. Type in and save Program 6-1 using the built-in monitor as explained in the Introduction. If the microprocessor's carry flag is set when this program begins, it sets the border, screen, and character colors according to the values in the accumulator and X and Y registers, respectively. If the carry is clear, the registers are loaded with the current color values. (Do *not* type in the semicolons and the comments following them; they merely provide extra information about how the program works.)

Program 6-1. Color Settings in ML

```
0C00  BCC $0C0B ;Test carry flag
0C02  STA $D020 ;Set colors
0C05  STX $D021
0C08  STY $F1
0C0A  RTS       ;Return to BASIC
0C0B  LDA $D021 ;Read colors
0C0E  AND #$0F
0C10  TAX
0C11  LDA $D020
0C14  AND #$0F
0C16  LDY $F1
0C18  RTS       ;Return to BASIC
```

For example, BANK 15:SYS 3072,14,6,14,33 sets the colors to imitate 64 mode. To read the 128's normal color values, press RUN/STOP–RESTORE, then enter SYS 3072,,,,32. The RREG command lets you assign the contents of the accumulator, X register, Y register, and status register to BASIC variables. For instance, after issuing the last command, enter RREG A,X,Y:PRINT A,X,Y.

Like SYS, the USR command lets you jump to an ML routine and optionally pass information from the BASIC environment to ML. Though USR makes it somewhat more convenient to pass variables, it requires an extra setup operation. Before calling USR, you must POKE locations 4633 and 4634 with the low byte and high byte of the address where your ML program starts.

USR must be followed by a numeric expression within parentheses. If you don't want to pass anything to the ML routine, you can put any number in the parentheses—the value is simply a dummy parameter like the 0 in POS(0). If you want to pass significant information, any numeric expression may be used; USR(6), USR(X), and USR(PEEK(LO)+256*PEEK(HI)) are all valid. Before passing control to the ML routine, the computer evalutes the expression in parentheses and stores the result in floating-point accumulator 1 (FAC1). Your ML routine may then retrieve the result from FAC1 (see "ROM Routines" later in this chapter) and use it however you like.

USR also lets you pass information in the opposite direction—from an ML routine back to BASIC. Store appropriate values in FAC1, then terminate the machine language program with RTS. When you return to BASIC, USR returns the new value from FAC1. In other words, FAC1 serves as the conduit between BASIC and ML. The following program uses USR to calculate square roots.

```
10 FOR L=3072 TO 3080:READ N:POKE L,N:NEXT :REM STORE
   MACHINE LANGUAGE
20 POKE 4633,0:POKE 4634,12 :REM STORE STARTING
   ADDRESS
30 PRINT USR(2) :REM PRINT SQUARE ROOT OF 2
40 DATA 169,0,141,0,255,32,48,175,96 :REM MACHINE
   LANGUAGE
```

Here is a disassembly of the ML routine used in the last example:

```
0C00  LDA #$00   ;Set bank 15
0C02  STA $FF00
0C05  JSR $AF30  ;Call BASIC SQR routine
0C08  RTS        ;Return to BASIC
```

Advanced Techniques

Several BASIC and Kernal routines pass through RAM vectors so that they can be changed to point to a customized routine. A vector is a pair of memory addresses that hold an address. In addition to the direct JMP opcode, which transfers control directly to the specified address, the 8502 can also perform a JMP indirectly through the vector, which transfers control to the address contained in the vector. For example, instead of using JMP $FA65 to go directly to the IRQ service routine, the 128 can JMP ($0314), where locations $0314–$0315 together contain the address $FA65. The great advantage of this technique is that you can change the vectors to point to your own routines, and thus add extra functions to those built into the 128's ROM. After you change the vector to point to the start of your routine, whenever the corresponding BASIC routine is executed, the altered vector sends control to your routine. This routine may be a complete substitute, bypassing the normal BASIC or Kernal routines altogether. However, most routines end by jumping to the normal vector destination.

The following example illustrates the technique. Whenever you press RUN/STOP–RESTORE, the 128 executes an NMI (Non-Maskable Interrupt) routine which, among other things, resets the screen, border, and character colors, and then jumps to the BASIC warm start routine. By altering the BASIC warm start vector at $0A00–$0A01, you can intercept that routine and change the colors to those you prefer.

Type in and save Program 6-2 using the monitor (don't type the comments on the right.) To use the program, BLOAD it from BASIC and enter SYS 3072. From now on, when you press RUN/STOP–RESTORE the colors will be set to the 64 colors: blue screen with light blue border and characters.

Program 6-2. RESTORE

```
0C00  LDA #$0B   ;Change the low byte
0C02  STA $0A00
0C05  LDA #$0C   ;and the high byte to point to $0C0B
0C07  STA $0A01
0C0A  RTS        ;Return to BASIC
0C0B  LDA #$0E   ;Light blue border
0C0D  STA $D020
0C10  LDA #$06   ;Blue screen
0C12  STA $D021
0C15  LDA #$0E   ;Light blue characters
0C17  STA $F1
0C19  JMP $4003  ;Jump to BASIC warm start
```

Another powerful ML technique is to run programs during the computer's hardware (IRQ) interrupt intervals, which occur 60 times per second. The 128 uses the IRQ interrupt to execute tasks that must be done continuously, such as updating the internal clock and reading the keyboard. Every 1/60 second the computer stops whatever it's doing, executes the interrupt routine, and then continues where it left off. This slows execution of the main routines slightly. But 1/60 second is about 17,000 machine cycles, or roughly 5000 instructions, so provided the interrupt routine is not too long, 99 percent of the 8502's time is spent on the main routines.

You can use the IRQ interrupt to run programs in the backround. For example, you could have music playing in the backround while another program runs. The next program installs an interrupt-driven routine to display a digital clock on the screen. The general technique is similar to that used in the last program. The IRQ vector is changed to point to a custom routine, which ends by jumping to the normal IRQ routine at the end. Note that you must disable interrupts with SEI before changing the vector to make sure that no interrupts occur while you're changing it. Remember to enable interrupts with CLI before returning to BASIC.

Enter the following machine language program (Program 6-3) with the monitor and save it with the name CLOCK.ML. Then type in and save the BASIC program (Program 6-4) which appears immediately after it. The BASIC portion allows you to set the clock to any starting time. To use the programs together, run the BASIC program and enter the time as a six-digit number (093015 for 9:30:15, and so on). The time is displayed in the upper-right corner of the screen. Since the ML routine executes in the background, you can use the computer normally as the clock ticks away.

Pressing RUN/STOP–RESTORE turns off the clock by resetting the IRQ vector. The time is still updated, however, and the clock can be made to reappear with SYS 3072. You could modify Program 6-2 to change the IRQ vector back again so that RUN/STOP–RESTORE doesn't turn off the clock.

Program 6-3. CLOCK.ML

```
0C00  SEI             ;Disable interrupts
0C01  LDA  #$0D       ;Change the low byte
0C03  STA  $0314
0C06  LDA  #$0C       ;and the high byte to point to $0C0D
0C08  STA  $0315
0C0B  CLI             ;Enable interrupts
0C0C  RTS             ;Return to BASIC
0C0D  LDA  #$BA       ;Display colons
0C0F  STA  $0422
0C12  STA  $0425
0C15  LDA  $DC0B      ;Calculate ten's digit of hour
0C18  AND  #$10
0C1A  LSR
```

```
0C1B  LSR
0C1C  LSR
0C1D  LSR
0C1E  ORA  #$B0
0C20  STA  $0420
0C23  LDA  $DC0B  ;Calculate one's digit of hour
0C26  AND  #$0F
0C28  ORA  #$B0
0C2A  STA  $0421
0C2D  LDA  $DC0A  ;Calculate ten's digit of minute
0C30  AND  #$F0
0C32  LSR
0C33  LSR
0C34  LSR
0C35  LSR
0C36  ORA  #$B0
0C38  STA  $0423
0C3B  LDA  $DC0A  ;Calculate one's digit of minute
0C3E  AND  #$0F
0C40  ORA  #$B0
0C42  STA  $0424
0C45  LDA  $DC09  ;Calculate ten's digit of second
0C48  AND  #$F0
0C4A  LSR
0C4B  LSR
0C4C  LSR
0C4D  LSR
0C4E  ORA  #$B0
0C50  STA  $0426
0C53  LDA  $DC09  ;Calculate one's digit of second
0C56  AND  #$0F
0C58  ORA  #$B0
0C5A  STA  $0427
0C5D  LDA  $DC08  ;Read tenth of second to start clock again
0C60  JMP  $FA65  ;Jump to IRQ routine
```

Program 6-4. CLOCK

```
10 BANK 15:BLOAD"CLOCK.ML"
20 INPUT"ENTER TIME (HHMMSS):";T$
30 POKE 56331,16*VAL(MID$(T$,1,1))+VAL(MID$(T$,2,1)) :REM
   SET HOUR
40 POKE 56330,16*VAL(MID$(T$,3,1))+VAL(MID$(T$,4,1)) :REM
   SET MINUTE
50 POKE 56329,16*VAL(MID$(T$,5,1))+VAL(MID$(T$,6,1)) :REM
   SET SECOND
```

```
60 POKE 56328,0 :REM TENTH OF SECOND = 0
70 SYS 3072
```

When BASIC executes a program, it reads characters one at a time using a routine at $0380 called CHRGET. By replacing the first instruction in this routine with a JMP to a custom routine, you can intercept characters before they're executed. With this sort of program (often called a *wedge)*, you can easily add your own commands to BASIC, causing the computer to perform a special function whenever it encounters a character such as @, !, or &.

Program 6-5 wedges into CHRGET and tests for the @ character. If one is found, it increments the value for the border color. The program may look complicated, but it can be easily modified to test for any character and perform any function. The value $40 in line $0C19 is the ASCII value of the special character (@ in this case). Lines $0C2A–$0C2F contain the routine that executes when that character is found. Note that in order to avoid interfering with CHRGET, you should save the X and Y registers when this routine begins, and restore them when it ends.

Type in Program 6-5 from the monitor and save a copy (don't type in the semicolons or the comments that follow them). Then activate the wedge with SYS 3072. Now whenever the computer finds an @ in a program, it changes the border color. For instance, enter and run this line:

```
10 @:GOTO 10
```

You should see a multicolored border. The @ command is executed so quickly that the border color is changed several times while the screen is being drawn. Also note that the wedge is not disabled by RUN/STOP–RESTORE.

Program 6-5. Test for @ Character

```
0C00  LDA  #$4C   ;Put JMP $0C10 into CHRGET
0C02  STA  $0380
0C05  LDA  #$10
0C07  STA  $0381
0C0A  LDA  #$0C
0C0C  STA  $0382
0C0F  RTS         ;Return to BASIC
0C10  INC  $3D    ;Get next character
0C12  BNE  $0C16
0C14  INC  $3E
```

```
0C16  JSR  $0386
0C19  CMP  #$40   ;Test for @ character
0C1B  BEQ  $0C20
0C1D  JMP  $0386  ;Not @ so jump to CHRGOT to continue
                  normally
0C20  LDA  $3E    ;Check if in program mode
0C22  CMP  #$02
0C24  BEQ  $0C1D
0C26  TYA         ;In program mode so use wedge
0C27  PHA         ;Save X and Y
0C28  TXA
0C29  PHA
0C2A  LDA  #$00   ;Set to bank 15
0C2C  STA  $FF00
0C2F  INC  $D020  ;Increment border color
0C32  PLA         ;Restore X and Y
0C33  TAX
0C34  PLA
0C35  TAY
0C36  JMP  $0380  ;Jump to CHRGET for next character
```

ROM Routines

The following is a list of BASIC, Editor, and Kernal ROM routines. Like other Commodore computers, the 128 accesses major routines through a standard jump table to insure compatibility among different ROM versions (and to a lesser degree, among different computers). Some routines require certain parameters to be set up before calling the routine. Except in a few cases, all of these routines end with RTS, meaning they can be called with JSR from your own program. The two floating-point accumulators are abbreviated FAC1 and FAC2. You must be in bank 15 to access these routines. In bank 15, RAM from bank 0 appears in all addresses below $4000 and is available for your machine language programming. See Chapter 7 for more information on banking.

BASIC Routines

AF00	AYINT	Convert floating point to integer
AF03	GIVAYF	Convert integer to floating point
AF06	FOUT	Convert floating point to ASCII string
AF09	VAL 1	Convert ASCII string to floating point
AF0C	GETADR	Convert floating point to an address
AF0F	FLOATC	Convert address to floating point

AF12	FSUB	Subtract FAC1 from a number in memory
AF15	FSUBT	Subtract FAC1 from FAC2
AF18	FADD	Add a number in memory to FAC1
AF1B	FADDT	Add FAC1 to FAC2
AF1E	FMULT	Multiply a number in memory by FAC1
AF21	FMULTT	Multiply FAC1 by FAC2
AF24	FDIV	Divide a number in memory by FAC1
AF27	FDIVT	Divide FAC2 by FAC1
AF2A	LOG	Calculate the natural log of FAC1
AF2D	INT	Take the integer portion of FAC1
AF30	SQR	Calculate the square root of FAC1
AF33	NEGOP	Negate FAC1
AF36	FPWR	Raise FAC2 to the power of a number in memory
AF39	FPWRT	Raise FAC2 to the FAC1 power
AF3C	EXP	Calculate EXP of FAC1
AF3F	COS	Calculate the cosine of FAC1
AF42	SIN	Calculate the sine of FAC1
AF45	TAN	Calculate the tangent of FAC1
AF48	ATN	Calculate the arctangent of FAC1
AF4B	ROUND	Round off FAC1
AF4E	ABS	Take the absolute value of FAC1
AF51	SIGN	Test the sign of FAC1
AF54	FCOMP	Compare FAC1 with a number in memory
AF57	RND 0	Generate a random floating-point number
AF5A	CONUPK	Move a number in RAM to FAC2
AF5D	ROMUPK	Move a number in ROM to FAC2
AF60	MOVFRM	Move a number in RAM to FAC1
AF63	MOVFM	Move a number in ROM to FAC1
AF66	MOVMF	Move FAC1 to memory
AF69	MOVFA	Move FAC2 to FAC1
AF6C	MOVAF	Move FAC1 to FAC2
AF6F	OPTAB	Math operator vector table
AF7B	RUN	Perform RUN
AF7E	RUNC	Reset the current-text-character pointer to the beginning of the program
AF81	CLEAR	Perform CLR
AF87	LNKPRG	Relink program lines
AF8A	CRUNCH	Tokenize line in input buffer
AF8D	FNDLIN	Search for line number
AF90	NEWSTT	Set up next program line for execution
AF93	EVAL	Convert a number from ASCII text to a floating-point number
AF96	FRMEVL	Evaluate expression
AF9F	LINGET	Convert a number from ASCII text to a two-byte line number
AFA2	GARBA2	Perform string garbage collection

Editor Routines

C000	CINT	Initialize editor and screen
C003	DISPLY	Display character in .A using color in .X
C006	LP2	Load .A with key in keyboard buffer
C009	LOOP5	Load .A with character from screen line
C00C	PRINT	Print character in .A
C00F	SCRORG	Load .X and .Y with number of rows and columns of window
C012	SCNKEY	Read the keyboard
C015	REPEAT	Repeat key
C018	PLOT	Set or read cursor position in .X and .Y
C01B	CURSOR	Move 80-column cursor
C01E	ESCAPE	Perform escape function using character in .A
C021	KEYSET	Define a function key
C024	IRQ	Perform IRQ functions
C027	INIT80	Initialize 80-column character set
C02A	SWAPPER	Switch between 40- and 80-column screen
C02D	WINDOW	Set top-left or bottom-right corner of window

Kernal Routines

The Kernal is Commodore's term for the BIOS (Basic Input/Output System). Located in ROM at $E000–$FFFF, it contains routines to perform all input/output functions, from printing a character on the screen to loading and saving programs. Since it uses a standardized jump table, it's compatible with earlier versions of the Kernal used in the VIC-20, 64, Plus/4, and 16 computers.

Note that Commodore has introduced a few slight name changes. In these cases, the name used in earlier versions of the Kernal appears in parentheses. Certain other routines are new, specifically designed for the 128, and are not permanent additions to the standard jump table. These routines are marked with an asterisk (*).

ACPTR
Input a byte from the serial bus
Call address: $FFA5 65445
Registers changed: .A
Error number: Use READSS

Before calling this routine, you must tell a device on the serial bus to talk by calling TALK. If the device requires a secondary address, you must also call TKSA. ACPTR accepts a byte from the talker using full handshaking and puts it in the accumulator. Be aware that this is a low-level routine; in nearly every case BASIN or GETIN is preferable.

BASIN (CHRIN)
Input a byte from the input channel
Call address: $FFCF 65487 (indirect RAM vector at $324–$325)
Registers changed: .A
Error number: In .A if carry set, or use READSS

BASIN gets a byte from the current input device and puts it in the accumulator. The default input device is the keyboard. If you want to input from a device other than the keyboard, you must call CHKIN first to define the input device.

BOOT CALL*
Boot a program from disk
Call address: $FF53 65363
Registers changed: .A, .X, .Y
Error number: I/O error if carry set

Load the accumulator with the ASCII value of the drive number, load the X register with the device number (0–31), and then call this routine. BOOT CALL loads and executes the boot sector from an autoboot disk. If an error occurs, the "UI" command is sent to the disk drive, and control returns to either the calling program or the booted program, depending on the error.

BSOUT (CHROUT)
Output a byte to the output channel
Call address: $FFD2 65490 (indirect RAM vector at $326–$327)
Registers changed: .A
Error number: In .A if carry set, or use READSS

Load the accumulator with the byte to send, then call this routine to send the byte to the current output device. The default output device is the screen. If you want to output to a device other than the screen, you must call CKOUT first to define the output device.

CHKIN
Set channel to input
Call address: $FFC6 65478 (indirect RAM vector at $31E–$31F)

Registers changed: .A, .X, .Y
Error number: In .A if carry set, or use READSS

OPEN must be called before CHKIN. Load the X register with the logical file number corresponding to the channel opened by OPEN, then call this routine to set the channel to input. This prepares for BASIN and GETIN.

CINT
Initialize screen editor
Call address: $FF81 65409
Registers changed: .A, .X, .Y
Error number: None

Do an SEI before calling this routine: CINT initializes the Editor indirect vectors which are used during IRQ interrupts. If bit 6 of location $0A04 is clear, CINT does a full initialization including setting the 40- and 80-column screens, keyboard, character ROM, and SID registers to normal operation. It does not do I/O initialization (see *IOINIT*). If that bit is set, it will not initialize the keyboard.

CIOUT
Output a byte to the serial bus
Call address: $FFA8 65448
Registers changed: .A
Error number: Use READSS

Before calling this routine, you must tell a device on the serial bus to listen by calling LISTN. If the device requires a secondary address, you must also call SECND. Then load the accumulator with the byte to send and call this routine which sends the byte to the listener with full handshaking. Be aware that this is a low-level routine; you should almost always use BSOUT instead.

CKOUT (CHKOUT)
Set channel to output
Call address: $FFC9 65481 (indirect RAM vector at $320–$321)
Registers changed: .A, .X, .Y
Error number: In .A if carry set, or use READSS

OPEN must be called before CKOUT. Load the X register with the logical file number corresponding to the channel opened by OPEN, and then call this routine to set the channel to output. This prepares for BSOUT.

CLALL
Close all files and channels
Call address: $FFE7 65511 (indirect RAM vector at $32C–$32D)
Registers changed: .A, .X
Error number: None

This routine closes all open files by resetting the file table index (location $0098), and also calls CLRCH. Do not use this routine as a substitute for CLOSE when closing a disk write file. The result will be a poison (unclosed) file.

CLOSE
Close a logical file
Call address: $FFC3 65475 (indirect RAM vector at $31C–$31D)
Registers changed: .A, .X, .Y
Error number: In .A if carry set, or use READSS

Load the accumulator with the file number to close, then call this routine to close it. Files open to the keyboard or screen cannot be closed. If the carry is set when CLOSE is called and the device number of the file is 8 or greater, and the secondary address is 15, then the file is removed from the logical file table, but a "close" command is not sent to the device. This solves the problem of all disk files being closed when the command channel is closed.

CLOSE ALL*
Close all files to a device
Call address: $FF4A 65354
Registers changed: .A, .X, .Y
Error number: None

Load the accumulator with the device number (0–31) and then call this routine to close all files open to that device. If one of those files corresponds to the current I/O channel, the default channel (keyboard or screen) is restored.

CLRCH (CLRCHN)
Restore default channels
Call address: $FFCC 65484 (indirect RAM vector at $322–$323)
Registers changed: .A, .X
Error number: None

Call this routine to clear all open channels and restore the keyboard and screen as input and output devices, respectively. If the input channel is to a serial device, UNTLK is called first. If the output channel is to a serial device, then UNLSN is called first.

C64MODE*
Enter 64 mode
Call address: $FF4D 65357
Registers changed: None
Error number: None

This routine reconfigures the system as a 64 and does not return. The MMU and 128 ROM cannot be accessed from 64 mode. If the 128 is in an unusual MMU or I/O configuration when you call C64MODE, unpredictable results may occur.

DLCHR*
Initialize 80-column characters
Call address: $FF62 65378
Registers changed: .A, .X, .Y
Error number: None

DLCHR copies the VIC-II character set from ROM at $D000–$DFFF in bank 14 to RAM at $2000–$3FFF in the 80-column video chip, padding each 8 × 8 character with zeros to fill the 8 × 16 character cells.

DMA CALL*
Send command to DMA device
Call address: $FF50 65360
Registers changed: .A, .X
Error number: None

This routine is used to communicate with an expansion RAM cartridge. Before calling DMA CALL, store the low byte and high byte of the 128 address to access in locations $DF02–$DF03, then store the low byte, high byte, and bank of the expansion RAM to access in locations $DF04–$DF06. Store the low and high bytes of the number of bytes in locations $DF07–$DF08. Then load the X register with the 128 bank to address, load the Y register with the DMA (Direct Memory Access) command, and call this routine. For the expansion module, the command values are 0 to stash, 1 to fetch, 2 to swap, and 3 to verify.

GETCFG*
Get byte to configure MMU for any bank
Call address: $FF6B 65387
Registers changed: .A
Error number: None

Load the X register with the bank number (0–15) and call this routine. The MMU configuration data for that bank is returned in the accumulator. You can then switch to that bank with STA $FF00.

GETIN
Get a byte from the input buffer
Call address: $FFE4 65508 (indirect RAM vector at $32A–$32B)
Registers changed: .A, .X, .Y
Error number: In .A if carry set, or use READSS

The 128's default input device is the keyboard. If you want to input from another device, you must call CHKIN first to define the device. Input from the keyboard and RS-232 is read from the buffers associated with those devices. GETIN calls BASIN for serial, cassette, and screen input.

INDCMP*
CMP (pointer),Y to any bank
Call address: $FF7A 65402
Registers changed: .X
Error number: None

Store the low byte and high byte of the base address in a zero page pointer, store the address of the pointer in location $02C8, load the accumulator with the byte to compare, load the X register with the bank number, load the Y register with the index, and call this routine. The result is returned in the processor status register.

INDFET*
LDA (pointer),Y from any bank
Call address: $FF74 65396
Registers changed: .A, .X
Error number: None

Store the low byte and high byte of the base address in a zero page pointer, load the accumulator with the address of the pointer, load the X register with the bank number, load the Y register with the index, and call this routine.

INDSTA*
STA (pointer),Y to any bank
Call address: $FF77 65399
Registers changed: .X
Error number: None

Store the low byte and high byte of the base address in a zero page pointer, store the address of the pointer in location $02B9, load the accumulator with the byte to store, load the X register with the bank number, load the Y register with the index, and call this routine.

IOBASE
Get location of I/O block
Call address: $FFF3 65523
Registers changed: .X, .Y
Error number: None

This routine returns the low byte of the I/O block in the X register and the high byte in the Y register. Unused by the 128 itself, it allows programs to be compatible with other Commodore computers.

IOINIT
Initialize I/O devices
Call address: $FF84 65412
Registers changed: .A, .X, .Y
Error number: None

Do an SEI before calling this routine because IOINIT initializes I/O devices which are used during IRQ interrupts. If bit 7 of location $0A04 is clear, CINT does a full initialization including setting CIA, VIC-II, SID, and 80-column chips to normal operation. If that bit is set, it will not initialize the 80-column character set.

JMPFAR*
JMP to any bank
Call address: $FF71 65393
Registers changed: None
Error number: None

Store the bank number in location 2, high byte of destination in 3, low byte of destination in 4, status register in 5, accumulator in 6, X register in 7, Y register in 8, and call this routine.

JSRFAR*
JSR to any bank
Call address: $FF6E 65390
Registers changed: None
Error number: None

Store the bank number in location 2, high byte of destination in 3, low byte of destination in 4, status register in 5, accumulator in 6, X register in 7, Y register in 8, and call this routine. On return, load the status register, accumulator, X register, and Y register with locations 5, 6, 7, and 8, respectively.

KEY (SCNKEY)
Read the keyboard
Call address: $FF9F 65439
Registers changed: None
Error number: None

This routine checks if a key is pressed and, if so, puts the character code value in the keyboard buffer. KEY is normally called during the IRQ interrupt.

LISTN (LISTEN)
Send listen command to serial device
Call address: $FFB1 65457
Registers changed: .A
Error number: Use READSS

Load the accumulator with the device number (0–31) and call this routine to command a serial device to begin reading data. This is a low-level routine; you should almost always use CKOUT instead.

LKUPLA*
Look up logical file number in file tables
Call address: $FF59 65369
Registers changed: .A, .X, .Y
Error number: File not found if carry set

Load the accumulator with the logical file number to search for and call this routine. The file number, device number, and secondary address are returned in the accumulator, X register, and Y register, if found.

LKUPSA*
Look up secondary address in file tables
Call address: $FF5C 65372
Registers changed: .A, .X, .Y

Error number: File not found if carry set

Load the Y register with the secondary address to search for and call this routine. The file number, device number, and secondary address are returned in the accumulator, X register, and Y register, if found.

LOAD
Load or verify data from device
Call address: $FFD5 65493 (indirect RAM vector at $330–$331)
Registers changed: .A, .X, .Y
Error number: In .A if carry set, or use READSS

Call SETNAM, SETBNK, and SETLFS first. Then load the accumulator with 0 to do a load, or any nonzero number to do a verify. If the secondary address specified by SETLFS is 0, load the X register with the low byte of the starting address, and the Y register with the high byte. If the secondary address is 1, the starting address is read from the device. The data is automatically loaded in burst mode if a burst handshake is received from the device.

MEMBOT
Set or read bottom of RAM
Call address: $FF9C 65436
Registers changed: .X, .Y
Error number: None

To set the bottom-of-memory pointer ($0A05–$0A06), clear the carry, load the X register with the low byte and the Y register with the high byte, and call this routine. To read the pointer, set the carry and call MEMBOT. The low and high bytes are returned in the X and Y registers, respectively. Due to memory banking, MEMBOT is not very useful on the 128, but is included for the sake of compatibility.

MEMTOP
Set or read top of RAM
Call address: $FF99 65433
Registers changed: .X, .Y
Error number: None

To set the top-of-memory pointer ($0A07–$0A08), clear the carry, load the X register with the low byte and the Y register with the high byte, and call this routine. To read the pointer, set the carry and call MEMTOP. The low and high bytes are returned in the X and Y registers, respectively. Because of memory banking, MEMTOP is not very useful on the 128, but is included for the sake of compatibility.

OPEN
Open a logical file
Call address: $FFC0 65472 (indirect RAM vector at $31A–$31B)
Registers changed: .A, .X, .Y
Error number: In .A if carry set, or use READSS

Call SETNAM, SETBNK, and SETLFS first. Then call this routine to prepare a logical file for I/O operations. As many as ten files can be open simultaneously.

PFKEY*
Program a function key
Call address: $FF65 65381
Registers changed: .A, .X, .Y
Error number: No room if carry set

Store the ASCII string in RAM, store the address of the string (low byte, high byte, bank) in three consecutive zero page locations, load the accumulator with the address of the three-byte pointer, load the X register with the key number (1–10), load the Y register with the string length, and call this routine.

PHOENIX*
Initialize function ROM cartridges
Call address: $FF56 65366
Registers changed: .A, .X, .Y
Error number: None

This aptly named routine calls the cold start vectors for all installed function ROM cartridges and then calls BOOT CALL.

PLOT
Set or read cursor position
Call address: $FFF0 65520
Registers changed: .X, .Y
Error number: Position outside window if carry set

To set the cursor position, clear the carry, load the X register with the row number, load the Y register with the column number, and call this routine. To read the cursor position, call this routine with the carry set. The row and column numbers are returned in the X and Y registers, respectively. Note that the position is relative to the current window, not the screen.

PRIMM*
Print string immediately following
Call address: $FF7D 65405
Registers changed: None
Error number: None

This routine prints an ASCII string which is imbedded in the code immediately after the call, and then continues with the code which appears immediately after the string. The string can be up to 255 characters long and must end with a zero byte. Since PRIMM uses the return address of the JSR to find the string, you cannot JMP to it.

RAMTAS
Initialize RAM and buffers
Call address: $FF87 65415
Registers changed: .A, .X, .Y
Error number: None

This routine clears zero page, allocates the cassette and RS-232 buffers, initializes the pointers to the top and bottom of system RAM, and sets the system vector ($0A00–$0A01) to point to $4000 (BASIC cold start).

RDTIM
Read jiffy clock
Call address: $FFDE 65502
Registers changed: .A, .X, .Y
Error number: None

This routine returns the low, middle, and high bytes of the jiffy clock in the accumulator, X register, and Y register, respectively.

READSS (READST)
Read the I/O status
Call address: $FFB7 65463
Registers changed: .A
Error number: None

This routine returns the status of the last I/O operation in the accumulator. Refer to ST in Chapter 1 for a description of the error numbers.

RESTOR
Restore Kernal indirect RAM vectors
Call address: $FF8A 65418
Registers changed: .A, .X, .Y

Error number: None

Do an SEI before calling this routine, which restores the default values of the Kernal indirect vectors.

SAVE
Save memory to a device
Call address: $FFD8 65496 (indirect RAM vector at $322–$323)
Registers changed: .A, .X, .Y
Error number: In .A if carry set

Call SETNAM, SETBNK, and SETLFS first. Then store the starting address of the block to be saved in a zero page pointer, load the accumulator with the address of the pointer, load the X and Y registers with the low and high address (plus one) of the end address of the block, and call this routine. Burst mode is not used.

SCRORG (SCREEN)
Get size of current screen window
Call address: $FFED 65517
Registers changed: .A, .X, .Y
Error number: None

This routine returns the screen width in the accumulator, the current window width in the X register, and the current window height in the Y register.

SECND (SECOND)
Send secondary address
Call address: $FF93 65427
Registers changed: .A
Error number: Use READSS

Call LISTN first, then load the accumulator with the secondary address and call this routine to send it to the listening device. This is a low-level routine; you should almost always use OPEN and CKOUT instead.

SETBNK*
Set banks for I/O operations
Call address: $FF68 65384
Registers changed: None
Error number: None

Call SETNAM first; then load the accumulator with the bank number (0–15) for the save, load, or verify; load the X register with the bank number containing the filename; and call this routine.

SETLFS
Set logical file number, device number, and secondary address
Call address: $FFBA 65466
Registers changed: None
Error number: None

Load the accumulator and X and Y registers with the logical file number, device number, and secondary address, respectively. If a secondary address is not needed, load the Y register with $FF.

SETMSG
Enable/disable Kernal messages
Call address: $FF90 65424
Registers changed: None
Error number: None

To enable Kernal error messages (I/O ERROR #), call this routine with bit 6 of the accumulator set. To enable control messages (LOADING, PRESS PLAY ON TAPE, and so on), set bit 7.

SETNAM
Set filename
Call address: $FFBD 65469
Registers changed: None
Error number: None

Call SETBNK first, then store the filename in RAM as an ASCII string, load the accumulator with the length of the filename, load the X and Y registers with the low and high bytes of the location of the filename, and call this routine. If a filename is not needed, you should still call SETNAM, but specify a name length of zero.

SETTIM
Set jiffy clock
Call address: $FFDB 65499
Registers changed: None
Error number: None

Load the accumulator and X and Y registers with the low, middle, and high bytes, and call this routine to set the time.

SETTMO
Enable/disable IEEE timeouts
Call address: $FFA2 65442
Registers changed: None

Error number: None

This routine is for the IEEE communication cartridge in 64 mode. Call this routine with bit 7 of the accumulator set to disable timeouts on the IEEE bus.

SPIN SPOUT
Set fast serial ports for input or output
Call address: $FF47 65351
Registers changed: .A
Error number: None

SPINP and SPOUT are two routines used to set up fast serial communication between the 128 and 1571 drive for input and output. Call this routine with the carry clear to select SPINP, or the carry set to select SPOUT. SPIN SPOUT is required only when using low-level routines. Fast serial I/O is automatically used by LOAD and SAVE.

STOP
Read RUN/STOP key
Call address: $FFE1 65505 (indirect RAM vector at $328–$329)
Registers changed: .A, .X
Error number: None

This routine checks whether the RUN/STOP key is pressed and, if so, calls CLRCH, clears the keyboard buffer, and returns with the Z flag set so you can branch with BEQ.

SWAPPER*
Switch between 40 and 80 columns
Call address: $FF5F 65375
Registers changed: .A, .X, .Y
Error number: None

This routine toggles the display mode between 40 and 80 columns. Bit 7 of location $D7 is set if 80-column mode is in effect.

TALK
Send talk command to serial device
Call address: $FFB4 65460
Registers changed: .A
Error number: Use READSS

Load the accumulator with the device number (0–31) and call this routine to command a serial device to begin sending data.

This is a low-level routine; you should almost always use CHKIN instead.

TKSA
Send secondary address to talker
Call address: $FF96 65430
Registers changed: .A
Error number: Use READSS

Load the accumulator with the secondary address and call this routine. This is a low-level routine; you should almost always use OPEN or CHKIN instead.

UDTIM
Update jiffy clock
Call address: $FFEA 65514
Registers changed: .A .X
Error number: None

Normally executed during the IRQ interrupt, this routine increments TIME, a three-byte counter at $00A0–$00A2, and decrements TIMER, a three-byte counter at $0A1D–$0A1F.

UNLSN
Send unlisten command to serial device
Call address: $FFAE 65454
Registers changed: .A
Error number: Use READSS

This routine commands all listeners on the serial bus to stop reading data. This is a low-level routine; you should almost always use CLRCH instead.

UNTLK
Send untalk command to serial device
Call address: $FFAB 65451
Registers changed: .A
Error number: Use READSS

This routine commands all talkers on the serial bus to stop sending data. This is a low-level routine; you should almost always use CLRCH instead.

VECTOR
Set or copy Kernal indirect RAM vectors
Call address: $FF8D 65421
Registers changed: .A, .Y
Error number: None

To copy the vectors to another RAM location, set the carry, load the X and Y registers with the low and high bytes of the RAM area, and call this routine. You can change the vectors to point to customized routines. Then to set the vectors to your altered values, clear the carry, load the X and Y registers with the address of the RAM area, and disable interrupts before calling this routine.

Chapter 7

System Architecture

System Architecture

In computer jargon, *system architecture* refers to the internal organization of the machine—the way that its various integrated circuit chips fit together to make a whole, functioning device. The 128 is unique in the microcomputer world because it can rearrange itself into three distinctly different computers: a 128 with BASIC 7.0, a Commodore 64, and a Z80-based CP/M machine. This chapter examines each of the 128's three operating modes, with particular emphasis on the memory management hardware that makes these metamorphoses possible.

128 Mode Overview

The native mode of the system—128 mode—is the one that makes most complete use of the system features. As Figure 7-1 shows, there's quite a lot of hardware packed into this mode: 128K of main RAM memory (in two 64K banks), 32K of BASIC ROM, 8K of Kernal operating system ROM, 4K of screen editor ROM, 4K of character set ROM, an 8502 microprocessor, a 40-column video chip, an 80-column video chip (which has its own private 16K of video memory), a SID sound synthesis chip, and CIA I/O chips. A powerful memory management chip orchestrates the entire operation, controlling how all these items work together. One striking feature of the 128 is that it's really a 256K computer that comes with 128K: The operating system provides for four 64K banks of RAM, but only two are currently installed. It's also possible to add up to 32K of extra ROM on the system board, and to connect external ROM cartridges with up to 32K more.

Entering 128 mode is as simple as turning on the computer. The 128 always comes up in 128 mode unless you hold down the Commodore key to go directly to 64 mode, have a 64 cartridge installed, or have a CP/M disk in the drive when you switch on the computer. At the start of the initialization process, the computer checks the status of the GAME and EXROM lines of the expansion port. If these lines are grounded, a 64 cartridge is assumed to be present and the system enters 64 mode. Next, the computer checks for 128 cartridges, which—if present—may or may not take control (see the section on cartridges later in this chapter). The computer then checks to see if the SHIFT key is held down. If so the computer comes up in 128 mode, but in the monitor rather than BASIC. This is followed by a check for the Commodore key, which—if held down—forces the system to come up in 64 mode. Finally, the computer checks the disk drive for a disk with autoboot information on sector 0 of the first track. If no boot disk is detected, the computer then comes up in 128 mode with BASIC 7.0. If a boot disk is found, the computer checks whether it is a CP/M boot disk. If so, the computer surrenders control to the Z80 microprocessor, which then brings the computer up in CP/M mode. Otherwise, the computer remains in 128 mode and boots the disk.

Figure 7-1. 128 Mode System Configuration

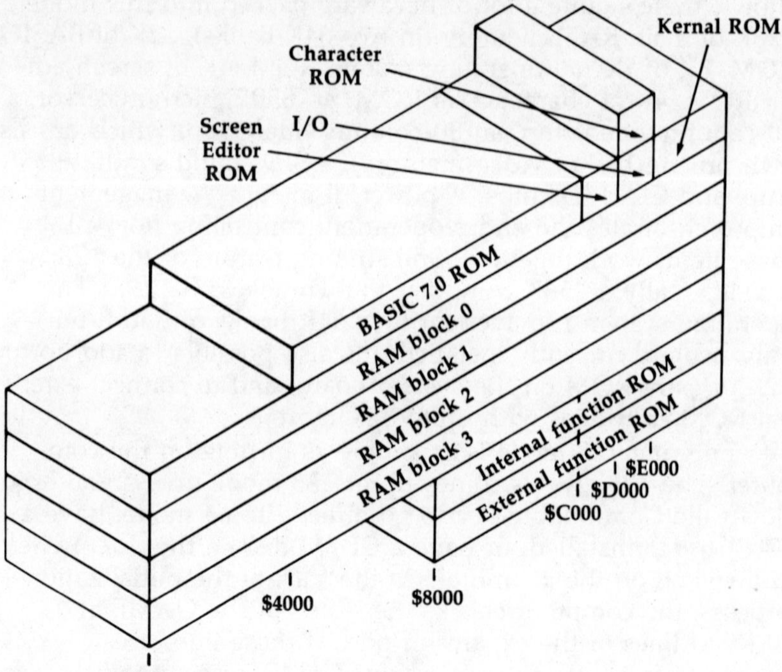

You can go from 128 mode into either of the other two operating modes. To switch to 64 mode, enter the command GO 64 (or SYS 65357). To go to CP/M mode, place a CP/M disk in the drive and enter the command BOOT. However, neither of the other modes provides a way to get back to 128 mode short of resetting the computer or turning it off and back on.

In the most common case, then, turning on the 128 puts you in 128 mode, with BASIC 7.0. You'll see the start message which identifies this version of BASIC and states that 122,365 bytes of memory are available for BASIC programming. This huge number is somewhat misleading, since you can't write a BASIC program that's 122K long. Instead, the available memory is split into two parts: 58,109 bytes for program text and 64,256 bytes for variable storage. (By comparison, the Commodore 64 offers 38,911 bytes for program text and variables combined.) The 8502 microprocessor can't "see" 122,356 bytes of memory at one time; the biggest chunk it can deal with at once is 64K (65536 bytes). Because of this, the 128 divides memory into 64K segments called *banks*. Since banks are an essential concept of the 128 system, we'll return to them later in this chapter.

If only 122,365 of the 128K (131,072 bytes) of RAM are available for BASIC, you may wonder what happens to the other 8707 bytes. In the BASIC text area (bank 0), 6144 bytes must be allocated to the Kernal operating system and to BASIC itself (remember that BASIC is really a long machine language program, so it must have storage locations in the same way that BASIC programs must have variables). Another 1024 bytes are given up to provide screen memory for the 40-column display. In the variable storage area, 1024 bytes are lost at the bottom of the bank because the memory management unit (MMU) always forces the system to look to block 0 of RAM for the first 1K of memory. And the top 256 bytes of every bank are also set aside for the memory management unit. That accounts for 8704 bytes: The remaining 3 bytes are three zeros in the BASIC text area which mark the start and end of a program. Figure 7-2 shows how the computer's resources are arranged for BASIC operations.

If you are not familiar with computer hardware or machine language programming, it may be hard to appreciate that the memory arrangement shown in Figure 7-2 represents quite a feat of engineering. Remember, the 8502 microprocessor can only see 64K of memory at a time. To run a BASIC program you obviously need the BASIC language, which is located in ROM in one 64K bank. The program text itself is in another bank, and the variable values referred to in the program text are in yet a third bank. This would seem to be an impossible situation.

Figure 7-2. BASIC Memory Organization

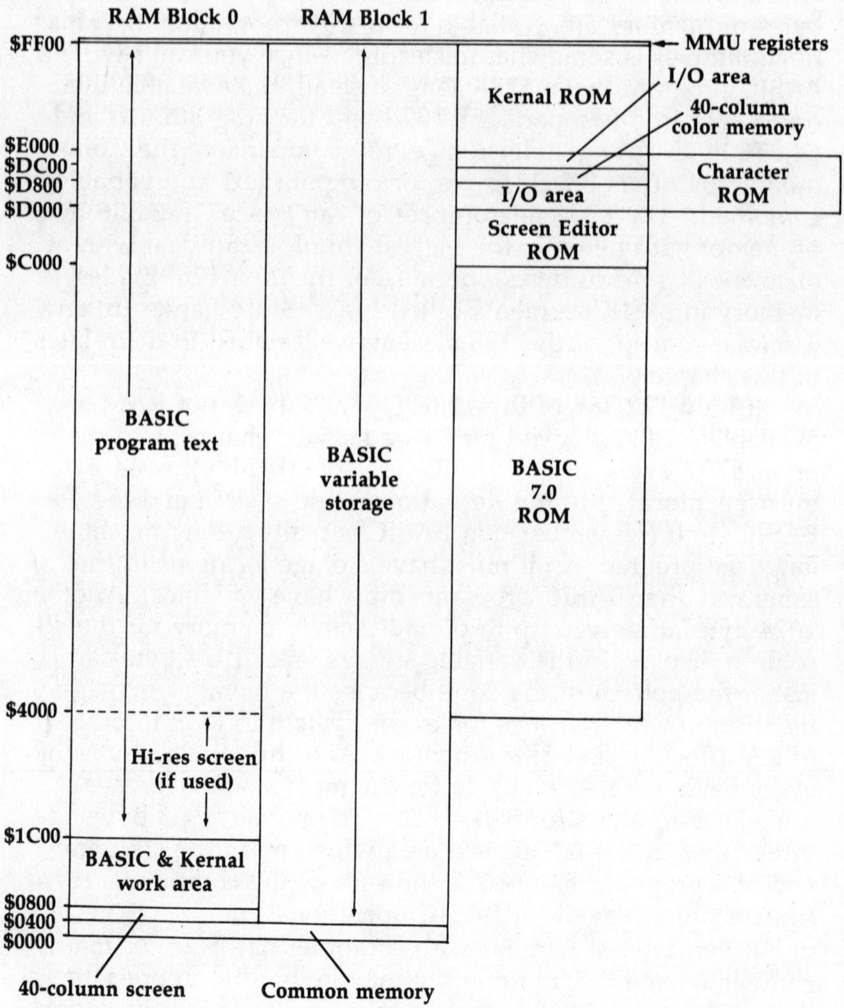

The key is the MMU and the common areas of memory it establishes. Since the computer always sees the same RAM in the low 1024 bytes of memory, a BASIC ROM routine can jump to a routine in the common block of RAM that switches the system to the bank where program text is stored, then reads a character from program text. When that's done, the character is stored in a special area (the BASIC input buffer) which is also within the first 1024 bytes of memory. At this point the routine switches back to the bank containing BASIC ROM. While in this bank, the computer can access the character we retrieved from program text, because the character is now stored in RAM that's visible in every bank. The 128 uses a similar system to jump from bank to bank when handling BASIC variables. The bank-switching is possible because the MMU itself appears in the top 256 bytes of *every* bank, starting at location $FF00.

This memory banking technique allows the 8502 processor to access many times more memory than its 64K addressing space normally allows. In fact, although the current 128 design only provides for up to 256K of memory, the MMU chip specifications hint at a design capable of managing up to 1 megabyte (1,048,576 bytes); perhaps a "Commodore 1024" will someday replace the 128. We'll examine the MMU chip in more detail later in this chapter.

64 Mode Overview

Figure 7-3 shows the system configuration in 64 mode. As mentioned earlier, a 128 in 64 mode isn't merely compatible with the Commodore 64; for all practical purposes, it *is* a Commodore 64. The BASIC and Kernal ROMs are identical, byte for byte, to the versions found in the most recent 64s. All I/O chips appear in the same locations and have the same functions. The ROM and I/O chips can be switched out for access to underlying RAM, just as in the 64. This should allow any Commodore 64 software to run unaltered in 64 mode.

The ability to run all Commodore 64 software without modification is, of course, the main feature of 64 mode. The huge supply of 64 software will allow you to keep your 128 busy until more programs are developed to take full advantage of the power of 128 mode. And if you have moved up to the 128 from a Commodore 64, then 64 mode may be reassuringly familiar. However, with all the enhancements added to the 128, there's very little reason to use 64 mode for any purpose other than running existing 64 software. Why figure out all the POKEs necessary for sound in 64 mode when you have SOUND and PLAY statements available in 128 mode's BASIC 7.0? Why write all the code needed to set up and move a sprite in 64 mode, when 128 mode offers SPRDEF, MOVSPR, BUMP, and COLLISION? Unless you have a strong need for your BASIC or ML programs to be totally compatible with the Commodore 64, you'll probably want to do all your original programming in 128 mode.

Figure 7-3. 64 Mode Configuration

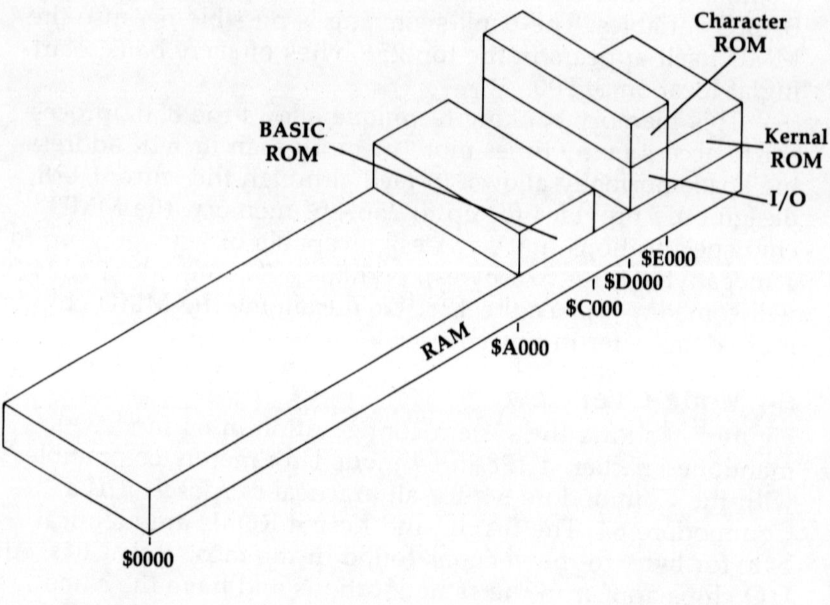

Although most of the enhancements of 128 mode disappear when the computer enters 64 mode, some do remain available. The biggest differences between a true Commodore 64 and a Commodore 128 operating in 64 mode are that the 128 uses an 8502 microprocessor in place of the 64's 6510, and an 8564 40-column video chip in place of the 64's 6567 VIC-II chip. The 8502 executes all the same machine language opcodes as the 6510, but adds additional pins to the built-in I/O port and is capable of changing clock rates. The 8564 is functionally equivalent to the 6567, but adds two more control registers. One of these registers is used to read the additional 24 keys on the 128 keyboard; the other controls the system clock rate. These may seem unusual features to add to a video chip, but Commodore owns MOS Technology, the company that makes most of the major chips in the 128. This enables them to add new features to existing chips rather than add entirely new chips, which would increase the cost of the system.

Because the extra features of the 8502 and 8564 are available in 64 mode, you can simulate some of the 128 enhancements. Consider this not-very-useful example: Bit 6 of location 1, the 8502 built-in I/0 port, reflects the status of the CAPS LOCK key, so that 128 key can easily be read in 64 mode. PRINT PEEK(1) AND 64 returns a value of 64 if the key is up, and 0 if the key is down. The two new registers on the 8564 provide more useful features. For example, Program 7-1 shows you how to read the numeric keypad from 64 mode. The keys can't be read by simply PEEKing the contents of a register. Rather, you must set up an interrupt-driven keyscan routine that mimics the way the computer reads the rest of the keyboard—as a matrix of rows and columns. Program 7-1 defines only the keys of the numeric keypad and the new row of cursor keys, but you could add definitions for the other extra keys. (See Appendix A for more details of the keyboard layout.)

Program 7-1. 64 Numeric Keypad

```
100 FOR AD=830 TO 949:READ BY:CK=CK+BY
110 POKE AD,BY:NEXT
120 IF CK<>13099 THEN PRINT TAB(7)"{RVS} ERROR IN
    DATA STATEMENTS ":STOP
130 SYS 830:PRINT"{2 DOWN}** NUMERIC KEYPAD IS NOW
     ACTIVE **{2 DOWN}"
140 NEW
830 DATA 120,169,75,141,20,3,169,3,141,21
840 DATA 3,88,96,169,248,141,47,208,169,255
850 DATA 141,0,220,205,1,220,208,10,141,47
860 DATA 208,74,141,0,220,76,49,234,160,0
870 DATA 140,141,2,169,251,141,47,208,162,8
880 DATA 173,1,220,205,1,220,208,248,74,144
890 DATA 9,200,202,208,249,110,47,208,176,234
900 DATA 185,157,3,16,7,162,1,142,141,2
910 DATA 41,127,133,203,169,255,141,47,208,32
920 DATA 72,235,76,126,234,64,35,44,135,7
930 DATA 130,2,64,64,40,43,64,1,19,32
940 DATA 8,64,27,16,64,59,11,24,56,64
```

To activate the numeric keypad, simply load and run the program. (Since it resides in the cassette buffer, this program can only be loaded from disk.) Be sure to save a copy of this program before running it for the first time, since it erases itself after it runs. The keypad keys now function exactly like the regular number keys, except that they are unaffected by CTRL, SHIFT, or the Commodore key. Like all IRQ routines, this one is disconnected when you use RUN/STOP–RESTORE. Enter SYS 830 to reenable it. Like all routines that use addresses below 1024 ($0400), this one is erased by a system reset: You must reinstall it after a reset.

It's also possible to use the fast operating mode from 64 mode. Bit 0 of location $D030 (53296) in the 8564 determines whether the system operates at the normal 1 MHz clock rate or the double-speed 2 MHz rate. However, since the 64 wasn't designed to operate at this speed, there are some limitations on what you can do in the faster mode. For one thing, you can't access disk, tape, or RS-232 while operating at the fast speed. These operations all require precise timing, and the 64's controlling ROM routines do not compensate for the different clock rate. Also, the 40-column screen display flashes randomly while operating at the faster speed. In 128 mode, you can still use the 80-column display, but in 64 mode you simply have to do without a display screen. Thus, you would only use the faster speed when performing long, slow operations that don't require a screen display. For example, in a high-resolution graphics plotting program that requires many complex calculations, you could enter fast mode to do the calculations and plot the figure, then return to normal speed to display the results. Try this example program:

```
10 INPUT N
20 FOR I=1 TO 2000
30 N=N+1/I
40 NEXT
50 PRINT N
```

Run the program and note how long it takes to print the result. Now add these two lines:

```
15 POKE 53296,1: REM FAST
45 POKE 53296,0: REM SLOW
```

The program now prints the result in approximately half the time. However, the screen goes crazy while the program is operating in fast mode. If you find this side effect distracting, you can do what the FAST command in BASIC 7.0 does—disable the screen display so that it shows only a blank field of the border color during fast mode. Make the following modifications to the program above:

```
15 POKE 53265,PEEK(53265)AND 239:POKE 53296,1:REM FAST
45 POKE 53265,PEEK(53265)OR 16:POKE 53296,0: REM SLOW
```

Be sure that any program you wish to use in fast mode is completely debugged before you add these lines. If your program crashes with an error message while the screen is disabled, you may not be able to recover without resetting the computer. (RUN/STOP–RESTORE *does not* restore the system to slow mode. That's the risk of using a nonstandard operating mode.)

You can enter 64 mode in several ways. First, the 128 enters 64 mode if you hold down the Commodore key when you turn the computer on. From BASIC in 128 mode you can type GO 64 (or SYS 65357 to bypass the ARE YOU SURE? and go directly to 64 mode). In machine language, you can JMP to the Kernal C64MODE routine at $FF4D. However, it's a one-way trip. There's no way out of 64 mode short of either pressing the reset switch or turning the computer off and back on, and you can even prevent the computer from returning to 128 mode when reset is pressed.

If you will be working in 64 mode, you may find it desirable to have the computer return directly to 64 mode when you press the reset button. From 128 mode, enter the monitor (press F8), then enter the following line:

```
>1FFF8 4D FF
```

Locations $FFF8–$FFF9 in bank 1 constitute the 128 operating system vector, which determines which system will be set up after a reset. The normal value here is $E224, the address of the routine which configures the computer for 128 mode. The monitor line above changes the vector to $FF4D, the Kernal C64MODE vector. Pressing reset now switches the computer to 64 mode, and it will remain locked in that mode until you turn it off. Pressing reset again simply kicks the system back into 64 mode. (You must also press RUN/STOP–RESTORE after each reset to complete the reinitialization. Otherwise, the computer will be unable to access the disk drive.)

CP/M Mode Overview

CP/M mode is radically different from the other two. In this mode, the 128 transfers primary control of the system from the 8502 to a second microprocessor, a Z80. All the ROM layers of 128 and 64 modes are switched away, and the system is configured as shown in Figure 7-4. Refer to Chapter 5 for a more thorough discussion of CP/M features.

Figure 7-4. CP/M Mode System Configuration

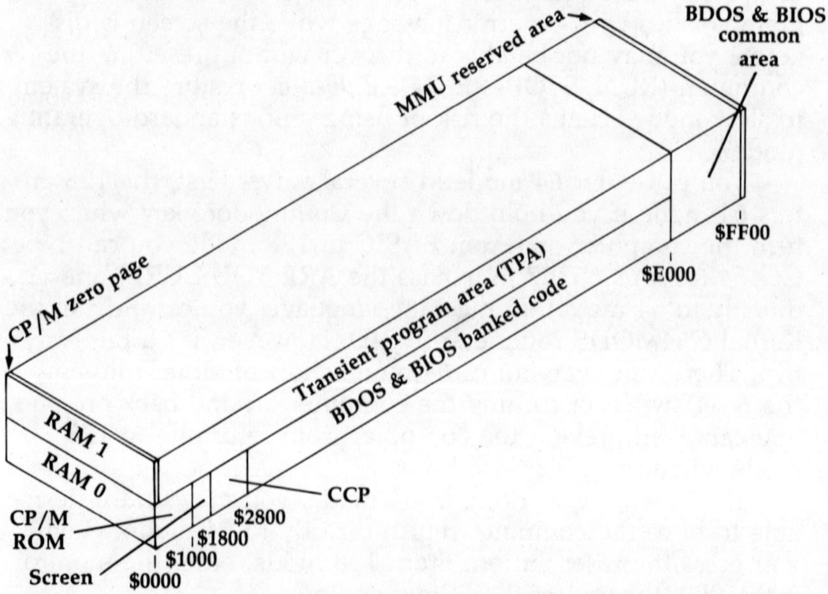

CP/M mode may seem the foreign element in the 128 system, and you may wonder why Commodore chose to include it. First of all, CP/M is widely used—dozens of different companies make CP/M-based computers and thousands of CP/M programs are available. Many of these are business programs—professional word processors, accounting packages, and the like—an area in which Commodore 64 software has been notably lacking. Secondly, CP/M was a comparatively simple system to implement. The 128 already had plenty of memory, I/O chips for video displays, disk access, and telecommunications, and a powerful memory management system to distribute these resources. Thus, the only additional hardware required was a Z80 microprocessor (CP/M is written in

Z80 machine language) and supporting ROM. Since CP/M is primarily disk-based, only a small amount of additional ROM was required. Finally, Commodore already had experience in adding CP/M compatibility to its machines, since a CP/M cartridge was developed for the Commodore 64.

The CP/M cartridge for the Commodore 64 was never particularly useful because the 1541 disk drive cannot read non-Commodore disk formats, and little if any serious CP/M software was available in Commodore's unique CP/M format. If you use a 1541 with the 128 you still face this problem, but the 1571 is able to read other disk formats and gives you true CP/M capabilities.

As discussed in Chapter 5, the 128's designers took some interesting shortcuts in implementing CP/M mode. Instead of writing all the new routines that would have been required to allow the Z80 to handle disk access or telecommunications, the system instead lets the 8502 handle those chores. The computer must be able to temporarily step out of CP/M mode into 128 mode to perform the operation, then switch back to CP/M mode when the operation is completed. This feat is made possible by the memory management system's capacity to make features appear almost anywhere in memory. For example, the ROM that the Z80 sees at locations 0–4095 is physically located at locations 53248–57343 in the 8502 address space. Letting the Z80 see the ROM at the lower addresses allows the 8502 to preserve its zero page and stack (locations 0–511), an area vital to 128-mode operations.

To enter CP/M mode, simply insert a CP/M boot disk in the drive and turn on the system. If you are already up and running in 128 mode, insert a CP/M boot disk and enter the command BOOT. To return to 128 mode, remove the CP/M disk from the drive and press the reset button. (If you press reset with a CP/M disk in the drive, you'll just restart CP/M.) There's no direct route from CP/M to 64 mode or vice versa. Either case involves turning the computer off and back on.

128-Mode Memory Management

The design of the 128 defines 372K of address space for this mode, as shown in Figure 7-1. However, the 8502 microprocessor has only 16 address lines, and thus can directly address only 2↑16 = 65536 bytes (64K) at any one time. Obviously, some sophisticated techniques are required to manipulate the way the microprocessor sees memory. The system used in the 128 is to divide memory into 16 logical *banks.* Grasping the concept of banks is central to understanding 128 mode. This can be confusing, since the banks don't represent 16 physical 64K blocks of memory. Rather, they are 16 different 64K selections from the buffet of available features. Banks are illusions created by the MMU that permit the microprocessor to see physically disjointed sections of memory as continuous blocks. Table 7-1 shows exactly what appears in each bank:

Table 7-1. Memory Banks

Bank Decimal	Hex	Locations	Contents
0	0	$0000–$FFFF	RAM block 0 (except for MMU registers at $FF00–$FF04)
1	1	$0000–$03FF	RAM from block 0
		$0400–$FFFF	RAM block 1 (except for MMU registers at $FF00–$FF04)
2	2	$0000–$03FF	RAM from block 0
		$0400–$FFFF	RAM block 2 (except for MMU registers at $FF00–$FF04)
3	3	$0000–$03FF	RAM from block 0
		$0400–$FFFF	RAM block 3 (except for MMU registers at $FF00–$FF04)
4	4	$0000–$7FFF	RAM from block 0
		$8000–$CFFF	Internal function ROM
		$D000–$DFFF	I/O block
		$E000–$FFFF	Internal function ROM (except for MMU registers at $FF00–$FF04)
5	5	$0000–$03FF	RAM from block 0
		$0400–$7FFF	RAM from block 1
		$8000–$CFFF	Internal function ROM
		$D000–$DFFF	I/O block
		$E000–$FFFF	Internal function ROM (except for MMU registers at $FF00–$FF04)

6	6	\$0000–\$03FF	RAM from block 0
		\$0400–\$7FFF	RAM from block 2
		\$8000–\$CFFF	Internal function ROM
		\$D000–\$DFFF	I/O block
		\$E000–\$FFFF	Internal function ROM (except for MMU registers at \$FF00–\$FF04)
7	7	\$0000–\$03FF	RAM from block 0
		\$0400–\$7FFF	RAM from block 3
		\$8000–\$CFFF	Internal function ROM
		\$D000–\$DFFF	I/O block
		\$E000–\$FFFF	Internal function ROM (except for MMU registers at \$FF00–\$FF04)
8	8	\$0000–\$7FFF	RAM from block 0
		\$8000–\$CFFF	External function ROM
		\$D000–\$DFFF	I/O block
		\$E000–\$FFFF	External function ROM (except for MMU registers at \$FF00–\$FF04)
9	9	\$0000–\$03FF	RAM from block 0
		\$0400–\$7FFF	RAM from block 1
		\$8000–\$CFFF	External function ROM
		\$D000–\$DFFF	I/O block
		\$E000–\$FFFF	External function ROM (except for MMU registers at \$FF00–\$FF04)
10	A	\$0000–\$03FF	RAM from block 0
		\$0400–\$7FFF	RAM from block 2
		\$8000–\$CFFF	External function ROM
		\$D000–\$DFFF	I/O block
		\$E000–\$FFFF	External function ROM (except for MMU registers at \$FF00–\$FF04)
11	B	\$0000–\$03FF	RAM from block 0
		\$0400–\$7FFF	RAM from block 3
		\$8000–\$CFFF	External function ROM
		\$D000–\$DFFF	I/O block
		\$E000–\$FFFF	External function ROM (except for MMU registers at \$FF00–\$FF04)

12	C	$0000–$7FFF	RAM from block 0
		$8000–$BFFF	Internal function ROM
		$C000–$CFFF	Kernal ROM
		$D000–$DFFF	I/O block
		$E000–$FFFF	Kernal ROM (except for MMU registers at $FF00–$FF04)
13	D	$0000–$7FFF	RAM from block 0
		$8000–$BFFF	External function ROM
		$C000–$CFFF	Kernal ROM
		$D000–$DFFF	I/O block
		$E000–$FFFF	Kernal ROM (except for MMU registers at $FF00–$FF04)
14	E	$0000–$3FFF	RAM from block 0
		$4000–$BFFF	BASIC 7.0 ROM
		$C000–$CFFF	Kernal ROM
		$D000–$DFFF	Character ROM
		$E000–$FFFF	Kernal ROM (except for MMU registers at $FF00–$FF04)
15	F	$0000–$3FFF	RAM from block 0
		$4000–$BFFF	BASIC 7.0 ROM
		$C000–$CFFF	Kernal ROM
		$D000–$DFFF	I/O block
		$E000–$FFFF	Kernal ROM (except for MMU registers at $FF00–$FF04)

Several important features you should notice in Table 7-1 are that the same block of memory—RAM from block 0—appears in locations $0000–$03FF (0–1023) *for all banks,* that the MMU configuration register appears at $FF00 (65280) in the top page (256 bytes) of memory *in every bank,* and that the RAM banks (0 and 1) contain copies of the ROM routines to redirect interrupts and reset to the Kernal interrupt- and reset-handling routines ($FF05–$FF16 for NMI, $FF17–$FF32 for IRQ, $FF33–$FF3C for return from interrupts, and $FF3D–$FF44 for reset), as well as copies of the hardware IRQ, reset, and NMI vectors. The common low area of memory provides a way for a routine from one bank to call a routine in another, or to access data from another bank. Without this common area to pass information, there would be no way for the system to keep track of which bank it had been in before a switch. Also, if the MMU did not appear in every bank it would not be possible to change freely from bank to bank; there would be no way out if you switched into a bank where the MMU was not accessible (as is the case in 64 mode, where the MMU is invisible). If the RAM banks did not contain copies of the routines to redirect the NMI and IRQ interrupts and system reset, the system would crash whenever an interrupt occurred while the processor was looking at a RAM bank.

Don't panic at the prospect of having to learn the details of all 16 banks; in most cases, you'll only need to know four to use your 128 effectively. First, there's not really any RAM in RAM blocks 2 and 3. As mentioned earlier, the 128 has all the features of a 256K computer except for the second 128K of memory. These two blocks are where that additional 128K will go, but for now they're just duplicate images of the existing RAM. Bank 2 is identical to bank 0, and bank 3 is identical to bank 1. Thus, you should never have a reason to use banks 2 or 3.

Banks 4–7 feature RAM from banks 0–3, respectively, in the lower 32K of memory and internal function ROM—plus the I/O chips—in the upper 32K. *Internal function ROM* is Commodore's designation for the ROM which occupies a free chip socket on the 128's circuit board. This is a throwback to Commodore's original PET designs, which included empty ROM sockets for users to add their own special features. Right now the socket is empty, and locations $8000–$CFFF and $E000–$FF00 in these banks show only randomly fluctuating values. Until someone introduces ROMs for this socket, you can ignore banks 4–7.

Banks 8–11 are the same as banks 4–7, except that the upper 32K of address space contains *external function ROM*, the designation for ROM on a cartridge plugged into the memory expansion port. Like the empty internal ROM socket in banks 4–7, locations $8000–$CFFF and $E000–$FF00 in banks 8–11 show random and unstable values if no cartridge ROM is present. Thus, banks 8–11 can be ignored unless you have a cartridge you wish to use. This applies only to 128 cartridges: Plugging a Commodore 64 cartridge into the port forces the system into 64 mode.

Banks 12 and 13 contain 32K of RAM from block 0 and the lower 16K ($8000–$BFFF) of internal or external function ROM, respectively, plus the Kernal ROM and I/O block at

$C000–$FFFF. Like banks 4–11, these two can be ignored if no internal (chip) or external (cartridge) ROM is present.

Banks 14 and 15 are very similar, but both are important. Both contain 16K of RAM (from block 0) at locations $0000–$3FFF, 32K of BASIC 7.0 ROM at $4000–$BFFF, the 40- and 80-column screen editor portion of the Kernal at $C000–$CFFF, and Kernal ROM at $E000–$FFFF. The two banks differ only in the contents of locations $D000–$DFFF. In bank 14, this area contains the character ROM, while in bank 15 this area is the I/O block, where the video, sound, and other I/O chips are addressed.

Thus, until you start plugging in extra ROM, you only need to worry about banks 0, 1, 14, and 15.

When programming in BASIC, bank 15 is the default. Unless you specify otherwise with a BANK statement, all POKE, PEEK, and SYS addresses refer to bank 15. Since bank 15 includes locations 0–16383 of bank 0 RAM (where most important BASIC pointers and 40-column screen memory reside) as well as ROM and the I/O chips, you can probably leave out the BANK statement most of the time. However, there may be times when you will want to have access to other banks. As shown in Figure 7-2, program text is located in bank 0 and program variables will reside in bank 1. Bank 14 is used when you need to access the character set ROM (for instance, when designing custom characters as explained in Chapter 2). A BANK statement is required to gain access to any of these banks. For example, these lines copy character patterns from ROM into the corresponding locations in bank 1 for redefinition:

```
100 POKE 58,208:CLR: REM RESERVE SPACE IN BANK 1
110 FOR AD=53248 TO 55295
120 BANK 14:CH=PEEK(AD)
130 BANK 1:POKE AD,CH:NEXT
```

Unless you know that you will be accessing the same bank again, it's a good idea to add a BANK 15 after each routine like the one above, so that the computer always returns to its standard state. Of course, the BANK statement only affects the operation of BASIC statements that deal directly with memory, not the internal operation of the system. Regardless of what BASIC BANK is in effect, the microprocessor is constantly jumping from bank to bank as it interprets and executes BASIC program lines.

When programming in machine language, you need to pay close attention to the bank you are operating in. The default bank for the built-in machine language monitor is bank 0—one of the banks that is composed entirely of RAM. If you don't specify otherwise, any code you enter will be placed in this bank. For example, if you specify a four-digit hex address, bank 0 will be assumed:

A 0C00 LDA #$41

is assembled as:

A 00C00 A9 41 LDA #$00

However, remember that you must be in bank 15 (bank F in monitor parlance) to use the Kernal routines or to have direct access to the I/O chips. Thus, adding this code causes a system lockup, since the Kernal BSOUT vector (at $FFD2 in Kernal ROM) does not appear in bank 0:

A 0C02 JSR $FFD2
G 0C00

Switching banks in machine language is accomplished by storing values in the MMU configuration register at $FF00, or at $D500 if the I/O block is present in the current bank. Figuring out the proper value for the desired bank can be a challenge. See the next section for information on configuration register values. One you probably should memorize is that the configuration register setting for bank 15 is simply 0. If you disassemble system ROM, you'll see the lines LDA #$00:STA $FF00 sprinkled throughout. These are places where the system is being redirected to ROM after accessing another bank. Fortunately, you usually don't have to calculate configuration register values if you don't want to. The Kernal routine GETCFG (at $FF6B; see Chapter 6) can find the proper value for you: Simply specify the bank you wish to access in the X register and call GETCFG. The value returned in the accumulator is the proper MMU configuration register value for the desired bank. For example, here is the machine language equivalent of the BASIC statement BANK 14:

LDX #$0E
JSR $FF6B
STA $FF00

Bank 15 is often the most convenient bank for machine language programming with the monitor, since this bank also includes bank 0 RAM from $0000–$3FFF. That's enough free memory for most programming projects.

The Kernal JMPFAR and JSRFAR routines also let you get to routines in other banks without worrying about bank-switching at all. And if you simply need to read, compare, or store data in another bank, you can use the Kernal INDFET, INDCMP, and INDSTA routines. Chapter 6 explains these routines in greater detail.

As mentioned earlier, the top page (locations $FF00–$FFFF) of both RAM banks (0 and 1) contains copies of the ROM routines that direct interrupts and resets to the appropriate ROM routines. The routines are not a permanent part of the banks—the system sees RAM in all locations in this page except $FF00–$FF04, where MMU registers appear—so they must be copied from ROM into RAM during power-on/reset initialization. Two additional routines are copied to the top page of bank 0 during system initialization. One, at $FFD0–$FFDE, lets the 8502 surrender control of the system to the Z80. The other is a Z80 machine language routine at $FFE0–$FFEE with the opposite purpose: It allows the Z80 to surrender control to the 8502. These routines are necessary because CP/M mode uses the 8502 to perform a variety of I/O operations such as reading from and writing to the disk drive or modem. The routines are placed here because memory above $FF00 is unaffected by the change from 128 to CP/M mode or vice versa.

There's one more special use for the top page of bank 1. During initialization, the system copies the codes for the characters CBM into locations $FFF5–$FFF7 of bank 1. This is done to show that preliminary initialization steps such as copying routines from ROM into RAM have been completed. Locations $FFF8 and $FFF9 are then initialized as the system vector. Future resets check for the CBM characters at $FFF5. If they are present, the system performs a "soft" reset which skips the preliminary steps by jumping through the system vector at $FFF8. As explained in the section on 64 mode, the system vector at $FFF8 can be redirected to other addresses so that reset need not always return the system to 128 mode. If the CBM characters are not found, a complete or "hard" reset is performed, just as if you turned the computer off and back on. In this case, the address in $FFF8–$FFF9 is irrelevant. Thus, you could force a complete power-on reset by changing the characters at $FFF5–$FFF7, then jumping to the reset-handling routine at $FF3D.

The Memory Management Unit

The special chip called the memory management unit (MMU) is the device that makes the entire 128 possible. Together with a companion chip called the programmable logic array (PLA), the MMU manipulates the microprocessor's addressing lines to arrange the system's resources in banks as described in the preceding section. It also controls which processor (8502 or Z80) has control of the system, and which set of ROM chips (64 or 128) the computer uses. Other MMU control lines can detect whether a 64 cartridge is present, whether fast serial disk access is being used, and even whether or not the 40/80-column display selection switch is depressed.

The main MMU registers appear in the 128 memory map at locations $D500–$D50B. Another set of registers appears at locations $FF00–$FF04. Since the MMU must be present in every bank to allow switching, this split addressing scheme lets the system see the upper set of registers in all banks, without sacrificing too much continuous memory: Only the top 256 bytes of each bank are lost.

The MMU's *configuration register* appears in both register sets, at locations $D500 and $FF00. This location controls the memory layout of the entire system by selecting what combination of RAM and ROM will appear in the 64K of available address space. The 16 banks in 128 mode are merely 16 different predefined settings for this register; other nonstandard arrangements are possible, but BASIC may not be able to use them. Figure 7-5 shows the function of each bit in the configuration register.

As an example, bank 14 contains bank 0 RAM from $0000–$3FFF, BASIC ROM from $4000–$BFFF, Kernal ROM from $C000–$CFFF and $E000–$FFFF, and character set ROM from $D000–$DFFF. Its configuration setting can be calculated as follows:

Bit	**Setting**	**Selects**
0	1	ROM at $D000–$DFFF
1	0	BASIC ROM (low) at $4000–$7FFF
2–3	00	BASIC ROM (high) at $8000–$BFFF
4–5	00	Kernal ROM at $C000–$CFFF and $E000–$EFFF
6–7	00	RAM at $0000–$3FFF comes from block 0

This setting corresponds to %00000001 or $01. Thus, storing a 1 in location $D500 or $FF00 sets the system to look at bank

Figure 7-5. MMU Configuration Register

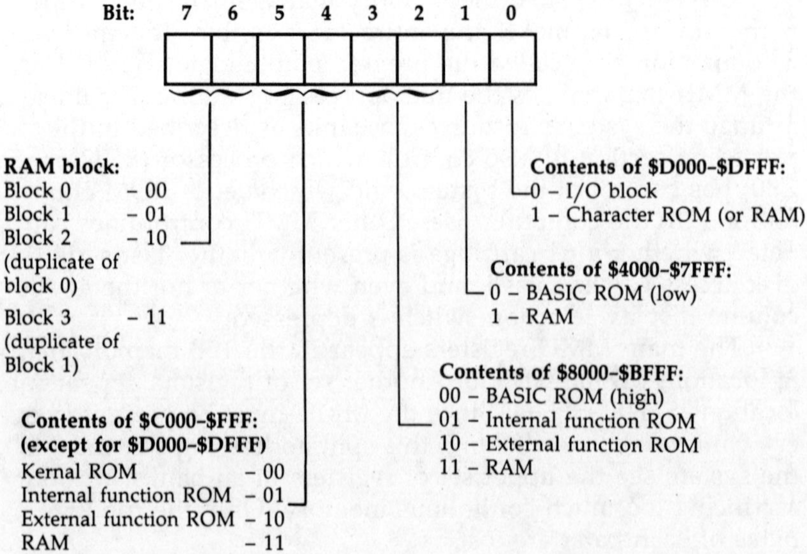

14. Location $FF00 (65280) is more commonly used because it is visible in all banks.

There is an alternative to storing values directly in the configuration registers. Locations $D501–$D504 are called *preconfiguration* registers: You can store values here for later transfer to the configuration register itself. Each preconfiguration register has a corresponding *load* configuration register at $FF01–$FF04. Storing a value in a load configuration register has the effect of transferring the contents of the matching preconfiguration register into the configuration register. For example, storing a value in $FF03 transfers the contents of $D503 to the configuration register. (Note that the value stored in $FF03 is irrelevant: It's the store operation, not the value, which triggers the transfer.) This allows a number of MMU values to be predefined and selected by a simple store. Reset your 128, then enter the monitor and enter the following:

M FF01 FF04

You should see the following in the first four positions:

3F 7F 01 41

Reading a load configuration register returns the contents of its matching preconfiguration register, so the values in $FF01–$FF04 show the predefined settings currently held in $D501–$D504. The first three numbers shown correspond to standard banks 0, 1, and 14. Thus, a simple way to select bank 1 is to store a value (remember, it can be any value) in $FF02. To select bank 0, store a value in $FF01, and so on.

The other MMU registers serve a variety of purposes. The *mode* configuration register at $D505 governs the operating mode of the 128. Bit 0 controls which processor is in control (0 = Z80, 1 = 8502); selecting the Z80 also makes the 4K of CP/M ROM (physically at $D000–$DFFF) visible to the Z80 at addresses $0000–$0FFF of its address space. Bit 3 controls fast serial disk communications, bits 5–6 are used to indicate the presence of 64 cartridges, and bit 7 reads the 40/80-column switch. In BASIC, PRINT PEEK(54533) AND 128 returns 128 if the switch is up (40 columns) and 0 if the switch is down (80 columns), so a line like this would let a program adjust itself to the current switch setting:

```
100 BANK 15:IF (PEEK(54533) AND 128)=PEEK(215) THEN
PRINT CHR$(27)"X"
```

(Location 215 indicates the current display mode, but has values opposite those returned from location 54533: 0 = 40 columns, 128 = 80 columns.)

Location $D506 is the RAM configuration register. Bits 0–3 of this register determine how much, if any, RAM is shared among banks, and whether the shared RAM is at the top or bottom of memory. In 128 mode, this is the register that establishes the common 1K at the bottom of memory. Bits 4–5 are unused in the current MMU, but Commodore's design specifications call for these to be used in future versions to select from among four separate 256K banks of memory (creating the tantalizing prospect of a 128-compatible computer with a full megabyte of memory). The leftmost two bits determine in which RAM bank the VIC chip's screen memory is located (its color memory is always in 1K of 4-bit RAM at $D800–$DBFF in the I/O block). Program 7-2 shows how you can create an alternate 40-column screen in bank 1:

Program 7-2. Alternate Screen Demo

```
10 POKE 48,8:CLR:REM RESERVE SPACE IN BANK 1
20 PRINT"{CLR}{2 DOWN}SETTING UP ALTERNATE SCREEN"
   :PRINT"{2 DOWN}PLEASE WAIT ..."
```

```
30 BANK 1:FOR J=1024 TO 2023:POKE J,32:NEXT:BANK 1
   5:REM CLEAR ALTERNATE SCREEN
40 XX=7:YY=10:M$="THIS SCREEN IS IN BANK 1":RV=0:G
   OSUB 1000
50 XX=2:YY=12:M$="(PRESS [RETURN] TO SWITCH SCREEN
   S)":RV=0:GOSUB 1000
100 PRINT"{CLR}"
110 CHAR 1,7,11,"THIS SCREEN IS IN BANK 0",1
120 CHAR 1,2,13,"(PRESS [RETURN] TO SWITCH SCREENS
    )",1
130 GETKEY K$:IF K$<>CHR$(13) THEN 130
140 POKE 54534,PEEK(54534)OR 64:REM SWITCH TO SCRE
    EN IN BANK 1
150 GETKEY K$:IF K$<>CHR$(13) THEN 150
160 POKE 54534,PEEK(54534)AND 63:REM SWITCH TO SCR
    EEN IN BANK 0
170 GOTO 130
997 REM: THE FOLLOWING ROUTINE SIMULATES THE BASIC
     CHAR STATEMENT FOR BANK 1
998 REM: XX IS COLUMN (0-39), YY IS ROW (0-24), M$
     IS STRING TO DISPLAY
999 REM: RV IS REVERSE FLAG (0=NORMAL, 1=REVERSE)
1000 CP=1023+(YY*40)+XX:BANK 1:FOR CC=1 TO LEN(M$)
     :CH=ASC(MID$(M$,CC,1))
1010 IF CH>63 AND CH<96 THEN CH=CH-64
1020 IF CH>191 AND CH<224 THEN CH=CH-128
1030 IF RV THEN CH=CH+128
1040 IF (CP+CC)>2023 THEN CC=LEN(M$):GOTO 1060
1050 POKE CP+CC,CH
1060 NEXT:BANK 15:RETURN
```

Note that you can only POKE characters to this alternate screen. BASIC's PRINT and CHAR statements still send all characters to the normal screen in bank 0. (Since the 40-column screen is in bank 0 RAM below address $4000, the BASIC routines can display characters on the screen without leaving banks 14 or 15, where the ROMs reside.) The subroutine at line 1000 simulates CHAR for the screen in BANK 1. You cannot change character colors on this alternate screen independently of the original screen in bank 0—both use the same color memory.

The next four registers ($D507–$D50A) let the system see pages zero or one at any memory location. The ability to relocate these pages is a very powerful feature, as that part of memory is very important. Page zero ($0000–$00FF) is very heavily used because many of the 8502 microprocessor's most powerful instructions refer to this page. Page one is important because it is the stack, the area where return addresses are stored during JSRs and interrupts. The MMU allows you to set up *virtual* pages—pages that aren't really where they say they are. Locations $D507–$D508 define the starting location of the new page zero, and locations $D509–$D50A define the starting location of the new page one.

In either case, the first location specifies the new page of memory where the relocated page will appear. The second location should allow the selection of either bank 0 or 1, but has no effect in the current version of the 128 and can be ignored (or set to zero). The new page must be in bank 0. As a side effect, any reference to an address within the zone where you put the page is translated into a reference to the original page. To avoid wiping out the original page zero or one, you must be careful not to use any addresses in the area where you have relocated the page. There's one important exception to this rule: The first two locations in zero page *cannot* be relocated. A reference to location $0000 or $0001 always affects the built-in I/O port directly, regardless of where the system currently sees page zero. Similarly, the system ignores any reference to the first two addresses in the zone where you have relocated the zero page.

The concept of virtual pages may seem confusing at first, but it gives you even more control over the system's configuration. To take an example, say that you relocate page zero to locations $3C00–$3CFF (by placing the value $3C in $D507), and then store the value 1 in location $00B0 with LDA #$01:STA $B0. Though the store instruction refers to the zero page, the value 1 is actually stored in location $3CB0. When you perform LDA $A4, the computer returns the contents of $3CA4, and so on. Note that you still *refer* to zero-page locations with zero-page addresses—just like always—but the actual operations take place elsewhere in memory. For all practical purposes, the zero page *is* elsewhere in memory, even though you access it exactly as you would in any other case. When would this be useful? For one thing, virtual paging makes it possible to switch rapidly between two or more different applications, maintaining a separate virtual zero page and stack area for each application.

But don't forget the other effects of relocating pages. In the example above (zero page relocated to page $3C), the system translates any reference to locations $3C02–$3CFF into a reference to locations $0002–$00FF. Thus, LDA #$FF:STA

$3C81 actually places the value $FF in location $0081. You must avoid using locations $3C02–$3CFF if you wish to preserve the original zero page (often a major reason for relocating it in the first place). References to locations $3C00–$3C01 have no effect on either those locations or $0000–$0001.

Finally, location $D50B is the version register, which contains a permanent value that identifies which MMU version this is and how much RAM should be present. In the 128, this register contains $22, indicating version 2 of the MMU in a system with two 64K banks of RAM. By checking the value in this location, programs will be able to adjust themselves for the amount of available memory. This will be important when future compatible systems with more than 128K are introduced.

Input and Output

The 128 uses a group of special input/output (I/O) chips for communicating with the outside world. These chips provide the video displays, read the keyboard, and handle data transfers to and from tape or disk drives and modems. The I/O chips are controlled by writing data into their *registers* (locations) or reading the registers to see what they contain. The 128 uses *memory-mapped* I/O, meaning that the I/O chip registers can be addressed just like normal memory locations. The *I/O block* (see Figure 7-1) is simply the area of memory where all the I/O chip registers appear.

The 128's I/O block—addresses $D000–$DFFF (53248–57343)—includes the VIC 40-column video chip at addresses $D000–$D030 (53248–53296), the SID sound chip at locations $D400–$D41C (54272–54300), the MMU memory management unit at $D500–$D50B (54528–54539), the 80-column video chip at $D600–$D601 (54784–54785). A 1K (1024 byte) block of memory occupies locations $D800–$DBFF (55296–56391), the area where color information for the 40-column text screen is stored. Unlike the other sections of RAM in the computer, only the lower four bits of each location in this block contain valid data. (A group of four bits is called a nybble, so you may also see these locations referred to as the color RAM nybbles.) Since the high bits may contain unpredictable values, you should always use AND to mask out all but the lower four bits when reading the contents of locations in this area. For example, you would use PRINT PEEK(55296) AND 15 to find the true color value of the character in the home position (upper-left corner) of the 40-column screen.

The two general-purpose CIA I/O chips appear at locations $DC00–$DC0F (56320–56335) and $DD00–$DD0F (56576–56591). Two other I/O areas—locations $DE00–$DEFF (56832–57087) and $DF00–$DFFF (57088–57343)—are also defined, although not used by built-in chips. The add-on memory expansion module is designed to be addressed in the second unused slot, and uses addresses $DF00–$DF0A (57088–57098). Chapter 2 has more information on the video chips, and Chapter 3 discusses the SID sound chip in detail. The MMU is discussed in the preceding section on memory management. We'll examine the memory expansion module more closely in the next section of this chapter.

Most of the 128's input and output operations are handled by the pair of 6526 Complex Interface Adapter (CIA) chips. Since nearly every computer operation requires some sort of I/O operation, these versatile chips are almost always busy. CIA #1, at locations $DC00–$DC0F (56320–56335) in the I/O block, reads the keyboard as well as joysticks, mice, and the buttons of paddle controllers. It also generates an IRQ interrupt every 1/60 second (to provide for keyboard reading and other housekeeping tasks) and helps out with fast serial communications with the 1571 disk drive. CIA #2, at locations $DD00–$DD0F (56576–56591) in the I/O block, handles normal-speed serial communications with the 1541 or 1571, RS-232 transmission and reception, and the user port. It is also the source for the NMI interrupts that provide proper timing for RS-232. In addition, this chip controls memory banking for the VIC-II 40-column video chip. Since these are exactly the same CIA chips used in the 64, most if not all 64 CIA programming techniques should transfer directly to the 128. The 64's CIA chips are discussed in considerable detail in COMPUTE!'s *Mapping the Commodore 64*.

The most significant I/O enhancement of the 128 is its faster serial data transfer rate. The CIAs in the Commodore 64 are also capable of faster operation, but since all 64 peripherals were designed to be compatible with the VIC-20, no attempt has been made to enhance the data transfer speed. The 1571 disk drive allows the 128 to step beyond this limitation, since it can operate in either a slow 1541 mode compatible with the 64 or 128, or in a fast mode compatible with the 128 alone. In the slower mode, the computer uses software to divide each byte into bits and send these bits one at a time to the CIA for transmission over the serial bus. Likewise, it uses a software routine to read bits one at a time from the serial bus and assemble them back into bytes. This is inefficient, since the CIA has the built-in ability to take whole bytes, break them into bits, and send the bits. Likewise, the CIA can receive bits and reassemble them into bytes on its own. The fast serial mode relies on the CIA's hardware to perform tasks that are done by software in slow serial mode—which speeds up the process dramatically. Refer to Chapter 4 for more information on the fast serial mode.

Because the same CIA chip is used to read both the keyboard and the joysticks, several conflicts are possible. For instance, using a joystick in control port 1 has the same effect as typing on the keyboard. Moving the joystick to the right is the same as typing CRSR-left, moving it down is equivalent to pressing insert (SHIFT-INST/DEL), and moving it left corresponds to pressing RETURN. Pressing the firebutton is equivalent to F8 (which kicks you into the monitor if no program is running). For this reason, it is preferable to use control port 2 in programs that require only one joystick. Even though the light pen is not actually read by the CIA, it affects keyboard reading because it shares an input line on joystick port 1 that is connected to the CIA. Thus, when a light pen is plugged in, you cannot type the period, M, B, C, Z, F1, or right SHIFT keys or the space bar (if you're familiar with keyboard scanning, you may notice that all of these keys are located on the same row of the keyscan matrix).

One additional feature of the CIA chip is its time-of-day clock. Since the clock is driven by the highly stable frequency of the power line, it should be significantly more accurate than the software-driven jiffy clock, which stops whenever IRQ interrupts are disabled (most notably during tape saves or loads). Moreover, the time-of-day clocks count in hours, minutes, and seconds instead of jiffies—the 1/60-second ticks recorded by software clock. However, neither 64 nor 128 mode takes advantage of this capability. Both the BASIC TI and TI$ reserved variables and the Kernal RDTIM routine use the jiffy clock instead. (The system time function in CP/M mode does make use of the CIA clocks.) Chapter 6 shows how to set and read the time-of-day clocks.

A few I/O operations are handled by chips other than the

CIAs. The SID chip reads paddle controllers (see Chapter 3), and the VIC-II chip is used to scan 24 of the new 128 mode keys on the keyboard. The VIC-II and 80-column chips each read the light pen for their respective screens.

Memory Expansion

One new peripheral announced for the 128 is the 512K memory expansion module. The system handles access to the extra memory provided by the module in a unique manner. Since the expansion memory isn't connected directly to the address or data buses, it can't be read and written to directly by the 8502. Instead, the module is governed by a special new chip called the 8726 RAM Expansion Controller (REC). When you plug in an expansion module, the REC appears in the 8502's address space at locations $DF00–$DF0A (57088–57098).

The REC is capable of direct memory access (DMA), meaning that the 8502 can temporarily surrender control of the computer to the REC. While the REC is in charge, it can perform one of four operations: saving the contents of a portion of 128 memory into expansion module memory; loading the contents of a portion of expansion module memory into 128 memory; verifying that the contents of a portion of 128 memory are identical to the contents of a portion of expansion module memory; and swapping the contents of a portion of expansion module memory and 128 memory.

Note that the first three operations listed above are equivalent to those performed by a disk drive. Hence, the expansion module is also referred to as a RAMdisk. Using expansion memory as a RAMdisk is much faster than conventional disk operations (even the 1571's fast serial mode). Of course, since the contents of expansion memory are erased when you turn the computer off, it is still necessary to save programs to tape or disk at some point.

The 128 has ROM routines to transfer data to and from the expansion module. In BASIC, the commands STASH, FETCH, and SWAP are available to save, load, and swap data with the expansion module (however, BASIC has no VERIFY command for expansion memory). For transfers in machine language, the Kernal routine DMA_CALL (see Chapter 6) handles access to the REC.

Because an expansion module has such large memory capacity, it opens up a number of exciting possibilities. For example, you can fill the module with dozens of high-resolution screen images representing different background displays for a game, then load a new screen almost instantly whenever you want a change of scenery. Or you can keep several of your favorite programs in the module and swap them in or out of memory at will. Of course, you still have to load the programs from disk in order to stash them in the module, but after that point loading from the module is nearly instantaneous.

An interesting programming challenge would be to write a program that loads an entire group of programs—perhaps programming aids—from disk into the module. By making this into an autobooting program (see Chapter 4), you can automate the entire process: In effect, the computer will boot up with your favorite utilities already in memory.

Cartridges

The 128 has the same cartridge connector (memory expansion port) as the Commodore 64, and all 64 ROM cartridges should work properly on the 128. Those 64 cartridges that ground the GAME and EXROM lines on the memory expansion port (almost all 64 cartridges work this way) should take effect immediately. The MMU checks these lines and forces the 128 into 64 mode if a cartridge is detected.

A different system is used to detect 128 cartridges. During the initialization sequence, a Kernal routine checks the four possible function ROM starting addresses ($8000 and $C000 for both external and internal ROM) for entry vectors, an identifier byte, and the character pattern CBM, which indicates that ROM is present. The computer notes the location of any ROMs which it detects. The identifier byte determines whether or not the ROM routines autostart (take effect immediately). Any routines that don't autostart are called later in the initialization sequence (by the Kernal routine PHOENIX).

If more than one ROM is found, the 128 calls them in this order: $8000 external, $C000 external, $8000 internal, and $C000 internal. This system (similar to the one used in the Plus/4 and 16) allows for greater flexibility, since it allows function ROMs to occupy the same address space as BASIC and the Kernal without disabling those built-in ROMs. As noted earlier in this chapter (see the section on 128-mode memory management), the internal function ROM appears in banks 4–7 and 12, and external function ROM appears in banks 8–11 and 13.

Appendices

Character, Screen, and Keyboard Codes

The Commodore 128 represents characters in several different manners: as characters, as screen codes, and as keyboard codes. This appendix covers each of these possible representations.

Character Codes

An individual memory location in the Commodore 128 has eight bits, each of which can be either off (0) or on (1). This means that 2^8 (or 256) different patterns of ones and zeros can be represented, which can be interpreted as 256 different characters. The 128 actually has two separate sets of 256 characters. The set that is normally activated when the computer is turned on is called the uppercase/graphics set. It has only uppercase (capital) letters, but includes many graphics characters. The alternative lowercase/uppercase set has both lowercase and uppercase letters, but includes substantially fewer graphics characters. It is useful for creating more attractive text displays, and is essential for tasks like word processing. You can switch manually between sets by pressing the SHIFT and Commodore keys simultaneously. You can also switch to the lowercase/uppercase set within a program by printing character 14—PRINT CHR$(14). To switch back to the normal uppercase/graphics set, print character 142.

In the 40-column display mode, switching character sets affects all characters currently on the screen. For example, uppercase letters printed from the uppercase/graphics set will change to lowercase characters after CHR$(14) is printed. However, any character set switching in 80-column mode affects only those characters printed after the switch. In this case, uppercase letters printed from the uppercase/graphics set will remain in uppercase after a CHR$(14) is printed.

The lowercase/uppercase character set has two identical groups of uppercase letters, characters 97–122 and characters 193–218. When using this set, PRINT CHR$(97) and PRINT CHR$(193) both cause an A to be displayed on the screen. However, you should be aware that the ASC function always returns values from the higher group—in lowercase/uppercase, PRINT ASC("A") always gives 193 instead of 97. In machine language, the Kernal GETIN routine also returns values 193–218 for shifted letters in the lowercase/uppercase set.

The following table lists the codes for the 128 character sets. There are no characters for codes 0, 1, 3, 4, 6, 16, 21–23, 25, 26, 128, 131, and 132.

Dec	Hex	Uppercase/Graphics Set	Lowercase/Uppercase Set
2	02	underline on[1]	
5	05	white	
7	07	bell tone[2]	
8	08	disable SHIFT-Commodore[3]	
9	09	tab[2]	
		enable SHIFT-Commodore[3]	
10	0A	linefeed[2]	
11	0B	disable SHIFT-Commodore[2]	
12	0C	enable SHIFT-Commodore[2]	
13	0D	RETURN	
14	0E	switch to lowercase	
15	0F	flash on[1]	
17	11	cursor down	
18	12	reverse on	
19	13	home	
20	14	delete	
24	18	tab set/clear[2]	
27	1B	ESCape	
28	1C	red	
29	1D	cursor right	
30	1E	green	
31	1F	blue	
32	20	space	
33	21	!	!
34	22	"	"
35	23	#	#
36	24	$	$
37	25	%	%

Dec	Hex	Uppercase/Graphics Set	Lowercase/Uppercase Set
38	26	&	&
39	27	'	'
40	28	(	(
41	29	)	)
42	2A	*	*
43	2B	+	+
44	2C	,	,
45	2D	-	-
46	2E	.	.
47	2F	/	/
48	30	0	0
49	31	1	1
50	32	2	2
51	33	3	3
52	34	4	4
53	35	5	5
54	36	6	6
55	37	7	7
56	38	8	8
57	39	9	9
58	3A	:	:
59	3B	;	;
60	3C	<	<
61	3D	=	=
62	3E	>	>
63	3F	?	?
64	40	@	@
65	41	A	a
66	42	B	b
67	43	C	c
68	44	D	d
69	45	E	e
70	46	F	f

Dec	Hex	Uppercase/Graphics Set	Lowercase/Uppercase Set
71	47	G	g
72	48	H	h
73	49	I	i
74	4A	J	j
75	4B	K	k
76	4C	L	l
77	4D	M	m
78	4E	N	n
79	4F	O	o
80	50	P	p
81	51	Q	q
82	52	R	r
83	53	S	s
84	54	T	t
85	55	U	u
86	56	V	v
87	57	W	w
88	58	X	x
89	59	Y	y
90	5A	Z	z
91	5B	[	[
92	5C	£	£
93	5D	]	]
94	5E	↑	↑
95	5F	←	←
96	60		
97	61		A
98	62		B
99	63		C
100	64		D
101	65		E
102	66		F
103	67		G

Dec	Hex	Uppercase/Graphics Set	Lowercase/Uppercase Set
104	68		H
105	69		I
106	6A		J
107	6B		K
108	6C		L
109	6D		M
110	6E		N
111	6F		O
112	70		P
113	71		Q
114	72		R
115	73		S
116	74		T
117	75		U
118	76		V
119	77		W
120	78		X
121	79		Y
122	7A		Z
123	7B		
124	7C		
125	7D		
126	7E		
127	7F		
129	81	orange[4]	
		dark purple[1]	
130	82	underline off[1]	
133	85	F1	
134	86	F3	
135	87	F5	
136	88	F7	
137	89	F2	
138	8A	F4	

Dec	Hex	Uppercase/Graphics Set	Lowercase/Uppercase Set
139	8B	F6	
140	8C	F8	
141	8D	SHIFT–RETURN	
142	8E	switch to uppercase	
143	8F	flash off[1]	
144	90	black	
145	91	cursor up	
146	92	reverse off	
147	93	clear screen	
148	94	insert	
149	95	brown[4]	
		dark yellow[1]	
150	96	light red	
151	97	dark gray[4]	
		dark cyan[1]	
152	98	medium gray	
153	99	light green	
154	9A	light blue	
155	9B	light gray	
156	9C	purple	
157	9D	cursor left	
158	9E	yellow	
159	9F	cyan	
160	A0	SHIFT-space	
161	A1		
162	A2		
163	A3		
164	A4		
165	A5		
166	A6		
167	A7		
168	A8		
169	A9		

Dec	Hex	Uppercase/Graphics Set	Lowercase/Uppercase Set
170	AA		
171	AB		
172	AC		
173	AD		
174	AE		
175	AF		
176	B0		
177	B1		
178	B2		
179	B3		
180	B4		
181	B5		
182	B6		
183	B7		
184	B8		
185	B9		
186	BA		
187	BB		
188	BC		
189	BD		
190	BE		
191	BF		
192	C0		
193	C1		A
194	C2		B
195	C3		C
196	C4		D
197	C5		E
198	C6		F
199	C7		G
200	C8		H
201	C9		I
202	CA		J

Dec	Hex	Uppercase/Graphics Set	Lowercase/Uppercase Set
203	CB		K
204	CC		L
205	CD		M
206	CE		N
207	CF		O
208	D0		P
209	D1		Q
210	D2		R
211	D3		S
212	D4		T
213	D5		U
214	D6		V
215	D7		W
216	D8		X
217	D9		Y
218	DA		Z
219	DB		
220	DC		
221	DD		
222	DE		
223	DF		
224	E0		
225	E1		
226	E2		
227	E3		
228	E4		
229	E5		
230	E6		
231	E7		
232	E8		
233	E9		
234	EA		
235	EB		

Dec	Hex	Uppercase/Graphics Set	Lowercase/Uppercase Set
236	EC		
237	ED		
238	EE		
239	EF		
240	F0		
241	F1		
242	F2		
243	F3		
244	F4		
245	F5		
246	F6		
247	F7		
248	F8		
249	F9		
250	FA		
251	FB		
252	FC		
253	FD		
254	FE		
255	FF		

Notes
1. *For 80-column display only*
2. *For 128 mode only*
3. *For 64 mode only*
4. *For 40-column display only*

Screen Codes

There are 256 screen codes for each character set; codes 128–255 are the reverse images of codes 0–127. To display any character in reverse video, simply add 128 to its screen code value. Thus, POKE 1024,1:POKE 1025,1+128 displays an A and a reverse A.

The character ROM has a total of 153 different characters. In the uppercase/graphics set, the character patterns for codes 32 and 96 are identical, as are those for 64 and 67, 66 and 93, 101 and 116, and 103 and 106.

Dec	Hex	Uppercase/Graphics Set	Lowercase/Uppercase Set
0	00	@	@
1	01	A	a
2	02	B	b
3	03	C	c
4	04	D	d
5	05	E	e
6	06	F	f
7	07	G	g
8	08	H	h
9	09	I	i
10	0A	J	j
11	0B	K	k
12	0C	L	l
13	0D	M	m
14	0E	N	n
15	0F	O	o
16	10	P	p
17	11	Q	q
18	12	R	r
19	13	S	s
20	14	T	t
21	15	U	u
22	16	V	v
23	17	W	w

Dec	Hex	Uppercase/Graphics Set	Lowercase/Uppercase Set
24	18	X	x
25	19	Y	y
26	1A	Z	z
27	1B	[	[
28	1C	£	£
29	1D	]	]
30	1E	↑	↑
31	1F	←	←
32	20	space	
33	21	!	!
34	22	"	"
35	23	#	#
36	24	$	$
37	25	%	%
38	26	&	&
39	27	'	'
40	28	(	(
41	29	)	)
42	2A	*	*
43	2B	+	+
44	2C	,	,
45	2D	-	-
46	2E	.	.
47	2F	/	/
48	30	0	0
49	31	1	1
50	32	2	2
51	33	3	3
52	34	4	4
53	35	5	5
54	36	6	6
55	37	7	7
56	38	8	8

Dec	Hex	Uppercase/Graphics Set	Lowercase/Uppercase Set
57	39	9	9
58	3A	:	:
59	3B	;	;
60	3C	<	<
61	3D	=	=
62	3E	>	>
63	3F	?	?
64	40		
65	41		A
66	42		B
67	43		C
68	44		D
69	45		E
70	46		F
71	47		G
72	48		H
73	49		I
74	4A		J
75	4B		K
76	4C		L
77	4D		M
78	4E		N
79	4F		O
80	50		P
81	51		Q
82	52		R
83	53		S
84	54		T
85	55		U
86	56		V
87	57		W
88	58		X
89	59		Y

Dec	Hex	Uppercase/Graphics Set	Lowercase/Uppercase Set
90	5A		Z
91	5B		
92	5C		
93	5D		
94	5E		
95	5F		
96	60	SHIFT-space	
97	61		
98	62		
99	63		
100	64		
101	65		
102	66		
103	67		
104	68		
105	69		
106	6A		
107	6B		
108	6C		
109	6D		
110	6E		
111	6F		
112	70		
113	71		
114	72		
115	73		
116	74		
117	75		
118	76		
119	77		
120	78		
121	79		
122	7A		

Dec	Hex	Uppercase/Graphics Set	Lowercase/Uppercase Set
123	7B		
124	7C		
125	7D		
126	7E		
127	7F		

Keycodes

The 128 keyboard is arranged electrically as a matrix of 11 columns × 8 rows of keys (8 columns × 8 rows, in 64 mode). Every 1/60 second, the computer scans the keyboard to see if a key is pressed. If a key is pressed, the keyscan routine generates a value that corresponds to the key's position in the matrix. (The formula is keycode = *column* * 8 + *row*, where *column* has a value from 0 to 10, and *row* has a value from 0 to 7.) If no key is pressed, a value of 88 is generated. (The "no key pressed" value in 64 mode is 64.) This value is stored in location 212 (location 203 in 64 mode). Location 213 (location 197 in 64 mode) will also hold the same value. The contents of this location can be used to determine which key is currently being pressed, as an alternative to using GET (or the Kernal GETIN routine in machine language). For example, these two lines have the the same effect—to pause the program until any key is pressed:

```
100 GET K$:IF K$="" THEN 100
100 IF PEEK(212)=88 THEN 100
```

Figure A-1 gives the keyscan codes for the 128 keyboard. Notice that the figure shows no values for the left and right SHIFT keys, CONTROL, the Commodore key, and ALT. They are the keys which use the missing codes 15, 52, 58, 61, and 80, respectively. These keys are detected later in the keyscan routine, and another location is used to record their status. In 128 mode, the location used is 211; the corresponding location in 64 mode is 653. The values found in that location are shown in the following table:

No shift key pressed	0
SHIFT	1
Commodore	2
CONTROL	4
ALT (128 mode only)	8

Figure A-1. Commodore 128 Keycodes

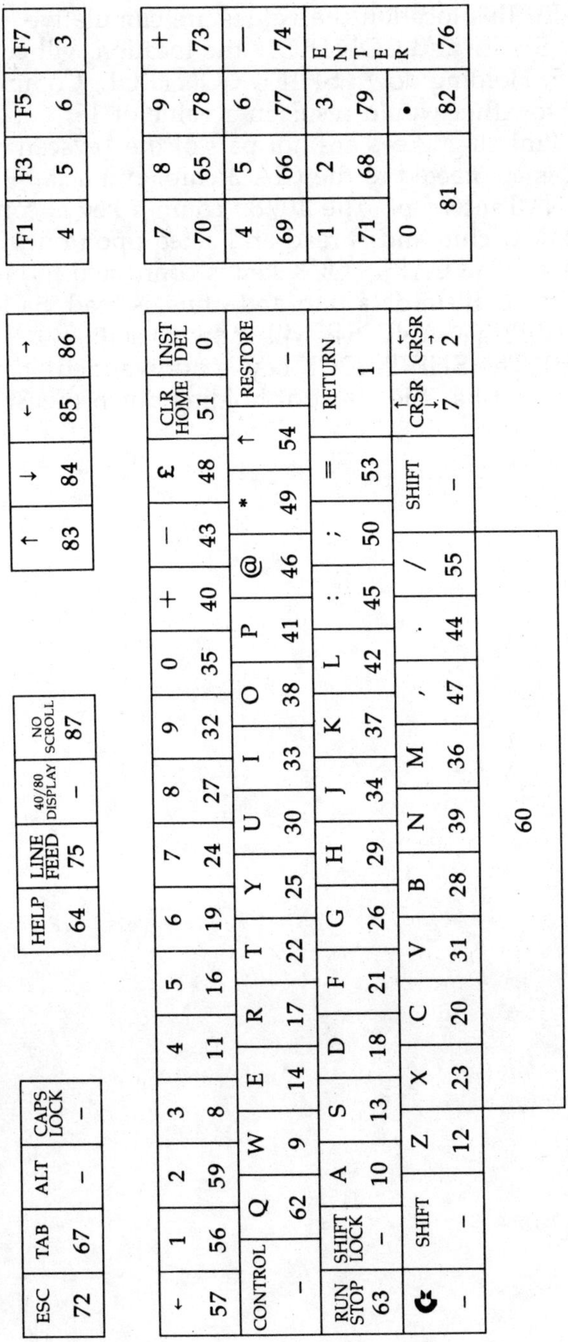

Note that for this location the values are cumulative. If you press both SHIFT and CONTROL, the location will contain 1 + 4 = 5. Holding down SHIFT, CONTROL, Commodore, and ALT together would result in a value of 15.

The other "missing" keys are not part of the keyscan matrix. RESTORE is connected to the CIA 2 chip, and acts by generating an NMI interrupt. The 40/80 column key is connected to the MMU chip and is read and acted upon only at power on or reset. The CAPS LOCK key is connected to bit 6 of the 8502 chip's built-in data port and, thus, is read via location 1. PRINT (PEEK(1) AND 64) will show its status (0 = down, 64 = up). The SHIFT LOCK key is not scanned; it's merely a switch that has the effect of holding down the SHIFT key.

Escape Codes

In 128 mode, each of the letter keys has a special function when preceded by an ESCape keypress. These escape functions perform certain actions on the screen and are especially helpful when you're writing a program. To activate an escape function, press the ESC key, release it, and then press the key associated with the function desired. (You must release ESC before you press the other key; otherwise, the function won't work.) To access escape codes from within a program, PRINT CHR$(27) followed by the appropriate unshifted character—PRINT CHR$(27)"E", for example—would disable the flashing cursor.

Key	Function
ESC-@	Clear from current cursor position to end of screen display.
ESC-A	Enable autoinsert mode (remains active until disabled with ESC-C).
ESC-B	Define bottom of screen window at current cursor position.
ESC-C	Cancel autoinsert mode.
ESC-D	Delete current logical line (may be more than one screen line).
ESC-E	Disable cursor blinking.
ESC-F	Enable cursor blinking.
ESC-G	Enable bell tone when CHR$(7) is printed.
ESC-H	Disable bell tone.
ESC-I	Insert a blank line.
ESC-J	Position cursor at start of line.
ESC-K	Position cursor at end of line.
ESC-L	Enable screen scrolling.
ESC-M	Disable screen scrolling.
ESC-N	Switch to normal video output mode—the opposite of ESC-R (80-column display only).
ESC-O	Disable quote mode and insert modes.
ESC-P	Erase line from current cursor position to start of line.
ESC-Q	Erase line from current cursor position to end of line.
ESC-R	Switch to reverse-video output mode (80-column display only).
ESC-S	Switch to block cursor (80-column display only).
ESC-T	Define top-of-screen window top at current cursor position.
ESC-U	Switch to underline cursor (80-column only).
ESC-V	Scroll display up one line (cursor does not move).
ESC-W	Scroll display down one line (cursor does not move).
ESC-X	Switch display (from 40 to 80 column, or from 80 to 40 column).
ESC-Y	Define tab as eight spaces.
ESC-Z	Clear tab.

Standard ASCII Codes

The most widely recognized character code is ASCII (American Standard Code for Information Interchange). ASCII is a seven-bit code and, thus, can represent 2^7 (128) different characters. CP/M mode uses standard ASCII (although it does add special definitions for the additional characters 128–255).

Most microcomputer telecommunication is also conducted in ASCII. Unfortunately, neither of the two character sets in 128 or 64 mode follows the ASCII standard exactly, so unless you are communicating with another Commodore computer, you'll have to translate the characters you send into ASCII and translate those you receive back into Commodore character codes.

Dec	Hex	Character	Dec	Hex	Character
0	00	NUL	29	1D	GS
1	01	SOH	30	1E	RS
2	02	STX	31	1F	US
3	03	ETX	32	20	space
4	04	EOT	33	21	!
5	05	ENQ	34	22	"
6	06	ACK	35	23	#
7	07	BEL	36	24	$
8	08	BS	37	25	%
9	09	HT	38	26	&
10	0A	LF	39	27	'
11	0B	VT	40	28	(
12	0C	FF	41	29	)
13	0D	CR	42	2A	*
14	0E	SO	43	2B	+
15	0F	SI	44	2C	,
16	10	DLE	45	2D	-
17	11	DC1	46	2E	.
18	12	DC2	47	2F	/
19	13	DC3	48	30	0
20	14	DC4	49	31	1
21	15	NAK	50	32	2
22	16	SYN	51	33	3
23	17	ETB	52	34	4
24	18	CAN	53	35	5
25	19	EM	54	36	6
26	1A	SUB	55	37	7
27	1B	ESC	56	38	8
28	1C	FS	57	39	9

Character, Screen, and Keyboard Codes

<table>
<tr><th>Dec</th><th>Hex</th><th>Character</th></tr>
<tr><td>58</td><td>3A</td><td>:</td></tr>
<tr><td>59</td><td>3B</td><td>;</td></tr>
<tr><td>60</td><td>3C</td><td><</td></tr>
<tr><td>61</td><td>3D</td><td>=</td></tr>
<tr><td>62</td><td>3E</td><td>></td></tr>
<tr><td>63</td><td>3F</td><td>?</td></tr>
<tr><td>64</td><td>40</td><td>@</td></tr>
<tr><td>65</td><td>41</td><td>A</td></tr>
<tr><td>66</td><td>42</td><td>B</td></tr>
<tr><td>67</td><td>43</td><td>C</td></tr>
<tr><td>68</td><td>44</td><td>D</td></tr>
<tr><td>69</td><td>45</td><td>E</td></tr>
<tr><td>70</td><td>46</td><td>F</td></tr>
<tr><td>71</td><td>47</td><td>G</td></tr>
<tr><td>72</td><td>48</td><td>H</td></tr>
<tr><td>73</td><td>49</td><td>I</td></tr>
<tr><td>74</td><td>4A</td><td>J</td></tr>
<tr><td>75</td><td>4B</td><td>K</td></tr>
<tr><td>76</td><td>4C</td><td>L</td></tr>
<tr><td>77</td><td>4D</td><td>M</td></tr>
<tr><td>78</td><td>4E</td><td>N</td></tr>
<tr><td>79</td><td>4F</td><td>O</td></tr>
<tr><td>80</td><td>50</td><td>P</td></tr>
<tr><td>81</td><td>51</td><td>Q</td></tr>
<tr><td>82</td><td>52</td><td>R</td></tr>
<tr><td>83</td><td>53</td><td>S</td></tr>
<tr><td>84</td><td>54</td><td>T</td></tr>
<tr><td>85</td><td>55</td><td>U</td></tr>
<tr><td>86</td><td>56</td><td>V</td></tr>
<tr><td>87</td><td>57</td><td>W</td></tr>
<tr><td>88</td><td>58</td><td>X</td></tr>
<tr><td>89</td><td>59</td><td>Y</td></tr>
<tr><td>90</td><td>5A</td><td>Z</td></tr>
<tr><td>91</td><td>5B</td><td>[</td></tr>
<tr><td>92</td><td>5C</td><td>\</td></tr>
<tr><td>93</td><td>5D</td><td>]</td></tr>
<tr><td>94</td><td>5E</td><td>^</td></tr>
<tr><td>95</td><td>5F</td><td>_</td></tr>
<tr><td>96</td><td>60</td><td>`</td></tr>
<tr><td>97</td><td>61</td><td>a</td></tr>
<tr><td>98</td><td>62</td><td>b</td></tr>
<tr><td>99</td><td>63</td><td>c</td></tr>
<tr><td>100</td><td>64</td><td>d</td></tr>
<tr><td>101</td><td>65</td><td>e</td></tr>
<tr><td>102</td><td>66</td><td>f</td></tr>
<tr><td>103</td><td>67</td><td>g</td></tr>
<tr><td>104</td><td>68</td><td>h</td></tr>
<tr><td>105</td><td>69</td><td>i</td></tr>
<tr><td>106</td><td>6A</td><td>j</td></tr>
<tr><td>107</td><td>6B</td><td>k</td></tr>
<tr><td>108</td><td>6C</td><td>l</td></tr>
<tr><td>109</td><td>6D</td><td>m</td></tr>
<tr><td>110</td><td>6E</td><td>n</td></tr>
<tr><td>111</td><td>6F</td><td>o</td></tr>
<tr><td>112</td><td>70</td><td>p</td></tr>
<tr><td>113</td><td>71</td><td>q</td></tr>
<tr><td>114</td><td>72</td><td>r</td></tr>
<tr><td>115</td><td>73</td><td>s</td></tr>
<tr><td>116</td><td>74</td><td>t</td></tr>
<tr><td>117</td><td>75</td><td>u</td></tr>
<tr><td>118</td><td>76</td><td>v</td></tr>
<tr><td>119</td><td>77</td><td>w</td></tr>
<tr><td>120</td><td>78</td><td>x</td></tr>
<tr><td>121</td><td>79</td><td>y</td></tr>
<tr><td>122</td><td>7A</td><td>z</td></tr>
<tr><td>123</td><td>7B</td><td>{</td></tr>
<tr><td>124</td><td>7C</td><td>|</td></tr>
<tr><td>125</td><td>7D</td><td>}</td></tr>
<tr><td>126</td><td>7E</td><td>~</td></tr>
<tr><td>127</td><td>7F</td><td>DEL</td></tr>
</table>

Notes

1. Codes 0–31 are transmission control codes, and only a few are commonly used in microcomputer telecommunications. These include character 13, the carriage return (RETURN) character, and character 27, the ESCape character (which is frequently used to indicate a command). Some non-Commodore computers require that RETURN be followed by character 10, the linefeed character. Many terminal programs recognize character 19 as XOFF, a signal to halt transmission temporarily. Transmission resumes when character 17, also known as XON, is received. File transfer protocols such as XMODEM use some of the other control codes.
2. For character 94, Commodore uses the up-arrow (↑) in place of the caret (^).

BASIC and Disk Error Messages

This Appendix contains explanations for all of the possible BASIC and disk error messages. Each entry discusses the most likely cause(s) of that particular error and offers some advice (in italics) about how to prevent it.

BASIC Error Messages

This list of error messages includes both the cause of the error and some suggestions for how to fix it. The entries under DS, DS$, EL, ER, ERR$, RESUME, TRAP, TRON, and TROFF in Chapter 1 provide additional information about finding and correcting errors.

BAD DATA (No error number)
This error happens only in 64 mode. It's the same as the 128's FILE DATA error (see below).

BAD DISK (Error 36)
Something is wrong with the disk you're trying to format. The "quick format" command can reformat a previously formatted disk, but it doesn't work on brand new, unformatted disks. You may also have a physically defective disk. *Try again, but include the disk ID (see HEADER for the syntax). If that doesn't work, the disk may be defective, in which case it should be discarded.*

BAD SUBSCRIPT (Error 18)
The subscript used in an array variable is too big or too small. *Look for a variable name followed by a number or variable inside parentheses—the subscript. If the array was not DIMensioned, the subscript must be in the range 0–10. If there is a DIM statement, the subscript was either outside the range specified or the subscript was incorrectly calculated.*

BEND NOT FOUND (Error 37)
Within IF-THEN or IF-THEN-ELSE statements, you can define a BEGIN-BEND block that will execute after a THEN or an ELSE. But each BEGIN must have a corresponding BEND. *Check back for a BEGIN statement that has no BEND.*

BREAK (Error 30)
This isn't really an error message. It means that you've pressed the RUN/STOP key or the program has encountered a STOP statement. *To resume execution after a program has stopped, use the CONT (continue) command.*

CAN'T CONTINUE (Error 26)
After a soft break—caused by the STOP or END statement or by pressing the RUN/STOP key—you can type CONT to make the program continue. But after an error (or if you've edited a line), you can't use CONT. *If you know where the program stopped, you may be able to continue with the GOTO command. If that fails, fix any errors and run the program again.*

CAN'T RESUME (Error 31)
RESUME allows you to continue after an error has occurred, but you must TRAP errors first. If TRAP is not active when you try to RESUME, this error message is printed. *Add a TRAP to your program, preferably near the beginning.*

DEVICE NOT PRESENT (Error 5)
A "device" can be a printer, Datassette, disk drive, or other peripheral you connect to the computer. "Not present" usually means the device hasn't been turned on. *Check the power switch on the disk drive or printer. If it's on, turning it off and then on sometimes works. Otherwise, make sure that it's plugged in and that the cables are inserted correctly.*

DIRECT MODE ONLY (Error 34)
Some BASIC keywords, like AUTO, can be used in immediate (direct) mode only. They cannot be part of a program. *Press the HELP key to see which command is causing the problem.*

DIVISION BY ZERO (Error 20)
It is mathematically impossible to divide by zero. Trying to divide five by zero, for example, should return a number that when multiplied by zero gives five (if 5/0 = X then X*0 = 5). But multiplying by zero always returns a zero, so there's no such number that fits the equation X * 0 = 5. Division by zero is not possible. *If the numbers are being input by the user, use a TRAP statement to check for error 20 and then RESUME back to the input statement. If the numbers are built into the program, you may have to rewrite the formulas being used.*

EXTRA IGNORED (No error number)
This means that an INPUT statement received a line that included a comma. The 128 ignores any input following a comma. This error does not stop program execution and cannot be trapped.

FILE DATA (Error 24)
The program is using INPUT or GET# to read data from a tape or disk file. It's expecting numeric information, but receiving strings or other nonnumeric characters. *Either the file was written incorrectly or something is amiss in the program's input routine. Remember that names of string variables must end in a dollar sign ($).*

FILE NOT FOUND (Error 4)
An attempt to load a program or read a file did not succeed. If you have a disk drive, you may have used the wrong filename, you may have the wrong disk in the drive, or the disk may be brand new and not formatted yet. If you own a cassette drive, it may be that the previous file ended with an end-of-tape marker. *Check the filename and try again. Disk users can type the DIRECTORY command (or just press F3) to see if the desired file is on the disk.*

FILE NOT OPEN (Error 3)
Before you can read from or write to a file, you must OPEN it. And the logical file number (the first number after OPEN) must be specified in PRINT#, INPUT#, and GET# commands. *You may have forgotten to OPEN or DOPEN the file. Or you may have used one logical file number in the OPEN, but a different number after the file-handling statement.*

FILE OPEN (Error 2)
If you try to open a file that's already open, this error appears. Note that it's not illegal to CLOSE a file that's already closed. The simplest fix is to add a CLOSE statement right before the OPEN that led to this error.

FILE READ (Error 41)
Something went wrong when a file was being read. *Check the disk drive door to make sure it is properly closed and try again.*

FORMULA TOO COMPLEX (Error 25)
This error is fairly rare. When you write an equation that uses

a lot of parentheses, the computer has to start with the innermost calculation. There's a limited amount of memory for keeping track of nested calculations, so too many parentheses will lead to this error. *Either simplify the calculation by breaking it down to a few intermediate steps or delete unnecessary parentheses.*

ILLEGAL DEVICE NUMBER (Error 9)
Some peripherals can be used only for input or only for output. You can save a program to disk or tape, but you can't save to the screen or to a printer. *Check the second number after the OPEN statement to make sure you're using the correct device number.*

ILLEGAL DIRECT (Error 21)
This is the opposite of the DIRECT MODE ONLY error. It means that you tried to use in direct mode a command that works only in program mode. Keywords like GET, INPUT, GET#, and INPUT# can appear only inside a program.

ILLEGAL QUANTITY (Error 14)
Certain functions or statements have limits on the range of numbers they can handle. There's no such thing as LOG(0), for example. *If the cause of the error is not immediately obvious, print the numeric variables that appear in the line. A common cause for this error is a READ followed by a POKE. The address being POKEd has to be in the range 0–65535, and the number being POKEd there has to be within 0–255. If you get this message while POKEing values READ from DATA, it's virtually certain that your error is actually in the DATA, not the line with the READ or POKE.*

LINE NUMBER TOO LARGE (Error 38)
The lines in a BASIC program can include whole numbers from 0 to 63999. If you RENUMBER, and the renumbered program would include a line number 64000 or higher, this error results. *Try renumbering with a smaller starting number or a smaller increment.*

LOAD (Error 29)
This error generally occurs when loading programs from tape. When you save to tape, two copies of the program are put on the tape. In a load, the first copy is compared with the second, and if they don't match, this error is returned. *Try again. It*

often helps to move the tape drive away from the magnetism generated by the TV or monitor. You can also try fast-forwarding the tape to the end and then rewinding to the start to remove slack. If load errors continue, either the tape is bad or the read/write heads in the tape drive need to be cleaned and demagnetized.

LOOP NOT FOUND (Error 32)
Every DO that starts a loop needs a corresponding LOOP to mark the end. If a WHILE statement becomes false, an UNTIL becomes true, or an EXIT is executed, the program tries to find a LOOP that marks the end of the DO-LOOP. *Count the number of DOs: There should be an equal number of LOOPs. Also, look for DO-LOOPs inside other DO-LOOPs and make sure they're properly nested.*

LOOP WITHOUT DO (Error 33)
The LOOP statement sends the program back to the DO that initiated the loop. If there's no DO there, it causes this error message. *Add a DO at the beginning of the loop.*

MISSING FILE NAME (Error 8)
You don't need a filename for certain peripherals like printers. And with tape, the filename is optional (but recommended). But when information is read from or written to a disk file, you must provide a name. *Check the OPEN or DOPEN command, and add a filename if it's not there.*

NEXT WITHOUT FOR (Error 10)
A FOR-NEXT loop must begin with a FOR-TO-STEP statement and end with a NEXT. A NEXT by itself doesn't make sense: How can the computer continue a loop that hasn't started? *First check for improperly nested loops. If you have a FOR-NEXT loop inside another, the inner loop should end before the outer loop (the first loop to begin must be the last to finish). Or you may have used GOTO or GOSUB to send the program to the middle of a loop, causing it to perform a NEXT when no FOR is in effect.*

NO GRAPHICS AREA (Error 35)
The GRAPHIC command, followed by a number 1–4, establishes 9K of memory for use by the hi-res graphics screen. CIRCLE, DRAW, and other hi-res commands won't work unless the graphics screen has been set up in advance. Note that hi-res commands will work when the screen is in text mode

(to draw on the hidden graphics screen), as long as GRAPHIC has been used previously. Since GRAPHIC CLR gets rid of the hi-res screen and frees up the 9K of memory, it can lead to this error if you later try to draw something in hi-res.

NOT INPUT FILE (Error 6)
When a sequential or program file is opened, you specify whether you'll be reading or writing. A file opened for writing cannot be read and vice versa. See the next error message.

NOT OUTPUT FILE (Error 7)
You can read a file opened for input with the GET# and INPUT# statements. But you can't use PRINT# to write to such a file. Simply put, an input file won't accept output and an output file can't provide input. Relative files are an exception to this rule; you can read from and write to a relative file at any time.

OUT OF DATA (Error 13)
The READ statement gets information from DATA statements, which are read sequentially from first to last. After the last DATA statement has been read, attempts to READ more data will return this error, unless the RESTORE command has reset the data pointer. *You may have accidentally left out a DATA statement or two, or forgotten a comma. Or you may have typed a period instead of a comma. Look through the DATA statements for typing mistakes.*

OUT OF MEMORY (Error 16)
There are three possible causes for this error. The program (in bank 0) may be too long; the variables (bank 1) may have filled up available memory; or you may have used too many nested FOR-NEXT loops, GOSUBs, or DO-LOOPs. *First PRINT FRE(0), FRE(1) to see how much memory remains for programs and variables. If there's enough memory, the stack has overflowed because of unfinished loops and subroutines. Using GOTO to jump out of loops and subroutines can lead to this error.*

OVERFLOW (Error 15)
The biggest number a 128 can handle is approximately 10↑38—a one followed by 38 zeros. Numbers larger than this cause an OVERFLOW error. *If the overflow happens in the middle of a calculation, you may be able to rewrite the equation, for example, to divide before multiplying.*

REDIM'D ARRAY (Error 19)
The DIM statement establishes the size (DIMension) of an array of variables. Once you set the size of an array, you cannot redimension it while the program is running, unless all variables have been erased with the CLR statement.

REDO FROM START (No error number)
The program is asking for numeric input, but the user has mistakenly entered a string. This error does not stop the program, nor can it be TRAPped. *You can avoid this message by inputting a string and converting it to a number with the VAL function. Or insert a prompt for the user indicating that only numbers should be entered.*

RETURN WITHOUT GOSUB (Error 12)
GOSUB temporarily transfers program flow to a subroutine. RETURN marks the end of the subroutine and sends the program back to the line following the GOSUB. If no GOSUB is in effect, RETURN leads to this error condition. *If you've placed subroutines at the end of the program, it's possible to "drop through" to the first subroutine after the end of the program. The solution is to add an END statement to separate the subroutines from the main program.*

STRING TOO LONG (Error 23)
Strings are not allowed to be longer than 255 characters. *If the line with the error is concatenating strings with the plus (+) sign, the error is caused by a string exceeding 255 characters. If there's an INPUT# in the line, the program is trying to read a file that contains a string longer than 255 characters.*

SYNTAX ERROR (Error 11)
This is one of the most commonly encountered errors. It means that the 128 can't translate what you typed into a legal BASIC command. *Typing HELP (or pressing the HELP key) should show you where the error is. Check the spelling and syntax of the keyword in reverse (in 80-column mode, the mistake is underlined). Make sure you have the right number of opening and closing parentheses and check the punctuation marks—quotation marks, commas, colons, and semicolons. You may also have imbedded a keyword in a variable name. MAINT = 4, for example, would not be allowed, because the INT function is part of the variable name.*

TOO MANY FILES (Error 1)
The 128 can keep track of a maximum of ten files open at the same time. *You'll have to avoid opening more than ten files. Better yet, remember to CLOSE files when you're finished using them.*

TYPE MISMATCH (Error 22)
String functions are designed to handle only strings and string variables. You can't put a numeric variable into a string function. The same goes for numeric functions: You can't find the square root of the word "CLOUD" or set the sound volume to "THUMB." *If you get this message in a line that READs from DATA into a numeric variable, it's virtually certain that your error is actually in the DATA, not the line with the READ. Look for a nonnumeric character in your DATA—the letter O typed where the numeral 0 should appear, for instance.*

UNDEF'D FUNCTION (Error 27)
DEF FN allows you to define a function to be used later in the program. If the program runs into an FN that hasn't been defined, it stops with this error message. *Setup procedures like DIMensioning arrays, establishing a graphics area, and defining functions are best handled in a one-shot routine at the beginning of the program.*

UNDEF'D STATEMENT (Error 17)
An instruction to GOTO, GOSUB, or otherwise transfer control to another line in the program includes a line number that does not exist in the program.

UNIMPLEMENTED COMMAND (Error 40)
The 128 recognizes a keyword as a command that was not added to BASIC 7.0. *You may be able to cause this error by typing QUIT or OFF. Some additional commands were apparently planned, but never added to BASIC.*

UNRESOLVED REFERENCE (Error 39)
When programs are renumbered, GOTOs, GOSUBs, and other related commands are modified. So, if line 200 is renumbered to 170, any instance of GOTO 200 is changed to GOTO 170. But the RENUMBER command will not work if there's a GOTO or GOSUB to a line that does not exist. *Either delete the command referring to a nonexistent line number or add a line, even a simple REM statement, with that number.*

VERIFY (Error 28)
The VERIFY command compares the program in memory with a program saved to tape or disk. If they're not the same, a VERIFY error is returned. *Verifying immediately after saving is a way of testing the reliability of the save. It's especially valuable for checking programs on tape. However, if you execute a GRAPHIC statement to establish a hi-res screen or enter a GRAPHIC CLR to deallocate the screen, the beginning of BASIC can move to a new location. Saving from one location and verifying from another can give you a spurious VERIFY error.*

Disk Error Messages

This is a complete list of all possible disk error messages. Only a few of them appear in ordinary programming. Disk error messages may be read in 128 mode by entering PRINT DS$. In 64 mode, enter and run this short program:

```
10 OPEN 15,8,15:INPUT#15, DS,DS$,T,S
20 PRINT DS,DS$,T,S:CLOSE 15
```

Every disk error message consists of four parts: an error number (0–74), a string of text which explains the error in English, and two numbers which indicate the track and sector locations on the disk which the drive was accessing when the error occurred. The track and sector numbers are important only in certain cases. Some messages don't signal an error. Error 0 shows that all is well; error 1 simply tells you how many files were SCRATCHed; and error 73 usually means that the drive was turned on or reset. Though you're not likely to see them, errors 2–19 are meaningless and can safely be ignored.

0 OK
The most recent disk operation was successful (no errors).

1 FILES SCRATCHED
The last SCRATCH command was successful. The number after the text indicates the number of files scratched. *If you intended to SCRATCH one or more files, but the message indicates no files were scratched, you may need to check the filename and retry the SCRATCH operation.*

(Note: Errors 20–29 are accompanied by two numbers following the text of the error message. These numbers indicate the track and sector the drive was trying to access at the time the error occurred.)

20 READ ERROR
The drive cannot locate the header portion of the sector you tried to access. *You have tried to access a nonexistent sector, or the sector header has been damaged. Make sure that your disk command refers to a legal track and sector.*

21 READ ERROR
The drive cannot find a sync marker for the track that you tried to access. *Make sure you are using a formatted disk, that the drive contains a disk, and that the disk has been properly inserted. This error can also indicate a misaligned disk drive.*

22 READ ERROR
The drive detected a checksum error when reading or writing the header portion of a sector. *You have tried to access a nonexistent track or sector, or the block was written incorrectly. Make sure that your disk command refers to a legal track and sector.*

23 READ ERROR
The drive sensed a checksum error while reading data into its internal memory. *This is not usually a serious error condition. You may be able to read the data into memory and rewrite it to the same sector with a disk editor program; copy the file to another disk (if possible) before attempting this operation. This error can also indicate a simple problem with electrical grounding.*

24 READ ERROR
A hardware error occurred while the drive was reading data or header information into its internal memory. *Check the drive's electrical grounding.*

25 WRITE ERROR
This message is really a VERIFY error. After it writes data to disk, the drive reads it back and compares it with the data in internal memory. *Try repeating the command that caused the error. If it fails again, you may have a bad quality disk, in which case you should copy all files to a new disk and discard the bad one.*

26 WRITE PROTECT ON
You tried to put data on a disk which has tape over the write-protect notch. *Remove the write-protect tape or insert another disk.*

27 READ ERROR
A checksum error occurred while the drive was reading the header of a sector. *This may occur because of electrical grounding problems in the drive.*

28 WRITE ERROR
After the drive wrote data to the disk, it was not able to find sync marks for the next sector. *Either the drive has a mechanical problem or the disk was improperly formatted.*

29 DISK ID MISMATCH
The ID in the drive's internal memory does not match the ID on the disk. *The disk may contain a bad header, or you may simply need to initialize the disk. Try repeating the operation after initializing the disk.*
(Note: In error messages 30–64 the track and sector values are both zero; you may safely ignore the zeros.)

30 SYNTAX ERROR
You sent something over the command channel (15) which DOS does not recognize as a command. *Check the syntax of the disk command and send it again.*

31 SYNTAX ERROR
You sent a command containing a syntax error over the command channel (15). *Check the syntax of the disk command and send it again.*

32 SYNTAX ERROR
You sent a command containing more than 58 characters over the command channel (15). *Split the command into two separate commands or use abbreviations.*

33 SYNTAX ERROR
You used wildcard symbols (* or ?) in a SAVE or OPEN command. *Wildcards are illegal when creating a new file; reissue the command, using the full filename.*

34 SYNTAX ERROR
You left a filename or a colon out of a disk command, or made another syntax error. *Check the syntax of the disk command and send it again.*

39 SYNTAX ERROR
You sent a command containing a syntax error over the command channel (15). *Check the syntax of the disk command and send it again.*

50 RECORD NOT PRESENT
You accessed a relative file record that did not previously exist. *This does not signal an error condition when you are creating a new relative file or expanding an existing relative file. In other cases, it usually means you have failed to position the record pointer correctly before accessing a record. See Chapter 4 for additional details.*

51 OVERFLOW IN RECORD
You tried to write more characters in a relative file record than the record can contain. *Records in relative files have a predetermined length, established when you create the file. Check the record length used in your program, keeping in mind that the carriage return counts as a character. See Chapter 4 for additional details.*

52 FILE TOO LARGE
The disk does not have enough free space to contain the next relative file record. *Either split the file into two separate files (on separate disks) or rewrite your program so that it uses shorter records.*

60 WRITE FILE OPEN
You tried to OPEN a file for reading when it is still open for writing. *CLOSE the file immediately to avoid making it into a splat file. Only relative files can be open for reading and writing at the same time.*

61 FILE NOT OPEN
You tried to read or write to a file before it was OPENed. *OPEN the file properly and reissue the command.*

62 FILE NOT FOUND
You tried to LOAD or BLOAD a program, or OPEN or DOPEN a file for reading, which does not exist on the current disk. *Make sure that the correct disk is in the drive and that you spelled the filename correctly.*

63 FILE EXISTS
You tried to SAVE or BSAVE a program, or OPEN or DOPEN a file for writing, which already exists on the current disk. *Check the spelling of the filename and make sure that you have the correct disk in the drive. Every file on the disk must have a different name.*

64 FILE TYPE MISMATCH
The current disk contains a file with the name you gave, but the file type is different (SEQ, PRG, etc.) from what you specified. *Check the syntax of the command and try it again. Note that certain BASIC commands default to one file type or another.*

(Note: Errors 65–71 are accompanied by two numbers following the text of the error message. These numbers indicate the track and sector the drive was trying to access at the time the error occurred.)

65 NO BLOCK
You issued a Block-Allocate command for a block that's already allocated. *If the disk is not already full (indicated by track number 0), you may be able to use a lower track and sector. The track and sector numbers indicate the next highest available track and sector.*

66 ILLEGAL TRACK AND SECTOR
You tried to access a track and/or sector that does not exist on the disk. *Check the syntax of the disk command and try it again. Chapter 4 explains the organization of Commodore disks.*

67 ILLEGAL SYSTEM T OR S
Illegal system track or sector. *You will probably never see this in ordinary programming.*

70 NO CHANNEL
You tried to open or access more channels than the drive can currently provide. *This error can result from your forgetting to CLOSE a file after it's not needed, or from trying to handle too many files at once (for instance, only one relative file can be open at a time). It can also occur when you use advanced disk commands which require an extra channel in addition to the command channel (15). Either your program contains a logic error or you are trying to do something that's impossible. The zeros after the error text can be ignored.*

71 DIRECTORY ERROR
The BAM (Block Availabilty Map) currently recorded in the drive's internal memory does not match up with the BAM on the current disk. *You may simply need to initialize the disk. If that does not cure the situation, you may have garbled the BAM. Copy all readable files to another disk before attempting to write anything new to the current disk.*

(Note: You may ignore the track and sector values in the following messages.)

72 DISK FULL
You have tried to SAVE or BSAVE a program (or write data to a file) which would take more disk space than is currently available. Or, you have tried to put more than 144 files on the disk. *Scratch unnecessary files or begin using another disk.*

73 DOS VERSION NUMBER
Either you have just turned on or reset the drive (in which case, this simply tells you what version of DOS the drive uses), or you tried to write to a disk that was formatted in a write-incompatible Commodore format. *In most cases this message is harmless. If it occurs after an attempted write operation on a disk which you formatted on your own drive, it probably means you have garbled the DOS version bytes in the disk BAM (see explanation in Chapter 4).*

74 DRIVE NOT READY
The drive contains no disk, or you have left the drive lever or door open, or you are trying to use a disk that was never formatted.

8502 and Z80 Machine Language Opcodes

8502 Instruction Set

Instruction	Description	Flags Affected
ADC	Add to accumulator with carry	N Z C V
AND	AND with accumulator	N Z
ASL	Shift left one bit, bit 0=0	N Z C
BCC	Branch if carry clear (less than)	
BCS	Branch if carry set (greater than)	
BEQ	Branch if equal to zero (Z=1)	
BIT	AND with accumulator, V=bit 6, N=bit 7	N Z V
BMI	Branch if minus (N=1)	
BNE	Branch if not equal to zero (Z=0)	
BPL	Branch if plus (N=0)	
BRK	Break: forced interrupt to IRQ	I
BVC	Branch if overflow clear	
BVS	Branch if overflow set	
CLC	Clear carry	C
CLD	Clear decimal mode	D
CLI	Clear interrupt disable (enable interrupts)	I
CLV	Clear overflow	V
CMP	Compare with accumulator	N Z C
CPX	Compare with X register	N Z C
CPY	Compare with Y register	N Z C
DEC	Decrement	N Z
DEX	Decrement X register	N Z
DEY	Decrement Y register	N Z
EOR	Exclusive-OR with accumulator	N Z
INC	Increment	N Z
INX	Increment X register	N Z
INY	Increment Y register	N Z
JMP	Jump to new address	
JSR	Jump to new address, saving return address	
LDA	Load accumulator	N Z
LDX	Load X register	N Z
LDY	Load Y register	N Z
LSR	Shift right one bit, bit 7=0	N Z C
NOP	No operation	
ORA	OR with accumulator	N Z
PHA	Push accumulator on stack	
PHP	Push status register (flags) on stack	

Instruction	Description	Flags Affected
PLA	Pull accumulator from stack	N Z
PLP	Pull status register (flags) from stack	N Z C I D V
ROL	Rotate one bit left, bit 0=C, C=bit 7	N Z C
ROR	Rotate one bit right, bit 7=C, C=bit 0	N Z C
RTI	Return from interrupt	N Z C I D V
RTS	Return from subroutine	
SBC	Subtract from accumulator with borrow	N Z C V
SEC	Set carry	C
SED	Set decimal mode	D
SEI	Set interrupt disable (disable interrupts)	I
STA	Store accumulator	
STX	Store X register	
STY	Store Y register	
TAX	Transfer accumulator to X register	N Z
TAY	Transfer accumulator to Y register	N Z
TSX	Transfer stack pointer to X register	N Z
TXA	Transfer X register to accumulator	N Z
TXS	Transfer X register to stack pointer	
TYA	Transfer Y register to accumulator	N Z

Addressing Modes

Instruction	Addr Mode	Example	Opcode	Bytes	Cycles
ADC	immediate	ADC #$FF	69	2	2
	zero page	ADC $FF	65	2	3
	zero page, X	ADC $FF,X	75	2	4
	absolute	ADC $FFFF	6D	3	4
	absolute, X	ADC $FFFF,X	75	2	4*
	absolute, Y	ADC $FFFF,Y	79	3	4*
	(indirect, X)	ADC ($FF,X)	61	2	6
	(indirect), Y	ADC ($FF),Y	71	2	5*
AND	immediate	AND #$FF	29	2	2
	zero page	AND $FF	25	2	3
	zero page, X	AND $FF,X	35	2	4
	absolute	AND $FFFF	2D	3	4
	absolute, X	AND $FFFF,X	3D	3	4*
	absolute, Y	AND $FFFF,Y	39	3	4*
	(indirect, X)	AND ($FF,X)	21	2	6
	(indirect), Y	AND ($FF),Y	31	2	5
ASL	accumulator	ASL	0A	1	2
	zero page	ASL $FF	06	2	5
	zero page, X	ASL $FF,X	16	2	6
	absolute	ASL $FFFF	0E	3	6
	absolute, X	ASL $FFFF,X	1E	3	7

8502 and Z80 Machine Language Opcodes

Instruction	Addr Mode	Example	Opcode	Bytes	Cycles
BCC	relative	BCC $FFFF	90	2	2†
BCS	relative	BCS $FFFF	B0	2	2†
BIT	zero page	BIT $FF	24	2	3
	absolute	BIT $FFFF	2C	3	4
BMI	relative	BMI $FFFF	30	2	2†
BNE	relative	BNE $FFFF	D0	2	2†
BPL	relative	BPL $FFFF	10	2	2†
BRK	implied	BRK	00	1	7
BVC	relative	BVC $FFFF	50	2	2†
BVS	relative	BVS $FFFF	70	2	2†
CLC	implied	CLC	18	1	2
CLD	implied	CLD	D8	1	2
CLI	implied	CLI	58	1	2
CLV	implied	CLV	B8	1	2
CMP	immediate	CMP #$FF	C9	2	2
	zero page	CMP $FF	C5	2	3
	zero page, X	CMP $FF,X	D5	2	4
	absolute	CMP $FFFF	CD	3	4
	absolute, X	CMP $FFFF,X	DD	3	4*
	absolute, Y	CMP $FFFF,Y	D9	3	4*
	(indirect, X)	CMP ($FF,X)	C1	2	6
	(indirect), Y	CMP ($FF),Y	D1	2	5*
CPX	immediate	CPX #$FF	E0	2	2
	zero page	CPX $FF	E4	2	3
	absolute	CPX $FFFF	EC	3	4
CPY	immediate	CPY #$FF	C0	2	2
	zero page	CPY $FF	C4	2	3
	absolute	CPY $FFFF	CC	3	4
DEC	zero page	DEC $FF	C6	2	5
	zero page, X	DEC $FF,X	D6	2	6
	absolute	DEC $FFFF	CE	3	6
	absolute, X	DEC $FFFF,X	DE	3	7
DEX	implied	DEX	CA	1	2
DEY	implied	DEY	88	1	2
EOR	immediate	EOR #$FF	49	2	2
	zero page	EOR $FF	45	2	3
	zero page, X	EOR $FF,X	55	2	4
	absolute	EOR $FFFF	4D	3	4
	absolute, X	EOR $FFFF,X	5D	3	4*
	absolute, Y	EOR $FFFF,Y	59	3	4*
	(indirect,X)	EOR ($FF,X)	41	2	6
	(indirect),Y	EOR ($FF),Y	51	2	5*
INC	zero page	INC $FF	E6	2	5
	zero page, X	INC $FF,X	F6	2	6
	absolute	INC $FFFF	EE	3	6
	absolute, X	INC $FFFF,X	FE	3	7

Instruction	Addr Mode	Example	Opcode	Bytes	Cycles
INX	implied	INX	E8	1	2
INY	implied	INY	C8	1	2
JMP	absolute	JMP $FFFF	4C	3	3
	indirect	JMP ($FFFF)	6C	3	5
JSR	absolute	JSR $FFFF	20	3	6
LDA	immediate	LDA #$FF	A9	2	2
	zero page	LDA $FF	A5	2	3
	zero page, X	LDA $FF,X	B5	2	4
	absolute	LDA $FFFF	AD	3	4
	absolute, X	LDA $FFFF,X	BD	3	4*
	absolute, Y	LDA $FFFF,Y	B9	3	4*
	(indirect,X)	LDA ($FF,X)	A1	2	6
	(indirect),Y	LDA ($FF),Y	B1	2	5*
LDX	immediate	LDX #$FF	A2	2	2
	zero page	LDX $FF	A6	2	3
	zero page, Y	LDX $FF,Y	B6	2	4
	absolute	LDX $FFFF	AE	3	4
	absolute, Y	LDX $FFFF,Y	BE	3	4*
LDY	immediate	LDY #$FF	A0	2	2
	zero page	LDY $FF	A4	2	3
	zero page, X	LDY $FF,X	B4	2	4
	absolute	LDY $FFFF	AC	3	4
	absolute, X	LDY $FFFF,X	BC	3	4*
LSR	accumulator	LSR	4A	1	2
	zero page	LSR $FF	46	2	5
	zero page, X	LSR $FF,X	56	2	6
	absolute	LSR $FFFF	4E	3	6
	absolute, X	LSR $FFFF,X	5E	3	7
NOP	implied	NOP	EA	1	2
ORA	immediate	ORA #$FF	09	2	2
	zero page	ORA $FF	05	2	3
	zero page, X	ORA $FF,X	15	2	4
	absolute	ORA $FFFF	0D	3	4
	absolute, X	ORA $FFFF,X	1D	3	4*
	absolute, Y	ORA $FFFF,Y	19	3	4*
	(indirect,X)	ORA ($FF,X)	01	2	6
	(indirect),Y	ORA ($FF),Y	11	2	5*
PHA	implied	PHA	48	1	3
PHP	implied	PHP	08	1	3
PLA	implied	PLA	68	1	4
PLP	implied	PLP	28	1	4
ROL	accumulator	ROL	2A	1	2
	zero page	ROL $FF	26	2	5
	zero page, X	ROL $FF,X	36	2	6
	absolute	ROL $FFFF	2E	3	6
	absolute, X	ROL $FFFF,X	3E	3	7

Instruction	Addr Mode	Example	Opcode	Bytes	Cycles
ROR	accumulator	ROR	6A	1	2
	zero page	ROR $FF	66	2	5
	zero page, X	ROR $FF,X	76	2	6
	absolute	ROR $FFFF	6E	3	6
	absolute, X	ROR $FFFF,X	7E	3	7
RTI	implied	RTI	40	1	6
RTS	implied	RTS	60	1	6
SBC	immediate	SBC #$FF	E9	2	2
	zero page	SBC $FF	E5	2	3
	zero page, X	SBC $FF,X	F5	2	4
	absolute	SBC $FFFF	ED	3	4
	absolute, X	SBC $FFFF,X	F5	2	4*
	absolute, Y	SBC $FFFF,Y	F9	3	4*
	(indirect, X)	SBC ($FF,X)	E1	2	6
	(indirect), Y	SBC ($FF),Y	F1	2	5*
SEC	implied	SEC	38	1	2
SED	implied	SED	F8	1	2
SEI	implied	SEI	78	1	2
STA	zero page	STA $FF	85	2	3
	zero page, X	STA $FF,X	95	2	4
	absolute	STA $FFFF	8D	3	4
	absolute, X	STA $FFFF,X	9D	3	5
	absolute, Y	STA $FFFF,Y	99	3	5
	(indirect,X)	STA ($FF,X)	81	2	6
	(indirect),Y	STA ($FF),Y	91	2	6
STX	zero page	STX $FF	86	2	3
	zero page, Y	STX $FF,Y	96	2	4
	absolute	STX $FFFF	8E	3	4
STY	zero page	STY $FF	84	2	3
	zero page, Y	STY $FF,X	94	2	4
	absolute	STY $FFFF	8C	3	4
TAX	implied	TAX	AA	1	2
TAY	implied	TAY	A8	1	2
TSX	implied	TSX	BA	1	2
TXA	implied	TXA	8A	1	2
TXS	implied	TXS	9A	1	2
TYA	implied	TYA	98	1	2

Notes

* Add one if index crosses a page boundary.

† Add one if branch is taken; add one more if branch crosses a page boundary.

Z80 Instruction Set*

Data Movement Instructions

Z80 Mnemonic	8080 Mnemonic	Object Code	Description
			8-bit load operations
LD reg,reg	MOV reg,reg	01rrrrrr	Copy second register into first
LD reg,(HL)	MOV reg,M	01rrr110	Copy contents of location addressed by HL into register
LD (HL),reg	MOV M,reg	01110rrr	Store register in location addressed by HL
LD reg,data	MVI reg,data	00rrr110 dd	Load register with value
LD (HL),data	MVI M,data	$36 dd	Store value in location addressed by HL
LD A,(addr)	LDA addr	$3A ll hh	Load A register from memory location
LD A,(BC)	LDAX B	$0A	Copy contents of location addressed by BC into A register
LD A,(DE)	LDAX D	$1A	Copy contents of location addressed by DE into A register
LD reg,(IX+disp)	————	$DD 01rrr110 ii	Load register using relative addressing with IX register
LD reg,(IY+disp)	————	$FD 01rrr110 ii	Load register using relative addressing with IY register
LD (IX+disp),reg	————	$DD 01110rrr ii	Store register using relative addressing with IX register
LD (IY+disp),reg	————	$FD 01110rrr ii	Store register using relative addressing with IY register
LD (IX+disp),data	————	$DD $36 ll hh	Store value using relative addressing with IX register
LD (IY+disp),data	————	$FD $36 ll hh	Store value using relative addressing with IX register
LD (addr),A	STA addr	$32 ll hh	Store A register in memory location
LD (BC),A	STAX B	$02	Store A register in memory location addressed by BC register pair
LD (DE),A	STAX D	$12	Store A register in memory location addressed by DE register pair

Z80 Mnemonic	8080 Mnemonic	Object Code	Description
			16-bit load operations
LD rp,data	LXI rp,data	00pp0001 ll hh	Load register pair with value
LD HL,(addr)	LHLD addr	$2a ll hh	Load HL register pair from memory location
LD rp,(addr)	————	$ED 01pp1011 ll hh	Load register pair from memory location
LD IX,data	————	$DD $21 ll hh	Load IX register with 16-bit value
LD IY,data	————	$FD $21 ll hh	Load IY register with 16-bit value
LD IX,(addr)	————	$DD $2A ll hh	Load IX register from memory locations
LD IY,(addr)	————	$FD $2A ll hh	Load IY register from memory locations
LD (addr),HL	SHLD	$22 ll hh	Store HL register pair in memory locations
LD (addr),BC	————	$ED $43 ll hh	Store BC register pair in memory locations
LD (addr),DE	————	$ED $53 ll hh	Store DE register pair in memory locations
LD (addr),SP	————	$ED $73 ll hh	Store stack pointer in memory locations
LD (addr),IX	————	$DD $22 ll hh	Store IX register in memory locations
LD (addr),IY	————	$FD $22 ll hh	Store IY register in memory locations
LD SP,HL	SPHL	$F9	Copy HL register pair into stack pointer
LD SP,IX	————	$DD $F9	Copy IX register into stack pointer
LD SP,IY	————	$FD $F9	Copy IY register into stack pointer
PUSH rp	PUSH rp	11pp0101	Stack contents of register pair
PUSH IX	————	$DD $E5	Stack contents of IX register
PUSH IY	————	$FD $E5	Stack contents of IY register
POP rp	POP rp	11pp0001	Unstack contents of register pair
POP IX	————	$DD $E1	Unstack contents of IX register
POP IY	————	$FD $E1	Unstack contents of IY register

Z80 Mnemonic	8080 Mnemonic	Object Code	Description
			8-bit I/O
IN A,port	IN port	$DB port	Load A register from I/O port
IN reg,(C)	————	$ED 01rrr000	Load register from port address by C register
OUT port,A	OUT port	$D3 port	Output value in A register to I/O port
OUT (C),reg	————	$ED 01rrr001	Output value in register to I/O port addressed by C register
			16-bit exchange operations
EX DE,HL	XCHG	$EB	Exchange contents of DE and HL register pairs
EX (SP),HL	XTHL	$E3	Exchange contents of HL register pair with value at top of stack
EX (SP),IX	————	$DD $E3	Exchange contents of IX register with value at top of stack
EX (SP),IY	————	$FD $E3	Exchange contents of IY register with value at top of stack
EX AF,AF′	————	$08	Exchange program status word with alternate status word
EXX	————	$D9	Exchange BC, DE, and HL register pairs with alternate pairs (BC′, DE′, and HL′)
			Block move operations
LDI	————	$ED $A0	Copy a byte from location addressed by HL register pair to location addressed by DE, increment DE and HL, decrement BC
LDIR	————	$ED $B0	Perform LDI operations until BC register pair is zero
LDD	————	$ED $A8	Copy a byte from location addressed by HL register pair to location addressed by DE, decrement DE and HL, decrement BC
LDDR	————	$ED $B8	Perform LDD operations until BC register pair is zero

Z80 Mnemonic	8080 Mnemonic	Object Code	Description
INI	————	$ED $A2	Store byte from I/O port addressed by C register in memory location addressed by HL register pair, increment HL, decrement B
INIR	————	$ED $B2	Perform INI until B register is zero
IND	————	$ED $AA	Store byte from I/O port addressed by C register in memory location addressed by HL register pair, decrement HL, decrement B
INDR	————	$ED $BA	Perform IND until B register is zero
OUTI	————	$ED $A3	Store byte from memory location addressed by HL register pair in I/O port addressed by C register, increment HL, decrement B
OTIR	————	$ED $B3	Perform OUTI until B register is zero
OUTD	————	$ED $AB	Store byte from memory location addressed by HL register pair in I/O port addressed by C register, decrement HL, decrement B
OTDR	————	$ED $BB	Perform OUTD until B register is zero

Control Transfer Instructions

Z80 Mnemonic	8080 Mnemonic	Object Code	Description
			Subroutine call instructions
CALL addr	CALL addr	$CD ll hh	Call subroutine, saving program counter on stack
CALL C,addr	CC addr	$DC ll hh	Call subroutine if carry flag is set
CALL NC,addr	CNC addr	$D4 ll hh	Call subroutine if carry flag is clear
CALL Z,addr	CZ addr	$CC ll hh	Call subroutine if zero flag is set
CALL NZ,addr	CNZ addr	$C4 ll hh	Call subroutine if zero flag is clear
CALL M,addr	CM addr	$FC ll hh	Call subroutine if minus flag is set

Z80 Mnemonic	8080 Mnemonic	Object Code	Description
CALL P,addr	CP addr	$F4 ll hh	Call subroutine if minus flag is clear
CALL PE,addr	CPE addr	$EC ll hh	Call subroutine if parity is even
CALL PO,addr	CPO addr	$E4 ll hh	Call subroutine if parity is odd
			Absolute jump instructions
JP addr	JMP addr	$C3 ll hh	Jump to address
JP C,addr	JC addr	$DA ll hh	Jump if carry
JP NC,addr	JNC addr	$D2 ll hh	Jump if no carry
JP Z,addr	JZ addr	$CA ll hh	Jump if zero
JP NZ,addr	JNZ addr	$C2 ll hh	Jump if not zero
JP M,addr	JM addr	$FA ll hh	Jump if minus
JP P,addr	JP addr	$F2 ll hh	Jump if plus
JP PE,addr	JPE addr	$EA ll hh	Jump if parity is even
JP PO,addr	JPO addr	$E2 ll hh	Jump if parity is odd
JP (HL)	PCHL	$E9	Jump to address in HL register pair
JP (IX)	———	$DD $E9	Jump to address in IX register
JP (IY)	———	$FD $E9	Jump to address in IY register
			Relative jump instructions
JR disp	———	$18 ii	Relative jump—add signed offset to program counter and jump to resulting address
JR C,disp	———	$38 ii	Jump relative if carry
JR NC,disp	———	$30 ii	Jump relative if no carry
JR Z,disp	———	$28 ii	Jump relative if zero
JR NZ,disp	———	$20 ii	Jump relative if not zero
DJNZ disp	———	$10 ii	Decrement B register and jump relative if result is not zero
			Return instructions
RET	RET	$C9	Return from subroutine call
RET C	RC	$D8	Return from subroutine if carry
RET NC	RNC	$D0	Return from subroutine if no carry
RET Z	RZ	$C8	Return from subroutine if zero
RET NZ	RNZ	$C0	Return from subroutine if not zero
RET M	RM	$F8	Return from subroutine if minus
RET P	RP	$F0	Return from subroutine if plus
RET PE	RPE	$E8	Return from subroutine if even parity
RET PO	RPO	$E0	Return from subroutine if odd parity
RST n	RST n	11nnn111	Jump to restart vector

Z80 Mnemonic	8080 Mnemonic	Object Code	Description
RETI	———	$ED $4D	Return from maskable hardware interrrupt
RETN	———	$ED $45	Return from non-maskable hardware interrupt

Arithmetic and Logical Instructions

Z80 Mnemonic	8080 Mnemonic	Object Code	Description
			8-bit arithmetic operations
ADC reg	ADC reg	10001rrr	Add register to A register and increment A register if carry flag is set
ADC (HL)	ADC M	$8E	Add carry flag and memory location addressed by HL register pair to A register
ADC data	ACI data	$CE dd	Add value and carry flag to A register
ADC (IX+disp)	———	$DD $8E ii	Add memory location and carry flag to A register using relative addressing with IX register
ADC (IY+disp)	———	$FD $8E ii	Add memory location and carry flag to A register using relative addressing with IY register
ADD reg	ADD reg	10000rrr	Add register to A register
ADD (HL)	ADD M	$86	Add memory location addressed by HL register pair to A register
ADD data	ADI data	$C6 dd	Add value to A register
ADD (IX+disp)	———	$DD $86 ii	Add memory to A register using relative addressing with IX register
ADD (IY+disp)	———	$FD $86 ii	Add memory to A register using relative addressing with IY register
AND reg	ANA reg	10100rrr	Logical AND register with A register
AND (HL)	ANA M	$A6	Logical AND memory location addressed by HL register pair with A register
AND data	ANI data	$E6 dd	Logical AND value with A register
AND (IX+disp)	———	$DD $A6 ii	Logical AND memory location with A register using relative addressing with IX register

Appendix C

Z80 Mnemonic	8080 Mnemonic	Object Code	Description
AND (IY+disp)	————	$FD $A6 ii	Logical AND memory location with A register using relative addressing with IY register
CP reg	CMP reg	10111rrr	Compare A register with another register
CP (HL)	CMP M	$BE	Compare A register with memory location addressed by HL register pair
CP data	CPI data	$FE dd	Compare A register with value
CP (IX+disp)	————	$DD $BE ii	Compare A register with memory location using relative addressing with IX register
CP (IY+disp)	————	$FD $BE ii	Compare A register with memory location using relative addressing with IY register
OR reg	ORA reg	10110rrr	Logical OR register with A register
OR (HL)	ORA M	$B6	Logical OR memory location addressed by HL register pair with A register
OR data	ORI data	$F6 dd	Logical OR value with A register
OR (IX+disp)	————	$DD $B6 ii	Logical OR memory location with A register using relative addressing with IX register
OR (IY+disp)	————	$FD $B6 ii	Logical OR memory location with A register using relative addressing with IY register
SBC reg	SBB reg	10011rrr	Subtract register and carry flag from A register
SBC (HL)	SBB M	$9E	Subtract carry flag and memory location addressed by HL register pair from A register
SBC data	SBI data	$DE dd	Subtract value and carry flag from A register
SBC (IX+disp)	————	$DD $9E ii	Subtract memory location and carry flag from A register using relative addressing with IX register
SBC (IY+disp)	————	$FD $9E ii	Subtract memory location and carry flag from A register using relative addressing with IY register

Z80 Mnemonic	8080 Mnemonic	Object Code	Description
SUB reg	SUB reg	10010rrr	Subtract register from A register
SUB (HL)	SUB M	$96	Subtract memory location addressed by HL register pair from A register
SUB data	SUI data	$D6 dd	Subtract value from A register
SUB (IX+disp)	________	$DD $96 ii	Subtract memory location from A register using relative addressing with IX register
SUB (IY+disp)	________	$FD $96 ii	Subtract memory location from A register using relative addressing with IY register
XOR reg	XRA reg	10101rrr	Exclusive-OR register with A register
XOR (HL)	XRA M	$AE	Exclusive-OR memory location addressed by HL register pair with A register
XOR data	XRI data	$EE dd	Exclusive-OR value with A register
XOR (IX+disp)	________	$DD $AE ii	Exclusive-OR memory location with A register using relative addressing with IX register
XOR (IY+disp)	________	$FD $AE ii	Exclusive-OR memory location with A register using relative addressing with IY register
DEC reg	DCR reg	00rrr101	Decrement register
DEC (HL)	DCR M	$35	Decrement memory location addressed by HL register pair
DEC (IX+disp)	________	$DD $35 ii	Decrement memory location using relative addressing with IX register
DEC (IY+disp)	________	$FD $35 ii	Decrement memory location using relative addressing with IY register
INC reg	INR reg	00rrr100	Increment register
INC (HL)	INR M	$34	Increment memory location addressed by HL register pair
INC (IX+disp)	________	$DD $34 ii	Increment memory location using relative addressing with IX register
INC (IY+disp)	________	$FD $34 ii	Increment memory location using relative addressing with IY register
CPL	CMA	$2F	Complement A register
DAA	DAA	$27	Adjust A register for decimal arithmetic

Z80 Mnemonic	8080 Mnemonic	Object Code	Description
NEG	————	$ED $44	Negate A register
			16-bit arithmetic operations
ADC HL,rp	————	$ED 01pp1010	Add register pair and carry flag to HL register pair
ADD HL,rp	DAD rp	00pp1001	Add register pair to HL register pair
ADD IX,rp	————	$DD 00pp1001	Add register pair to IX register
ADD IY,rp	————	$FD 00pp1001	Add register pair to IY register
SBC HL,rp	————	$ED 01pp0010	Subtract register pair and carry flag from A register
DEC rp	DCX rp	00pp1011	Decrement register pair
DEC IX	————	$DD $2B	Decrement IX register
DEC IY	————	$FD $2B	Decrement IY register
INC rp	INX rp	00pp0011	Increment register pair
INC IX	————	$DD $23	Increment IX register
INC IY	————	$FD $23	Increment IY register
			Rotate and shift operations
RLA	RAL	$17	Rotate A register left through carry bit
RL reg	————	$CB 00010rrr	Rotate register left through carry bit
RL (HL)	————	$CB $16	Rotate memory location addressed by HL register pair left through carry bit
RL (IX+disp)	————	$DD $CB ii $16	Rotate memory location left through carry bit using relative addressing with IX register
RL (IY+disp)	————	$FD $CB ii $16	Rotate memory location left through carry bit using relative addressing with IY register
RLCA	RLC	$07	Rotate A register left, circular (without carry bit)
RLC reg	————	$CB 00000rrr	Rotate register left, circular
RLC (HL)	————	$CB $06	Rotate memory location addressed by HL register pair left, circular
RLC (IX+disp)	————	$DD $CB ii $06	Rotate memory location left using relative addressing with IX register, circular
RLC (IY+disp)	————	$FD $CB ii $06	Rotate memory location left using relative addressing with IY register, circular

Z80 Mnemonic	8080 Mnemonic	Object Code	Description
RRA	RAR	$1F	Rotate A register right through carry bit
RR reg	___________	$CB 00011rrr	Rotate memory location addressed by HL register pair right through carry bit
RR (HL)	___________	$CB $1E	Rotate register right through carry bit
RR (IX+disp)	___________	$DD $CB ii $1E	Rotate memory location right through carry bit using relative addressing with IX register
RR (IY+disp)	___________	$FD $CB ii $1E	Rotate memory location right through carry bit using relative addressing with IY register
RRCA	RRC	$0F	Rotate A register right, circular (without carry bit)
RRC reg	___________	$CB 00001rrr	Rotate register right, circular
RRC (HL)	___________	$CB $0E	Rotate memory location addressed by HL register pair right, circular
RRC (IX+disp)	___________	$DD $CB ii $0E	Rotate memory location right, circular using relative addressing with IX register
RRC (IY+disp)	___________	$FD $CB ii $0E	Rotate memory location right, circular using relative addressing with IY register
SLA reg	___________	$CB 00100rrr	Shift A register left
SLA (HL)	___________	$CB $2E	Shift memory location addressed by HL register pair left
SLA (IX+disp)	___________	$DD $CB ii $2E	Shift memory location left using relative addressing with IX register
SLA (IY+disp)	___________	$FD $CB ii $2E	Shift memory location left using relative addressing with IY register
SRA reg	___________	$CB 00101rrr	Shift A register right with sign extension
SRA (HL)	___________	$CB $3E	Shift memory location addressed by HL register pair right with sign extension
SRA (IX+disp)	___________	$DD $CB ii $3E	Shift memory location right with sign extension using relative addressing with IX register

Z80 Mnemonic	8080 Mnemonic	Object Code	Description
SRA (IY+disp)	________	$FD $CB ii $3E	Shift memory location right with sign extension using relative addressing with IY register
			Decimal rotate operations
RLD	________	$ED $6F	Rotate left decimal (unpack binary coded decimal)
RRD	________	$ED $67	Rotate right decimal (pack binary coded decimal)
			Bit manipulation operations
BIT bit,reg	________	$CB 01nnnrrr	Test value of a bit in register
BIT bit,(HL)	________	$CB 01nnn110	Test bit in byte addressed by HL
BIT bit,(IX+disp)	________	$DD $CB ii 01nnn110	Test bit using relative addressing with IX register
BIT bit,(IY+disp)	________	$FD $CB ii 01nnn110	Test bit using relative addressing with IY register
RES bit,reg	________	$CB 10nnnrrr	Clear (reset) a bit in register
RES bit,(HL)	________	$CB 10nnn110	Clear bit in byte addressed by HL
RES bit,(IX+disp)	________	$DD $CB ii 10nnn110	Clear bit using relative addressing with IX register
RES bit,(IY+disp)	________	$FD $CB ii 10nnn110	Clear bit using relative addressing with IX register
SET bit,reg	________	$CB 11bbbnnn	Set bit in register
SET bit,(HL)	________	$CB 11nnn110	Set bit in byte addressed by HL
SET bit,(IX+disp)	________	$DD $CB ii 11nnn110	Set bit using relative addressing with IX register
SET bit,(IY+disp)	________	$FD $CB ii 11nnn110	Set bit using relative addressing with IY register
CCF	CMC	$3F	Complement carry flag
SCF	STC	$37	Set carry flag

Processor Control Instructions

Z80 Mnemonic	8080 Mnemonic	Object Code	Description
HALT	HALT	$76	Stop executing instructions
NOP	NOP	$00	Fetch this byte and increment program counter, but do nothing else
DI	______	$F3	Inhibit hardware interrupt
EI	______	$FB	Enable hardware interrupt
LD A,I	______	$ED $57	Move contents of interrupt base vector to A register
LD I,A	______	$ED $47	Move contents of A register to interrupt base vector
LD A,R	______	$ED $5F	Move contents of DRAM refresh register to A register
LD R,A	______	$ED $4F	Move contents of A register ro DRAM refresh register
IM 0	______	$ED $46	Set interrupt mode 0
IM 1	______	$ED $56	Set interrupt mode 1
IM 2	______	$ED $5E	Set interrupt mode 2

***Legend for Object Code Subfields**

addr—Instruction contains the two-byte address (ll hh) of a memory location.

bit—The bit-handling instructions (BIT, RES, and SET) contain a three-bit field (bbb) to select one of the eight bits in the target byte.

data—Included in object code as one (dd) or two (ll hh) bytes.

disp—Data contained in the object code represents a one-byte, signed integer (ii) to be added to either the program counter, on relative jumps, or an index register. Possible values range from −128 ($80) to 127 ($7F).

n—There are possible Restart instructions, numbered 0–7, indicated with three bits (nnn).

port—One byte of data in the object code indicates which I/O port (0—255) is to be used.

reg—Three-bit field (rrr) which selects an eight-bit register. Here are the possible values:

B	000	H	100
C	001	L	101
D	010	(HL)	110
E	011	A	111

rp—Sixteen-bit register pairs are selected with a two-bit field (pp). Here are the possible values:

BC	00
DE	01
HL	10
SP	11

Memory Map

The numbers in brackets ([ ]) following each entry show the corresponding Commodore 64 locations. An asterisk in brackets ([*]) indicates that the location is the same as in the 64.

0–255 ($0000–$00FF) Zero Page

0	$00	8502 I/O port data direction register [*]
1	$01	8502 I/O port data register [*]
2	$02	Bank value storage for JMPFAR and JSRFAR
3–4	$03–$04	Program counter storage for JMPFAR and JSRFAR
5	$05	Stack register storage for JMPFAR and JSRFAR
6	$06	Accumulator storage for JMPFAR and JSRFAR
7	$07	X register storage for JMPFAR and JSRFAR
8	$08	Y register storage for JMPFAR and JSRFAR
9	$09	Stack pointer storage for JMPFAR and JSRFAR
45–46	$2D–$2E	Pointer to start of BASIC program text (in bank 0) [43–44/$2B–$2C]
47–48	$2F–$30	Pointer to start of variables (in bank 1) [45–46/$2D–$2E]
49–50	$31–$32	Pointer to start of arrays (in bank 1) [47–48/$2F–$30]
51–52	$33–$34	Pointer to start of free memory (in bank 1) [49–50/$31–$32]
53–54	$35–$36	Pointer to bottom of dynamic string storage (in bank 1) [51–52/$33–$34]
55–56	$37–$38	Pointer to most recently used string (in bank 1) [53–54/$35–$36]
57–58	$39–$3A	Pointer to top of dynamic string storage (in bank 1) [55–56/$37–$38]
59–60	$3B–$3C	Current BASIC line number [57–58/$39–$3A]
61–62	$3D–$3E	Pointer to current BASIC text character [122–123/$7A–$7B]
65–66	$41–$42	Current DATA line number [63–64/$3F–$40]
67–68	$43–$44	Pointer to current DATA item [65–66/$41–$42]
71–72	$47–$48	Pointer to current BASIC variable name [69–70/$47–$48]
73–74	$49–$4A	Pointer to current variable contents
99–104	$63–$68	Floating-point accumulator 1 (FAC1) [97–102/$61–$66]
106–111	$6A–$6F	Floating-point accumulator 2 (FAC2) [105–110/$69–$6E]
125–126	$7D–$7E	Pointer into BASIC runtime stack at $0800–$09FF
144	$90	Status byte for tape and serial I/O (see discussion of ST in Chapter 1) [*]
145	$91	STOP key flag (127 = RUN/STOP key pressed) [*]
152	$98	Number of files currently opened [*]
153	$99	Current input device [*]
154	$9A	Current output device [*]
157	$9D	Kernal message flag (192 = Kernal control and error messages displayed, 128 = only control messages displayed, 64 = only error messages displayed, 0 = no messages displayed) [*]

160–162	$A0–$A2	Software jiffy clock [*]
172–173	$AC–$AD	Working pointer for LOAD, SAVE, and VERIFY [*]
174–175	$AE–$AF	Ending address for LOAD, SAVE, and VERIFY [*]
178–179	$B2–$B3	Pointer to cassette buffer [*]
183	$B7	Length of current filename [*]
184	$B8	Current logical file number (channel) [*]
185	$B9	Current secondary address [*]
186	$BA	Current device number [*]
187–188	$BB–$BC	Address of current filename [*]
193–195	$C1–$C2	Starting address for SAVE, LOAD, and VERIFY [*]
195–196	$C3–$C4	Starting address of memory to be loaded or saved to tape [*] Also used as a pointer during block memory moves
198	$C6	Bank for current LOAD, SAVE, or VERIFY operation
199	$C7	Bank where current filename is found
200–201	$C8–$C9	Pointer to RS-232 input buffer [247–248/$F7–$F8]
202–203	$CA–$CB	Pointer to RS-232 output buffer [249–250/$F9–$FA]
204–204	$CC–$CD	Pointer to current keyboard lookup table (in ROM) [243–244/$F3–$F4]
208	$D0	Number of characters in keyboard buffer [198/$C6]
211	$D3	Current SHIFT, CONTROL, Commodore, and ALT key status (see Appendix A) [653/028D]
212	$D4	Matrix coordinate of current key pressed (see Appendix A) [203/$CB]
213	$D5	Matrix coordinate of last key pressed [197/$C5]
215	$D7	Screen width flag (0 = 40 columns, 128 = 80 columns)
216	$D8	Text/graphics mode flag for 40-column screen: 224 = graphic 4 (split multicolor bitmapped and text) 160 = graphic 3 (multicolor bitmapped) 96 = graphic 2 (split bitmapped and text) 32 = graphic 1 (bitmapped) 0 = graphic 0 (text)
217	$D9	Shadow register for CHREN bit of location $01 (4 = I/O block at $D000–$DFFF, 0 = Character ROM at $D000–$DFFF)
224–225	$E0–$E1	Pointer to current text screen line [209–210/$D1–$D2]
226–227	$E2–$E3	Pointer to current color (attribute) line [243–244/$F3–$F4]
228	$E4	Bottom line of current window
229	$E5	Top line of current window
230	$E6	Left margin of current window
231	$E7	Right margin of current window
232	$E8	Line for input [201/$C9]
233	$E9	Starting logical column for input [202/$CA]
234	$EA	Ending logical column for input [200/$C8]
235	$EB	Current cursor line [214/$D6]
236	$EC	Current cursor column [211/$D3]

237	$ED	Maximum number of lines in screen
238	$EE	Maximum number of columns in a line [213/$D5]
243	$F3	Reverse mode flag (if nonzero, characters are printed in reverse video) [199/$C7]
244	$F4	Quote mode flag (if nonzero, quote mode is in effect) [212/$D4]
245	$F5	Insert mode flag (if nonzero, number of inserts pending) [216/$D8]
247	$F7	Enable/disable character set switching with SHIFT-Commodore (128 = disable switching, 0 = enable switching) [657/$0291]
248	$F8	Enable/disable screen scrolling (128 = no scrolling, 0 = allow scrolling)
250–254	$FA–$FE	Unused [251–245/$FB–$FE]

256–511 ($0100–$01FF) Page One—System Stack

512–1023 ($0200–$03FF) Common RAM Vectors and Routines

512–673	$0200–$02A1	BASIC input buffer (161 bytes) [512–600/$0200–$0258]
674–686	$02A2–$02AE	INDFET routine to get a character from any bank
687–701	$02AF–$02BD	INDSTA routine to store a character in any bank
702–716	$02BE–$02CC	INDCMP routine to compare characters in any banks
717–738	$02CD–$02E2	JSRFAR routine to jump to a subroutine in any bank and return to the calling bank
739–761	$02E3–$02F9	JMPFAR routine to jump to a routine in any bank without return
768–769	$0300–$0301	IERROR vector to BASIC error message routine [*]
770–771	$0302–$0303	IMAIN vector to main BASIC immediate mode loop [*]
772–773	$0304–$0305	ICRNCH vector to routine that tokenizes a line of BASIC text [*]
774–775	$0306–$0307	IQPLOP vector to routine that lists a token as characters [*]
776–777	$0308–$0309	IGONE vector to routine that executes a BASIC statement token [*]
778–779	$030A–$030B	IEVAL vector to outine that evaluates an arithmetic expression [*]
780–781	$030C–$030D	Vector to routine that tokenizes a two-byte token
782–783	$030E–$030F	Vector to routine that lists a two-byte token as characters
784–785	$0310–$0311	Vector to routine that executes a two-byte BASIC statement token
788–789	$0314–$0315	CINV vector to IRQ handler routine [*]
790–791	$0316–$0317	CBINV vector to BRK handler routine [*]
792–793	$0318–$0319	NMINV vector to NMI handler routine [*]
794–795	$031A–$031B	IOPEN vector to the Kernal OPEN routine [*]
796–797	$031C–$031D	ICLOSE vector to the Kernal CLOSE routine [*]

798–799	$031E–$031F	ICHKIN vector to the Kernal CHKIN routine [*]
800–801	$0320–$0321	ICKOUT vector to the Kernal CKOUT routine [*]
802–803	$0322–$0323	ICLRCH vector to the Kernal CHRCH routine [*]
804–804	$0324–$0325	IBASIN vector to the Kernal BASIN routine [*]
806–807	$0326–$0327	IBSOUT vector to the Kernal BSOUT routine [*]
808–809	$0328–$0329	ISTOP vector to the Kernal STOP routine [*]
810–811	$032A–$032B	IGETIN vector to the Kernal GETIN routine [*]
812–813	$032C–$032D	ICLALL vector to the Kernal CLALL routine [*]
814–815	$0330–$0331	ILOAD vector to the Kernal LOAD routine [*]
816–817	$032C–$032D	ISAVE vector to the Kernal SAVE routine [*]
842–851	$034A–$0353	Keyboard input buffer [631–640/$0277–$0280]
866–875	$0362–036B	Table of logical file numbers [601–610/$0259–$0262]
876–885	$036C–$0375	Table of device numbers for open files [611–620/$0263–$026C]
886–895	$0376–$037F	Table of secondary addresses for open files [621–630/$026D–$0276]
896–926	$0380–$039E	Routine to get next character of BASIC program text from bank 0 (CHRGET) [115–138/$73–$8A]
902	$0386	Entry point in CHRGET to retrieve previous character (CHRGOT) [121/$79]
927–938	$039F–$03AA	Indirect fetch from bank 0 for ROM routines
939–950	$03AB–$03B6	Indirect fetch from bank 1 for ROM routines
951–959	$03B7–$03BF	Fetch from bank 1 for ROM routines; uses $24–$25 as pointer
960–968	$03C0–$03C8	Fetch from bank 0 for ROM routines; uses $26–$27 as pointer
969–977	$03C9–$03D1	Fetch from bank 0 for ROM routines; uses $3D–$3E as pointer

1024–2047 ($0400–$07FF) 40-Column Text Screen Memory

2048–7167 ($0800–$1BFF) Bank 0: BASIC and Kernal Working Storage

2048–2559	$0800–$09FF	BASIC stack: pointers for DO-LOOP, BEGIN-BEND, etc.
2560–2561	$0A00–$0A00	System restore vector (points to BASIC warm-start routine)
2562	$0A02	Flag to indicate that system vector has been initialized
2563	$0A03	PAL/NTSC flag (0 = NTSC video, 1 = PAL video) [678/$02A6]
2565–2566	$0A05–$0A06	Bottom of memory used for program text (in bank 0) [641–642/$0281–$0282]
2567–2568	$0A07–$0A08	Top of memory used for variables (in bank 1) [643–644/$0283–$0284]
2576	$0A10	RS-232 control register [659/$0293]
2577	$0A11	RS-232 command register [660/$0294]
2578–2579	[4]$0A12–$0A13	RS-232 user-defined baud rate [661–662/$0295–$0296]

2580	$0A14	RS-232 status register [663/$0297]
2582–2583	$0A16–$0A17	RS-232 baud timing constant value [665–666/$0299–$029A]
2584	$0A18	Index to last character in the RS-232 input buffer [667/$029B]
2585	$0A19	Index to first character in the RS-232 input buffer [668/$029C]
2586	$0A1A	Index to last character in the RS-232 output buffer [669/$029D]
2587	$0A1B	Index to first character in the RS-232 output buffer [670/$029E]
2592	$0A20	Maximum number of characters in the keyboard buffer [649/$0289]
2594	$0A22	Enable/disable key repeating (128 = all keys repeat, 64 = no keys repeat, 0 = space, INST/DEL, and cursor keys delete) [650/$028A]
2624–2687	$0A40–$0A7F	Storage area for screen editor variables during 40/80-column screen display exchanges
2752	$0AC0	Number of function ROMs present
2753–2756	$0AC1–$0AC4	Table of function ROM identifier bytes
2816–3007	$0B00–$0BBF	Cassette buffer [828–1019/$33C–$03FB]
2816–3071	$0B00–$0BFF	Holds image of boot sector during disk boot
3072–3327	$0C00–$0CFF	RS-232 input buffer
3328–3583	$0D00–$0DFF	RS-232 output buffer
3584–4095	$0E00–$0FFF	Sprite definition area
4096–4105	$1000–$1009	Table of indexes to function key definitions
4106–4351	$100A–$10FF	Storage area for function key definitions
4616	$1208	Error number for last error
4617–4618	$1209–$120A	Line number where last error occurred
4624–4625	$1210–$1211	Pointer to end of BASIC program text (in bank 0)
4626–4627	$1212–$1214	Pointer to top of memory for BASIC program text (in bank 0)
4632–4634	$1218–$121A	JSR and address for USR statement

2024–65279 ($0800–$FEFF) Bank 1: BASIC Variable Storage

7168–65279 ($1C00–$FEFF) Bank 0: BASIC Program Text Storage

7168–16383 ($1C00–$3FFF) Bank 0: 40-Column High-Resolution Screen and Color Memory (if used)

7168–8191	$1C00–$1FFF	Color memory for bitmapped screen
8192–16383	$2000–$3FFF	Bitmap for high-resolution screen

16348–45055 ($4000–$AFFF) BASIC ROM

16343	$4000	BASIC cold-start vector
16346	$4003	BASIC warm-start vector
16349	$4006	BASIC IRQ entry vector

45056–49151 ($B000–$BFFF) Machine Language Monitor ROM

45056	$B000	Monitor cold-start vector
45059	$B003	Monitor BRK entry vector

49152–53247 ($C000–$CFFF) Screen Editor ROM

Editor Jump Table

49152	$C000	Initialize screen editor and video chips (Kernal CINT)
49155	$C003	Display a character
49158	$C006	Get a key from keyboard buffer (GETIN from keyboard)
49161	$C009	Get a character from the screen (BASIN from screen)
49164	$C00C	Print a character on the screen (BSOUT to screen)
49167	$C00F	Return number of lines and columns in current window (Kernal SCRORG)
49170	$C012	Scan keyboard for keypress (Kernal KEY)
49173	$C015	Check for key repeat
49176	$C018	Read or set cursor position (Kernal PLOT)
49179	$C01B	Move cursor on 80-column screen
49182	$C01E	Handle ESC key sequences
49185	$C021	Define a programmable key (Kernal PFKEY)
49188	$C024	Editor IRQ entry vector
49191	$C027	Initialize character set for 80-column display (Kernal DLCHR)
49194	$C02A	Switch between 40- and 80-column displays (Kernal SWAPPER)
49197	$C02D	Set window boundaries

53248–57343 ($D000–$DFFF) Character ROM

53248–54271	$D000–$D3FF	Uppercase/graphics set definitions (normal)
54272–55295	$D400–$D7FF	Uppercase/graphics set definitions (reverse video)
55296–56319	$D800–$DBFF	Lowercase/uppercase set definitions (normal)
56320–57343	$DC00–$DFFF	Lowercase/uppercase set definitions (reverse video)

53248–57343 ($D000–$DFFF) I/O Block

53248–53296	$D000–$D030	VIC 40-column video chip
54272–54300	$D400–$D41C	SID sound chip
54528–54539	$D500–$D50B	MMU memory management chip
54784–54785	$D600–$D601	8563 80-column video chip
55296–56319	$D800–$DBFF	Color memory for 40-column screen
56320–56335	$DC00–$DC0F	CIA input/output chip 1
56576–56591	$DD00–$DD0F	CIA input/output chip 2
56832–57087	$DE00–$DEFF	Expansion I/O slot (unused)
57088–57098	$DF00–$DF0A	REC expansion memory controller chip in memory expansion module

57344–65535 ($E000–$FFFF) Kernal ROM

New Kernal Jump Table Entries for the 128

65351	$FF47	SPIN_SPOUT	Set serial ports for fast input or output
65354	$FF4A	CLOSE_ALL	Close all files to a device
65357	$FF4D	C64MODE	Enter 64 mode
65360	$FF50	DMA_CALL	Send command to DMA device
65363	$FF53	BOOT_CALL	Boot a program from disk
65366	$FF56	PHOENIX	Initialize function ROM cartridges
65369	$FF59	LKUPLA	Look up logical file number in file tables
65372	$FF5C	LKUPSA	Look up secondary address in file tables
65375	$FF5F	SWAPPER	Switch between 40- and 80-column displays
65378	$FF62	DLCHR	Initialize character set for 80-column display
65381	$FF65	PFKEY	Assign a string to a function key
65384	$FF68	SETBNK	Set banks for I/O operations
65387	$FF6B	GETCFG	Get byte to configure MMU for any bank
65390	$FF6E	JSRFAR	Jump to a subroutine in any bank, with return to the calling bank
65393	$FF71	JMPFAR	Jump to a routine in any bank, with no return to the calling bank
65396	$FF74	INDFET	Load a byte from an address (offset of Y) in any bank
65399	$FF77	INDSTA	Store a byte to an address (offset of Y) in any bank
65402	$FF7A	INDCMP	Compare a byte to the contents of an address (offset of Y) in any bank
65405	$FF7D	PRIMM	Print the string in memory immediately following the JSR to this routine

Standard Commodore Kernal Jump Table
(Also found on the Commodore 64, VIC-20, 16, and Plus/4)

65409	$FF81	CINT	Initialize screen editor and video chips
65412	$FF84	IOINIT	Initialize I/O devices
65415	$FF87	RAMTAS	Initialize RAM and buffers
65418	$FF8A	RESTOR	Restore default values for Kernal indirect RAM vectors
65421	$FF8D	VECTOR	Set or copy Kernal indirect RAM vectors
65424	$FF90	SETMSG	Enable or disable Kernal messages
65427	$FF93	SECND	Send secondary address
65430	$FF96	TKSA	Send secondary address to talker
65433	$FF99	MEMTOP	Set or read top of RAM
65436	$FF9C	MEMBOT	Set or read bottom of RAM
65439	$FF9F	KEY	Read the keyboard
65442	$FFA2	SETTMO	Enable/disable IEEE timeouts (unused in the 128)
65445	$FFA5	ACPTR	Input a byte from the serial bus
65448	$FFA8	CIOUT	Output a device to the serial bus
65451	$FFAB	UNTLK	Send untalk command to serial device
65454	$FFAE	UNLSN	Send unlisten command to serial device
65457	$FFB1	LISTN	Send listen command to serial device
65460	$FFB4	TALK	Send talk command to serial device

65453	$FFB7	READSS	Read the I/O status
65466	$FFBA	SETLFS	Set channel, device number, and secondary address
65469	$FFBD	SETNAM	Specify length and address of current filename
65472	$FFC0	OPEN	Open a logical file
65475	$FFC3	CLOSE	Close a logical file
65478	$FFC6	CHKIN	Set a specified channel for input
65481	$FFC9	CKOUT	Set a specified channel for output
65484	$FFCC	CLRCH	Clear all channels
65487	$FFCF	BASIN	Retrieve a byte from the input channel
65490	$FFD2	BSOUT	Send a byte to the output channel
65493	$FFD5	LOAD	Load or verify data from device
65496	$FFD8	SAVE	Save contents of memory to a device
65499	$FFDB	SETTIM	Set jiffy clock
65502	$FFDE	RDTIM	Read jiffy clock
65505	$FFE1	STOP	Read RUN/STOP key status
65508	$FFE4	GETIN	Get a byte from the input buffer
65511	$FFE7	CLALL	Close all files and channels
65514	$FFEA	UDTIM	Update jiffy clock
65517	$FFED	SCRORG	Get size of current screen window
65520	$FFF0	PLOT	Set or read cursor position
65523	$FFF3	IOBASE	Get location of I/O block

65280–65284 ($FF00–$FF04) Common MMU Registers

Musical Note Values

Musical Note		Frequency	
Pitch	Octave	High Byte	Low Byte
C	0	1	12
C♯(D♭)	0	1	28
D	0	1	45
E♭(D♯)	0	1	62
E	0	1	81
F	0	1	102
F♯(G♭)	0	1	123
G	0	1	145
A♭(G♯)	0	1	169
A	0	1	195
B♭(A♯)	0	1	221
B	0	1	250
C	1	2	24
C♯(D♭)	1	2	56
D	1	2	90
E♭(D♯)	1	2	125
E	1	2	163
F	1	2	204
F♯(G♭)	1	2	246
G	1	3	35
A♭(G♯)	1	3	83
A	1	3	134
B♭(A♯)	1	3	187
B	1	3	244
C	2	4	48
C♯(D♭)	2	4	112
D	2	4	180
E♭(D♯)	2	4	251
E	2	5	71
F	2	5	152
F♯(G♭)	2	5	237
G	2	6	71
A♭(G♯)	2	6	167
A	2	7	12
B♭(A♯)	2	7	119
B	2	7	233
C	3	8	97
C♯(D♭)	3	8	225
D	3	9	104
E♭(D♯)	3	9	247
E	3	10	143

Musical Note		Frequency	
Pitch	Octave	High Byte	Low Byte
F	3	11	48
F♯(G♭)	3	11	218
G	3	12	143
A♭(G♯)	3	13	78
A	3	14	24
B♭(A♯)	3	14	239
B	3	15	210
C	4	16	195
C♯(D♭)	4	17	195
D	4	18	209
E♭(D♯)	4	19	239
E	4	21	31
F	4	22	96
F♯(G♭)	4	23	181
G	4	25	30
A♭(G♯)	4	26	156
A	4	28	49
B♭(A♯)	4	29	223
B	4	31	165
C	5	33	135
C♯(D♭)	5	35	134
D	5	37	162
E♭(D♯)	5	39	223
E	5	42	62
F	5	44	193
F♯(G♭)	5	47	107
G	5	50	60
A♭(G♯)	5	53	57
A	5	56	99
B♭(A♯)	5	59	190
B	5	63	75
C	6	67	15
C♯(D♭)	6	71	12
D	6	75	69
E♭(D♯)	6	79	191
E	6	84	125
F	6	89	131
F♯(G♭)	6	94	214
G	6	100	121
A♭(G♯)	6	106	115
A	6	112	199
B♭(A♯)	6	119	124
B	6	126	151

Musical Note		Frequency	
Pitch	Octave	High Byte	Low Byte
C	7	134	30
C♯(D♭)	7	142	24
D	7	150	139
E♭(D♯)	7	159	126
E	7	168	250
F	7	179	6
F♯(G♭)	7	189	172
G	7	200	243
A♭(G♯)	7	212	230
A	7	225	143
B♭(A♯)	7	238	2489
B	7	253	46

CP/M Basic Disk Operating System Service Calls

BDOS services are requested by loading the C register with the number of the desired service, then calling the request handler located at 0005H. Register usage for other information is less uniform. The following 8080 ML code illustrates how to print a single A character on the console device (usually the 128's video screen):

```
BDOS     EQU  0005H ;SYMBOL FOR ADDRESS OF SERVICE
                     HANDLER
;
PRINTA   MVI  E,'A'  ;PUT CHARACTER IN E REGISTER
         MVI  C,2    ;PUT SERVICE NUMBER IN C REGISTER
         CALL BDOS   ;REQUEST SERVICE
```

Note: this table contains only a brief description of each service. For complete information, consult Digital Research's *CP/M Programmer's Guide.*

0	Terminate Program	Restart CCP, ending current program.
1	Console Input Byte	Wait for a character from console, return in A.
2	Console Output Byte	Send character in E to console.
3	Auxiliary Input	Wait for a character from auxiliary device, return in A.
4	Auxiliary Output	Send character in E to auxiliary device.
5	Print Output	Send character in E to LST: device.
6	Direct Console I/O	Perform raw character I/O to console, control characters are not intercepted. Action performed depends on value in E (0FFH, read a char if one is ready; 0FEH, return status; 0FDH, wait for a char; other, print value in E). Return status or input byte in A.
7	Auxiliary Input Status	Check status of AUXIN: device. On return, A=0 if not ready, 0FFH if ready.
8	Auxiliary Output Status	Check status of AUXOUT: device. Returns same as BDOS7.
9	Print String to Console	Print string addressed by DE, terminated by $.
10	Input Line from Console	Input string from console to buffer addressed by DE.

11	Console Status	Return A=1 if a character has been typed, A=0 if not.
12	Get CP/M Version	On return, HL=0031H for CPM 3.0.
13	Reset Disk Drives	Reinitialize all disk drives.
14	Select Disk Drive	Change default disk to drive code in E. If unsuccessful, A is set to 0FFH, and H contains the error code.
15	Open File	DE points to FCB of file, A indicates success or error, H holds error code.
16	Close File	Same register usage as BDOS15.
17	Search for First	Search for file indicated by FCB addressed by DE.
18	Search for Next	Search for file, starting at location of the last match.
19	Delete File	DE points to the FCB of the file to be erased.
20	Sequential Read	Read a record from file indicated by FCB addressed by DE.
21	Sequential Write	Write a record to file indicated by FCB addressed by DE.
22	Create File	Create a directory entry from FCB indicated by DE.
23	Rename File	Rename file from FCB indicated by DE.
24	Get Active Drives	Return 16-bit value in HL, each bit of which represents the status of a disk drive.
25	Get Default Drive	Return the number of the current disk drive in A.
26	Get Buffer Address	Change the location of disk data buffer to address in DE.
27	Get Allocation Vector	Return the address of the allocation vector for the current drive in HL.
28	Write-Protect Drive	Set current drive to read-only status.
29	Get Read-only Drives	Return 16-bit value in HL, each bit of which represents the read-only status of a disk drive.
30	Set File Attributes	Change attibute bits of file indicated by FCB addressed by DE.
31	Get Disk Parameter Block	Return the address of the current drive's DPB in HL.
32	Get or Set User Number	If E contains 0FFH, return current user number in A; otherwise, set user number to value in E.
33	Direct-Access Read	Read a particular record from the file indicated by the FCB addressed by DE.

34	Direct-Access Write	Write a particular record to the file indicated by the FCB addressed by DE.
35	Get Address of File End	Return length of file in FCB pointed to by DE.
36	Set Direct-Access Address	Return record number for next record to be accessed by FCB addressed by DE.
37	Reset Disk Drive	Reset one or several drives. The 16-bit value in HL indicates which drives to reset.
40	Direct-Access Zero Fill	Same as 34 except that newly allocated sectors are initialized to zero.
44	Set Record Count	Set number of disk records to be transferred by disk operations to value in E.
45	Set Error Mode	If E=0FFH, handle disk errors by returning error code in H. If E=0FEH, display an error message before returning. On any other value, display message and terminate program.
46	Get Free Space on Disk	Return amount of available space on drive indicated by E in the first three bytes of the file buffer.
47	Chain to Program	Run transient program from command line in file buffer.
48	Flush Disk Buffers	Forces CP/M to write disk sectors which may be buffered in RAM to the disks.
49	Get/Set System Control Block	Directly access the SCB, which holds various system variables.
50	Call BIOS	Call a BIOS function.
59	Load Overlay	Load a .PRL file indicated by the FCB addressed by DE.
60	Call RSX	Resident System Extensions can perform services in response to this call.
98	Release Free Blocks	Recover allocated data blocks which belong to no file on all active drives.
99	Truncate File	Set the last record of a file to the record number in the FCB address by DE.
100	Set Directory Info	Use FCB addressed by DE to set a directory's label.
101	Get Directory Info	Use FCB addressed by DE to read a directory's label.
102	Get Timestamp and Password	Use FCB addressed by DE to read a directory's password and timestamp.

103	Set Timestamp and Password	Use FCB addressed by DE to set a directory's label.
104	Set System Date and Time	Set the time and date to value addressed by DE.
105	Get System Date and Time	Store the time and date in the location addressed by DE.
106	Set Default Password	8-byte string addressed by DE becomes the current password.
107	Get Serial Number	Store BDOS's serial number in 6-byte field addressed by DE.
108	Get/Set Program Return Code	If DE contains 0FFFFh, set HL to current return code; otherwise, set return code to value in DE.
109	Get/Set Console Mode	If DE contains 0FFFFh, set HL to current console mode; otherwise, set console mode to value in DE.
110	Get/Set Output Delimeter	If DE contains 0FFFFh, return the current end-of-string character for BDOS9 in A; otherwise, set string terminator to value in E.
111	Print Block	DE points to a 4-byte structure which contains the address and length of a block of text to be displayed on the console.
112	List Block	DE points to a 4-byte structure which contains the address and length of a block of text to be displayed on the LST: device.
152	Parse File Name	DE points to a 4-byte structure which contains the address of an ASCII string to be analyzed and the address of an FCB to be initialized based on the file reference in the ASCII string.

Basic Input/Output System Service Calls

0	BOOT	Perform cold start.
1	WBOOT	Perform warm start.
2	CONST	Check if console has a character waiting; return $FF (yes) or $00 (no) in A.
3	CONIN	Read a character from the console and return it in A.
4	CONOUT	Send character in C to console.
5	LIST	Send character in C to list device.
6	AUXOUT	Send character in C to auxiliary device.
7	AUXIN	Read a character from auxiliary device and return it in A.

8 HOME — Set the current track of the selected disk drive to track 0.

9 SELDSK — Select the disk drive whose ID is in C and return the address of its Disk Parameter Header in HL.

10 SETTRK — Set current track to value in BC.

11 SETSEC — Set current sector to value in BC.

12 SETDMA — Set file buffer to location in BC.

13 READ — Read from current disk, track, and sector; store data in the file buffer; and return $00 (OK), $01 (error), or $FF (disk changed) in A.

14 WRITE — Write from buffer to current disk, track, and sector, returning $00 (OK), $01 (error), $02 (R/O disk), or $FF (disk changed) in A.

15 LISTST — Return status of list device—$00 (not ready) or $FF (ready)—in A.

16 SECTRN — Convert logical sector number in BC to physical sector number in HL, using translation table at address in DE.

17 CONOST — Return status of console—$00 (not ready) or $FF (ready)—in A.

18 AUXIST — Return status of auxiliary input—$FF if character is waiting, $00 if not ready—in A.

19 AUXOST — Set A to $FF if auxiliary output can accept a character, else set A to $00.

20 DEVTBL — Return the address of the character I/O table in HL.

21 DEVINI — Initialize the device specified by C to values in I/O table.

22 DRVTBL — Return the address of the disk drive table in HL.

23 MULTIO — Set number of sectors for a multisector transfer to value in C.

24 FLUSH — Flush sector deblocking buffers.

25 MOVE — Move block of length BC from address in DE to address in HL.

26 TIME — Set system clock if C=$FF, get system time if C=$00.

27 SELMEM — Switch between memory banks to bank indicated by A.

28 SETBNK — Set the memory bank of the file buffer.

29 XMOVE — Set the source (C) and destination (B) banks for the MOVE (BIOS25) operation.

Index